"Andrew Diamond's wide-ranging and significant book movingly tells the history of Chicago, how it has become a tale of two cities from the shimmering and branded opulence of the Loop to the poverty-filled and underserved streets of the South Side. And this isn't, as Diamond makes clear, a matter of chance or culture, but of deliberate and long-standing policy decisions. This is an honest and truthful book for this difficult moment in history."

—BRYANT SIMON, author of *Boardwalk of Dreams: Atlantic City and the Fate of Urban America*

"Original and sophisticated, Diamond's *Chicago on the Make* offers a fresh take on a city, country, and indeed a concept we thought we knew. We've taken of late to using 'neoliberalism' to describe any number of entrepreneurial impulses and austerity measures shaping our contemporary political culture. But as Diamond's probing look at the twentieth-century city so brilliantly instructs, when it comes to market-based approaches and state violence shaping political outcomes, there's really nothing 'neo' about 'neoliberalism.' Excellent."

—N. D. B. CONNOLLY, author of *A World More Concrete: Real Estate and the Remaking of Jim Crow South Florida*

"*Chicago on the Make* is a forcefully wrought and persuasive synthetic account of race, ethnicity, and power in modern Chicago. Diamond brilliantly ties together the histories of machine politics and social movements, of major figures like both Mayor Daleys, and of ordinary Chicagoans—black, white, and Latino. This is the indispensable history of the Windy City, a work of urban history at its best."

—THOMAS J. SUGRUE, author of *Sweet Land of Liberty: The Forgotten Struggle for Civil Rights in the North*

"With the attention to detail and narrative depth that only a historian can bring, *Chicago on the Make* explains how and why Chicago has become a city of extremes: wealth and poverty, power and resignation. Its grand scope—which stretches across time, from downtown to the neighborhoods, and from grassroots organizing to City Hall—makes it a definitive, must-read account."

—MARY PATTILLO, author of *Black on the Block: The Politics of Race and Class in the City*

"Few American cities have been as subject to neoliberal transformation as Chicago. Fewer still have seen leaders so adept at absorbing the discontent generated by such policies. But as Andrew Diamond makes clear in this sweeping, highly readable history, the roots of such policies run deep. Anyone interested in understanding how Chicago became the racially and economically stratified metropolis that it is today—or, more ambitiously, how to resist such stratification—should read this book."

—MICAH UETRICHT, *Jacobin* magazine, author of *Strike for America: Chicago Teachers against Austerity*

Chicago on the Make

MAP 1. Chicago's community areas. All maps by Bill Nelson.

Chicago on the Make

POWER AND INEQUALITY IN
A MODERN CITY

Andrew J. Diamond

UNIVERSITY OF CALIFORNIA PRESS

University of California Press, one of the most distinguished university presses in the United States, enriches lives around the world by advancing scholarship in the humanities, social sciences, and natural sciences. Its activities are supported by the UC Press Foundation and by philanthropic contributions from individuals and institutions. For more information, visit www.ucpress.edu.

University of California Press
Oakland, California

French versions of chapters 3–7 were originally published as *Histoire de Chicago,* by Andrew Diamond and Pap Ndiaye. © Librairie Arthème Fayard, 2013.

Parts of chapters 1 and 5 originally appeared in a somewhat different form in *Mean Streets: Chicago Youths and the Everyday Struggle for Empowerment in the Multiracial City, 1908–1969* (Berkeley and Los Angeles: University of California Press, 2009).

Library of Congress Cataloging-in-Publication Data

Names: Diamond, Andrew J., author.
Title: Chicago on the make : power and inequality in a modern city / Andrew J. Diamond.
Description: Oakland, California : University of California Press, [2017] | Includes bibliographical references and index.
Identifiers: LCCN 2017026928| ISBN 9780520286481 (cloth : alk. paper) | ISBN 9780520286498 (pbk. : alk. paper) | ISBN 9780520961715 (ebook)
Subjects: LCSH: Chicago (Ill.)—Politics and government—20th century. | Chicago (Ill.)—History—20th century. | Chicago (Ill.)—Social conditions—20th century.
Classification: LCC F548.5 .D525 2017 | DDC 977.3/1104—dc23
LC record available at https://lccn.loc.gov/2017026928

26 25 24 23 22 21 20 19 18 17
10 9 8 7 6 5 4 3 2 1

To my family, near and far, past and present

CONTENTS

ILLUSTRATIONS

FIGURES

MAPS

Introduction

Former president Barack Obama joined a long line of observers when, while addressing officials gathered at the 2012 NATO Summit in Chicago, he referred to the host city as "a quintessentially American town." Perhaps the first recorded expression of this idea came from British ambassador James Bryce, who in 1888 mused that Chicago was "perhaps the most typically American place in America." Years later Sarah Bernhardt opined it was "the pulse of America" and H. L. Mencken quipped that it was "American in every chitling and sparerib." By contrast, few have made similar claims about either New York or Los Angeles. New York has long remained the "great" American city, but its greatness has rested more upon a sense of particularity than typicality. Most Americans residing between the two coasts think of the Big Apple as a somewhat strange and daunting place. Moreover, if Hollywood has played a leading role in exporting American values and norms throughout the planet, it has also made Los Angeles into a surreal and idiosyncratic place in the minds of most Americans living east of the San Fernando Valley.

Chicago, on the other hand, has evoked so much that is patently American, and it continues to do so today even after President Trump attempted to make it into an aberration by evoking the "carnage" on its streets. First and foremost, with its 2.7 million residents (nearly 10 million in the entire metropolitan area), it is the clear-cut capital of the Midwest and thus of the fabled American "heartland"—a nebulous place that politicians of every stripe appeal to in order to convince voters that they represent the "real" people. And Chicago strikes this populist chord in ways that other "great" American cities do not. In contrast with the dominant image of the good people residing in the older, educated cities of the eastern seaboard, for example, the stereotypical Chicagoan speaks in a thick accent, pronouncing words like *the* and *these* as "da" and "dese."[1] While notions of class justice (and injustice) now struggle for legitimacy within the realm of mainstream political discourse in the United States, American patriotism nonetheless remains infused with celebrations of average working men and women—which keeps Chicago a working-class town in the American imagination, even if it now ranks among the most economically powerful global cities in the world.

Although nobody knows with certainty why Chicago popularly became known as the Windy City around the 1880s, the city has taken numerous other nicknames since its rise to national prominence in the late nineteenth century, and some of the most recognized and enduring of these have related to its working-class identity. Carl Sandburg coined two such monikers in a single stanza of his 1914 poem "Chicago," when he referred to the city as both the "Hog Butcher for the World" and the "City of the Big Shoulders." The latter still resonated several decades later, when Chicago had picked up yet another slogan seeming to pay tribute to its industriousness: "the city that works." Currently, in the postindustrial era, when jobs in the service sector are far more plentiful than those in factories and mills, such homages to the city's industrial strength seem anomalous. If Chicago still possesses a considerable industrial labor force, its packinghouses and steel mills have shut down, and many of its warehouses have been converted into galleries, lofts, and condos. But when Sandburg was penning his famous lines, Chicago was emerging as *the* symbol of American industrial power worldwide. Americans are nostalgic for this golden age of global leadership, and such yearnings further support Chicago's bid to be the "quintessentially American town."

Moreover, as the symbol of a triumphant industrial past, Chicago also emblematizes another of the country's grand narratives: its long tradition of immigration and cultural pluralism. If in recent years the increasing economic insecurity of middle-class Americans has fueled the growth of anti-immigration sentiments, especially in the southwestern states along the Mexican border, the cherished idea of the United States as a country of immigrants persists. Well recognized is the fact that waves of immigrants and African American migrants worked many of the jobs that made Chicago and the United States with it an industrial giant during the American Century. The urban landscape in the minds of most Americans is a multiethnic place that mixes distinct ethnoracial communities and cultures, and in this sense Chicago once more appears as the prototypical American city. Its folklore is filled with many of the things that conjure up the multiethnic urban experience: gangsters, hot dogs and sausages, pizza, jazz and the blues. The city's recent campaign to brand itself as "the city of neighborhoods" represents an attempt to renew its association with this dimension of the urban experience, even if not *every* neighborhood mapped by this campaign was an ethnic or racial community per se.

Thus, Chicago has meshed with key cultural and ideological currents that have shaped mainstream conceptions of the American city. Its central location within the landscape of popular culture has mirrored its geographical position in the midst of the American heartland. Yet, Chicago's centrality to the U.S. urban experience also owes a great deal to the key role it has played in the production of knowledge about urban society. The University of Chicago was the birthplace of modern urban sociology in the 1920s and 1930s, when scores of researchers associated with the Chicago School of sociology plunged into the city's ethnic working-class neighborhoods to produce ethnographies that demonstrated—among other things—that poverty, crime, family dysfunction, and immorality were due more to social structures and physical environmental factors than to biological or cultural characteristics.[2] By 1930 the University of Chicago had trained over half of all the sociologists in the world, and the behavioral and ecological models of its faculty soon structured the way a generation of social scientists viewed the American city and its problems— for better or for worse. Using the city of Chicago as a laboratory, Chicago School pioneer Robert Park conceptualized the "race relations" paradigm that would come to shape the country's understanding of its racial "dilemma" into the distant future, and two University of Chicago graduate students, St. Clair Drake and Horace Cayton, gave the social sciences the first book on the "black ghetto" with their 1945 classic *Black Metropolis*.[3] By midcentury, Chicago had become the case study for the rest of the nation.

It was not until somewhat recently that scholars began to challenge this paradigmatic status, arguing that its emphasis on concentric zones surrounding a central business district no longer captured the decentered, postmodern arrangement of numerous American cities in the twenty-first century.[4] Many of these criticisms have come from researchers identifying themselves with the so-called Los Angeles School of urbanism. In 2002, geographer Michael Dear claimed that Los Angeles was more paradigmatic than Chicago for understanding the evolution of the metropolitan United States.[5] Dear's argument rested on the idea that Chicago's spatial logic of a centrally organized, modernist city, in which the economic and political activities of the central business district organize the surrounding metropolitan region was outdated.

Much more prototypical, he asserted, was the kind of sprawl and fragmentation exhibited by the postmodern metropolis of Los Angeles, where cores of economic activity have sprung up with little relation to any kind of city center. Proponents of the Los Angeles School, moreover, claimed that the case of Los Angeles aptly demonstrated that forces of globalization were far more powerful than local politics in shaping the city, and pointed to Los Angeles's gated communities patrolled by private security forces—a common feature of many southern U.S. cities that has been largely absent from the Chicago scene. Such claims also reflected a key development in the history of the postwar United States. In the decades following the Second World War, massive federal government spending on military, aerospace, and other high-tech programs in the country's southern, Sun Belt regions accelerated the political and economic decline of the northeastern and midwestern industrial cities belonging to what, by the 1980s, became known as the Rust Belt. Los Angeles, far more than Chicago, resembled the sprawling Sun Belt cities that rose to prominence during this era.

The Los Angeles School critique provoked a strong reaction among researchers working on Chicago, a number of whom came together to establish what they referred to as the New Chicago School of urbanism. While most of these political scientists and sociologists concurred that the old Chicago School model of concentric rings around a central business district needed to be updated to reflect the new realities of decentralization in the urban United States, they reasserted the relevance of Chicago's model of development by arguing that "the city center is critical (even as there is growth on the metropolitan periphery) and that public services are a core organizing element in such a global city."[6] Another fundamental point of agreement among this school's scholars, moreover, was that while global forces have had a strong impact on the city's evolution, the local political structure, from the neighborhood level up to City Hall, continues to play a major role in determining how the city develops and how it is governed.[7] "Politics," as two of the New Chicago School's leading proponents put it, "still matters and . . . it does in other cities as well."[8] This quintessentially Chicago School (old and new) emphasis on local context recently received further validation with the publication of Robert Sampson's widely acclaimed *Great American City,* a book that marshals an enormous body of data gleaned from decades of fieldwork in Chicago to convincingly defend the critical importance of "neighborhood effects"—the roles of neighborhoods and communities in shaping the lives of those living within them.[9]

While settling the debate between the Los Angeles and New Chicago Schools is decidedly not one of the stakes of the narrative to follow, there is much about *Chicago on the Make* that will be welcomed by those who continue to view the story of Chicago politics as somehow emblematic of the American urban experience. In contrast with an increasing tendency among scholars of contemporary U.S. cities to look beyond the grassroots to the forces of global capital, local politics, broadly defined, lies near the center of this new history of Chicago. Politics for my purposes here is not merely something that happens during elections, city council sessions, and in the meetings of labor unions and a range of other political and civic organizations; politics also transpires on street corners, in parks, corner bars, stores, coffee shops, and restaurants, around schools, at block meetings and parties, and in nearly every place in which people come together to share stories, discuss the issues that are important to them, and, ultimately, to form ideas about themselves, their neighbors, and their neighborhood. Such an approach unavoidably veers onto the terrains of local culture and everyday life, for it is here that average residents of the city have most commonly engaged in political activities and formed their political views.

Chicago on the Make thus draws some of its inspiration from Robert Sampson's more recent turn towards neighborhoods and communities as vital forces in shaping urban life at the grassroots, as well as from older "bottom-up" approaches pioneered by British Marxist historians like E. P. Thompson. It is, above all, a "people's history" of Chicago—an attempt to capture the city as it was lived by its ordinary residents. Yet, telling the story from this perspective by no means entails marginalizing the more formal, institutional dimensions of policy making, governance, and electoral politics. Nor does it mean looking past economic circumstances, technological changes, and demographic shifts—the broader structural forces that so powerfully shaped Chicago's political culture, social context, neighborhoods, communities, and built environment. The goal here is to integrate the bottom up with the top down, to combine total history and microhistory, to bring the political, social, cultural, and economic into the same frame.

Taking this kind of approach over more than a century, as Chicago grew from an unruly tangle of railyards, slaughterhouses, factories, tenement houses, state-of-the-art skyscrapers, and fiercely defended ethnic neighborhoods into one of the world's mightiest global cities, comes with its share of pitfalls. Certain celebrated facets of Chicago's past have been slighted and even omitted in the effort to fit this grand narrative between the front and back covers of this book. For one thing, the orientation from below entails devoting a great deal of attention to the work, community, and leisure activities of Chicago's laboring classes—to what was going on in its neighborhoods of African Americans, immigrants, and ethnics—at the expense of the city's more prosperous districts. As a consequence, this particular history overlooks some related facets of Chicago's history that may be of great interest to some readers. For example, while it would be impossible to deny the enormous impact that the famed Chicago and Second Chicago Schools has had on the broader architectural history of the United States, the interest in the majestic buildings that have defined Chicago's skyline here relates mostly to their role in the city's political economy and in the structural transformation of its neighborhoods. When references are made to Chicago's great literary works, moreover, it is usually as a way into understanding social conditions. And when Chicago's art scene comes into the story, it is mainly in relation to the popular art forms emerging out of the city's vibrant neighborhoods—such as jazz and the blues or the striking wall murals that began appearing in Chicago's black, Mexican, and Puerto Rican neighborhoods beginning in the 1960s.

Chicago on the Make seeks to move beyond such fables of exceptionalism to highlight a range of historical dynamics and processes that have, to one extent or another, characterized much of the metropolitan United States. Unlike most of the other biographies of U.S. cities, this book endeavors to make a new and much-needed contribution to reflections on the "history of the present" for both Chicago and the urban United States in general.[10] By traversing a period of more than a century and devoting substantial coverage to the more immediate twenty-first-century past, it seeks to accomplish what historian Joan Scott has defined as the crucial burden of this historiographical project—to unearth the historical processes behind structures, policies, and ideas that now appear "inevitable, natural or culturally necessary."

Nothing has seemed more natural and inevitable in Chicago over the past several decades than authoritarian mayors and racial segregation. According to some measures, Chicago is "the most segregated city in the United States" and has ranked high on the list for much of the last century. Only one other thing has rivaled its level of segregation as a distinguishing feature of the city's history: the extraordinarily long dynasty of Mayor Richard J. Daley and his son Richard M. Daley, whose respective styles of authoritarian "machine" rule, taken together, dominated Chicago's political scene for forty-three years between 1955 and 2011. For over four decades of Daley rule—a period that spanned the rise and fall of the modern civil rights movement, the spectacular growth of white middle-class suburbs outside the city limits, the ghettoization of huge swaths of its West and South Sides, a massive wave of immigration from Latin America, and the transformation of the city from a motor of industry to a postindustrial node of the global service economy—Chicago scarcely witnessed a legitimate mayoral election or heated city council vote.[11] While it is tempting to view Chicago's rigid racial order and its particularly undemocratic political culture as pure products of the Daley dynasty, these problems, as the story to follow seeks to reveal, had deeper roots.

Excavating the conditions of demobilization and political quiescence that prevailed in Chicago between the 1970s and the first decade of the twenty-first century—a period that saw the city's racial order hardening and its social inequalities widening—lies at the heart of this history of Chicago. I was living in Chicago during Congressman Bobby Rush's 1999 mayoral primary run, when the former Black Panther tried to challenge the all-powerful regime of Richard M. Daley, which had spent the previous decade pursuing a global-city agenda that had left all but a handful Chicago's working-class black and Latino neighborhoods in shambles, by evoking the idea that there were, in fact, "two Chicagos." The result: Daley defeated Rush by 73 to 27 percent. Eight years later, with corruption scandals mounting and Daley pursuing an austerity program that was essentially punishing the poor for the city's exploding debt, it was hard to argue that things had not gotten worse. One of these scandals, it should be remembered, involved revelations that the police had been systematically torturing African Americans at the Area 2 police station on the South Side for years. And yet in the 2007 election, Daley's last, overall voter turnout barely surpassed 30 percent, with 70 percent of black voters and 80 percent of Latino voters casting their votes for Richard M. Daley.

Most scholars attempting to explain this state of demobilization have focused on the more than four decades of autocratic machine rule that shaped the city's political institutions, modes of governance, and political culture. To be sure, the fact that Chicago's machine outlasted its analogues in other major cities by decades must enter into any reckoning with politics and power in the Windy City, and *Chicago on the Make* pays particular attention to this story as well. Where this new history of Chicago diverges from most political histories of the American city in the twentieth century is in its effort to view the dynamics of inequality and demobilization as manifestations of a process of neoliberalization, which in the antidemocratic, political-machine context of Chicago advanced somewhat more rapidly and more aggressively than it did elsewhere. The term *neoliberalization* is invoked not merely to connote the implementation of a package of economic-minded policies that had inadvertent social and political consequences—such policies were in fact implemented and they did have important social and political consequences, especially beginning in the early 1990s under Richard M. Daley. A more important dimension of the story of neoliberalization being told here involves revealing how market values and economizing logics penetrated into the city's political institutions and beyond them into its broader political culture.[12] This political history of Chicago seeks to understand from both the top down and the bottom up how this happened and how the advance of neoliberalization crippled the political forces standing in opposition to it: labor unions, municipal reformers, neighborhood planning boards, civil rights organizations, and a range of other political organizations that sought to challenge injustices within the prevailing social and political order.

The interpretive thread that weaves together the seven chapters of *Chicago on the Make* unravels out of the broader project of tracing the evolution of urban societies during the neoliberal moment of late capitalism. It seeks to historicize and delineate the social, political, and cultural conditions of City Hall's transformation into what Eric Klinenberg refers to as an "entrepreneurial state"—characterized by deregulation, fiscal austerity, outsourcing of city services, market solutions to public problems, and the overriding view of residents as consumers (rather than citizens).[13] But my account of Chicago's neoliberal turn takes the discussion in three somewhat new directions.

First, as perhaps the first book-length history of neoliberalization at the urban grassroots over the *longue durée,* this study makes a historiographical intervention in a field thus far dominated by sociologists, geographers, and political scientists. The Reagan revolution's neoliberal takeover in the 1980s did not happen overnight but rather developed out of an ideological and cultural framework that had been decades in the making. While scholars like David Harvey have viewed the context of the mid-1970s as pivotal to the neoliberal turn, this history of Chicago views neoliberalization as a process that unraveled gradually and unevenly over much of the twentieth century.[14] In Chicago, the mid-1950s proved to be a critical moment in the city's neoliberal turn. If some of the guiding principles of neoliberalism are the supremacy of free market values, the placement of the state at the disposition of private enterprise, and the attenuation of expansive notions of "the public good," then Mayor Richard J. Daley's administration fit the description quite well for most of its more than two decades in power. Beginning in the late 1950s, when Daley took the city council out of the game and turned over the task of planning the city's future development to an alliance of downtown business interests and technocrats, "Boss" Daley presided over a municipal government in which key policy decisions had been moved out of the hands of the public and into corporate boardrooms. In Daley's Chicago, a federally funded urban renewal program intended to uplift the poor ended up subsidizing downtown development projects that reinforced the walls around the black ghetto. It was Richard J. (not Richard M.) Daley who brokered the deals that built the John Hancock Center, the Sears Tower, and many of the other iconic skyscrapers that launched Chicago into the global age—all this while the South and West Sides were turning into depopulated hyperghettos. But the Daley administration's ability to push this agenda forward depended on the *inability* of democratizing forces to gain traction within Chicago's political culture during the interwar years, when progressive labor and grassroots forces fought what was ultimately a losing battle against business elites striving to economize the city's governance criteria, align their own economic interests with "the public interest," and prescribe entrepreneurial values as the cure for pressing social problems.

Second, unlike most of what has been written on the neoliberal turn, this book places the local politics of race at the center of the story. "Economics are the method," Margaret Thatcher once remarked, "but the object is to change the soul." These words suggest that to view neoliberalism too narrowly as simply a policy regime that rose to international prominence beginning in the mid-1970s is to misunderstand how much its triumph rested upon the construction of what David Harvey has referred to as "a neoliberal market-based populist culture of differentiated consumerism and individual libertarianism."[15] *Chicago on the Make* seeks to show that racial issues often played crucial roles in changing the "souls" of many Chicagoans—that the politics of race, in effect, pulled residents into the political sphere and shaped feelings, sensibilities, and ideas that paved the way for the acceptance of neoliberal values and policies. This was true on both sides of the color line throughout the long twentieth century, even in the decades prior to the pivotal 1950s. In the city's white ethnic neighborhoods the formation of an increasingly more inclusive white identity during the interwar era worked to weaken the voice of organized labor, disrupt the efforts of reformers, and, more generally, to enable the administrations of Mayors Cermak, Kelly, and Kennelly to preside over political machines that effectively submerged the politics of social justice beneath a progrowth, antilabor agenda between the 1930s and

1950s. And, in black Chicago, a range of businessman race heroes, religious leaders, and syndicate kingpins managed to tether the politics of racial advancement to the gospel of black capitalism, an achievement that worked to stifle political organizations seeking to organize working-class African Americans around housing and labor issues and to challenge the relationship between the businessmen of the "Black Metropolis" and the white power structure. Tragically, such developments paralyzed the forces opposing the prevailing racial and social order at the very moment when the system of American capitalism was most vulnerable to attack.

Of course the rest of the story does not follow a straight line towards neoliberal domination. There were some big bumps in the road. The 1960s and 1970s witnessed significant challenges to the Daley machine in the form of powerful identity-based mobilizations. And yet, if these movements posed real threats to the machine, they ended up accelerating the process of neoliberalization in their own ways. On the one hand, working-class white Chicagoans took to the streets against racially integrated public housing projects and the black drive for civil rights between the 1950s and 1970s, articulating languages of whiteness, antistatism and consumer rights—the building blocks of a neoliberal populist culture. On the other hand, minority empowerment movements emerged out of black, Puerto Rican, and Mexican neighborhoods, challenging the Daley machine's downtown agenda and demanding political rights and representation. While these minority rights movements did manage to create a tradition of antimachine activism that stretched across racial and ethnic lines—a situation that bore fruit in the 1983 election of the city's black reformist mayor Harold Washington—my story about their ultimate fate is not a triumphant one.

In fact, *Chicago on the Make* reveals how the politics of racial identity and recognition these movements put into practice came to be powerfully incorporated into the neoliberal project of Richard M. Daley in the 1990s. Unlike his father, Richard M. Daley understood the importance of the politics of recognition for different ethnoracial communities, and he bestowed this recognition in the forms of strategic minority appointments within his administration and official acknowledgement of the physical boundaries and cultural significance of key ethnoracial neighborhoods. Such policies enabled him to create local "brokers" and "middlemen" whose ethnoracial legitimacy allowed them to advance the larger neoliberal agenda, especially in the form of progentrification and protourism policies that worked to the disadvantage of renters and public housing residents. Along with the new economy of tourism, the gentrification imperative has driven a range of policies that have ushered in neoliberal sensibilities and forms of governance. It has given private developers an even larger role in the planning process, transformed more and more homeowners into individualistically minded investors, and turned many middle-class Chicagoans against public housing and other state programs that appear to threaten their property values.

This form of incorporation was but one facet of a larger story that constitutes the third somewhat new contribution that this book offers: an attempt to examine at the grassroots level how neoliberalization combined with other forces to create the conditions of political quiescence in Chicago over much of the twentieth century. Part of my explanation for this quiescence builds upon Wendy Brown's thinking on how the "business approach to governing" and the "market rationality" that characterize neoliberalism militate against democratic governance and a democratic political culture.[16] In Chicago, moreover, the de-democratizing forces of neoliberalization were augmented by a political context that worked to effectively depoliticize many of the city's most pressing issues—segregation, gang-related murders, drug trafficking, failing public schools, and high minority unemployment and poverty rates— by attributing them to cultural rather than political causes. Mahmood Mamdani has referred to this process as the "culturization of politics": the transfer of political acts and events onto the terrain of culture, where they become dissociated from questions of structure, power, and, ultimately, political mobilization.[17] Like neoliberalization, the culturization of politics is part of a story that has transcended the borders of Chicago, but these trends had particularly powerful de-democratizing effects during the more than four decades of Daley rule.

And yet, if *Chicago on the Make* seeks to shed new light on how the interplay of race and neoliberalization shaped Chicago's political culture, this by no means suggests that the more traditional story of demobilization and repression should be discarded. Of course other factors worked to dampen the forces of grassroots democracy in Chicago—for one, the city's patronage machine, which Richard J. Daley was building up to its full potential as cities across the nation were dismantling theirs. Daley distributed patronage resources to his loyal aldermen based on the votes their wards added to his margin of victory, and as chairman of the Cook County Democratic Party he controlled the entire war chest for waging reelection campaigns. An alderman could thus not hope to remain in power without devoting unconditional support to the Boss, a situation that explains how Daley was able to maintain his base in black Chicago even as a local civil rights movement was agitating actively for rights and justice. All this has been well detailed in a number of studies on the Daley machine.[18]

But observers of the Daley machine have paid too much attention to the carrot and not enough to the stick, thereby omitting a key factor behind Daley's ability to weather the great political insurgencies of the 1960s and 1970s. Historians have generally undervalued the decisive role that state-sponsored countersubversion played in many major U.S. cities in the postwar era. A quick inventory of the massive collection of surveillance files produced by the Chicago Police Department's Red Squad division between the 1950s and 1970s suggests that this is a particularly serious blind spot in the case of Chicago.[19] Hence, the story here will revise the city's well-known history of postwar political struggle by better incorporating the part played by the Daley machine's repressive apparatus. Saul Alinsky's and Florence Scala's movements against unjust urban renewal plans in the 1950s and 1960s, the politicization of Chicago gangs by black power militants and federal grant programs, Martin Luther King's open-housing marches in 1966, the notorious student protests outside the 1968 Democratic National Convention, and the Black Panther Party's efforts to form a "rainbow coalition" with the Puerto Rican Young Lords Organization in 1969—all these campaigns fell short of their objectives, in part, because of Red Squad countersubversion. Sometimes the effects of this repression were all too direct, as in the police assassination of Black Panther leader Fred Hampton or in the well-documented infiltration and harassment of Chicago street gangs and black power groups during the civil rights challenges of the late 1960s. In other instances the impact of repression was more abstract and must be construed by reflecting on what could have (or should have) happened but did not. Why did the movements of Alinsky and Scala fail to snowball? Why didn't Chicagoans come out in the tens of thousands to participate in the demonstration at the 1968 Democratic National Convention? Why didn't Martin Luther King succeed in mobilizing several thousand (rather than several hundred) African Americans for the open-housing marches? The answer to all of these questions, *Chicago on the Make* contends, has to do with the fact that forces of state repression hindered the development of a vibrant culture of dissent that could link up universities, labor unions, and progressive political organizations.

And yet the Red Squad was not solely responsible for Chicago entering the momentous years of the mid-1960s with a somewhat anemic left political culture in comparison to cities like New York and San Francisco. The city's entrenched pattern of racial segregation imposed significant barriers to political collaboration across racial lines, and Daley's policy of directing urban renewal funds into downtown development projects only made the situation worse. Other important factors also contributed to the political quiescence of the Richard J. Daley era—policies that fit within the neoliberal framework this book lays out. For one thing, Daley's very early turn to a global-city agenda had an important cultural component. In an era when groups associated with the New Left were offering scathing critiques of the materialism and meaninglessness of white-collar, middle-class society, Chicago was quickly casting off its working-class identity and morphing into the kind of city white-collar professionals felt good about living in. By 1968 it possessed the country's second tallest skyscraper, the world's highest apartment building, and a range of luxurious middle-class housing complexes, one of which had its own marina, gymnasium, movie theater, swimming pool, ice rink, and *parfumerie*. Major transnational corporations like John Hancock, Standard Oil, Chase, and Sears were putting their names on its tall buildings downtown, and the city's Playboy Club had well over 100,000 members. By the early 1970s Chicago's two commodities exchanges were recording nearly $200 billion in transactions.

Certainly, Daley's efforts to attract corporate capital and make the city desirable for white-collar workers responded to some grim economic realities related to the rapid loss of Chicago's industrial base and the flight of capital and people to the suburbs. Yet the choices he made when faced with this situation followed a pattern he had established early on of handing the task of planning the city's future development to the business community—as far away as possible from public scrutiny and democratic process. And this trend dovetailed with the gradual evaporation of federal urban renewal and housing funds after the 1960s, which meant that private capital would increasingly drive the city's development. Richard M. Daley's administration brought this style of governance to a whole new level, devising innovative outsourcing and privatization schemes while shifting nearly a quarter of the city's tax revenues into a tax increment financing program (TIF) that constituted a virtual shadow budget for financing infrastructural improvements and subsidizing private sector investments. Moreover, unlike his father, Daley embraced the politics of identity and recognition, essentially buying out the emerging segment of middle-class minority homeowners, who, like their white counterparts, wanted to realize the gains that came with the gentrification of their neighborhoods. And unlike his father, he used a slick public relations machine that told Chicagoans that their schools were the best in the nation and that everyone had a fair chance to succeed in the city. The result of all these circumstances, *Chicago on the Make* seeks to demonstrate, was the formation of a political culture in which the forces of dissent and reform were much less capable of identifying the political, structural, and historical sources of injustice and inequality. And in this, Chicago was and still is a lot like many other American cities.

ONE

Capital Order

GROWING CHAOS

In 1903 renowned muckraking journalist Lincoln Steffens traveled to Chicago in search of a scoop on the graft, corruption, and brutality that Americans across the nation associated with the country's second largest metropolis. He did not exactly find the story he was expecting to write. After all, this was a city run by Carter Harrison II, a mayor who had proven his reformist mettle by working with the "goo-goos" in the Municipal Voter's League (MVL)—a group of upright businessmen, professionals, and social workers unified by the mission of bringing "good government" to their city— to appoint city council committees on a nonpartisan basis. And Harrison had just a year earlier taken an unequivocal stand in defense of the public interest in his dealings with the traction magnates—the robber barons looking to cash in on their soon-to-expire franchises on the tangle of streetcar lines inflicting impossible traffic jams downtown. If, for his part, Steffens judged Harrison a reluctant reformer, the mayor nonetheless advocated municipal ownership of mass transit and a popular referendum to decide the issue—a stance that certainly did not win him favor with railroad tycoon Charles Tyson Yerkes and the so-called Gray Wolves on the city council who had enabled him to amass a fortune of some $30 million since his arrival in Chicago more than a decade earlier. What impressed Steffens most of all were the earnest efforts of the MVL and its new secretary, Walter L. Fisher, which gave him cause to proclaim: "The city of Chicago is ruled by the citizens of Chicago." And yet Steffens did not leave Chicago without something sensational to report. If Chicago reformers seemed to Steffens to be fighting the good fight, they also seemed no match for the miasma of ills that plagued its residents: its tainted drinking water, its unpaved streets, its "stench of the stockyards," its "insufficient (and inefficient)" police force, its "mobs" and "riotous strikers," its "extra-legal system of controlling vice and crime." Summing it all up in the oft-repeated phrase that would come to identify Steffens's view of Chicago much more than any of his accolades about its engaged citizenry and reformers, he dubbed the city "[f]irst in violence, deepest in dirt; loud, lawless, unlovely, ill-smelling, irreverent, new; an overgrown gawk of a village, the "tough" among cities, the spectacle of a nation."[1]

While some may have thought Steffens was merely displaying the hyperbolic flair that was the signature of turn-of-the-century muckraking journalism, his claims were, in fact, right on the mark. By the early twentieth century, Chicagoans were killing each other at an astounding rate; its muddy streets were piled with trash, animal excrement, and seemingly all the detritus of humanity; its rivers were brown with sewage; and its skies black with coal soot. In fact, the vigorous civic engagement Steffens found so remarkable signified that an increasing number of its notables were beginning to reckon with these horrid conditions and with the idea that their city was quickly turning into the world's reference point for urban dystopia. Indeed, Steffens had arrived in Chicago at the dawning of a new era of reformist zeal, whose intensity had something to do with a growing sense among civic and political leaders that their city had fallen behind other great cities throughout the world in its manner of dealing with the social costs of laissez-faire capitalism. This new reformist spirit had taken shape within the context of what Daniel T. Rodgers has referred to as "the Atlantic Era," when "American social politics were tied to social political debates and endeavors in Europe through a web of rivalry and exchange."[2] For pioneering social worker Jane Addams, this meant traveling repeatedly to London's East End to observe the Toynbee Hall social settlement before launching her own Hull House settlement on Chicago's Near West Side. And for architect Daniel Burnham, who would set to work on his visionary *Plan of Chicago* several years later, it meant using the inspiration of Baron Haussmann and his renovation of nineteenth-century Paris "to bring order out of the chaos."[3]

It came as no surprise to most that Steffens had bestowed upon Chicago the dubious honor of being "first in violence"—certainly in the nation and perhaps in the world. By 1913, its murder rate was four times higher than New York's and was about fourteen times that of London. In fact, this situation had begun to arouse concern in 1903, when juvenile court judge Richard Tuthill had organized a group of businessmen, religious leaders, and other reform types into an "anti-crime committee" to put pressure on the police, whom they viewed as inefficient in fighting criminal activities, if not complicit with them.[4] Holding up Chicago's startling number of murders in comparison with London's, the editors of the *Chicago Tribune* spoke of "an attitude of mind which prevails in Chicago and which cannot be shaken except by long years of struggle on the part of individual Chicagoans to bring individual souls to a nobler conception of individual life." In the years to come, as racial theories and social Darwinism would take center stage in campaigns to close the country's borders, anticrime discourses would increasingly identify this "attitude of mind" with African Americans, Mexicans, Asian Americans, and a range of "races" that poured into the country from southern and eastern Europe between the 1880s and 1910s. But in turn-of-the-century Chicago, perceptions of criminality were still surprisingly democratic, more so, it seemed, than in comparable cities. "Crime in Chicago," the *Tribune*'s editors made sure to point out, "is a matter of individual tolerance of sharp, illegal, wrongful, violent practices, either at mahogany tables or in dark alleys."[5]

Chicago in the first decade of the twentieth century was certainly a place where even political officials at times settled their arguments with their fists, and one's ability to do so convincingly could earn respect. For example, when, as a young foreman for the Chicago Sanitary District in 1907, future mayor Edward Kelly punched out an insubordinate worker, his supervisor, Robert McCormick (a staunch Republican and future owner and publisher of the *Chicago Tribune*), granted him a raise and a promotion. McCormick told him he admired his "guts," as the story goes. Nonetheless, in most people's minds the violent crime problem that was the object of law-and-order campaigns and sensationalized newspaper reportage belonged almost exclusively to Chicago's laboring classes. "Homicide," as historian Jeffrey Adler has argued, "was a public and shockingly visible activity in late-nineteenth-century Chicago," where a good many murders took place in and around saloons, brothels, and other spaces defined by the male working-class "sporting culture" of the time.[6] And it was significant that a relatively large proportion of the city's rank and file worked in the most brutal of workplaces: the packinghouses, which, by the turn of the century, had become Chicago's largest sector of employment. The link between the bloody entrails on the killing floors and the bloody brawls in the streets was irresistible. "Men who crack the heads of animals all day," Upton Sinclair famously quipped in *The Jungle,* "seem to get into the habit, and to practice on their friends, and even on their families."[7] However, Chicago's national reputation for violence had also come, in part, from the spectacles of violence and destruction wrought by the Haymarket bombing of 1886 and the Pullman Strike of 1894, both of which witnessed striking workers battling the local forces of order and federal troops in its streets. These events were so threatening to Chicago's upper crust that a group of affluent businessmen living along Prairie Avenue's "Millionaire's Row" in the South Loop commissioned architects Daniel Burnham and John Wellborn Root to design the five-story, fortress-like First Regiment Armory at 1552 S. Michigan Avenue for the purpose of stationing troops and armaments just three blocks from their homes.

Hence, the civic-minded folks seeking to root out the sources of criminality in the first decade of the twentieth century, some of whom rubbed elbows with the residents of Prairie Avenue around mahogany tables, went first looking for them down "dark alleys." In 1900, for example, a group of concerned citizens and settlement workers constituted themselves into the Investigative Committee of the City Homes Association and fanned out into some of the city's impoverished Jewish, Italian, and Polish tenement districts around the Near West and Near North Sides with pencils and notepads. Among the six members of the committee were tireless social settlement worker Jane Addams and Anita McCormick Blaine, whose older brother Cyrus McCormick, Jr., had ordered Pinkerton thugs to attack strikers at his McCormick Harvesting Machine Company plant three days before the Haymarket bombing. McCormick Blaine, however, was no apologist for capitalism. She had just finished bankrolling John Dewey's new Laboratory School at the University of Chicago and its bold experiment of interactive pedagogical approaches in order to imbue in young children a sense of democratic citizenship. Addams, another daughter of a prominent Midwest businessman, was cut from the same cloth. Having cofounded Hull House a decade earlier to serve and better understand the needs of the largely Italian, Jewish, and Greek communities of the Near West Side, Addams thought of her work there as part of the same project of promoting social democratic principles at the grassroots. She placed special emphasis on the recreational programs offered to children, designing art, theater, and sports activities as means for instilling a spirit of democratic cooperation and civic consciousness. That these women had joined sociologist Robert Hunter on this committee demonstrated their belief that the living conditions prevailing in Chicago's tenement districts threatened the goals they held so dear.

Allowing no alley, privy, or manure box to escape their gaze, McCormick Blaine, Addams, and the other committee members recorded a seemingly endless litany of atrocities: raw sewage seeping into basements packed with families and into alleys where small children played; yards covered in manure and rotting garbage; chickens, horses, and cows living in and around apartments—all emitting unbearable odors and noises that forced residents to keep their windows closed, even during the suffocating heat of a Chicago summer. If Jacob Riis had made New York the emblem of tenement ills with his stunning photojournalism in *How the Other Half Lives* a decade earlier, the Investigative Committee of the City Homes Association, whose observations were gathered into a published report entitled *Tenement Conditions in Chicago,* insisted that conditions in Chicago were no less serious. Moreover, unlike older cities such as New York and London, which had been addressing tenement problems for years with an array of city ordinances, such legislation in Chicago was either nonexistent or unenforced. "There is probably no other city approximating the size of Chicago, in this country or abroad," they asserted, "which has as many neglected sanitary conditions associated with its tenement-house problem." "The conditions here," they concluded, "show how backward, in some respects, the City of Chicago is."[8]

To be sure, viewed from its tenement alleys, Chicago may have appeared backwards. But such perceptions also reflected the lofty standards of some of its leading reformers, who had already made the city a pioneer in some important ways. By the turn of the century Hull House represented the cutting edge of the nation's settlement house movement; Chicago's juvenile court—the world's first—was providing a widely recognized model for a new case-by-case approach that emphasized rehabilitation over punishment; and John Dewey was trying to revolutionize the country's educational system at the University of Chicago, which, when it had opened its doors in 1892, was the first university in the country to house a sociology department. Even on the tenement housing issue, Chicago was not exactly a laggard. In fact, the city's health department had been inspecting buildings and approving construction plans since the early 1880s. But the rapid spread of tenement districts overwhelmed its monitoring capacities. Chicago seemed backwards to reformers in large part because its authorities had failed to keep up with its breathtaking growth in the last quarter of the nineteenth century, when the population had more than quadrupled, from just over 400,000 to some 1.7 million.

While the many skyscrapers shooting upward from the bustling streets of the Loop business district during these decades attested to the new legions of white-collar workers making the city their home, industrialization was a key

FIGURE 1. The Union Stockyards. Courtesy of the Library of Congress.

driver of this spectacular growth. Indeed, if Chicago's breathtaking population growth made it an outlier in comparison with other large cities, the expansion of its industrial capacity was even more extraordinary. Between 1880 and 1900, the number of manufacturing workers in the city nearly quadrupled and the number of manufacturing establishments more than doubled.[9] Leading the way was the meatpacking sector, which by the turn of the century had captured an 80-percent share of the domestic market in packaged meat, making Chicago, in the words of local poet and journalist Carl Sandburg, "Hog Butcher for the World." At that time, Chicago's biggest meatpacking plants—Armour, Swift, and Morris—were among the thirty largest factories in the United States. Meatpacking workers constituted 10 percent of the city's wage labor force, and some 30 percent of Chicago's manufactures came out of the mammoth Union Stockyards at the southwestern edge of the city in the form of "Chicago dressed meat"—a brand that was shuttering butcher shops throughout the heartland. By 1900 the stockyards, perhaps the largest single industrial plant in the world, had expanded to 475 acres, with a pen capacity of more than 430,000 animals, 50 miles of road, and 130 miles of railroad track along its perimeter. During that year,

14,622,315 cattle, sheep, hogs, and horses passed through its pens, nine times the number of livestock herded through its gates in its first year of operation in 1866; by the 1920s, this number would surpass 18 million.[10]

Chicago's dramatic industrial growth, however, was also propelled by its massive steel works along the lakefront in the southeastern corner of the city. In 1889, most of Chicago's major steel mills merged to form Illinois Steel, making it, at the time, the world's largest steel manufacturer. In 1902, another merger engineered by New York banker J. P. Morgan saw Illinois Steel (then called Federal Steel) absorbed into the industrial giant U.S. Steel, the world's largest business enterprise. At that time the South Works site of steel production employed 3,500 men and covered some 260 acres; twelve years later, 11,000 people worked there. A number of other mills, such as Iroquois Steel, Wisconsin Steel, the Federal Furnace Company, and Interstate Iron and Steel Company, opened to the south of U.S. Steel around this time, and in 1906 U.S. Steel began operations in its massive Gary Works, which by the 1920s employed some 16,000. In the years to come, the steel corridor extending from the southern part of Chicago to Gary, Indiana, would make the region one of the world's top steel producers.

Moreover, a sizable amount of the millions of tons of steel being turned out in Chicago did not have to go very far. By the turn of the century the raw-materials needs of a number of Chicago's heavy industries were rising sharply, creating corresponding labor demands. In 1902, International Harvester—the by-product of the merger of McCormick Harvesting Machine Company with four other Chicago farm equipment makers—launched Wisconsin Steel to assure its steel supply as it gathered an 80-percent share of the world market in grain harvesting equipment. Within eight years the company was grossing about $100 million in annual sales and employing more than 17,000 workers in the Chicago area. Around this time, the Pullman Company became another big purchaser of Chicago-made steel as its production shifted from wooden to steel sleeper cars in its company town of Pullman fourteen miles south of the Loop, where its workforce increased from 6,000 to 10,000 between 1900 and 1910. In addition, a significant and growing portion of the steel produced within the Chicago-Gary corridor was hauled up to the Loop to be used in the construction of the steel skeletons holding up the city's many imposing skyscrapers.

Beginning in the 1880s, Chicago, along with New York, had quickly emerged as a pioneer in the construction of skyscrapers, with Chicago School architects such as Burnham, Root, and Louis Sullivan designing many of the city's landmark buildings. In the first two decades of the twentieth century, according to architectural historian Carol Willis, "the dominant aesthetic for office buildings in Chicago was to appear as big as possible by rising as a sheer wall above the sidewalks."[11] Often spanning a quarter of a city block and rising sixteen to twenty stories, these palazzo-style buildings typically contained ornate commercial courts with shops, services, and restaurants covered by glass canopies—signature features that sought to define the professionalism and class status of the white-collar workforce in the "City of Big Shoulders."[12] In fact, "big shoulders" by the tens of thousands were employed to construct these massive buildings, whose proliferation had, by the 1920s, moved Chicago into second place in the nation in number of headquarter offices.

Similar designs, moreover, characterized the swanky department stores that so elegantly displayed the wares of retailers such as Marshall Field and Carson Pirie Scott. The brisk expansion of Chicago's commercial, financial, insurance, real estate, and advertising sectors during this era created an enormous need for retail and office space. And leading the way were burgeoning mail-order retailers such as Montgomery Ward and Sears, Roebuck and Co., which, by bringing the fashions and necessities of modern life to folks in the hinterlands, had grown into some of the nation's largest business enterprises by the 1910s. Many of the fashions being mailed out, moreover, were produced right there in Chicago, which by the turn of the century had become the country's second largest production center for men's clothing. Making it possible to get all these workers and shoppers to the Loop was the rapid expansion of the city's elevated railroad system, which grew from 35 miles of line in 1900 to 70 miles by 1914, establishing Chicago's "L" as one of the longest metropolitan railways in the world.

All this to say that Chicago's economy and workforce expanded at breakneck speed in the late nineteenth and early twentieth centuries in comparison with most of the world's major cities. The city's phenomenal growth was due in part to its central location within the country's railroad network, which made it the "gateway" between east and west, in part to its extraordinarily diversified economy, and in part to the Great Fire of 1871, which by razing more than 18,000 structures across some 2,000 acres downtown, created the conditions for a building boom that worked to modernize the young city at a breathtaking pace. Yet the commercial forces unleashed in this perfect storm of redevelopment after the Great Fire had devastating effects on the city's infrastructure. They created a jumbled mess of railroad tracks, rail yards, and service buildings out of the lakefront; huddled poorly constructed wood-frame tenements around muddy, unpaved streets at the Loop's periphery; cut up the city with railroad tracks; and cluttered the Chicago River's banks with factories, smokestacks, and ramshackle warehouses. And this had all come to pass in a city that had shown it had the wherewithal to move mountains. Chicago, after all, had managed to put on the greatest spectacle in modern history when the city's brass had marshaled the resources and know-how to hastily conjure the majestic White City—the neoclassical fantasyland setting for the World's Columbian Exposition of 1893—out of some 600 acres of swamp and mud in Jackson Park. Over 27 million visitors had walked through the Beaux Arts pavilions of this city-within-a-city, marveling at wonders of modernity collected from the four corners of the world. Then, in 1900, the city had displayed its engineering prowess by permanently reversing the Chicago River's flow with the completion of the Sanitary and Ship Canal, thus stopping the outbreaks of cholera and typhoid caused by sewage pouring into the city's Lake Michigan drinking water. Yet, regardless of such technological feats, Chicago in the early 1900s nonetheless seemed like a city struggling in vain to make order out of the chaos that had taken it captive.

In addition to the built environment, this sense of chaos permeated the social fabric. Profound social instabilities grew out of the massive wave of immigrants and migrants that washed over Chicago between 1890 and 1910, when the city's foreign-born population increased from under half a million to almost 800,000. By 1910, the foreign born and their children made up almost 80 percent of the population. Moreover, the industrial juggernaut was pulling its immigrant laborers from other reaches of Europe than it had in the past. At the turn of the century, the Germans, the Irish, and the Poles had been the largest ethnic groups. By the 1910s, the Poles were on their way to becoming the most prominent white ethnic group; the Germans and the Irish were proportionally on the decline; and a range of new ethnic groups from points in southern and eastern Europe were exerting their presence in the streets and neighborhoods. While Chicago's population roughly doubled between 1890 and 1910, for example, its Italian-born population jumped eightfold and its Jewish population rocketed almost sixteenfold. Greeks and Czechs also poured into the city, which became the central destination in the United States for these groups.[13] Moreover, these decades also witnessed the arrival of an increasing number of African American migrants from the South. Between 1890 and 1910, Chicago's black population more than tripled, jumping from 14,271 to 44,103, which at the time represented 2 percent of the overall population.

The tendency for these new ethnic groups to form close-knit communities accentuated the great changes under way, as native-born Chicagoans saw whole neighborhoods being transformed before their eyes. In the late 1890s, for example, Swedes had dominated the Near North Side "Swede Town" neighborhood around Seward Park; just ten years later it would be commonly referred to as "Little Sicily." But nowhere was this phenomenon more readily apparent than on the Near West Side, in the immediate vicinity of Hull House, where a number of the city's most distinctive ethnic neighborhoods sprung up seemingly overnight. A short stroll to the north took one into the "Greek Delta" (later known as Greektown) at the triangle of Halsted, Harrison, and Blue Island Avenue; just to the south lay the "Jew Town" neighborhood around Maxwell Street, with its bustling outdoor market and ramshackle storefront synagogues; and a quick jaunt to the west along Taylor Street took one straight into the heart of Little Italy. To the northwest of Greektown, at the triangle formed by Division, Ashland, and Milwaukee Avenue lay the heart of Polish Downtown. South of Maxwell Street, in the Pilsen area, was the city's largest Czech community. To the east of Pilsen, Chicago's largest African American neighborhood, referred to as the "Black Belt," stretched from the Loop down to the Levee vice district between 18th and 22nd Streets and beyond to 39th Street, encompassing much of the 2nd and 3rd Wards. While such areas of the city came to be associated with a certain predominant group whose imprint appeared in the form of ethnically identifiable saloons, groceries, restaurants, retail shops, places of worship, and meeting spots, these neighborhoods were far from homogeneous. Jews, Italians, Greeks, and blacks collided on a daily basis on the Near West Side; Polish Downtown overlapped with well-defined enclaves of Jews, Italians, and Ukrainians; Czechs and Poles coexisted in Pilsen; and the Back of the Yards neighborhood adjacent to the stockyards mixed Germans, Irish, Poles, Slovaks, Lithuanians, and Czechs. Even African Americans were relatively well distributed throughout the city, settling among Italians and other white ethnics on the Near West and Near North Sides, as well as around the steel mills in the South Chicago community area. In fact, although the forces of segregation were gaining momentum by the early 1900s, as late as 1910 blacks remained less segregated from native-born whites than Italian immigrants.[14]

Nonetheless, by the early 1900s the social fabric seemed to be coming apart at the seams. Youth gangs and athletic clubs patrolled neighborhood boundaries, engaging in turf battles that reflected both simmering tensions between rival ethnoracial communities and the increasing precariousness of masculinity in a labor market characterized by Taylorist deskilling strategies on the part of employers and downward wage pressures caused by all of the new immigrants ready and willing to fill unskilled jobs. Such circumstances contributed to the wave of lethal violence that made Chicago the nation's leader in homicides by 1910, as well as to the rise of a new era in racially motivated aggression within the laboring class.[15] Particularly emblematic of the new times were the rancorous and vicious labor conflicts that shook the city in the summers of 1904 and 1905.

The first of these, the stockyards strike of 1904, began in the first week of July after the major meatpackers refused to guarantee the wage levels of unskilled packinghouse workers, whom unionists from the Amalgamated Meat Cutters and Butcher Workmen (AMCBW) believed were being used to undercut the pay and position of skilled butchers. The ensuing strike involved the immediate walkout of some 20,000 workers and lasted two months, with numerous violent clashes pitting strikers and their sympathizers against strikebreakers and the police. While the vast majority of the strikebreakers recruited by the packers were white, black strikebreakers occupied center stage in the drama from the outset. Antiblack violence associated with the strike quickly metastasized as white workers began referring to blacks in general as a "scab race." Suggestive of the rancorous racial hatred circulating around the affair was a polemic in one labor newspaper that referred to the strikebreakers as "a horde of debased, bestialized blacks . . . brought in[to] the labor market and shipped into the yards as hogs are shipped for the killing floors."[16] Over the summer, African Americans, whether involved in the strike or not, became frequent targets of violence around the stockyards, being pulled off streetcars by mobs or pelted with rocks in the streets. Such injuries were compounded by the strike's failure, which the butchers of course blamed on the black strikebreakers, who, for their part, lost their jobs as soon as the conflict ended.

The teamsters strike of the following year further escalated the racial situation. Beginning in April as a sympathy strike by the Brotherhood of Teamsters in support of the United Garment Workers (UGW), several of whose members had been fired by Montgomery Ward for a strike months before, the campaign quickly garnered the participation of several thousand workers and turned destructive. Days after the teamsters stopped deliveries to Montgomery Ward, the *Chicago Tribune* alarmingly reported the outbreak of "riotous demonstrations, blockading of streets, and clashes with the police force."[17] Once again, employers resorted to bringing in black strike-breakers, and once again racial hatred eclipsed class struggle, as attacks on African Americans spilled out of the context of the labor dispute and into the streets and neighborhoods. According to historian David H. Bates, the savage violence that followed was partly due to the race-baiting tactics of the Chicago Employers Association, an antiunion cabal led by Marshall Field's vice president John G. Shedd and Montgomery Ward executive Robert J. Thorne, which paraded black strikebreakers provocatively through the streets in broad daylight and circulated inflammatory pamphlets asserting that such events portended that blacks would soon "assume a responsible place in society ... upon equal terms with the whites."[18] The reportage of the main Chicago dailies fanned the flames of race hatred, publishing stories that highlighted the immorality and licentiousness of the black strikebreakers. One *Tribune* article, for example, characterized them as "Southern 'darkies,' who had loafed all their lives along the cotton bales of the Mississippi docks."[19] Although blacks constituted but a small minority of the strike-breakers, white workers were yet again only too eager to take the bait. Strikers threw bricks from rooftops and took to the streets wielding axes, shovels, clubs, and revolvers on an almost daily basis between late April and mid July, a situation that led the strikebreakers to fight back with revolvers and razors. The violence spiraled out of control on April 29th, when thousands of strikers confronted the police in a battle that resulted in three shootings and two stabbings, and then again on May 4th, when mobs broke off from a crowd of more than five thousand and carried out indiscriminate attacks on any blacks in sight. By July, as the strike broke down amidst allegations of bribes exchanged between union leaders and employers, twenty-one people had been killed and over four hundred seriously injured. As in the stockyards strike of the previous summer, workers suffered a crushing defeat. Stained by bribery accusations and the unbridled violence that had shaken the city, the local labor movement limped out of the summer of 1905 towards an uncertain future in which employers would continue to exploit racial fears to break unions.

And yet these tactics worked so effectively because such fears were, in the early 1900s, spreading like an epidemic through the city's working-class districts. A good many of those venting their rage at blacks during the labor campaigns of 1904 and 1905 were immigrants whose place in the city began to seem increasingly tenuous around this time. This situation was certainly not specific to Chicago. Immigrants from southern and eastern Europe encountered ethnoracial discrimination across the urban United States as they sought to claim their rightful place in their neighborhoods and workplaces during the early years of the twentieth century. Employers regularly refused to hire members of certain groups for higher-paying skilled jobs, both out of an effort to break the unity of the workforce and out of their own racialized sense of which groups were more suited to performing skilled tasks. In Chicago's packinghouses, the Irish and the Germans were the so-called butcher aristocracy, with Poles and other eastern European groups filling a range of semiskilled and unskilled jobs below them, and blacks performing the dirtiest, lowest-paid work available. Similar arrangements increasingly characterized the workforces of the city's steel mills and manufacturing plants. Such hierarchies were reproduced within the city's residential geography, as native-born landlords and realtors commonly refused housing opportunities to blacks and immigrants from southern and eastern Europe. An ethnoracial pecking order was also taking shape out on the streets, where certain groups found themselves to be more susceptible to attacks by street gangs and athletic clubs defending their turf. Here again, the Irish constituted, in the words of sociologist Frederic Thrasher, "the aristocracy of gangland," and their propensity to target Jews, blacks, and, to a somewhat lesser extent, Poles and Italians conveyed to these groups that their status within the city was far from secure.[20] As historians James Barrett and David Roediger have argued, all this constituted a process of "Americanization from the bottom up" in which the Irish served as the key "Americanizers."[21] The power of the Irish to perform this role came from their presence and influence in a range of institutions immigrants dealt with in their daily lives: the school system, the Catholic Church, labor unions, the police department, and the political world.

By the second half of the 1910s, this process of Americanization at the grassroots was increasingly informing immigrants that their proximity to blacks on the job and in their neighborhood placed them in jeopardy. Such feelings would only intensify in the years to come, as a massive wave of African American migrants arrived in the city, and blacks emerged as a new force to be reckoned with at work, in the neighborhoods, and in municipal politics. Between 1910 and 1920, Chicago's black population would more than double, and in the "red summer" of 1919, the city would witness the most violent and destructive race riot in the nation's history. But, as the savagery and bloodshed of the stockyards and teamsters strikes revealed, such events should not be viewed as the mere consequences of demographic forces—the reflexes of a tipping point reached. African Americans, after all, constituted a rather inconsequential segment of the city's turn-of-the-century workforce and a relatively small minority of the strikebreakers brought into the city in 1904 and 1905. And yet their presence aroused an unprecedented level of racial animosity—an animosity fed by the racial uncertainties faced by new immigrants during these years. But if the racial order of the city was evolving by the turn of the century, the events of 1904 and 1905 clearly worked to transform the role race would play in Chicago's political culture in the years to come, and the fact that some of the city's leading businessmen had pulled the strings should not be overlooked.

ORDER OUT OF CHAOS

If the stockyards and teamsters strikes of 1904 and 1905 seemed to signify the outbreak of race war for many white workers, such events had very different implications for the city's business community. For the city's longstanding power elites—Field, Armour, and Pullman, among others—these explosions of labor violence represented another peak moment in a longer pattern of class warfare that had witnessed epic confrontations between disgruntled workers and the forces of order in the middle years of every decade since the 1870s, when, during the Great Railroad Strike of 1877, Mayor Monroe Heath rounded up some five thousand vigilantes to take on striking railroad workers. While this more recent wave of strikes did not involve the intervention of federal troops, as had been the case in the Great Railroad Strike, the Haymarket affair of 1886, and the Pullman Strike of 1894, the seriousness of the situation was lost on few within Chicago's rather tight circle of business elites. A range of business interests—meatpackers, retailers, and the press— conspired to ignite the flames of race hatred in 1904 and 1905. The response to the teamsters strike, in particular, revealed the existence of a tight alliance of businessmen—brought together under the auspices of the Employers Association of Chicago—sworn to the task of defeating the unions and making Chicago an "open shop" town. Although the Employers Association had been led by retailing executives John G. Shedd and Robert J. Thorne during the teamsters strike, it had formed three years earlier with financing from a number of prominent bankers to take on strikers seeking to unionize manufacturing workers at Western Electric.[22] In managing the battle over public opinion, the Employers Association also clearly had the moral support of some key dailies. But the collusion of the press involved more than this. It is doubtful that the race-baiting tactics of the Employers Association would have met with the same success without the toxic press coverage provided by the supposedly progressive *Chicago Tribune* and the more avowedly reactionary *Chicago Daily News,* which painted unionists as hell-bent on destruction and black strikebreakers as moral degenerates.

Indeed, African Americans were not the only ones to suffer from the fallout of these events, and while broader currents were carrying along discourses linking the nation's decline to the racial others crowding out the "native Anglo-Saxon race," diatribes against immigrants seemed particularly virulent and somewhat more visible after the strikes. The city's homicide epidemic merged seamlessly with the vicious labor violence of previous years, shaping perceptions that immigrants were prone to such behavior. By 1907, this premise was guiding the work of the United States Immigration Commission (also known as the Dillingham Commission), which, after analyzing Chicago arrest records between 1905 and 1908, concluded in its 1911 report that southern and eastern Europeans committed more murders than "the peoples of northern and western Europe and the peoples of North America, with the exception of the American negroes."[23] In Chicago, however, this had been a foregone conclusion for years. Discussing the city's crime problem in the pages of the *Chicago Record-Herald* in July 1906, for example, police chief John Collins went so far as to refer to the city as a "dumping ground for the different nations of Europe" and a "rallying point for the scum of the earth."[24]

And yet, as the work of Jane Addams and Anita McCormick Blaine on Chicago's tenements revealed, some of the more enlightened middle-class Chicagoans did not put much stock into such ideas. In fact, the city's business elite was, politically speaking, a somewhat varied crowd, and even within individual families one could find opposing positions on the pressing issues of the day. As historian Maureen Flanagan has argued, middle-class men and women, in particular, tended to have markedly divergent perspectives on the city and its problems during this era.[25] But significant differences of opinion existed among men as well. A good many prominent Chicago men would answer the call of Jane Addams during the 1912 presidential election to break with old school Republicans and support the Progressive Party candidate, Theodore Roosevelt. *Chicago Tribune* vice president Joseph Medill McCormick, for example, signed on as vice chairman for the Progressive Party's national campaign committee. McCormick's progressive leanings, however, did not necessarily involve a warm embrace—at least when Chicago was involved—of the kind of lofty pro-labor principles espoused by the Progressive Party platform. Although the *Tribune*'s coverage of labor affairs had come a long way from the Haymarket era, when, under Joseph Medill's direction, the paper once referred to strikers as "the scum and filth of the city," the *Tribune*'s sensationalist, race-baiting reportage of the stockyards and teamsters strikes under Medill McCormick hardly displayed an unmitigated commitment to the working man.

Medill McCormick, it should not be forgotten, circulated within a milieu in which rabid antiunionism lingered in the air with the thick smoke of fine cigars. He was a loyal member of Chicago's most elite fraternity of business leaders, the Commercial Club of Chicago, which met each month in the glitzy dining hall of the Auditorium Hotel over an extravagant four-course dinner, concocted with the finest ingredients from overseas, to discuss the business of the city and to hear talks by illustrious guest speakers. The Commercial Club received presidents, senators, congressmen, and cabinet members, as well as the city's most influential reformers and civic leaders, and meetings were not to be missed. This exclusive club gathered among its members a good many of those leading the charge against the labor movement in the early 1900s: retailing executives like Shedd, Thorne, and John W. Scott of Carson Pirie Scott; wholesalers like John V. Farwell Jr. of Farwell & Company and Frank H. Armstrong of Reid, Murdoch & Company; captains of meatpacking like J. Ogden Armour and his right-hand man, Arthur Meeker; and leading newspapermen like Medill McCormick and Victor Lawson of the *Chicago Daily News*. To be admitted into the this elite fold, one of its founding members wrote, "a man must have shown conspicuous success in his private business, with a broad and comprehending sympathy with important affairs of city and state, and a generous subordinating of self in the interests of the community."[26] Such sympathy and generosity extended to the helpless and infirm—Farwell, for example, was a big benefactor of the Young Men's Christian Association (YMCA) and its orphan asylum—but stopped well short of able-bodied workers fighting for better living and working conditions. In fact, a great many of the philanthropic activities pursued by the Commercial Club's members figured somehow into the labor question. The YMCA's project of evangelizing working-class young men and offering them healthy recreational alternatives to keep them out of the saloons made it one of the Commercial Club's charities of choice. The great antilabor warriors of the late nineteenth century (all Commercial Club members)—Philip Armour, Cyrus McCormick, and George Pullman—were all generous benefactors of this organization.

Commercial Club members were also quite active as patrons and sponsors of the city's cultural institutions, with twelve serving on the board of the Art Institute of Chicago and eight on the board of the Chicago Symphony Orchestra by 1907. Yet the involvement of the captains of industry and finance in such endeavors was about more than obtaining marks of prestige and refinement. Between the 1890s and 1910s, both of these institutions, in line with the spirit of Hull House, were engaged in missions to uplift the laboring classes by bringing them into contact with the fine arts. Beginning in 1909, the Art Institute sponsored exhibitions of its works in public park field houses and other neighborhood settings, and in 1914 it worked with the Chicago Board of Education to bring exhibitions into some of the city's public schools. For its part, the Chicago Symphony Orchestra partnered with the Civic Music Association, an organization launched by the progressive-minded Chicago Women's Club, to fill the city's parks and neighborhoods with the refined sounds of classical music. Although banker, Art Institute president, and Commercial Club member Charles Hutchinson spearheaded these activities, they also reflected the fact that the spirit of progressivism embraced by Jane Addams had taken hold among a significant number of the city's power elites—more so, according to historian Paul DiMaggio, than in other major U.S. cities.[27] Within the context of the Commercial Club, this spirit translated into a marked open-mindedness in terms of the speakers chosen to enlighten its members. Jane Addams and pioneering black writer Alain Locke, for example, were among those invited to address the club during these years. Although Hutchinson may not have seen eye to eye with the hardcore antiunionists in the Commercial Club on some issues, he was largely after the same thing: a resolution of the class war that appeared to be threatening Chicago's place on the national and world stages. The Commercial Club discussed the labor question at a number of its banquets in the early 1900s. The very building in which it often met, the Auditorium Hotel, with its grandiose Auditorium Theater, was a monument to the mission of disarming the laboring classes. Conceived amidst the labor upheavals of the 1880s on a scale that would facilitate the sale of low-priced seats, the entrepreneur behind the Auditorium Theater's construction, Ferdinand Peck, once claimed that "magnificent music, at prices within the reach of all, would have a tendency to diminish crime and Socialism in our city by educating the masses to higher things."[28] Not surprisingly, Marshall Field and George Pullman were among the project's biggest investors.

However, amidst the troubling violence of the stockyards and teamsters strikes, it is likely that many of Chicago's civic and business leaders felt that more dramatic measures were necessary to bring order to the chaos—social and infrastructural—that seemed to be dragging the city down. Such feelings gained increasing expression, in particular, among the members of the Commercial Club and the Chicago Merchants Club, another exclusive organization of leading businessmen that distinguished itself from its homologue by restricting its membership to men under the age of forty-five. In 1907, the two organizations merged, taking the name of the older, more prestigious Commercial Club, in order to more effectively support the grand plan that was to save the city from the chaos enveloping it. The Commercial Club quickly raised the funds required to draft the plan, and the expertise behind it was provided by one of its own members: Chicago's star architect Daniel Burnham. The result of this private initiative, the *Plan of Chicago*, was released on July 4, 1909, amidst an aggressive public relations campaign that sought to make the ideas behind the plan building blocks of common sense. By January 1910 the Chicago Plan Commission, the body responsible for drafting and promoting the plan, had raised money for an abridged edition to be assigned to eighth graders as a part of their civics curriculum, the idea being that these adolescents would then educate their parents about the plan's merits. The *Plan of Chicago* would need to be sold to the public, the commission realized, if it stood any chance of being implemented.[29]

Using the city of Paris as its main source of inspiration, the plan called for a number of projects that would "bring order out of the chaos incident to rapid growth" and turn the city into "an efficient instrument for providing all its people with the best possible conditions of living": a green, uncluttered lakefront area that would facilitate views of the lake to inspire "calm thoughts and feelings"; a scheme for a metropolitan highway system; the consolidation of the intercity railroad passenger terminals into new centralized complexes around the Loop; the incorporation of forest areas around the city into a vast park system; the widening of existing thoroughfares into Parisian-style boulevards and the addition of new diagonal streets to improve the circulation of traffic around the city; and the construction of a massive neoclassical civic center downtown that would serve as a source of pride and unity for all.[30] Of course an unabashed commercial logic tied together all of these schemes. The goal of the whole project was to ensure the future "prosperity" of the city, a notion linked, in the final analysis, to the accumulation of wealth more than anything else, as the plan explained:

> In creating the ideal arrangement, everyone who lives here is better accommodated in his business and his social activities. In bringing about better freight and passenger facilities, every merchant and manufacturer is helped. In establishing a complete park and parkway system, the life of the wage-earner and of his family is made healthier and pleasanter; while the greater attractiveness thus produced keeps at home the people of means and taste, and acts as a magnet to draw those who seek to live amid pleasing surroundings. The very beauty that attracts him who has money makes pleasant the life of those among whom he lives, while anchoring him and his wealth to the city. The prosperity aimed at is for all Chicago.[31]

Clearly the objective of attracting, retaining, and generating capital lay at the center of the plan's moral universe. Tellingly, average citizens here were conceptualized only as wage-earners, and there was little doubt that their health and well-being mattered only in so much as they made them better workers. In this the plan reflected the ethos of the City Beautiful movement of the 1890s and 1900s, of which Burnham was a central figure. Beautification, proponents of this movement believed, would lead to a higher quality of life for the populace, which in turn would bring about social harmony, thereby ensuring optimal conditions for labor productivity. While the labor conflicts of previous years were referred to only obliquely as "frequent outbreaks against law and order," the plan, in the environmentalist spirit of reformers like Jane Addams, attributed such problems to the "narrow and pleasureless lives" led by the city's laborers.[32] The solution then was to create a city that would function on a grand scale in the same way as the fine arts and recreational initiatives behind which many in the Commercial Club were then throwing their support.

Reflecting on the plan today, it is tempting to interpret its vision of the city as "an efficient instrument" for the accumulation of wealth, its displacement of any sense of social justice by values of business efficiency, and its authorship by a group of businessmen representing an organization called the "Commercial Club" as symptoms of the kind of neoliberal mind-set that would increasingly shape Chicago's political culture during the postwar decades. And yet if the plan represented a seminal moment in a longer process of neoliberalization that would advance incrementally throughout the twentieth century, it also revealed how much resistance that process ran up against during this era. Moreover, as much as Burnham and his peers viewed business as occupying the driver's seat, they also invested in the idea of a protective and interventionist state using its power to improve the general welfare of city residents (rather than a truly neoliberal one whose only vocation was to unleash free market dynamics). "It is no attack on private property," the plan asserted, "to argue that society has the inherent right to protect itself against abuses."[33] Furthermore, strikingly expansive notions of "the people" and "the public interest" were seemingly everywhere to be found—a far cry from the privatized, individualized neoliberal mind-set of the late twentieth century. In perhaps its most definitive passage, for example, the plan characterized the very "spirit of Chicago" as "the constant, steady determination to bring about the very best conditions of city life for all the people, with full knowledge that what we as a people decide to do in the public interest we can and surely will bring to pass."[34] Such democratic ideals extended to some of the city's most valuable resources, such as the lakefront, which the plan affirmed in no uncertain terms "belong[ed] to the people." "Not a foot of its shores," it unambiguously specified, "should be appropriated by individuals to the exclusion of the people."[35] Finally, the great amount of energy and resources the Commercial Club brought to promoting the plan also suggested how far away the city was from where it would be by the late 1950s, when the major planning decisions shaping its future were moving further and further out of the public eye. The city's business interests would perhaps never again speak in such a unified voice about its planning priorities, and nevertheless the plan's implementation was far from a fait accompli.

Of course the plan faced other challenges beyond public acceptance. For one thing, raising the funds required by these massive infrastructural projects was going to be difficult because of state-level constitutional limitations on the city's home rule powers. In other words, Chicago would require authorization from the Illinois state legislature to borrow money or to initiate new tax policies. For another, although the Municipal Voters League had begun to take on the corrupt practices of the Gray Wolves on the city council, it was unable to remove them from office. Preventing the plan's infrastructural projects from becoming boondoggles was thus not going to be easy. Daniel Burnham and the rest of the Chicago Plan Commission had so little faith in the public authorities that they were ready to raise the necessary funds themselves in order to force the city to carry out the plan's projects. In fact, considering that the *Plan of Chicago* devoted an entire chapter to implementation, it is quite reasonable to conclude that practical considerations as well were behind its heartfelt embrace of the people. The people offered valuable leverage in the struggle to force the hand of the public authorities. And the Chicago Plan Commission continued to insist on the active participation of the people into the 1920s, when under the chairmanship of businessman and leading Commercial Club member Charles Wacker, it issued a pamphlet entitled *An S-O-S to the Public Spirited Citizens of Chicago.*

While the people never really took the cause to heart in the way Burnham and his cohorts had dreamed, the Chicago Plan Commission did manage to work closely and somewhat effectively with every mayoral administration between 1909 and 1931. Chicagoans approved numerous bond issues (some eighty-six between 1912 and 1931) that provided the city with more than $230 million during this era. Key thoroughfares like Michigan Avenue, Roosevelt Road, Western Avenue, and Ashland Avenue were widened; the double-level Wacker Drive was constructed so as to route traffic around the Loop; the new Union Station railroad terminal was built; a huge stretch of the lakeshore was filled and landscaped along with neighboring Grant Park; a recreational parkway was developed along the lakefront; numerous parks and playgrounds were added; and the Forest Preserve District of Cook County acquired several tens of thousands of acres of forest land around the outskirts of the city. Although most of these projects fell short of the plan's vision, and the majestic civic center in the heart of the city never materialized, Burnham's scheme had clearly served as a blueprint for these infrastructural changes. By the beginning of the 1930s, however, the role of the Chicago Plan Commission had diminished—in part because much of it had been taken over by the Zoning Commission after the enactment of the city's first zoning ordinance in 1923—and in 1939 the Chicago Plan Commission was incorporated into the city government as a somewhat powerless advisory body.

These changes corresponded with broader trends shaping municipal administrations across the urban United States, as city governments became active in the business of planning and zoning in the 1920s. According to geographer Robert Lewis, Chicago's 1923 zoning ordinance was pivotal in transforming the role that city government would play in the local economy. Zoning in Chicago emerged at the outset as more of "an expansionary tool" than an instrument of social reform, with the zoning commission increasingly focusing on economic matters—the promotion of industrial growth and the preservation of real estate values—over social ones.[36] Driving the decisions and policies of zoning officials from the outset were fears about competition from other cities. Such orientations reflected the Chicago plan's priorities of keeping the city's wealth and wealthy citizens from departing for greener pastures, and of boosting real estate values. Burnham, after all, was an architect, and the Commercial Club was, of course, propertied to the hilt. And yet, somewhat ironically, this private initiative to align the city's planning priorities with the interests of capital—backed by men who had waged a bloody war against the labor movement—looked to the people in a way that would soon seem foolishly nostalgic. Somewhat paradoxically, as the planning apparatus passed from private to public hands—to zoning and planning officials who were either democratically elected or appointed by officials who were—all the concern with the people and the public interest that Burnham and his cohorts had displayed began to fade. And as the very notion of the people itself slipped into obsolescence, so did concerns with improving the quality of their lives. Burnham's global vision of a "well-ordered, convenient, and unified city" could never survive within the piecemeal, fractured, political process that planning had become, and the unity and civic spirit he so cherished could never be achieved in the fragmented metropolis that Chicago was quickly becoming.

RACIAL ORDER, MACHINE ORDER

On a stiflingly hot Sunday at the end of July in 1919, the racial tensions that had been simmering since the stockyards strike of 1904 boiled over into a massive race riot that had people across the city throwing around the expression "race war." Fittingly, the whole affair began at the lakefront, the very place whose blue watery vistas, Burnham had believed, would inspire "calm thoughts." What transpired on the strip of sand between 25th and 29th Streets on July 27 was anything but serene. While differing accounts exist as to what sparked the week-long rampage of rage, violence, and arson, there is general agreement on three related events that occurred that day. The first concerned several African Americans daring to cross the imaginary color line in the sand to cool themselves in water fronted by a beach whites believed was reserved to them—an act that earned them a shower of rocks hurled by white beachgoers. The second, later in the day, involved a young white man in the breakwater around 26th Street lobbing rocks at three black teens on a makeshift raft, striking one of them, Eugene Williams, in the head and sending him to the bottom of the lake to his death. The third witnessed a mob of African Americans confronting police for refusing to arrest the man who had allegedly thrown the rock that had struck Williams, a situation that led

FIGURE 2. Homicidal violence around the stockyards during the 1919 riot. Photo by Jun Fujita. From The New York Public Library.

to an exchange of gunshots that left a police officer wounded and the civilian shooter dead. These were the first two casualties of a frenzy of homicidal violence that, in the final toll, left thirty-eight people dead, some five hundred wounded, and thousands homeless. Some notable incidents were reported in the Near West and Near North Sides, but the area around the stockyards was ground zero.

While the magnitude and duration of the explosion shocked many, few were particularly surprised. Two years earlier Chicagoans had read about the horror and bloodshed of a similar race riot downstate, in East Saint Louis, Illinois, and the local press made sure that nobody missed the point that it could happen here. Appearing next to coverage of the aftermath of the East Saint Louis riot in the *Chicago Tribune*'s edition of July 8, 1917, for example, was one story with the provocative headline "Half a Million Darkies from Dixie Swarm the North to Better Themselves" and another reporting on former Illinois governor Charles Deneen's suggestion that city authorities close the Black Belt's "saloons, vicious cabarets, disorderly houses ... as a safeguard against riots and mobs." "Conditions in East Saint Louis," the story made sure to point out, "were not unlike those prevailing in Chicago."[37] And there was certainly some truth to this. The series of events that had unraveled at the lakefront that scorching July day were perfectly consistent with general trends that had made Chicago into a tinderbox of racial conflict in the years leading up to the riot. In short, working-class white Chicagoans were becoming much more prone to lashing out against their African American neighbors and coworkers, and African Americans were becoming much more willing to resist and confront such aggression. In the past, collective acts of racial violence had crystallized mostly within the context of labor conflicts. But the scene at the lakefront revealed a new pattern of racial struggle over neighborhoods and recreational spaces that was becoming increasingly apparent as the city's black population grew, and with it the determination of African American residents to assert their rights to the city's spaces and resources. Further exacerbating the situation was the fact that the forces of order often refused to protect the rights of blacks, and, in some instances, actively aided white aggressors in their campaign to defend their neighborhoods against what they viewed as "black invasion."

This volatile mix of circumstances came together with the entrance of the United States into the First World War, which opened up unprecedented opportunities for blacks in the industrial workforce. In part due to the efforts of labor recruiters operating in the Deep South, over fifty thousand black migrants arrived in the city between 1916 and 1919, roughly doubling the city's black population.[38] Many of them had expected to find a friendlier racial climate up North, but such hopes were quickly dashed. Mingling with such frustrations, moreover, was a new sense of assertiveness and wounded pride on the part of black veterans returning to the city after risking their lives for their country in combat overseas. These conditions produced a new wave of racial violence around the boundaries of the South Side Black Belt, which in 1915 consisted of a quarter-mile-wide band running along State Street from 12th Street down to 39th Street and edging southward. Between July 1, 1917, and July 27, 1919—the first day of the riot—whites in neighborhoods bordering the Black Belt bombed twenty-four black homes and stoned or otherwise vandalized countless others.[39] The main perpetrators of such terror were young men organized into street gangs and so-called athletic clubs based in the Irish neighborhoods to the east of the stockyards. The most notorious of these organizations was Ragen's Colts, a club that provided muscle for Democratic Cook County commissioner Frank Ragen and boasted of having some two thousand members. Such groups, according to a study of the riot's

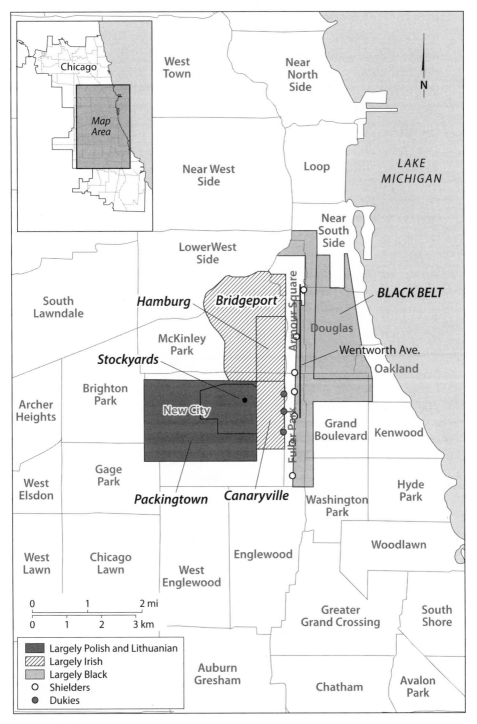

MAP 2. Communities, gangs, and boundaries on the South Side, ca. 1919.

causes by the Chicago Commission on Race Relations (CCRR), were instrumental in escalating the conflict and spreading it from the lakefront into the neighborhoods around the stockyards and the Black Belt. By the time of the riot, Irish gangs such as the Dukies and the Shielders claimed affiliates in a long stretch of city blocks from around 22nd Street all the way down to 59th Street, constituting a phalanx of hard-nosed street toughs bent on punishing any African American who dared cross the "dead line" of Wentworth Avenue and venture into the Irish neighborhoods of the Bridgeport area, Hamburg and Canaryville, which lay between the Black Belt and the stockyards. In the months preceding the riot, the antiblack intimidation carried out by these groups was so persistent and the sense of Irish pride motivating it so marked that, as historian James Grossman has noted, "many blacks mistakenly assumed that all the white gangs were Irish."[40]

Historians have generally agreed that Irish participation in the riot was strong, and more recent interpretations have put forward rather compelling evidence that some of the eastern European groups around the stockyards—Poles, Lithuanians, Czechs, and Jews—were reluctant to join in the hostilities, even at times comparing the attacks on blacks to forms of discrimination visited upon them by the Irish and other "Americans." For example, Arnold Hirsch's survey of a range of foreign-language newspapers—Polish, Lithuanian, Jewish, and Italian—in the period following the riot turned up a number of editorials that viewed the violence against African Americans as another ploy by the bosses to break the unions.[41] Such findings could be interpreted as running counter to the idea that the Irish served as Americanizers for southern and eastern Europeans occupying a racially in-between status during the interwar years. Why indeed would the aristocracy of the stockyards and streets feel the need to engage in such demonstrative and risky acts when they seemingly had little to prove, and why would the groups whose status in the racial order was most precarious refrain from following the example of their standard-bearers as a means to reaffirming their whiteness?

As for the matter of antiblack aggression on the part of the Irish, the explanation has perhaps more to do with the injuries of class than with the circumstances of race, though the two factors were of course hard to disentangle in interwar Chicago. Certainly recent political events had stirred up racial animosities. Only four months prior to the riot, Republican mayor "Big Bill" Thompson had won his reelection bid in a tight race with strong support from black voters. "NEGROES ELECT BIG BILL" was the headline of the

Democratic rag *The Chicago Daily Journal* on the eve of election day—a proclamation that elicited palpable outrage in Irish Bridgeport. That Thompson was a Republican was bad enough, but this particular Republican also displayed anti-Catholic tendencies in a moment when such tendencies were on the rise. Moreover, this slap in the face came at a time when working conditions around the stockyards were clearly deteriorating in the midst of the postwar recession everyone had feared. With the packinghouses laying off some fifteen thousand workers in the spring of 1919, employers looking to speed up the pace of production, and workers fearing competition from the tens of thousands of African Americans arriving in the city, tensions moved from the killing floors into the communities of Canaryville and Hamburg.

Canaryville and Hamburg were, in fact, separate neighborhoods with somewhat distinct and at times even rival identities. While each was home to families of packinghouse workers and industrial laborers, Hamburg, which extended from 31st to 39th Street between Halsted Avenue and the Penn Central Railroad tracks, had a leg up over its southern rival, which, with its western edge along Halsted between 39th and 49th Streets, offered too little distance from the smoke and odor of the stockyards. Canaryville was also too close to the increasingly overcrowded Back of the Yards (or Packingtown) area to the west of the stockyards, with its decrepit two-story wood-frame tenements packed with the Polish and Lithuanian immigrants whom Irish Bridgeport's experienced meat cutters and butcher workmen commonly accused of undercutting their wages. Such conditions produced a street subculture that turned teenagers into career criminals—the Canaryville School of Gunmen, as it was referred to.[42]

Hamburg was also hard-boiled, but it was more akin to the Bridgeport that would produce three mayors and numerous other political, civic, and business leaders out of the generation of 1919. One of these was the future "Boss" of Chicago, Richard J. Daley, who used the strict guidance provided by the Our Lady of Nativity Parish School and then the commercial orientation of nearby De La Salle High School to help him ascend the ranks of the city's political machine to the mayor's office. Yet when not in the classroom or at his summer job in the stockyards, the young Richard Daley was running with the Hamburg Athletic Club, an organization which, as Mike Royko opined, "never had the Colts' reputation for criminality, but [was] handy with a brick."[43] Like Ragen's Colts, the Hamburgs furnished muscle for neighborhood bosses, and, as such, represented a quasi-legitimate opportunity structure. In 1914, for example, the president of the Hamburg Club,

Tommy Doyle, used the club's leverage to unseat an alderman who had held the position for over twenty years. Four years later, Doyle won a seat on the state legislature, and another Hamburg president, Joe McDonough, took over as alderman. Daley became the club's president in 1924 and held the post for fifteen years while climbing the ranks of the Democratic Party machine.

While Canaryville was much less capable of producing this kind of political clout, what it lacked in political and social capital it made up for with syndicate ties. Questioned by the CCRR about this particular neighborhood, the state's attorney of Cook County claimed that "more bank robbers, pay-roll bandits, automobile bandits, highwaymen, and strong-arm crooks come from this particular district than from any other."[44] Canaryville was the breeding ground for some of the city's most notorious beer-running gangsters—people like "Moss" Enright, "Sonny" Dunn, Eugene Geary, and the Gentleman brothers—who drew much of their manpower from the pool of ready labor provided by the athletic clubs. The Chicago Crime Commission well understood this vital link between the crime syndicates and Canaryville's gangs, reporting in 1920: "It is in this district that 'athletic clubs' and other organizations of young toughs and gangsters flourish, and where disreputable poolrooms, hoodlum-infested saloons and other criminal hang-outs are plentiful."[45]

Criminal enterprises and machine politics thus offered some significant opportunities for young men in Canaryville and Hamburg, but there were not nearly enough to go around, and most of those coming of age in these neighborhoods were more proletarian than slick. Athletic club toughs were predominantly the sons of packinghouse workers and factory laborers, and the world they made on the streets was intimately linked to the affairs of the enormous meat-processing combine next door. Examining this world in the 1920s, sociologist John Landesco concluded that "the sons of Irish laborers in the packing houses and stockyards" joined gangs like the Ragen's Colts because "Americanization made them averse to the plodding, seasonal, heavy and odoriferous labor of their parents, beset with the competition of wave upon wave of immigrants who poured into the area and bid for the jobs at lesser wages."[46] In reality, it was perhaps as much Taylorism as Americanism that made the Irish youths of these neighborhoods unwilling to cast their lots in a career in the stockyards and killing floors: as packers sought to keep up with increasing demand, they quickened the pace of work, maintained closer supervision, and introduced division of labor and continuous-flow production methods.[47] Upton Sinclair's description of a packinghouse perhaps conveyed it best: "a line of dangling hogs a hundred yards in length; and for every yard there was a man, working as if a demon were after him."[48] Such was the nature of the work available to unskilled youths in this moment. Moreover, a job wrestling with hog carcasses in a room like the one Sinclair depicted would have meant working side by side with Poles, Lithuanians, or members of other new immigrant groups whose status, many of the Irish believed, was clearly below theirs.

Conditions of this sort explain a great deal about why Irish youths coming of age around the stockyards district in the first few decades of the twentieth century were eager recruits for the race war that broke out in 1919. To be an aristocrat in the stockyards was not what it used to be, and the unwillingness of these youths to fill degraded jobs in the increasingly rationalized mass-production workplaces of the city ultimately stemmed from their under-standing that other options were open to them—a situation that reflected the strong if embattled position of the Irish in the public sector. This was a large part of the "Americanization" that sociologists noted about them, and it was something that distinguished them from their immigrant neighbors, who had little choice in the matter of their employment in tedious, dangerous, low-wage labor. Yet for many working-class Irish youths, this perception of choice was something of an illusion. In fact, the Irish youths of the genera-tion of 1919 were not so far removed from the American Protective Association's "no Irish need apply" campaign of the 1900s, and they were now facing four more years under an anti-Catholic mayor who would certainly not be smothering this Democratic stronghold with patronage. Institutions like Daley's alma mater De La Salle were beginning to show the sons of Irish packinghouse workers the way to the white-collar world, but those enrolled in such schools were still a rather select group. If Irish Bridgeport was in the process of producing an illustrious cohort of political and business leaders, few growing up in Canaryville and Hamburg were very aware of it.

Such circumstances shaped the youth subculture of gangs and athletic clubs that served as the training ground for the white foot soldiers of the 1919 race riot. Politicians and syndicate kingpins circulated in this milieu, draw-ing upon neighborhood muscle to rally votes and intimidate rivals, but the brutal rituals of street violence that were so central to this world served other needs. The culture of physical combat that defined the athletic clubs of Hamburg and Canaryville represented a collective strategy of the disempow-ered to create a compensatory system of empowerment. As in nearly all male-dominated, fighting gang cultures that have been studied by historians and sociologists before and after this historical conjuncture, claims to vital manhood and the sense of honor or status it bestowed constituted the stakes of the street brawls in this area. "Status as a gang among gangs, as well as in the neighborhood and the community," Frederic Thrasher observed after surveying more than 1,300 Chicago gangs, "must . . . be maintained, usually through its prowess in a fight."[49] No other neighborhood area personified this idea more than the blocks of Hamburg and Canaryville, where demonstrations of "prowess in a fight" had been integral to the street culture since at least the 1880s. According to one resident, youths from these communities "thirsted for a fight," and Saturday night turf battles between "Canaryvillains" and "Hamburg lads" often produced "broken noses and black eyes that were . . . too numerous to count."[50] And in a period when handguns were rarely used in such street fights, the not infrequent fatalities came the hard way: from skull fractures and stab wounds. The fact that gangs arriving at designated fights during these years expected to see their enemies holding clubs, bats, blackjacks, and knives that they were not afraid to use suggests that the drive for manly prowess was anything but trivial—rather, it was something worth risking one's life for.

Although lads from Hamburg and Canaryville were perfectly willing to crack each other's skulls for the sake of honor and respect, they preferred the skulls of the outsiders who seemed to be closing in on them from all sides— namely, blacks from across the color line and Poles and Lithuanians from the Back of the Yards. In the years leading up to the riot, social workers associated with the University of Chicago Settlement directed by Mary McDowell recorded a pattern of violence between Polish and Irish gangs in this area. One Polish gang in particular, the Murderers, engaged in recurrent brawls with a nearby Irish gang named the Aberdeens, whose members, according to one of the Murderers, "was always punching our kids." A similar rivalry existed between another Polish gang of this vicinity, the Wigwams, and Ragen's Colts, who on more than one occasion destroyed the Wigwams' clubhouse at 51st and Racine, in the midst of a predominantly Polish area around Sherman Park. Apparently, when the Wigwams were unavailable for a beating, any Polish gang would do for the Colts, who, according to Polish residents in the area, cruised the area around Sherman Park, which lay right between Canaryville and Packingtown, looking for fights.[51]

Such battles, to be sure, were enmeshed within a process of Americanization in the streets that taught Poles and also Lithuanians the meaning of their "Polishness" within the city's racial order. While Lithuanians represented about 29 percent of the population of the Back of the Yards, their Irish aggressors tended to lump them with Poles, who, with a 43 percent share of Packingtown's population, dominated the neighborhood. And yet this process of Americanization did not have the effect—at least not yet—of bringing Poles and Lithuanians into a pact of whiteness with the Irish. While University of Chicago Settlement workers did observe the Murderers joining the offensive against African Americans during the riot and then later boasting about it, many Poles chose a place on the sidelines and some criticized the Irish for their actions.[52] When an arson fire during the riot left about a thousand Polish, Lithuanian, Czech, and Slovak residents homeless, many in the Back of the Yards claimed the Irish had set the fire in order to rouse Poles and Lithuanians to action. Although we will never know the verity of the rumor that whites in blackface were seen running from the scene as the flames grew, that many believed the story to be true is nonetheless suggestive. And yet, if many southern and eastern Europeans largely refrained from joining the white mob, they showed no signs of actively defending blacks or of engaging in any form of meaningful cooperation with them. If their visceral contempt for the Irish and an awareness of their own injuries of race kept them somewhat neutral during the riot, the injustices imposed from above turned them against rather than towards those below them—as has so often been the case in the American experience.

As Arnold Hirsch has convincingly argued, substantial evidence from the 1919 race riot reveals how new immigrant groups—Poles, Lithuanians, Italians, and Jews, among others—occupied a "third (or middle) tier" within Chicago's racial order at this time.[53] But the riot itself was also a watershed event in the undoing of this very same racial order—a spectacular demonstration of the new centrality of the ghetto in the city's political culture. The "third tier" did not disintegrate immediately, however. In the early 1920s, pop eugenicist Madison Grant's theories about "Nordic" (northern European) racial superiority were orienting the national debate on immigration policy, and Prohibitionists across the country were decrying the wayward social habits of new immigrants.

However, a different story was unfolding at the grassroots in Chicago, where the anxious activities taking shape in the "white" neighborhoods surrounding the rapidly expanding black ghetto pointed the way towards a more binary racial future. To be sure, new immigrants would still have to defend their Americanness in the years to come against those who would restrict further immigration from their homelands, prohibit them from a drink, and place a range of social ills on their shoulders, but a new racial order was in the process of being embedded within Chicago's social and physical geography. Providing the catalyst for this shift was the continuing flow of southern black migrants into the city during the 1920s. By the end of the decade the city's black population had more than doubled once again, with African Americans now constituting almost 7 percent of the city's residents. In 1917 the Chicago Real Estate Board had declared a block-by-block policy of racial separation, and now it engaged in an aggressive campaign in white neighborhoods to promote the formation of homeowners associations and the use of racially restrictive covenants to prevent residents from renting or selling their homes to blacks. By 1940, these legally binding agreements covered some 80 percent of Chicago's property—a "marvelous delicately woven chain of armor," as one official from the Chicago Real Estate Board referred to it in 1928.[54] When legal means were lacking, street gangs and thugs affiliated with local "improvement associations" used terror tactics—bombings and beatings—to police the color line throughout the first half of the 1920s.

The bonds of whiteness that were created from this project of black exclusion within the housing market were further solidified within the burgeoning sphere of mainstream commercial leisure—in movie theaters, dance halls, and sporting arenas—where different ethnic groups mixed in whites-only spaces. In the early 1910s, the boxing world had buzzed with anticipation about the "great white hope" who would manage to take the heavyweight crown away from Chicago resident Jack Johnson, the first black boxer ever to hold the title. By 1920, with interest in baseball at a peak following three consecutive years in which one of the city's two major league teams had won a championship pennant, Chicago was fielding two black baseball teams— the Chicago American Giants and Chicago Giants—in the country's first black professional baseball league. Moreover, religion played a part in this story. Catholic Church policies ushered in by Archbishop George Cardinal Mundelein contributed to breaking down ethnic rivalries and reinforcing a sense of shared destiny among different Catholic groups. By promoting territorial over ethnic parishes and the use of the English language in parochial schools, for example, the Church helped to pave the way towards a more universalizing sense of whiteness among Europeans. And many of those moving into these new territorial parishes were doing so as homeowners with a new sense of "investment" in the preservation of their neighborhoods.

Moreover, forces of upward social mobility during this era created new kinds of neighborhoods strongly identified by the middle-class aspirations rather than the ethnic solidarities of their residents. The 1920s witnessed the rapid growth of the "Bungalow Belt," a ring of white middle-class neighborhoods in the outlying neighborhoods and suburbs distinguished by the single-family detached homes neatly lining their streets. During this decade, for example, the population of the Gage Park area southwest of the stockyards more than doubled to over 31,000 residents, and that of nearby Chicago Lawn grew over 300 percent to 47,462 residents.[55] With designs inspired by Frank Lloyd Wright's Prairie School Architecture, the modern homes built in these neighborhoods attracted a range of strivers—Irish, German, Polish, Lithuanian, Bohemian, and Italian—looking to put some distance between themselves and the stink, grit, and angst of the stockyards. The strong sense of shared destiny that evolved out of these circumstances would make these neighborhoods into bastions of "white power" politics by the late 1960s, when marches into the fiercely defended neighborhoods of the Bungalow Belt led by the Reverend Martin Luther King transformed places like Gage Park and Chicago Lawn into the living embodiments of racial exclusion. But such sensibilities were long in the making. Even as early as 1927, an ad linked to the mayoral campaign of Democrat William Dever was urging residents of the West Side Bungalow Belt neighborhood of Austin to "protect" their "families" and "beautiful homes" by making sure that "no harmful influences invade them"—a message that, in the context of the incessant race-baiting of this mayoral race, could have had only one meaning.[56] Ethnicity was far from done as a force in Chicago politics, but as different ethnic groups increasingly lined up together as "whites" struggling to hold off the ghetto from their doorsteps, the problem of the ghetto moved to the center of the city's political system, and politics became yet another force creating a black-and-white world.

Hence, by the mid-1920s Chicago's political scene had become seemingly saturated with race. Racism ran rampant in aldermanic and mayoral elections as candidates sought to woo the city's emerging middle class by promising to "preserve" and "protect" their neighborhoods, and the substance of political discourse gravitated inexorably towards the problems of vice, gambling, criminality, and racial mixing in the Black Belt. Under the aegis of party boss George Brennan—a man whose determination was steeled by having lost his right leg at the age of thirteen while working as a rail switchman—Democrats continued to use race-baiting tactics to counter Mayor Big Bill Thompson's appeal in the Black Belt. While the incumbent Thompson's withdrawal from the 1923 mayoral election made for a particularly low-key race that saw the straitlaced Democrat reformer William Dever triumphing with relative ease, a much more vitriolic form of racism exploded during the hard-fought mayoral campaign of 1927, when Thompson jumped back into the fray. "There is just one issue in this campaign," Illinois State representative Michael Igoe notoriously claimed during a speech in support of Dever in the run-up to the election. "There is a south side issue; if you folks want to keep the south side white, you go out and vote election day."[57] Democrats plastered this Manichean vision of the election's stakes on walls throughout the city with posters bearing such provocations as "Is the Negro or the White Man to Rule Chicago?" and "Negroes First—William Hale Thompson for Mayor." They took out ads in the city's newspapers evoking the oft-repeated tale that Thompson had kissed a black child at a rally, and they engaged in a range of vaudevillian gags, like driving trucks around the city mounted with calliopes playing "Bye Bye Blackbird" over and over again. If, in the end, these antics failed to keep Dever in office, Thompson's victory by no means signified any kind of broad renunciation of antiblack racism. In fact, Dever's loss had more to do with his determination to stand between a Chicagoan and a beer, and Thompson's ability to use Dever's moral pretensions—"Dever and Decency" was his campaign slogan—to paint him as an aristocrat opposed to the common people. He proclaimed himself to be "wetter than the middle of the Atlantic Ocean," told his supporters that "we low-brows have got to stick together," and accused Dever's superintendent of schools, William McAndrew, of a plot to disseminate a pro-British, royalist view of American history through the textbooks used in the city's school system.

Yet somewhat ironically, if the election of 1927 would go down in history for its vicious race-baiting, perhaps even more striking, in the final analysis, was the extent to which it displayed the vitality of class pride and the edginess of class resentment within the city's political culture. Thompson was able to tap into such feelings, in part, because he had already made inroads into the city's laboring class during his first two terms. In Thompson's Chicago, the politics of school reform collided with the labor struggle, with the antilabor dogma of the Commercial Club crowd swaying businessmen and much of the professional class towards the view that the Chicago Teachers Federation (CTF) was all that prevented the city from reforming the school system to cost efficiently serve the interests of business. It was within this context that Thompson defended the right of teachers to join unions in the face of an antiunion campaign spearheaded by school board member Jacob Loeb in 1917, and the following year he created a stir by nominating (unsuccessfully) Chicago Federation of Labor (CFL) President John Fitzpatrick to the school board. By 1921, Mayor Thompson had substantially raised the salaries of teachers (as well as policemen) and his superintendent, Peter Mortenson, had created local councils to give teachers a greater say in school affairs. Moreover, he complemented such redistributive and democratizing policies with gestures intended to demonstrate to the city's laborers that his heart was in the right place. In 1922, for example, he stood up to reformer Louise DeKoven Bowen after she had publicly attacked the city's policy of sponsoring school field trips to the Riverview Amusement Park—a popular working-class leisure venue that DeKoven Bowen characterized as "filthy and indecent."[58]

Dever, on the other hand, committed a series of miscues to alienate the city's working-class base during his four years in the mayor's office. In fact, Dever had inherited a rancorous labor dispute that had begun in 1921, during his predecessor's second term, when the Chicago Building Trades Council had accepted arbitration after refusing deep wage cuts proposed by builders. The result was catastrophic for labor. The arbitrator in the dispute, Judge Kennesaw Mountain Landis, issued a decision that not only granted builders the wage reductions they had demanded but also established a number of principles that virtually banned strikes and permitted employers to more easily hire nonunion labor. The decision, which was applauded by the *Tribune* and the *Daily News,* provoked an angry reaction among the more than seventy thousand members of the Chicago Building Trades Council and unleashed the full wrath of the city's open-shop movement. The Chicago Association of Commerce and Industry quickly rallied business leaders around the project of forcing the unions to comply with the terms of the arbitration. Spearheading the organization that grew out of this effort, the Citizens' Committee to Enforce the Landis Award, were a number of Commercial Club notables, such as printing executive Thomas Donnelley, steel executive Joseph Ryerson, Commonwealth Edison's Samuel Insull, and *Daily News* editor Victor Lawson. With such supporters and donors, the Citizens' Committee was able to raise some $2 million to fund a range of activities to undermine the labor movement, which included running a trade school and employment bureau, as well as maintaining its own police force. Dever thus made few friends in the labor movement when he appointed Citizens' Committee (and Commercial Club) member A. A. Sprague to be his public works commissioner. The committee was trying to accomplish nothing short of excluding union labor from its construction sites, and Sprague was certainly in a position to help make this happen. Landis Award contractors would go on to build $400 million worth of projects, including the medical and theology buildings at the University of Chicago, which, with "progressives" like Julius Rosenwald and Charles Hutchinson on its board of trustees, approved a $5,000 donation to the Citizens' Committee.[59]

Dever's next series of gaffes was dealt to him by his superintendent of schools, who alienated the CTF by disbanding the popular teachers' councils as a cost-cutting measure and then wrangled with the teachers over the use of stigmatizing IQ tests and the imposition of a "platoon" system that created junior high schools and shifted students between classrooms (more cost-cutting measures that allowed the city to avoid constructing new facilities to deal with its school overcrowding problem). While such moves rankled the sensibilities of even the conservative *Chicago Tribune,* which in a 1924 editorial asserted that "schools are not steel mills," Superintendent McAndrew remained steadfast in his campaign to bring a hard business rationale to the administration of the city's school system.[60] "The purpose of a school system is not to please us who are in it," he proclaimed, "but as with all public service corporations, to satisfy the customers."[61] The key customer he had in mind was the Chicago Association of Commerce and Industry, whose help McAndrew enlisted in order to assess the school system's performance. McAndrew's words and the agenda they articulated were strikingly ahead of their time; they would not have seemed the least bit out of place more than eighty years later, when school superintendents were being called "CEOs" and school officials appointed by Mayor Richard M. Daley were taking aim at the Chicago Teachers' Union and the Local School Councils (LSC) created by Mayor Harold Washington to democratize the school system.

McAndrew's mission to align the objectives of public education with the profit-making motives of the business community and his adoption of an autocratic managerial approach could be read as more signs that Chicago was already in the throes of neoliberal hegemony by the mid-1920s. Yet, if it is reasonable to draw a long straight line between McAndrew's reform project and Daley's Renaissance 2010 plan of 2006—that is to say, to view it as an early manifestation of a privatizing business logic within the city's modes of governance and political culture—the fierce resistance it confronted in the public sphere warns against any kind of totalizing conclusions. This was a moment, it must be remembered, that witnessed voices like that of CTF leader Margaret Haley taking center stage to defend the public interest in the raging debate over public education. A frequent contributor to the columns of Chicago dailies, Haley hammered away in no uncertain terms at the class agenda behind McAndrew's policies, decrying the school board for "aping hard-boiled businessmen ... to whom 'efficiency' in the maximum use of 'plant and equipment' overshadows the human factor" and declaring that the schools under McAndrew constituted a "mechanized and regimented system which subordinates everything to the industrializing of infants."[62] The class struggle was thus out there for everyone to see, and Thompson was much more adept than Dever at riding the wave of working-class discontent.

And yet the apparent groundswell of class politics in the mid-1920s never translated into any meaningful campaign against social inequalities because the working-class sensibilities that drove it were becoming so thoroughly entangled with the anxieties and injuries of race. Between 1920 and 1928, the number of registered voters in the city increased by some 67 percent, and an overwhelming number of those casting votes for the first time during these years were new immigrants from southern and eastern Europe and their American-born children—the scourge of moralizing Prohibitionists and bigoted immigrant restrictionists. The new immigrant working class had emerged as the bedrock of Chicago politics, and Thompson's jibes against Anglo-Saxon snobbery helped to convince enough of these voters—a bit more than 50 percent of them—to make his dominance in black Chicago the deciding factor. In an era in which nationalist discourses of all kinds were drawing boundaries around a white Anglo-Saxon Protestant vision of the nation, Thompson's "America First" campaign offered an inclusive form of Americanism that, for the excluded, seemed to turn the world upside down. It was populist vaudeville of the first order, but it worked like a charm. And it coalesced powerfully with the resentment these same people felt about the Irish domination of the Democratic Party ticket, a complaint aired frequently in foreign-language newspapers across the city during the 1920s. In the final analysis, few were those casting a vote in the 1927 election, whether for the Democratic or Republican ticket, whose decision was not somehow touched by the forces of racial kinship, resentment, and fear.

These forces were certainly here to stay, but they would ebb and flow in relation to economic, demographic, political, and cultural circumstances in the years to come. In the years following the racial explosion of 1927, they seemed to be ebbing. For one thing, the cataclysmic economic crisis that struck the entire country in 1929 combined with the proliferation of restrictive covenants throughout the city helped to stabilize the situation along the color line. Although the black population did increase by some 44,000 (almost 19 percent) over the 1930s, the vast majority of migrants settled in existing black neighborhoods. "The period of the 1930s, consequently," according to Arnold Hirsch, "was an era of territorial consolidation for Chicago's blacks."[63] Moreover, by the turn of the new decade the exclusionary anti-immigrant rhetoric of restrictionists and Prohibitionists seemed to be receding towards the margins, and the Democratic Party's 1928 nomination of New York governor Al Smith, the country's first Catholic presidential candidate, had dulled the sting of anti-Catholicism.

Such circumstances opened the door for Czech immigrant Anton Cermak—a man who had begun his career as a horse-and-wagon teamster before building a power base in the West Side Pilsen area and then using it to climb the ranks of the Cook County Democratic Party—and the timely death of Irish party boss George Brennan pushed him across the threshold. In 1928 Cermak became the party's new chairman, and by 1931 he was running unopposed for the Democratic nomination for mayor. Taking on the incumbent Thompson in a general election that saw surprisingly little discussion of the problem along the city's color line, Cermak used his "wet" stance on Prohibition and his promise to break the Irish stranglehold on the Democratic Party to build a multiethnic coalition of Italians, Poles, Slovaks, Jews, and of course Czechs. And Thompson, making one of the worst miscalculations in the history of American politics, chose to play the anti-immigrant card in a city overwhelmingly dominated by immigrants and their children. In his classic vaudeville style, he poked fun at Cermak's name, referred to him repeatedly as a "bohunk," and ridiculed his modest working-class immigrant origins with the oft-quoted jibe: "Tony, Tony, where's your pushcart at?" He also tried to exploit Cermak's alleged rift with the Irish, another tactic that fell flat on its face. Cermak had certainly made a number of enemies among Irish machine politicians on his way up, on at least one occasion even challenging one to a fistfight. But he had also formed an alliance with a dissident Irish faction led by the formidable Pat Nash, who would go on to run the party until his death in 1943, and the respectable number of Irish names appearing on Cermak's ticket belied Thompson's claims. The Irish still had a place in Cermak's "house for all peoples," whose multiethnic structure would even, in the years to come, accommodate the city's rapidly increasing black population. It was Cermak, in fact, who began the practice of grooming black leaders and distributing just enough patronage to the black wards to secure their loyalty to the machine without provoking a backlash among the party's white base—a balancing act that would challenge his mayoral successors in the decades to follow.

Few at the time could have imagined that Cermak's decisive victory over Thompson by nearly 200,000 votes would enthrone the Democratic Party for all of eternity. Killed in storybook fashion by an assassin's bullet intended for President Franklin Delano Roosevelt in February 1933—"I'm glad it was me instead of you" he apparently uttered to the president while being rushed to the hospital—Cermak occupied City Hall for not much more than a year. But during his short time on the political stage, he had identified the formula that would, in the hands of Pat Nash and the party bosses after him, effectively transform Chicago into a one-party city, emptying politics of its ideological substance and reducing government to the management of power struggles between party rivals. Chicago's machine was powerfully taking form just as others across the nation were being dismantled, straitjacketing the vibrant working-class upsurge that had been building in the 1920s. And all this was happening when the system of free-market capitalism and the stark inequalities it generated had never been so exposed to public outrage. As Chicagoans packed into downtown hotels on December 31, 1931, to celebrate the new year on a cold, dreary night, flaunting Prohibition with a vengeance, Chicago's unemployment rate was hovering around 30 percent and the city remained unable to pay its schoolteachers, as well as a good many of its policemen and firemen. Government at all levels struggled to retain credibility. In 1931 the city's celebrity-gangster-turned-Robin-Hood, Al Capone, a loyal ally of Big Bill Thompson, opened a soup kitchen in the heart of the Loop, boasting that he was doing more for the poor than the whole United States government. The following year, the Chicago Teachers Federation drew over 27,000 people to Soldier Field on January 4 to demand their unpaid wages, and the Communist Party and the Chicago Workers' Committee on Unemployment (CWC) cosponsored a hunger march in October that drew some 50,000 demonstrators to the Loop to protest cuts in relief payments and the threatened closure of relief stations.

While Thompson had waffled in the face of the crisis, referring to the economic downturn as "psychological," Cermak acted much more decisively. He lobbied both the Illinois legislature and President Herbert Hoover for relief loans, got to work on procuring a public works loan from Hoover's Reconstruction Finance Corporation to build a subway system, and began planning for a world's fair to take place in 1933—all this while marshaling the city's forces of order against Capone and the other gangsters who had been given free rein under Thompson. He also kept pushing for an end to Prohibition. And yet, despite his stand on Prohibition and his efforts to procure relief loans for the bankrupt city, Chicago's first immigrant mayor—a man who had looked like a working-class hero in the face of Thompson's jeers about his humble origins—was, during his short stint in office, no champion of the working man.

Cermak's policies revealed that he was more attuned to the gospel of business than to the struggle for social justice. Most chalked it up as political payback when Cermak cut Thompson's patronage appointees from the city's payroll, but his handling of the school budget crisis revealed that the move was also consistent with a broader austerity program supported by many in the business community. Working closely with a citizens' committee of bankers and businessmen organized by Chicago and Northwestern Railroad president Fred Sargent to lobby for the reduction of government expenditures, the mayor promptly cut 17 percent from the 1933 school budget, a move intended to punish the board of education for resisting his campaign to cut costs and bring a businesslike efficiency to all branches of city government. Cermak also solicited the assistance of the business community for his civil service reform campaign, appointing Richard Collins, a former director of First National Bank, to join University of Chicago professor of public administration Leonard D. White, and ward committeeman J. V. Geary on the three-member civil service commission. Such measures earned the mayor praise from the editors of the *Chicago Tribune,* the good government types who had rallied around Dever, and the Commercial Club crowd, helping to build what amounted to nothing short of a cross-class multiethnic consensus.

Cermak had essentially neutralized the forces opposing the capitalist order, and he had been able to do this, in large part, because his working-class immigrant origins had disarmed his working-class base. To be sure, there were still plenty of hungry, disgruntled folks in the streets, and the teachers were certainly not lying down as the city continued to withhold their wages, but few seemed to recognize how much Cermak was picking up on McAndrew and Dever's program of imposing austerity and bringing a business rationale to municipal governance. Cermak's kinship with Dever as a crusader against organized crime and municipal corruption, for example, did not lie merely in the fact that he, like Dever, was cast in the ring against Big Bill Thompson and the gangsters and cronies in his corner; it also reflected a similar understanding of the role of city government in the capitalist order. Indeed, reform and law-and-order politics diverted attention from the structural forces that had filled the streets with the destitute and unemployed. The rhetoric of reformers pointed more to the moral failings of the people within the system than to fundamental flaws in the system itself—an ideological function performed on the terrain of popular culture by the blockbuster gangster films of the early Depression years, such as *Public Enemy* (1931) and *Scarface* (1932). But whereas Dever was never really able to rein in the forces of opposition, Cermak's multiethnic machine was the perfect antidote to the class struggle that had animated Chicago's political culture in the previous decade, when the injuries of class converged with the dilemma of ethnoracial exclusion. This was a moment when notions of social justice clashed directly with the market-driven rationale of the business community in debates over the role of the city's schools and the rights of workers to organize and bargain collectively. Cermak's incorporation of the formerly excluded ushered in a new era in which the power of ethnoracial bonds was placed squarely in the service of the machine. The man who had attended business school at night while spending his days hauling food waste from International Harvester and peddling it to the poor managed his party like a business. After the general election of 1932, he developed a statistical system that graded each ward's "vote getting" ability based on vote margin, turnout, and the percentage of straight Democratic Party voters.[64] Those producing for the machine stood to gain larger shares of the party's resources, and producing invariably meant rallying residents behind ward leaders who appeared to represent them—an appearance achieved as a natural consequence of ethnoracial affinities.

Cermak's successor, Edward J. Kelly, who, as the chief engineer of the Sanitary District had enriched himself with rampant cronyism during the so-called Whoopee Era, picked up exactly where he had left off. The Kelly-Nash machine cultivated a number of key ethnic middlemen to solidify their multiethnic coalition. If Jews, for example, had rallied behind Cermak after he had backed the election of the state's first Jewish governor, Henry Horner, in 1932, decades of tense relations between the Jews and the Irish in Chicago made them wary of losing what they had gained under the new mayor. Kelly and Nash moved quickly to assuage such fears, appointing West Side Jewish leader Jacob Arvey as chairman of the powerful city council finance committee and naming his law partner Barnet Hodes, another influential Jewish community leader, as the city's corporation counsel. As for the city's sizable German community, the Kelly-Nash machine continued the job begun by Cermak of eroding long-standing German loyalty to the Republican Party by elevating North Side German leaders like Forty-Third Ward alderman Matthias "Paddy" Bauler and Forty-Seventh Ward alderman Charlie Weber. Such tactics paid big dividends in the mayoral election of 1935, when Kelly confirmed the new dominance of the Democratic machine by crushing his Republican opponent, Emil Wetten, in the most lopsided election in Chicago's history. Surprisingly, Kelly had achieved this broad popularity despite having imposed sharp budget cuts that led to the dismissal of nearly 1,400 teachers while fending off scandalous accusations regarding the sources of the more than $570,000 he had made on top of his salary between 1919 and 1929.[65]

In his inaugural address following the election, Kelly assured the business community that had rallied around him that he would oppose increases in personal property and real estate taxes. But Kelly's fiscal conservatism was not all that explained his appeal with the business crowd. The mayor also demonstrated that he was ready to carry the union-busting torch. Under Kelly's watch, strikers in Depression-ravaged Chicago encountered systematic and often violent police repression, especially after 1935, when the Congress of Industrial Organizations (CIO) was making its push to organize the city's industrial workforce. In February 1937, a massive sit-down strike at Fansteel Metallurgical Corp. ended with police forcibly removing strikers from the building with tear gas. Then at the end of May, several weeks after a successful unionization drive by the Steelworkers Organizing Committee (SWOC) at U.S. Steel's Carnegie-Illinois plant, strikers at the Republic Steel mill in southeast Chicago felt the full brunt of the antiunion tactics countenanced by Kelly. After gathering on a humid Memorial Day afternoon at Sam's Place, a local tavern that served as the headquarters for the SWOC's organizing drive, well over a thousand strikers set out across a prairie towards the Republic Steel mill. If Mayor Kelly had issued a statement days earlier defending the right to picket peacefully, the forces of order that confronted the strikers before they arrived at the mill seemed unaware of it. They opened fire and then moved in with billy clubs swinging. When the dust settled and the tear gas cleared, ten strikers lay dead and many more were seriously injured. Kelly was on vacation in Wisconsin at the time, but his initial reaction to the news suggested where his priorities lay. He immediately defended the actions of police and blamed outside troublemakers for inciting the violence. Chicago's ideological apparatus quickly followed suit. The reactionary *Chicago Tribune* under the rabidly antilabor Republican Colonel Robert McCormick covered the event as a frontal attack on police officers by communist agitators, and the city's coroner's jury ruled the shootings "justifiable homicide."

Such a reaction by the Kelly-Nash machine and its allies created ripples of discontent within the CIO's burgeoning labor movement in Chicago, which by 1939 counted some 60,000 members. In retrospect, however, what is most striking about the Memorial Day massacre is how limited its consequences were for the Kelly-Nash machine. To be sure, Kelly had closer ties with the city's American Federation of Labor (AFL) unions, which possessed well over 300,000 members at the time, than with the rival CIO, but this does not tell the whole story of how Kelly was able to retain the support of the city's laborers in the wake of the Memorial Day massacre. Part of the explanation lay with Kelly's association with the Democratic Party and President Franklin D. Roosevelt's New Deal administration, which had reached out to organized labor in unprecedented ways, beginning with its sponsorship of the landmark Wagner Act of 1935 and its commitment to labor's right to organize free of harassment by employers. Kelly had worked hard to get out the vote for Roosevelt in the presidential election of 1936, helping the president to win an impressive 65 percent of the vote in Chicago—a margin of victory that the Kelly-Nash machine hoped would assure the continuing flow of federal work relief funds into the city. The Kelly-Nash machine had quickly capitalized on the federal funds funneled into the city through the Federal Emergency Relief Administration (FERA), the Civil Works Administration (CWA), and the Works Progress Administration (WPA), transforming these relief programs into political capital in the form of tens of thousands of patronage jobs. Certainly Kelly saw the need to mend his relations with the CIO in the wake of the Memorial Day massacre, intervening in a labor dispute on behalf of the Packinghouse Workers Organizing Committee (PWOC) in 1938 and guaranteeing no further interference from the police. But the CIO's active support for Kelly in the mayoral election of 1939, which was critical to his surprisingly tough victory over Republican Dwight Green during a moment when Democrats nationally were on the defensive in the face of a middle-class backlash against the New Deal's pro-labor stance, was largely secured by the mayor's ability to make workers and their families across the city indebted to him for their livelihoods. The machine had not fared well in the Bungalow Belt, but the working-class "river wards" had carried the day.

This is not to say that the workers had been duped. Kelly was quite frankly the best chance they had. Yet the Kelly-Nash machine had effectively incorporated a movement that held the potential of challenging its agenda and making it more accountable for the economic inequalities that were so starkly exposed by the economic crisis of the 1930s. The CIO's emergence owed to some of the same shifts in the racial order that had enabled Cermak and Kelly to reconfigure the Cook County Democratic Party into a multiethnic political machine. And yet these two structures were fundamentally at odds. The machine's drive to carve the city into ethnic blocs ran counter to the

CIO's project of spreading a culture of class unity from the factories and mills into working-class neighborhoods. Moreover, if ethnic differences between whites of European descent were disintegrating, this was in part because a universalizing sense of whiteness was increasingly organizing the world of workers living outside the Black Belt. Of course this was a project in the making during the 1930s, and ethnic animosities still raged within the machine's "house for all peoples." Nonetheless, the sensibilities of class unity that were developing during this era were intertwined with notions of white racial unity. The CIO was swimming against the tide. While many white workers were willing to embrace their black coworkers for pragmatic ends in the workplace, interracialism was a much different matter in the context of their communities. CIO locals tried picnics, and pioneer community organizers like Saul Alinsky sought to create councils and committees to negotiate tensions between rival groups in hard-core working-class areas like the Back of the Yards and South Chicago. But the machine had the better response to the new biracial political order in the making, convincing whites in a myriad of ways that blacks would remain subordinate and separate, and assuring blacks that what happened in the Black Belt was their own business.

TWO

Black Metropolis

ADVANCING THE RACE AND GETTING AHEAD

During the first weekend of April 1938, more than 100,000 black Chicagoans packed into the Eighth Regiment Armory in the heart of the Bronzeville district to behold the fruits of black enterprise displayed at the Negro Business Exposition. Those attending the exposition, as *Time* magazine reported, were there to "watch fashion shows, finger fancy caskets, see demonstrations of pressing the kink out of Negro hair, listen to church choirs and hot bands, munch free handouts or purchase raffle tickets from the 75 booths."[1] The event attracted the attention of the national news media because it signaled Chicago's emergence as the capital of black America. "Although Chicago has 100,000 fewer Negroes than New York," the *Time* story began, "it is the center of U.S. Negro business; last census figures showed Chicago's Negro establishments had annual net sales of $4,826,897, New York's were only $3,322,274." And of course the article did not miss the opportunity to insert the kind of condescending remark that was so characteristic of the white gaze upon black attempts to "uplift the race"—in this case a jibe about the "admiring pickaninnies" surrounding world heavyweight champion boxer Joe Louis in a ploy to get the dollar bills that his bodyguard apparently gave out "to moppets so they will leave Joe alone."[2]

Organized by a group of local businessmen and religious leaders, the Negro Business Exposition was part of a broader campaign that had picked up momentum in the midst of the Great Depression to promote support for black businesses as a means of "advancing the race." Speaking on Sunday to an admiring crowd, one of the event's key organizers, Junius C. Austin, the animated pastor of the famed Pilgrim Baptist Church (whose musical director

Thomas A. Dorsey was at that very moment creating Chicago's blues-inflected gospel sound), issued a declaration that left little doubt about what had motivated the exposition: "Tomorrow I want all of you people to go to these stores, have your shoes repaired at a Negro shoe shop, buy your groceries from a Negro grocer, patronize these Jones Brothers, and for God's sake buy your meats, pork chops and yes, even your chitterlings from your Negro butcher."[3] Austin's unabashed huckstering revealed that morale among black businessmen, eight years into the Great Depression, was at a low point. There were reasons to be hopeful—economic conditions had been picking up since the previous year, and the city's biggest syndicate kingpins, the Jones brothers, had invested some of the countless nickels and dimes they had procured from black Chicagoans chasing winning numbers in their illegal "policy" lotteries to open the country's largest black-owned retail establishment, the Ben Franklin store, in the heart of the Bronzeville business district. But if Austin's exhortation to "patronize" the Jones brothers suggested that African Americans could still look to their business leaders—regardless of the nature of their enterprises—as beacons of hope, the idea of the black businessman as a "race man" was desperately in need of reinforcement. Just two months prior to the exposition, former business magnate Jesse Binga, the founder of Chicago's first black-owned bank and thus a great symbol of racial progress, had been released from prison after serving five years for embezzlement—a broken man who would live out his life working as a janitor and handyman.

After observing the boosterism of black businessmen around the Negro Business Exposition, St. Clair Drake and Horace Cayton, the illustrious black scholars and authors of the definitive study of black life in interwar Chicago, *Black Metropolis,* issued a sober rejoinder to those who still sought to measure black progress "in terms of the positions of power and prestige which Negroes attain in the business world":

> No Negro sits on a board of directors in La Salle Street; none trades in the grain pit or has a seat on the Stock Exchange; none owns a skyscraper. Negro girls are seldom seen in the offices and stores of the Loop except as maids. Colored traveling salesmen, buyers, and jobbers are a rarity. The largest retail stores and half of the smaller business enterprises in Bronzeville are owned and operated by white persons, and until recently many of these did not voluntarily employ Negroes.[4]

Drake and Cayton compiled numerous figures to back up this assessment, the most striking of which showed that while black enterprises constituted nearly half of all the businesses in black Chicago, they received less than 10 percent of all the money spent within these areas. They also pointed out that the overwhelming majority of the some 2,600 black businesses in operation were small-scale enterprises—287 beauty parlors, 257 groceries, 207 barber shops, 163 tailors and cleaners, 145 restaurants, 87 coal and wood dealers, 70 bars, 50 undertakers, to name the most numerous—and they were located "on side streets, or in the older, less desirable communities."[5]

This vision of the decrepit state of the black business community contrasted somewhat with the overall picture these scholars painted of the impressive "Black Metropolis" that had developed around the Bronzeville district, with its bustling shopping area around 47th and South Parkway (now called King Drive), where the Ben Franklin store had opened its doors amidst much fanfare. Here, they pointed out, black Chicagoans could look upon an array of powerful and proud black institutions: "the Negro-staffed Provident Hospital; the George Cleveland Hall Library (named for a colored physician); the 'largest colored Catholic church in the country'; the 'largest Protestant congregation in America'; the Black Belt's Hotel Grand; Parkway Community House; and the imposing Michigan Boulevard Garden Apartments for middle-income families."[6] Chicago's Black Metropolis had become a veritable city within a city in the 1910s and 1920s, when nearly 200,000 black migrants took up residence within its borders, raising the total black population to just under 234,000. This influx of migrants transformed black Chicago, creating a "negro market" for goods and services and with it new forms of black market consciousness, which by the 1920s were intermingling with black nationalist currents circulating around Marcus Garvey's United Negro Improvement Association (UNIA) and the New Negro ideology emanating from the Harlem Renaissance. In this context, ordinary African Americans began to see in black purchasing power the promise of racial uplift, if not liberation, and looked towards an emerging generation of business magnates as the quintessential "race men"—a situation that caused great concern among the political forces of racial progress, from the National Association for the Advancement of Colored People (NAACP) and the Urban League to the Communist Party.

Certainly Drake and Cayton's gloomy assessment of black business stemmed, in part, from the concern being voiced by some political leaders that the allure of individual success in the business world could dampen support for collective strategies of racial struggle in the political sphere. Garveyism had sought to reconcile the gospel of private enterprise with more cooperative notions of racial progress throughout the 1920s, but the marriage of these ideals had come under considerable strain during the lean years of the Great Depression, even after the Don't Spend Your Money Where You Can't Work boycott of 1930 had demonstrated to black Chicagoans that they could use their buying power to force a national chain store like Woolworth's Five and Ten to change its discriminatory hiring practices. Triumphant as it was, the campaign had failed to blossom into a broader movement, and perhaps more significantly for the black business community, it had failed to alter the daily spending habits of Bronzeville residents. While black businessmen generally ascribed the continuing black predilection for patronizing white-owned businesses to the power of "the white man's psychology" learned in the South or else to some desire to magically invert the racial order by using their purchasing power to place whites in a subservient position, many working-class blacks referred merely to the lower prices and better services offered by white merchants.[7]

But Drake and Cayton's skepticism was also due to the fact that from the vantage point of the late 1930s and early 1940s, when they were collecting their data, black businesses were hardly thriving. If, as historian Christopher Robert Reed has claimed, the 1920s was the "golden decade of black business," many of the grand achievements of this era had been erased during the Depression years.[8] Black Chicago's banks had gone belly up, and its mighty business leaders had been brought down to size. In fact, by the time *Black Metropolis* was released in 1945, each figure in Chicago's triumvirate of black business heroes had been leveled in one way or another. Binga was working as a janitor; Robert Sengstacke Abbott, the founder of the *Chicago Defender*, the most widely circulated black newspaper in the country, was dead; and Anthony Overton, who in the 1920s had parlayed the revenues from his Overton Hygienic Company into a conglomerate that included the Douglass National Bank, the Victory Life Insurance Company, and a black weekly newspaper called the *Chicago Bee*, had reverted to his role as a seller of brown face powders.

And yet, even though the Great Depression had certainly humbled black businessmen and many of those who entrusted them with the future of the race, the crowds that packed into the Negro Business Exposition demonstrated that the gospel of black capitalism was relatively unshakable among ordinary residents of Bronzeville. This was due in part to the fact that the exclusion of blacks from trade unions and their relegation to low-wage, often dangerous jobs unleashed the spirit of entrepreneurialism in the Black

Metropolis. Utilizing occupational data gleaned from a New Deal–funded study on the black labor market in Chicago, Drake and Cayton painted a grim picture of a black population constrained by an impossibly low "job ceiling." Out of some 123,000 blacks in the workforce in 1930, 75,000 (61 percent) worked unskilled and service jobs, while only 12,000 (less than 10 percent) performed professional, proprietary, managerial, and clerical jobs— what Drake and Cayton referred to as "clean work." In fact, African Americans filled just 2 percent of all clean-work positions citywide, compared to 78 percent for whites and 20 percent for foreign-born immigrants. For black men, mail carriers (630) constituted by far the most common job in this category, followed by musicians (525), clergymen (390), and messengers and office boys (385); for women, restauranteurs (235) topped the list, followed by musicians (205) and actresses (145). As for the lower rungs of the occupational ladder, some 25 percent of all black male workers and 56 percent of all female ones were employed in some kind of servant work. For women, this mostly meant domestic service; for men, it involved a range of low-paying service jobs (janitors, elevator men, waiters, domestic service) as well as the relatively high-paying but somewhat demeaning job of Pullman porter (held by almost 14 percent of black male service workers). Black male manual laborers, for their part, were concentrated in the lowest paying and dirtiest unskilled jobs in factories, steel mills, and packinghouses, and black female manual laborers in poorly paid positions in laundry service and the needle trades.[9]

Starting one's own business thus seemed well worth a shot when faced with the prospect of working in the foundry of a steel mill or on the killing floor of a packinghouse. *Black's Blue Book,* black Chicago's first business directory catered to this burgeoning entrepreneurial spirit, urging black Chicagoans to "find your vocation and follow it" and warning them to "expect nothing on sympathy, but everything on merit."[10] Between 1916 and 1938 the number of black-owned businesses in Chicago jumped from 727 to over 2,600, outpacing the robust growth of the black population. Moreover, these figures did not even take into account black Chicago's most prevalent "business": the storefront church, which, with well over three hundred lining the streets of Bronzeville, topped beauty parlors as the most numerous type of black enterprise in the city.[11] During the Great Depression, according to Drake and Cayton, several hundred "jack-leg preachers" competed for pulpits in order "to escape from the WPA or the relief rolls"—a situation that resulted in a veritable "revolt against Heaven" by working-class churchgoers who accused their religious leaders of corrupting their spiritual lives or, more bluntly, of bilking them out of their money. As one congregant complained, "The average pastor is not studying the needs of his race. He's studying the ways to get more money out of the people."[12]

The stories concerning the iniquitous practices of some of the more entrepreneurially minded storefront preachers no doubt contributed disproportionately to the perception shared by many black Chicagoans that their churches were akin to rackets or businesses, but the larger, more established mainline Baptist and Methodist churches also engaged in practices that blurred the line between spiritual and monetary pursuits. By the early 1920s, with pews in Bronzeville packed with recently arrived southern migrants, many of the more prominent churches began building alliances with black businesses. "It was not uncommon for black churches to support black-owned businesses by carrying advertisements in their church bulletins and newspapers," historian Wallace Best has argued, "or by encouraging members to patronize certain retail stores, grocers, doctors, barbers, and undertakers."[13] While such exhortations were justified by broader appeals to "advancing the race" through the promotion of black enterprise, pastors also understood that businessmen would reciprocate with donations. In the fall of 1923 a group of black businessmen led by Robert Abbott and Jesse Binga organized the Associated Business Club (ABC) of Chicago for the purpose of adding a secular voice to the chorus of preachers singing the praises of black capitalism. With its membership expanding from fourteen to nearly one thousand in its first year of existence, the ABC sought to harness the efforts of pastors throughout Bronzeville by offering a free trip abroad for the pastor who brought the most customers to ABC-affiliated businesses.[14] Some fifteen years later, as Junius Austin's spirited involvement in the Negro Business Exposition suggests, pastors and businessmen were still rallying around the hopes and dreams of the black economy, and many ordinary black folks still seemed to want to believe.

This alliance of pastors and businessmen explains a great deal about the staying power of a business ethos oriented around the ideas of thrift, self-help, and racial uplift popularized by Booker T. Washington and his Negro Business League in the early years of the twentieth century. Certainly churches had their detractors, but they nonetheless continued to touch the hearts and minds of black Chicagoans as much as any other institution in the community. Yet African Americans also continued to believe in racial salvation through business success because a great many of them had lived through the not-so-distant heyday of the Black Metropolis, and there was plenty of reason to think that what had befallen their community was not due to any failings of the race or of the system of black capitalism itself but rather to broader forces that had struck U.S. society at large. The aura of the Black Metropolis as a place of excitement, innovation, and pride—immortalized in the canvasses of Archibald Motley, the writings of Langston Hughes, and the sounds of Louis Armstrong's trumpet—still lingered in the air.

For many, the promise of the Black Metropolis lay not in the rise of its vaunted black-owned banks, insurance companies, newspapers, and manufacturers but rather in the development in the 1910s and 1920s of the black entertainment district known as "the Stroll," a segment of State Street stretching from 26th Street on down to 39th Street, where, as Langston Hughes famously remarked, "midnight was like day." Here on the Stroll the bright glow emanating from countless cabarets, theaters, bars, and restaurants served as stage lighting for the swirling mass of black and white humanity jamming the sidewalks and spilling into the streets. The soundtrack was provided by the intermingling sounds of blues shouters, boogie-woogie piano romps, and hot jazz horn solos pulsating out of the numerous storefront jazz joints and cabarets. "If you held up a trumpet in the night air of the Stroll," bandleader Eddie Condon once claimed, "it would play itself!" In the 1910s and 1920s, as Chicago was assuming its place as the nation's leading center of heavy industry, the economy of its black city within was developing around the myriad commercial leisure ventures offered by the Stroll—its cabarets, nightclubs, dance halls, ballrooms, theaters, speakeasies, gambling halls, vaudeville houses, buffet flats, and brothels. By the late 1920s the Stroll began to decline rapidly, but its spirit migrated southward with the opening of the enormously successful Savoy Ballroom at 47th and South Parkway in 1927. In the early 1930s this area became the new bright-lights district of the Black Metropolis, and its happenings were, thanks to the publicity offered by the *Chicago Defender,* known to African Americans across the nation.

Such happenings did not figure into Drake and Cayton's rendering of Bronzeville—somewhat astonishingly given Chicago's importance as a fountain of Jazz Age black cultural expression. The omission suggests a lingering uneasiness among black middle-class civic leaders about black Chicago's transformation into a playground of desire, pleasure, and exoticism in the interwar years, when entrepreneurs, a good many of them white, opened up a number of black-and-tan cabarets catering to white "slummers" seeking the thrill of hot jazz, bootlegged liquor, and the black sexuality on display on the dance floor.[15] Even by the early 1940s, decades after Chicago's Black Metropolis had clearly established itself as the nation's "melting pot" of jazz and blues, its performing and recording scene helping to catapult the likes of Louis Armstrong, Jelly Roll Morton, Bessie Smith, Joe "King" Oliver, Duke Ellington, Cab Calloway, Ma Rainey, Ethel Waters, and Earl "Fatha" Hines to national prominence, a number of black community leaders were still unable to comfortably embrace this cultural heritage. This ambivalence stemmed from the fact that while many of the music venues of the Stroll were owned and run by blacks, they hardly embodied, in the eyes of many respectable civic leaders, the kinds of enterprises that contributed to "uplifting the race."[16] If the Stroll, according to historian Davarian Baldwin, "was more than simply a stretch of buildings, amusements, sidewalks, and signposts but the public showcase for black 'expressive behavior,'" the dancing, shouting, shimmying, and frolicking that was being showcased there flew squarely in the face of the codes of respectability promoted by the older, more established middle-class elements of the community.[17]

As Baldwin has argued, although most in the Black Metropolis invested in some idea of economic nationalism, the interwar years witnessed a struggle between an "old settler" ideology oriented around hard work, thrift, and sobriety and a "new settler" ideology that viewed in the Stroll's commercialized leisure enterprises the means not only to get ahead but also to create a new sense of racial pride and respectability.[18] The clash of these ideals appeared frequently in the black press during this era. On May, 17, 1919, for example, the *Chicago Defender* justified publishing a list of dos and don'ts directed at recent migrants with the explanation: "It is evident that some of the people coming to this city have seriously erred in their conduct in public places, much to the humiliation of all respectable classes of our citizens, and by so doing, on account of their ignorance of laws and customs necessary for the maintenance of health, sobriety and morality among the people in general, have given our enemies ground for complaint." Among the list of don'ts provided to the *Defender* by the Chicago Urban League were several explicitly targeting the Stroll nightlife: "Don't encourage gamblers, disreputable women or men to ply their business any time or place"; Don't congregate in crowds on the streets"; "Don't spend your time hanging around saloon doors or poolrooms."[19]

The *Defender*'s publisher, Robert Sengstacke Abbott, was the mouthpiece of the businessman race heroes of the daytime Stroll, who decried the pleasure-seeking and immorality that raged after nightfall. Abbott's Stroll by day, referred to at the time as "the black man's Broadway and Wall Street," offered a very different vision of black pride and autonomy. Rising amidst its famed nightspots—Motts Pekin Theater, the Apex Club, Elite No. 1, Elite No. 2, the Dreamland Ballroom, the Sunset Café, and the De Luxe Café—were brick-and-mortar monuments to the promise of black capitalism: the hulking Binga State Bank at 3452 South State with its marble, bronze, and walnut interior and imposing steel vaults; the *Chicago Defender* building at 3435 South Indiana, headquarters of a newspaper that, while occupying a converted synagogue, had the audacity to herald itself as "the world's greatest weekly"; and the Overton Hygienic Building at 3619–3627 South State, a massive six-story structure also housing Overton's Douglass National Bank and Victory Life Insurance Company, which Overton himself hailed as "a monument of negro thrift and industry."[20] The owners of these structures unabashedly assumed the role of preachers in the church of black capitalism. Although these reputed self-made captains of industry had established their enterprises in earlier years—Abbott founded the *Defender* in 1905, Binga opened his first bank in 1908, and Overton established his cosmetics company in Chicago in 1911—their stars began rising in the aftermath of the 1919 race riot, when their words of wisdom about hard work, thrift, and economic nationalism as the antidotes to systemic white racism were spread all over the pages of the black press.

More than anyone else, Jesse Binga incarnated the figure of the businessman race hero of the 1920s, a legend that his associate Robert Abbott—a major stockholder in Binga's bank—played a big part in creating. The *Defender* followed Binga's every move, giving him regular front-page exposure, and Binga used the pulpit offered to him to deliver sermon after sermon about how black businesses, with the proper support from black consumers, would lead the way towards racial progress. Announcing that his private bank would soon be reorganized under the protection of a state charter in April 1920, for example, Binga spoke of "an undercurrent of forces at play . . . gradually forcing the people of the great south side into an insoluble mass, which is to result in inestimable financial strength and resources."[21] More than three years later, addressing the Associated Business Club (ABC), a group that included Abbott, Overton, and Claude A. Barnett, founder of the Associated Negro Press news agency, Binga was still hammering away at the same ideas. "I would say to those aspiring to be of influence in our community," Binga asserted, "to remember that the banks and the business men are the bulwark of the community." "A race to achieve its independence," he

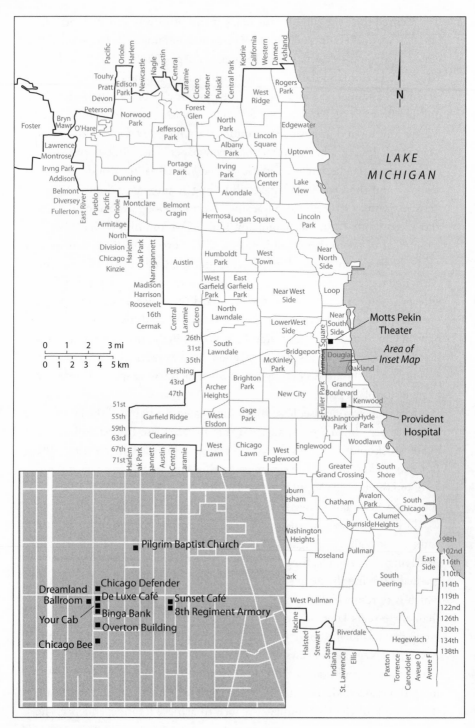

MAP 3. Bronzeville and the Stroll in 1920.

FIGURE 3. The Overton Hygienic Building at 3619–3627 South State Street. From The New York Public Library.

proclaimed, "must foster its own interests."[22] Such sentiments were intended not only to position businessmen as race leaders but also to counter the idea, shared by a range of white opinion makers, that African Americans as a race were out of step with the spirit of modern capitalism. Famed University of Chicago sociologist Robert Park went so far as to refer to blacks as "the lady of the races," attributing their deficiencies in the marketplace to temperament: "a disposition for expression rather than enterprise and action."[23] Although Park and many others of his ilk understood all too well that municipal zoning and law enforcement policies and the concatenations of machine politics—not any traits supposedly inherent in the race—had made the Stroll into a playground for gamblers, boozers, and sporting types in search of sexual adventure, the epic story of Chicago jazz, with all the artistic virtuosity and sensuality that came with it, seemed to confirm Park's essentialization of blacks as cultural producers.

Binga and the ABC crowd were thus somewhat adamant about drawing a sharp distinction between the earnest enterprise of the daytime Stroll and the frivolous *jouissance* of its nighttime alter ego, but the connection between these two worlds was, in reality, hard to deny. For one thing, there was no getting around the fact that the action of the nighttime Stroll produced revenues for some of the most important black businesses. Abbott's *Defender* may have stridently criticized the immoral ways of migrants cavorting on the Stroll, but it also profited enormously from showcasing these same activities. Amidst the *Defender*'s ads for the Stroll's hottest clubs, moreover, could be found others for a range of beauty services and products—Overton's face powders prominent among them—for revelers heading out for a night on the Stroll, and the burgeoning black-owned Your Cab Company at 3635 South State Street earned a good many of its fares from these same revelers. The activities of the daytime and nighttime Strolls were intertwined in other ways as well. As Davarian Baldwin has argued, "Better paying industrial jobs surely provided the disposable income for leisure activities, but it was the nickels and dimes used to buy drinks in local dance halls and put on lucky numbers at policy wheels that recirculated within the community to support the black metropolis."[24] It was, to be sure, hard to find a nickel or a dime in Bronzeville that had not touched the hands of a numbers runner. Brought to Chicago from New Orleans in the late 1880s by the legendary "Policy" Sam Young, policy wheels (illicit lotteries) multiplied rapidly in the high-paced atmosphere of the Black Metropolis, where, as Drake and Cayton claimed, a spirit of "getting ahead" joined that of "advancing the race" as one of the organizing axes of black life.

BY THE NUMBERS

By the late 1930s, the more reliable estimates had over 100,000 black Chicagoans placing some $18 million in bets at over 4,000 South Side policy stations, and while the policy syndicate was of course a pyramidal structure with limited redistributive possibilities (at least in a downward direction), policy wheels nonetheless provided thousands of jobs, and the profits they generated found their way into a range of legitimate ventures that created thousands more. Policy was thus the common denominator between the daytime and nighttime Strolls. Gambling and jazz (not to mention vice) were of course hard to disentangle on the nighttime Stroll, where policy kings underwrote the establishment of many of black Chicago's most revered jazz venues—the Pekin, the Dreamland, the Apex Club, Elite No. 1, and Elite No. 2—and where smoky gaming rooms were often appendages of the halls where Chicago's greatest musicians strutted their stuff. But policy proceeds lubricated the cogs of the daytime Stroll's economy as well. Binga's financial ventures, for example, were bankrolled in part by the gambling proceeds that passed into his hands through his marriage to Eudora Johnson, who had inherited more than half the substantial wealth of her brother, legendary policy kingpin John "Mushmouth" Johnson, upon his death in 1907.

The impact of policy could be felt in nearly every corner and alley of the Black Metropolis. Policy wheels offered supplemental revenue to beauty parlors, grocery stores, bars, and even funeral parlors, and many such legitimate businesses were built upon the nickels and dimes of its players. For example, in 1925 undertaker Dan Jackson, the "general manager" of the South Side's most powerful vice and gambling syndicate, used the profits from his illicit operations to launch the Metropolitan Funeral System Association—a thriving business that offered burial insurance to working-class black families for a fifteen-cent weekly premium. Two years later he sold it to another gambling kingpin, Robert Cole, who used his own profits to develop a sister company, Metropolitan Funeral Parlors, and move it into a modern office building he built at 4455 South Parkway in 1940. While Cole was no doubt looking to make a buck, this particular business venture aligned financial motives with more noble ideals. Denied proper funeral services by white undertakers, bereaved African Americans faced the humiliation of not being able to procure a respectable funeral, a situation that transformed Cole, whose companies offered insurance *and* burial services, into another of Bronzeville's self-made businessman race heroes. Yet Cole's contributions to the cause of black respectability did not stop at the funeral parlor. Beginning in the 1930s, he invested his financial resources in a number of visionary cultural ventures, providing office space for the pioneering *All-Negro Hour* radio show, the first to feature black performers exclusively, founding a popular black magazine called the *Bronzeman,* and purchasing the Chicago American Giants Negro League baseball team in 1932. Jackson served as Second Ward committeeman after helping Big Bill Thompson procure more than 91 percent of the black vote in his victorious 1927 mayoral election bid. As committeeman, he steered hundreds of thousands of graft dollars each year into Thompson's machine, assuring that South Side gambling operations would continue to irrigate the economy of the Black Metropolis.

The fact that policy wheels undergirded the financial, cultural, and political infrastructure of the Black Metropolis made many of the champions of middle-class respectability somewhat reluctant to include policy among the litany of vices allegedly setting back the race. One study of the numbers game in interwar Harlem revealed that business leaders there claimed that the viability of the community's policy banks had been critical in building business confidence among African Americans, and it is more than likely that such views were prevalent among business leaders in Chicago's Black Metropolis as well.[25] Moreover, the argument that policy provided thousands of jobs to black folks who were being denied employment in white businesses held plenty of water, transforming gambling kingpins into veritable race leaders. Bronzeville residents thus reacted with heated anger at the judgmental gaze of whites upon their alleged propensity to throw nickels and dimes at elusive numbers. The *Chicago Defender* was clearly seeking to channel such feelings of resentment, for example, during Mayor Cermak's 1931 campaign to close down South Side policy wheels, when it published a series of editorials decrying the mayor's characterization of a lawless "black belt," where, Cermak reportedly claimed, "95 percent of colored people over 14 years old" played the numbers.[26]

To be sure, policy was a sensitive issue in the Black Metropolis. A range of black ministers and civic leaders railed against it, pointing at all the people reduced to destitution because of their addiction and sardonically mocking those who sought to profit from this addiction—the so-called spiritual advisors and peddlers of "dream books" promising to extract winning combinations from the shadowy depths of a gambler's subconscious. However, such reproaches coming from the other side of the color line sparked the kind of outrage and proud defiance that made average residents of the Black Metropolis see heroism in the businessmen and syndicate kingpins who were exploiting them. For if policy was many things to many people, it was also a means of redistributing the increasing wealth of the Black Metropolis upward towards the point of the social pyramid, and, regardless of the numerous stories of winning "gigs" (three winning numbers out of twelve) pulling families out of tough circumstances, policy did, in fact, keep a good number of people down, though how many we will never know with any certainty.

But policy's impact went far beyond the economic realm. The penetration of policy into the fabric of everyday life in the Black Metropolis also had undeniable consequences for the political culture, especially in terms of how average residents made meaning of the dramatic inequalities prevailing there and of the possibilities for addressing them. Although historians have grappled with the role of policy gambling within the economies and labor markets of black ghettos in the first half of the twentieth century, they have largely overlooked its ideological power.[27] Policy was symptomatic of the conditions of life in the lower-class world of Bronzeville, and a good many of those who laid down their nickels and dimes for long-shot slips of paper lived

FIGURE 4. South Side kitchenette apartment. Photo by Russell Lee. Courtesy of the Library of Congress.

in the impossibly cramped "kitchenette" apartments that proliferated on the South Side during the interwar years (figure 4). These one-room living spaces, which real estate developers hastily carved out of basements and larger apartments, with little concern for proper ventilation and plumbing, often housed as many people as could find a space on the floor to stretch their legs for a night's sleep. "A building that formerly held sixty families," Drake and Cayton claimed, "might now have three hundred."[28] Richard Wright referred to the kitchenette as "our prison, our death sentence without a trial, the new form of mob violence that assaults not only the lone individual, but all of us, in ceaseless attacks."[29] Yet, if Wright's evocation of "mob violence" pointed to the white hand behind such conditions in northern ghettos like Harlem and Bronzeville, the ethos surrounding policy represented a countervailing force to such notions.

To be sure, discerning the psychology of habitual gamblers is slippery ground, and few scholars dealing with such issues have sought to do so in the tight-knit cultural context of a place like the Black Metropolis of interwar Chicago. Nonetheless, it is hard to argue with the idea that the fatalism inherent in the ritual could only have worked to deflect attention from the structural circumstances behind the rampant poverty of the Black Metropolis, even if the ethos of black capitalism offered constant reminders that the misery and toil there were due to the exclusion of blacks from white society. Besides, when players lost enough to make them stop to think about who was profiting from all the nickels and dimes they threw down, their reflection led them not to the other side of the color line but to their own policy-king race heroes, whom they simultaneously begrudged and admired. This is not to say that policy did not offer something valuable. It was a ritual of sociability that provided daily amusement, and the sense of camaraderie around the game sometimes saw players pooling their winnings and more often commiserating over their losses. Moreover, in addition to their role as an employer, policy banks served as a vital source of loans at a time when credit was scarce. Nonetheless, playing the numbers on a daily basis infused the common sense of working-class blacks with powerful notions of chance and risk that individualized or otherwise explained away the difficult conditions they faced as matters of fate and hard luck. And there were enough self-made success stories around the Black Metropolis and in the pages of the black press to confirm such notions.

However, policy's ideological force was not due only to the fact that it tended to normalize and legitimize the precariousness and risk that could have created, in the words of William Gamson, "the righteous anger that puts fire in the belly and iron in the soul"—the critical preconditions of political mobilization.[30] For the more serious players, it is important to remember, policy was more an investment strategy than a game, and even the most leisurely players understood the speculative, calculating nature of the venture. And in this it resembled another form of speculative activity that spread through the Black Metropolis during this same era: the purchase of insurance policies to protect families against a disabling or deadly industrial accident or simply to guarantee a respectable funeral. In fact, many of the same rationalities were at play in the insurance industry as in the world of policy.

Insurance magnates like Anthony Overton and Robert Cole became race heroes in Bronzeville because they challenged the injustices blacks suffered in paying high premiums for coverage provided by white-owned companies, and in so doing they created decent jobs for the African Americans staffing their expanding workforces. The client base of Cole's Metropolitan Funeral System Association (MFSA), for example, grew from 33,000 in 1935 to 52,000 by 1939, an increase that made MFSA a source of jobs when most firms in other sectors were scaling back. And, like policy kingpins, the captains of the insurance industry capitalized on their role as race men to maximize their profits, organizing boycotts of white insurers and advertising their contributions to the race on billboards and in the pages of the black press. Yet, after interviewing a number of prominent insurance men and Bronzeville residents, Drake and Cayton painted a grim picture of Bronzeville's insurance business, including executives speaking cynically and candidly about exploiting their capital of race pride to sell policies, and burial insurers working hand in hand with undertakers to provide minimal funeral services at exorbitant prices—a practice that continued even after state legislation to address the problem was supposed to have required insurers to pay their bereaved clients in cash.

Insurance, like policy, was of course an upwardly redistributive scheme, even if it did help some to make do under difficult circumstances. There was good reason that funeral parlors often served as policy stations, and that people like Cole and Jackson moved seamlessly between the worlds of policy wheels and insurance policies. But, like policy, the impact of the insurance business on the Black Metropolis went far beyond the economic realm. "Insurance's general model," François Ewald has written, "is the game of chance: a risk, an accident comes up like a roulette number, a card pulled out of the pack."[31] In the context of the interwar Black Metropolis, the insurance "game" was thus another activity that tended to cast the effects of structural inequalities as random events devoid of political meaning. Moreover, unlike the labor union or mutual aid society, insurance represented an individualized and privatized response to problems that might have otherwise been perceived as collective and public. The rationale that went with insurance transformed social injustices into "accidents," deflecting attention away from the reasons why African Americans in Chicago in the 1920s died at twice the rate whites did. Insurance, like policy, imposed a market logic on the affairs of everyday life, and all of the energy that black insurers put into organizing boycotts and emblazoning billboards with the promises of racial uplift suggested that the sense of "linked fate" they were offering with their policies was something of a hard sell.[32]

The explosion of policy and insurance in the 1920s thus reflected the ways in which the hegemony of black capitalism was working to "economize" the political culture and everyday life of the Black Metropolis.[33] How else to explain Jesse Binga's astonishing 1922 telegram to the secretary of the Illinois Bankers Association, published approvingly in the pages of the *Chicago Defender*, which, in urging "stronger ties of cooperation between the two races," boldly offered up black Americans as a resource to be better exploited:

The Negro is an industrial people. He furnishes two-fifths of the brawn and muscle of America: our wages return to whomsoever has the proper equivalent for those wages. You may get the Negro's dollar, but the question is, are you getting all you should from the Negro?

Should we not utilize to the extent of reaping millions out of him instead of getting merely thousands? Should we not develop the Negro in his desire for economic happiness to the extent of rendering his possessions worth a million instead of a thousand? That means more for your bank and for all the business institutions dependent upon it.

I admit that the Negro is not fully developed in business. He is at the same stage that your ancestors were during the opening of the Victorian era: but he is today the most promising undeveloped commercial material in America.[34]

Nor was this vision of the black population as a raw material for economic exploitation merely a rhetorical device for Binga and the business elite he spoke for; it was an idea that was put into practice in the ruthless pursuit of wealth in both the underground and formal economies of the Black Metropolis. In addition to marrying into policy money, Binga also gained some of his wealth in the real estate market. And, although he would build up his résumé as a race leader in the 1920s by using blockbusting tactics to open up formerly all-white areas for African Americans in desperate need of housing, Binga's business plan ultimately revolved around exploiting the people he was supposed to be uplifting. Instilling panic in white owners fearing the racial "invasion" of their neighborhoods, Binga was able to procure apartments in white-occupied buildings by offering a big advance to the owners on the rents, but, as was common practice among black real estate developers of the time, he then divided them up into kitchenettes and rented to poor black families at a sizable premium over the market price paid by white renters on the other side of the color line. The "boss" of the South Side's black "submachine," Oscar DePriest—who became the first African American elected to Chicago's city council (as Second Ward alderman) in 1915 and then the first black politician elected to the House of Representatives from a northern state in 1928—engaged in similar practices while amassing a personal fortune as a real estate broker. DePriest rose to prominence both locally and nationally as a race leader by defending the rights of African Americans on the floor of the House of Representatives, but his political career was dealt a blow in August 1931, when police responding to his call to stop Communist-led antieviction actions at one of his properties killed three black protestors.[35]

Along with Edward H. Wright, whom Mayor Thompson appointed to be the city's assistant corporation counsel as a reward for getting out the black vote in the 1915 election, DePriest sat atop a black submachine that funneled votes and funds from the South Side's 2nd and 3rd Wards into the Republican Party machine in return for political appointments for blacks, city jobs for Bronzeville residents, and a range of administrative and legislative favors for black businesses. As Second Ward alderman, DePriest served as intermediary between the Stroll's gambling clubs and the Republican machine, a role that led to his indictment on corruption charges in 1917. After eventually being acquitted the following year by arguing that the protection bribes he had taken were merely campaign contributions, DePriest lost the aldermanic election of 1919 to Louis B. Anderson, who had filled his seat on the city council after his indictment. By 1920, with DePriest returning to his real estate business, three politicians pulled the strings of the black submachine— Second Ward alderman Anderson, Third Ward alderman Robert Jackson, and Edward H. Wright, who had been named Second Ward committeeman, a position that gave him the power to nominate judges and a range of other political officials. Another black official of considerable influence was African Methodist Episcopal (AME) Church bishop Archibald Carey, whom Mayor Thompson named to the Civil Service Commission in 1927, giving him power over the city's pool of municipal jobs. Under Wright's leadership, the black submachine sought to use the electoral and financial resources of the Black Metropolis not only to increase patronage but also to increase the power of black politicians in the legislative process—a challenge that Wright took to heart. His refusal to accede to Mayor Thompson's pressure on the nomination of a First Ward committeeman in 1926 led to his withdrawal from politics, a void at the apex of the black submachine that was filled in 1928, when DePriest was elected to the House to represent the First Congressional District of Illinois (which included the Loop and the black South Side).[36]

Despite the best efforts of Wright and other well-meaning black political officials, the black submachine reproduced the bread-and-butter political style that characterized Chicago politics citywide during the interwar years. This does not mean that black politicians did not spearhead some considerable advances for black Chicagoans. As floor leader in the city council, for example, Anderson led an initiative to raise the wages of all city employees, a measure that helped thousands of black civil servants. Due to the efforts of black aldermen, by 1932 African Americans constituted 6.4 percent of the municipal workforce, which nearly matched their 7 percent proportion of the population.[37] Nevertheless, the leaders of the black submachine seldom weighed in publicly on the more systemic dimensions of racial injustice in the city, leaving the racial order intact. Although Thompson was hailed as a friend to blacks, he failed to act on the most pressing issues facing African Americans. For example, he refused to take any action, rhetorical or otherwise, against the campaign of bombings—fifty-eight incidents were recorded between July 1917 through April 1921—conducted by white homeowners' associations against black residents and the realtors who sought to provide them housing in white neighborhoods. Such terrorism, combined with the rampant use of restrictive covenants, greatly accelerated the advance of segregation, increasing Chicago's white-black dissimilarity index from 66.8 to 85.2 percent between 1920 and 1930.[38] And, in a moment when the education issue was at the heart of progressive politics, Thompson never gave much thought to appointing an African American to the highly politicized board of education.

In the final analysis, however, it is difficult to take Chicago's black political and economic establishment too rigorously to task for not advancing black aspirations in the political arena, in view of the enormous constraints they faced from the white political establishment, Republican and Democrat alike. Much more dubious was their influence in actively shaping a political culture and organizing a public sphere that proved highly resistant to grassroots political projects challenging the circumstances of social inequality within the Black Metropolis. The race men whose voices rang out loudest on the reigning issues of the day invested doggedly in the ideals of thrift, hard work, and entrepreneurial spirit, the lack of which, in their eyes, explained many of the problems working-class blacks faced in their daily lives. Oscar DePriest was perhaps behaving as a loyal member of the Republican Party—the party of Lincoln, one must not forget—when he declared on the floor of the House in 1930, "[I am not] asking for public funds to make mendicants of the American people, and I represent more poor people than any other man in America represents." But such sensibilities also reflected the ethos of black capitalism embraced by middle-class residents of his Chicago district, where a lack of public assistance was causing the forcible eviction of unemployed tenants in his properties. Addressing a crowd of protestors in Washington Park in the tense atmosphere following the deadly antieviction riot of August 3, 1931, Robert Abbott echoed these same ideas when he argued that their troubles had come about because they had not "saved for the lean years."[39]

Abbott's views were not only pronounced on soapboxes. Along with churches, the black press played a critical role in shaping the perceptions of ordinary residents about the political, economic, and social circumstances prevailing in the Black Metropolis, and Abbott's paper was certainly the most powerful of them all. While some scholars have described the *Defender*'s stance as "fluctuating" on certain issues (for example, in regard to labor unions), its coverage of grassroots movements for social and economic justice was normally colored by Abbott's pro-business, pull-yourself-up-by-your-bootstraps vision of the world. If the *Defender* supported unionization in cases when it seemed like the best means for advancing the race in the face of discriminatory actions by management, Abbott's weekly, notes historian James Grossman, "opposed anything that smelled of economic radicalism."[40] Hence, while Abbott praised the Communist Party for expelling one of its white members for segregating guests at a social function in 1933, his position on Communist efforts to defend evicted black residents two years earlier had been unequivocal: in a *Defender* editorial several days after the antieviction riots, he had opined, "Communism is not in the blood of the Negro."[41]

"POOR MAN'S BLUES"

Hence, while Abbott could embrace the racial egalitarianism of Communists, their efforts to uplift the poor were another matter altogether, which explains a great deal about his reluctance to throw the support of the "world's greatest weekly" behind black Chicago's most ambitious challenge to the political and economic arrangements of the Black Metropolis and the economizing logic of black capitalism: the Brotherhood of Sleeping Car Porters (BSCP). Following its successful unionization drive in New York in 1925, the BSCP, under the leadership of A. Philip Randolph, turned to the difficult task of organizing the many maids and porters living in Chicago. The BSCP was not a typical union in that porters were among Bronzeville's labor aristocracy. But their middle-class wages depended on gratuities, which placed them in a degrading and precarious position in relation to white customers, who could decide to withhold tips to those not displaying the requisite subservient demeanor. Moreover, the BSCP was an all-black union, and the Chicago Urban League, under the direction of T. Arnold Hill, had taken a position against separate unions since the 1919 race riot. An influential member of the Urban League was Associated Negro Press founder Claude Barnett, whose newswire was unwavering in its criticism of the BSCP. But the most significant impediment to the BSCP's success was the enormous power Pullman wielded on the South Side, where the company provided thousands of jobs and where it had bought considerable influence, in one way or another, with a good many of the race men of the Black Metropolis. Major black community institutions like the Provident Hospital and the Wabash YMCA, which provided a range of social services for Bronzeville's working-class residents, depended on Pullman's contributions for survival; the Pullman Porters' Benefit Association of America, the company union, had considerable funds deposited in Binga's bank; and Pullman money padded the revenues of both the *Chicago Defender* and the *Chicago Whip*. For these reasons, Chicago's leading race heroes—Binga, Abbott, Overton, DePriest, and Wright—withheld their support from the BSCP as it struggled for survival in the early years of its unionization drive.

Even the active backing of famed journalist Ida B. Wells-Barnett, whose antilynching campaign in the 1890s had won her national recognition as a "race woman" and who had emerged as a force to be reckoned with in South Side politics after her Alpha Suffrage Club had effectively mobilized thousands of women behind the triumphant aldermanic candidacy of Oscar DePriest in 1915, proved to be of little help in winning over the top brass of the Black Metropolis to the BSCP cause. When Wells-Barnett asked the exclusive Appomattox Club, black Chicago's version of the Commercial Club founded by Edward Wright in 1900, to give Randolph a hearing, she was told that the club could "not afford to have Mr. Randolph speak" because so many of the "men who are opposing him are members here and it would embarrass them with the Pullman Company."[42] A portrait of Pullman, it should be noted, hung in the club's stately three-story building at 3632 Grand Boulevard.

Opposition to Randolph was also strong among many of black Chicago's most influential religious leaders. Reverend Lacy Kirk Williams, who had allowed packinghouse and steel workers to use his Olivet Baptist Church for organizing efforts in 1919, voiced strong opposition to the BSCP, and Bishop Archibald Carey forbid Randolph access to any AME churches. Carey had a number of personal reasons to be loyal to Pullman. George Pullman had once helped stave off the foreclosure of his Quinn Chapel, and Carey's amicable relations with the company made him the man to see in the Black Metropolis about procuring one of the enviable positions in the Pullman workforce. Nonetheless, Carey articulated his aversion to challenges to the white business establishment in broader terms: "The interest of my people," he once proclaimed, "lies with the wealth of the nation and with the class of white people who control it."[43]

This was the very notion that Randolph had been publicly squaring off against since 1917, the year he cofounded the magazine *The Messenger* with fellow Socialist Party member Chandler Owen to serve as the mouthpiece of the black labor movement. It was within the pages of *The Messenger* that Randolph confronted the ethos of black capitalism, presenting his own vision of the New Negro spirit that replaced the values of thrift and self-reliance emanating from the black business heroes of the day with those of economic rights, brotherhood, and "collective organized action." "The social aims of the New Negro are decidedly different from the Old Negro," he wrote in his 1920 editorial "The New Negro—What is He?" "He insists that a society which is based upon justice can only be a society composed of *social equals*." Dismissing out of hand the emancipatory promises of black capitalism being celebrated by the *Defender* around the time of the opening of Binga's state bank, Randolph further argued that "there [were] no big capitalists" in black communities, only "a few petit bourgeoisie" whose position was untenable anyway because "the process of money concentration [was] destined to weed them out and drop them down into the ranks of the working class." As for the new political order of the Black Metropolis emerging at the time, Randolph proclaimed in the same editorial that "the New Negro, unlike the Old Negro, cannot be lulled into a false sense of security with political spoils and patronage."[44] This was a message he carried into the Chicago organizing campaign seven years later, when he unabashedly took on the pantheon of race men in the Black Metropolis—especially Robert Abbott, whose newspaper's support, tacit or otherwise, was critical to BSCP success. In October 1927, Randolph told a large Bronzeville crowd assembled at the People's Church and Metropolitan Community Center that Abbott had surrendered to "gold and power."[45]

Randolph extended such reproaches to Chicago's clergy as well—especially to the eminent Archibald Carey, who not only banned the BSCP from AME churches but also demanded that all AME ministers warn their congregants against the evils of labor unions. However, Randolph's opposition to the black religious establishment lay not only in its ties to big business and the political machine; it grew out of a broader critique of how black churches had fallen victim to the economizing logic of the Black Metropolis. As early as October 1919, he had argued in an editorial entitled "The Failure of the Negro Church" that the black church had been "converted into a business ... run primarily for profits" with an "interest ... focused upon debits and credits, deficits and surpluses."[46] In the face of such tendencies,

Randolph set out to devise an alternative theology that would align religion with a powerful language of social justice. Invited to the Yale Divinity School in 1931, he delivered a lecture entitled "Whither the Negro Church?" in which he urged black churches to develop "a working class viewpoint and program."[47]

While most religious leaders were unreceptive to such messages, Randolph's vision of working-class solidarity caught the attention of a handful of influential ministers. One of these was William Decatur Cook, the former pastor of Chicago's Bethel African Methodist Episcopal Church, who had become a rebel pastor after having been ousted from his pulpit by Archibald Carey upon his nomination as AME bishop for the Chicago area. In fact, Cook's removal indicated that he was already at odds with the more conservative church leadership. After holding services for a number of years in Unity Hall, the headquarters of DePriest's People's Movement Club, in 1927, the undaunted Cook took his some five hundred followers with him to the handsome sandstone Romanesque Revival church at 41st and Grand Boulevard, which had previously housed the First Presbyterian Church. Aligned with the Community Church movement, the Metropolitan Community Church defined its mission with the credo "non-sectarian, broadly humanitarian, serving all the people." Cook's church was thus a loyal friend to the BSCP.

In addition to Cook, Randolph had the unqualified support of Pilgrim Baptist Church pastor Junius Austin, a fervent Garveyite, who, having arrived in Chicago in 1926 from Pittsburgh, was relatively free of patronage entanglements and, presiding by 1930 over a congregation of some nine thousand faithful members, possessed the kind of power base that would allow him to remain free. Austin represented quite another version of black capitalism, one that shunned the competitive, profit-driven spirit articulated by Binga and his cohort. Back in Pittsburgh, he had developed a real estate cooperative that had enabled the purchase of some one thousand properties for black families. Once in Chicago, he quickly formed the Cooperative Business League, a venture that, according to the *Pittsburgh Courier,* "paved the way for the militant program that [gave] Chicago the largest number of Negro owned and operated enterprises of any city in the world."[48] And yet neither Austin nor his Cooperative Business League appeared in the pages of the *Defender* in 1926 and 1927, as Randolph and the BSCP were seeking to spread their vision of racial solidarity founded in a collective commitment to social equality.

By November 1927, however, the *Defender* had published a mea culpa regarding its stance on the BSCP:

> It is felt and asserted by some that the Defender is opposed to the porters' efforts at organization. . . . Whatever may be the merits of these charges, be it known by all whom it may concern that the Defender is a red-blooded four-square Race paper, which is unequivocally committed to the policy of supporting all bona fide Race movements. Therefore, we wish definitely to register that fact that we back and favor the right of Pullman porters and maids to organize into a bona fide union of their own choosing, untrammeled by the Pullman Company.[49]

Abbott's reversal represented a critical turning point in the BSCP's campaign. In 1935, the union would defeat the company union and win its charter from the AFL, paving the way for the Pullman Company's decision to grant it official recognition in 1937. Four years later, in 1941, when Randolph spearheaded the March on Washington movement to protest racial discrimination in the war industries, which were flourishing as a result of the United States entering the hostilities overseas, the BSCP rose to national prominence as a major player in the struggle for civil rights.

The BSCP's triumph had not come easily. By 1933, its total membership had dwindled to under seven hundred—a small fraction of the overall workforce—and were it not for the Roosevelt administration backing the Wagner Act of 1935, which outlawed company unions, it is doubtful the BSCP would have weathered the Pullman Company's offensive. Red-baiting tactics also played a role in the BSCP's struggles, especially after Randolph's election as president of the Communist-driven National Negro Congress (NNC). This alliance between the BSCP and the NNC caused rifts between the Communist-influenced CIO and the more conservative leadership of the AFL while subjecting Randolph to pressure from the Dies Committee. In 1940, Randolph resigned as NNC president, claiming: "Negroes cannot afford to add the handicap of being 'black' to the handicap of being 'red.'" And yet, what perhaps hampered the union most in Chicago was the continuing resistance from the city's black establishment.

Somewhat ironically, what support the BSCP was able to muster in order to overcome this resistance enough to win recognition came from a group of militant middle-class women who were no strangers to the black establishment crowd. Ida B. Wells-Barnett rallied the women of her Wells Club to canvas their neighborhoods in support of the BCSP. In fact, as a member of

Cook's congregation at the Metropolitan Community Church, Wells-Barnett sat in the same pews as Robert Abbott and under the same roof as DePriest's political headquarters—a building, as the story goes, that was provided to DePriest by telephone magnate and Commercial Club player Samuel Insull. Joining Wells-Barnett in her fight was another insider, Irene Goins, president of the Illinois Federation of Colored Women's Clubs (IFCWC) and founder of the Douglass League of Women Voters. Goins had the kind of pull that enabled her to bring Second Ward Republican committeeman Edward Wright and national Republican committeewoman Ruth Hanna McCormick to address the IFCWC. Like the old settler business crowd they were opposing, the influence these African American clubwomen wielded stretched across the color line, where it was entangled with the very patronage structure that Randolph had in his crosshairs. The involvement of such figures as Wells-Barnett and Goins on behalf of the BSCP was also critical to attracting prominent labor organizer and settlement worker Mary McDowell to the cause—the only white Chicagoan who took an active stand against the Pullman Company. McDowell made her support clear when on October 3, 1927, she addressed an audience of two thousand packed into Austin's Pilgrim Baptist Church for a BSCP meeting organized by Wells-Barnett, Goins, and BSCP organizer Milton Webster. This show of force for the BSCP, with its interracial cast of notables, was enough to push the hand of Abbott, who at the time was noting a drop in circulation due to talk of a boycott protesting his paper's stance. The BSCP had clearly hit Abbott where it hurt most by revealing, as Beth Tompkins Bates has argued, "the contradiction inherent in advocating black freedom through paternalistic relations."[50]

Certainly, something of a popular groundswell had been set in motion as clubwomen activists brought the BSCP's message of economic rights and racial dignity into the homes of working-class neighbors who, understandably, would have been receptive to such appeals. Historian Jeffrey Helgeson has recently argued that these circumstances represented a broader trend of community-based activism around quality-of-life issues led by women who were acting pragmatically to sustain the conditions of their households and neighborhoods in the interwar Black Metropolis.[51] Although Wells-Barnett and Goins were somewhat extraordinary race women, many of the more ordinary middle-class clubwomen who answered their call had entered the milieu of political activism as a means of addressing the ills of the city that were arriving at their doorsteps: crime, prostitution, and creeping slum conditions created by the spread of the nefarious kitchenettes. Whereas some scholars have viewed such bread-and-butter struggles to sustain the "home sphere" in a conservative light—as the individualistic reflexes of strivers and climbers seeking respectability and stature—the mobilization of clubwomen for the BSCP suggests that women engaging in the politics of home and neighborhood could also embrace more ambitious forms of collective activism.[52] Yet it would be misleading to overstate the power of such forms of activism to dilute the potent ideological brew produced by the intermingling notions of entrepreneurial initiative, personal responsibility, and racial uplift that were so central to the spirit of black capitalism in the interwar Black Metropolis. In the final analysis, the moral of the BSCP story is not its triumph but rather the dogged resistance it faced in achieving it. Regardless of the Urban League's position on race-based unions, the BSCP's approach was in line with the spirit of racial unity of the times, yet its collectivist appeal and its unabashed challenge to the ethos of black capitalism was hard to digest for the black power elite and enough members of the black middle class—professionals, small businessmen, and civil servants—who saw their interests as aligned with the Appomattox Club crowd.

Moreover, the politics of the home sphere that brought middle-class folks and their well-heeled neighbors together in church-based and neighborhood-based clubs seeking to lift up their impoverished neighbors and the race played out in the context of frantic real estate speculation—yet another force working to economize the fabric of neighborhood life in the Black Metropolis. By the late 1910s, seventeen South Side realtors were running listings in *Black's Blue Book,* with several of the more ambitious, such as DePriest and DePriest, taking out eye-catching ads. Sensing the trend in the making, one realtor, Dr. R. A. Williams, implored potential home buyers to "Make Your Dream Come True," warning them that "every rent day sees a little more money gone and you a little further behind."[53] By the mid-1920s, the black press was hailing what the *Defender* referred to as the black "obsession" with homeownership and the "friendly spirit of rivalry" motivating black homeowners to join "neighborhood improvement associations." In an editorial entitled "Neighborhood Pride," the paper's editors opined that the increasing number of blacks seizing "the opportunity to invest [their] earnings in property" was "the best thing that ever happened to [the race]."[54] At the start of the following year, Anthony Overton's *Half-Century Magazine* proudly announced that "$10,000,000.00 of Chicago real estate had gone over to Colored people in the past year."[55]

Indeed, like many other commercial activities in the Black Metropolis, the real estate industry held out great promises for advancing the race. Exemplifying this alignment of collective racial progress with individual property acquisition was a 1923 ad placed by the Sphinx Real Estate Improvement Corporation in the *Defender* reminding potential black homeowners that of the "fifty million dollars per year . . . paid out by the Colored renters of Chicago . . . less than 5 percent . . . is retained by the Colored race or controlled by them for the improvement of their own living conditions."[56] Such sentiments, according to the work of historian N. D. B. Connolly, reflected the critical importance of property and real estate to black politics in the first half of the twentieth century. Connolly argues, "Owning rental real estate and owning one's own home promised black people a measure of individual freedom from the coercive power of wage labor, landlords, and the state."[57] But Connolly also describes another side to this story—the contradictions that arose as black leaders seeking to uplift the race pursued economic activities that extracted resources from those they were seeking to uplift. And such contradictions also extended into the political sphere, as black landlords cooperated with white elites invested in maintaining a racially unjust status quo. While these circumstances certainly characterized the real estate dealings of Overton, Binga, and DePriest, perhaps even more significant for the Black Metropolis was the way in which its transformation into a real estate frontier in the 1920s reshaped its political culture. With residents increasingly bombarded with advertisements warning them not to miss the golden opportunity, an economizing ethos of "getting ahead" began to eclipse that of "advancing the race." "Have you invested in Chicago real estate?" asked another Sphinx Real Estate ad. "Those who have bought Chicago property in the last ten years have made money and values are increasing every year."[58] And yet another ad in the *Defender* from a Gary, Indiana, real estate agency implored potential buyers to get into the market there: "Putting things off has kept many men poor—perhaps this is your case. Action has made all rich men."[59]

The transformation of the family home into a financial investment—a critical development in the neoliberalization of the political cultures of metropolitan spaces, black and white alike, over the course of the twentieth century—was a phenomenon that was hardly specific to the Black Metropolis, Harlem, or any other of the country's larger black ghettos. Nor was the tendency of developers to take advantage of the situation. And African Americans were hardly alone in their tendency to imbue their property with a sense of racial and civic duty. Working- and middle-class whites buying into the hopes and promises of homeownership on the other side of the color line were also increasingly viewing their properties in such terms, as fears of black invasion increased and grassroots struggles to hold the line against block-busting real estate agents proliferated. And yet the blockbusters cynically betraying white homeowners for quick and substantial monetary gain were clearly regarded as villains, whereas the black developers who were ripping up buildings and charging exorbitant rents for substandard apartments were cast as race men and community leaders. This explains a great deal about how the clubwomen activists of the Black Metropolis could mobilize to help their poorer neighbors while embracing a pull-yourself-up-by-your-bootstraps view. If, as Helgeson has argued, these women did help to create "resilient local bases of power and a long and rich tradition of black liberal politics" that led blacks to make demands on the black submachine as well as New Deal relief agencies in the years to come, they also participated in shaping a political culture that proved hostile to many of the most assertive struggles for social justice in the early 1930s: the Communist-led actions against housing evictions, unemployment, and the lack of adequate welfare relief.[60] The political sympathies of a good many clubwomen activists lay not with such campaigns but with the more respectable Chicago NAACP, which, during the very moment antieviction protestors and Unemployment Councils were hitting the streets, was fighting for its survival. Indeed, if the local NAACP took on a more active role beginning in 1933 under the leadership of former *Chicago Whip* editor and Yale graduate A. C. MacNeal, one of the key forces behind the Don't Spend Your Money Where You Can't Work campaign, it had no real economic program in the midst of an economic catastrophe, and its reliance on the Appomattox Club crowd meant it would do little to become relevant to working-class blacks.

Hence, as on the other side of the color line, the political culture of the Black Metropolis could muster little opposition to the reigning political and economic order, even as that order lay in shambles. After 1929, most of what had been invested in black banks and businesses—in hope and money—had vanished, and even the likes of Edward Wright had kitchenettes on his block. Courageous were those agitating for jobs, housing, and relief in the 1930s, but their ranks were almost impossibly thin. By the mid-1930s, committed Communists in the city numbered about four hundred (although there were enough fellow travelers to swell the crowd to over a thousand when they demonstrated for relief). After dropping to 658 in 1933 from a 1928 peak of

1,150, membership in the Brotherhood of Sleeping Car Porters rebounded to over 1,000 by 1935, but there was no getting around the fact that seven years had passed with no gain.

It was within this context that the Black Metropolis played host in February 1936 to the first convention of the National Negro Congress (NNC), which brought over seven hundred delegates, including such notables as Harlem's famed Baptist pastor Adam Clayton Powell Jr.; James W. Ford, black vice presidential candidate for the Communist Party in 1932 and 1936; the National Urban League's Lester Granger; and the NAACP's Roy Wilkins, as well as a number of leading writers, artists, and intellectuals, including Richard Wright, Langston Hughes, and Arna Bontemps. The event was held at the Eighth Regiment Armory, whose interior hall was draped with banners, one of which read "Jobs and Adequate Relief for a Million Negro Destitute Families." Randolph could not attend the event but he sent another BSCP official to deliver a spirited speech proclaiming that "the problems of the Negro people [are] the problems of the workers, for practically 99 per cent of Negro people win their bread by selling their labor power."[61] "The NNC convention in Chicago proved unique," historian Erik Gellman has argued, "because its participants not only talked about working-class blacks but also looked to them for leadership."[62] Nevertheless, while receiving praise in the *Defender,* the convention also stirred up a great deal of controversy. Several religious leaders stormed out, and reporters covering the event noted undercurrents of discontent among the delegates concerning the radical tone of the proceedings, the large presence of whites and Communists, and the notable absence of old guard black leaders like W. E. B. Du Bois, James Weldon Johnson, and Charles S. Johnson.[63] In the end the NNC convention hardly left a footprint within the political culture of the Black Metropolis. Two years later, the scathing critiques of capitalism that had filled the Eighth Regiment Armory seemed like distant memories as Junius Austin urged the crowd gathered for the Negro Business Exposition in the very same building to take on racial oppression by buying black and supporting the retail business of the South Side's biggest policy kingpins.

Not even the stages of the nighttime Stroll, where jazz and blues performers sang about the trials of working-class city life to enthralled crowds of migrants, seemed to offer much spiritual opposition to the gospel of black capitalism. The blues, in particular, has long been associated with a "black cultural front" that brought together writers, artists, musicians, and labor activists in the interwar years, a perspective based, in part, on the number of blues standards circulating around the scene that articulated the injuries of class in northern ghettos—for example, Mamie Smith's "Lost Opportunity Blues" and Bessie Smith's "Poor Man's Blues." Hence, the blues and jazz opened up discursive spaces for migrants negotiating the difficulties of urban life in the North, and with the explosion of the race records industry in the 1920s, these spaces extended beyond the venues of the Stroll. Okeh Records, which had become a major race records label by the early 1920s, quickly set up recording operations in Chicago, seeking to tap the energy of the local scene there by recording some the Stroll's most prominent performers: King Oliver, Louis Armstrong, Ethel Waters, Alberta Hunter, and Duke Ellington, among others. Chicago blues and jazz performers transformed the bars, clubs, and theaters of the Stroll into their own churches, offering spiritual catharsis and fellowship to working-class blacks dealing with the cultural tensions and economic hardships of their new life in Chicago. Gospel great Thomas Dorsey, who worked the club scene before becoming the "father of black gospel music" as music director at Pilgrim Baptist Church, evoked such spiritual powers in describing a performance of blues queen Ma Rainey:

> When she started singing the gold in her teeth would sparkle. She was in the spotlight. She possessed her listeners; they swayed, they rocked, they moaned and groaned, as they felt the blues with her. A woman swooned who had lost her man. Men groaned who had given their week's pay to some woman who promised to be nice, but slipped away and couldn't be found at the appointed time.... As the song ends, she feels an understanding with her audience.... By this time everybody is excited and enthusiastic. The applause thunders for one more number. Some woman screams out with a shrill cry of agony as the blues recalls sorrow because some man trifled with her and wounded her to the bone.[64]

This ability to move the hearts and souls of black working-class audiences has led many to focus, almost single-mindedly, on the subversive undercurrents and oppositional power of the blues genre. "The blues," Ralph Ellison wrote in 1945 in a review of Richard Wright's novel *Black Boy,* "is an impulse to keep the painful details and episodes of a brutal experience alive in one's aching consciousness, to finger its jagged grain, and to transcend it, not by the consolation of philosophy but by squeezing from it a near-tragic, near-comic lyricism."[65] Though relatively few of the songs one heard on the Stroll were explicitly about racism, it was often a given in the stories of hardship and desperation they told. While many point to Billie Holliday's famed 1939 antilynching song "Strange Fruit" as the landmark contribution of black music to this movement on the national stage, local blues and jazz musicians had been for decades providing working-class blacks with a language that, in the words of Houston Baker, "connote[d] a world of transience, instability, hard luck, brutalizing work, lost love, minimal security, and enduring human wit and resourcefulness in the face of disaster."[66] Moreover, there is much to be said for the argument, advanced most notably by Angela Davis and Hazel Carby, that the women blues singers of the interwar era helped to build bonds among working-class black women around their challenges to the prevailing codes of patriarchy and respectability in black communities.[67] Ma Rainey and Bessie Smith, under the spotlight, bedecked in elegant satin gowns and covered in gold, jewels, and feathers, certainly projected images of power and autonomy, and their candor about subjects like domestic abuse, infidelity, turning the tables on the unfaithful, and female same-sex relations no doubt raised awareness about the myriad forms of gender oppression that had been naturalized as common sense.

But there was another side to the blues and jazz. The glamorously adorned, gilded, plumed bodies of the blues queens of the interwar years were dual signifiers. The aura of fame and wealth surrounding figures like Rainey, who earned the nickname of "Gold Necklace Woman of the Blues" for her practice of wearing a large chain of gold dollars around her neck, symbolically reinforced the dreams of social mobility that the likes of Binga, Abbott, and Overton were presenting as the logical by-products of black capitalism. The conspicuous taste of performers like Rainey and Smith was not a detail but rather was central to their star power, which was supported by extensive press coverage of their relatively lavish lifestyles. Such circumstances explain a great deal about the resonance of Bessie Smith's 1929 classic "Nobody Loves You When You're Down and Out," which famously begins: "Once I lived the life of a millionaire / Spendin' my money, I didn't care."

While lacking the extravagance of the blues queens, the Stroll's jazz greats—Louis Armstrong, King Oliver, Cab Calloway—also dressed sharply in order to project an unmistakable image of entrepreneurial ambition and success in the big city. This dress code responded, in part, to accusations frequently heard on the other side of the color line that jazz was immoral, baseless, and devoid of artistic value. Yet it also reflected notions of respectability among the race men of the daytime Stroll. Such values, for example, suffused the widely read weekly *Defender* column "The Musical Bunch," which was intended to publicize the jazz scene but which also ended up serving as a sounding board for

FIGURE 5. Louis Armstrong looking sharp. Public domain.

columnist (and former bandleader) Dave Peyton's moralizing diatribes about the lack of professionalism and sobriety exhibited by Stroll musicians. "When the public learns you are ratty and without culture," Peyton exhorted in 1928, "they learn to dislike your work."[68] In fact, Peyton even went so far as to list his own "don'ts" and to dispense fatherly financial advice to temper the extravagant spending habits of musicians, imploring them to forego the purchase of cars and to invest their money in real estate, save their money in the bank, and purchase proper insurance.[69] While Peyton was certainly an admirer of Louis Armstrong, he celebrated Armstrong's image as much as his artistic virtuosity, referring to him as a "fine example of ambition and thrift."[70] True to the spirit of the newspaper he was working for, Peyton mixed such moralizing middle-class condescension with strong condemnations regarding the racism stigmatizing black musicians and limiting their careers. Nonetheless, the great influence his columns wielded ultimately indicates that the Stroll's jazz and blues scene hardly represented an escape from middle-class values of respectability or from the cultural racism of the white gaze.

It was perhaps for this reason that when Chicago's jazz front men took to words, they often sang of the pomp and splendor of the Stroll and the Black

Metropolis around it in ways that conveyed possibility, opportunity, and mobility. Although Louis Armstrong, perhaps Chicago's most renowned jazz figure of the era, conveyed the constraining power of racism in his recording of Fats Waller and Andy Razaf's "(What Did I Do to Be So) Black and Blue," this was an aberration.[71] In fact, he was more recognized for his fun-loving scat singing style, popularized by his 1926 hit "Heebie Jeebies." Indeed, Armstrong's simple lyrics often sought to escape the hard realities of working-class black life by conveying the liberatory excitement of the nighttime Stroll in such songs as "Sunset Café Stomp"—named after the popular Stroll venue. Moreover, Armstrong's canvases of the nighttime Stroll were juxtaposed in his sets with portrayals of the respectability and bravado that came with financial success, in such numbers as "Struttin' with Some Barbecue" and "Big Butter and Egg Man." Such tunes were understood within a lexical field in which the cash economy was front and center. Bessie Smith's evocation of the crass opportunism displayed by "friends" taking advantage of another's financial success and then turning their backs during hard times made her hit "Nobody Loves You When You're Down and Out" one of the era's classics, but such tales of material considerations shaping interpersonal relations were commonplace within the lyrical landscape of the jazz and blues in the 1920s and 1930s. Louis Armstrong, for example, evoked a similar sentiment in his 1927 song "S.O.L. Blues," in which the narrator proclaims:

> Now I'm with you sweet mama / as long as you have the bucks
> (Bucks, bucks, bucks . . . I mean money, mama!)
> I'm with you sweet mama / as long as you have ba-rucks, bucks, bucks
> When the bucks run out, sweet mama you're out of luck (out of luck, luck, luck).

Cab Calloway's 1932 hit "Minnie the Moocher" turned on a related motif with its story of a gold-digging woman who "had a million dollars' worth of nickels and dimes" and who "counted them all a million times."

Yet perhaps even more significant than what was conveyed when blues and jazz performers in the Black Metropolis sang was what they left unsung. Virtually nonexistent within the moral universe of the blues and jazz were sentiments and feelings that aligned with the anticapitalist critiques and appeals for class-based collective action being made by those on the frontlines of struggles over labor and housing in the interwar Black Metropolis. While it was perhaps understood that the power of white racism lingered somewhere in the background of the stories of sorrow and hardship being staged on the Stroll, the more specific explanations being offered up revolved largely around bad luck, personal failings, and betrayal. In the end, the spirit of the nighttime Stroll, as it was lived by its habitués in the bars, clubs, and theaters, was not much more than a caricature of its daytime counterpart.

THREE

White and Black

CITY AT WAR

On June 14, 1942, an estimated 400,000 Chicagoans marched in a parade that snaked through more than fifty miles of the city's streets and lasted more than seventeen hours. The event was held to commemorate Flag Day, a holiday that would not attain official status until 1949 but had been celebrated by cities and towns across the nation since at least the 1880s. In fact, Chicago's first recorded Flag Day celebration was in 1894, when a reported 300,000 children from its public schools rallied around American flags in parks across the city. But this was the first such celebration since the Japanese attack on Pearl Harbor, and thus there was a much more pronounced sense of purpose in the air. Coming in the twilight of an era of bitter labor strife, Chicago's Office of Civilian Defense organized the affair so as to demonstrate the city's irreproachable spirit of national unity. While few in the labor movement had forgotten the horror of the Memorial Day Massacre of 1937, when police had gunned down ten members of the Steel Workers Organizing Committee on a prairie near Republic Steel, the procession saw nearly every branch of organized labor marching in step with thousands of local manufacturers and business organizations. Moreover, the patriotic spirit on display in this parade was hardly exclusive to the world of business and work. Every neighborhood affiliated with the Office of Civilian Defense marked its proud participation by contributing a float representing some aspect of the Civilian Defense movement.

Chicago was certainly not alone in its enthusiasm for supporting the war effort on the home front. No war in American history had ever witnessed such a clear consensus of support, nor has any since. While World War I saw some 12 percent of draftees refusing to report or deserting training camps, only 0.5 percent tried to avoid serving during the Second World War. Even black leaders who were vocal critics of the American racial order during the war years, calling upon the government to fight racism at home as zealously as it fought fascism overseas, seldom publicly staked out positions opposing the war itself. World War II was already being mythologized as the "good war" even before American troops set foot on overseas battlegrounds. Although some sense of a national mission in the world had been a fixture of American political life since the revolutionary era, World War II was perhaps the first moment when such ideas became popular heartfelt sentiments rather than merely the rhetorical flourishes of statesmen and civic leaders. And they were sentiments felt in the hearts of a range of ethnic Americans who not so long before, in the years prior to the Democratic Party's New Deal embrace of "new" immigrants and ethnics from southern and eastern Europe, had found themselves on the outside of American mainstream culture and political life. Prohibition, the antivice crusades, and the moral panic around real-life and filmic gangsters in the 1920s and 1930s all reflected the outsider status of these immigrants and their American-born children. But now their association with the "good war" was promising to deliver them into the ranks of "good" Americans, a message Hollywood drove home on the big screen with a spate of war films like *Sahara* (1943) and *Purple Heart* (1944) that depicted multiethnic bands of Americans overcoming their cultural differences and pulling together to save the day.[1]

What was playing out on the streets of Chicago during this Flag Day parade, however, was as much a managed form of civic boosterism as some kind of interethnic solidarity. Regardless of the importance of national unity on the home front to the cause of winning the war, Chicago found itself competing with other industrial cities for a slice of the war production pie being served up by the federal government. Chicago's industrial production, after all, had not rebounded from the depths of the Great Depression as quickly as that of many other cities across the nation, and some still feared a renewal of the bitter labor conflict of past years. In fact, in the months leading up to the parade, Mayor Kelly had complained publicly that while the city had received defense orders in steel, railway car construction, and food processing, Chicago was still not getting its fair share. Attracting more defense contracts, as Kelly and the Cook County Democratic Party leadership well understood, hinged on demonstrating that Chicago was a city in which employers and employees knew how to work together to keep production flowing smoothly. This became especially critical as its neighbor to the east, Detroit, began to witness a wave of labor disputes, wildcat strikes, and production slowdowns that led a reporter for *Life* magazine to exclaim, "Detroit can either blow up Hitler or it can blow up the U.S."[2] Chicago, by contrast, would boast at war's end that not one single labor stoppage had prevented a shipment of goods from going out on time, a situation attributable, on the one hand, to the local influence of the less militant American Federation of Labor, and on the other, to Mayor Kelly's excellent rapport with union leaders. Kelly had so thoroughly wiped from his hands the blood of the Memorial Day Massacre that in the 1939 mayoral elections a steelworker whose eye had been shot out by police in the affair had gone on the radio to endorse his candidacy. Moreover, Kelly's tolerance of vice and gambling had earned him the blessings—not to mention the kickbacks—of organized crime kingpins, which also contributed to his appeal to the labor movement.

Yet Chicago's bid for a leadership role in the national war effort rested not merely on the cooperation of its workforce. The Kelly administration had strived to show from the war's outset that war mobilization in Chicago did not begin and end on the factory floors. Having moved into its Loop headquarters scarcely one week after the war had been declared, Chicago's Office of Civilian Defense (OCD) lost little time in launching war bond promotions, enlistment campaigns, salvage collection initiatives, and blood drives. Women planted victory gardens, gathered old kitchen utensils, siphoned off cooking fats, baked cakes for soldiers staying at one of the city's servicemen centers, and eagerly participated in preparedness drills. The public school system ran a salvaging drive for tin, rubber, and scrap metal that had schoolchildren bringing 1,500,000 pounds of scrap to school in toy wagons and wheelbarrows.

The enormous success of these efforts—Chicago led the nation in enlistments, war bond sales, blood donations, and salvage materials collected—was due, in part, to the fact that the city already possessed a vertical chain of command structure par excellence. Since elections were fought like wars in Chicago, the Democratic Party machine was already set up for regimented, block-level mobilization. Chicago's OCD thus broke up the city into divisions, zones, and finally blocks, each of which was led by a block captain. The block captain was to be elected and was supposed to hold meetings with his neighbors to apprise them of new developments. The mayor's office referred to these as "New England town meetings," but the modus vivendi here was, in reality, much more homegrown.[3] That is to say, the roughly twenty thousand block captains in wartime Chicago were much less community organizers than operatives in the chain of command; they enforced participation in blackouts and preparedness drills, helped the OCD investigate the background of citizens, and looked out for draft dodgers, black marketeers, and suspicious characters.[4]

Chicago's mobilization plan was so effective that the federal government adopted it as the model for the entire nation. And yet, despite such impressive results and despite Kelly's frequent lobbying trips to Washington, federal dollars were still not flowing into Chicago at a rate satisfactory to its political and business establishment. That began to change, however, in the second half of 1942, when the city began to see more of the $24 billion that the federal government would spend on military supply orders by the end of the war. This money was divided between more than 1,400 contractors in the Chicago region, leading to a broad-based industrial boom that saw the construction of more than three hundred new manufacturing facilities and the expansion or improvement of nearly one thousand others. Pullman built tanks; International Harvester produced military tractors, torpedoes, and artillery shells; Douglas Aircraft turned out C-54 transport planes; and Dodge-Chicago built engines for the famed B-29 Superfortress bombers in a new plant that employed 31,000 people and cost nearly $100 million. Nor was such high-paced economic activity restricted to the heavy industries. Baxter Laboratories, for example, developed the first sterile, vacuum-type blood collection and storage container, the enormous demand for which required the construction of two temporary plants; its main competitor in that area, Abbott Laboratories, shipped millions of water purification tablets overseas and began the first mass commercial production of penicillin. The communications technology firm Western Electric developed military radar systems, while forty of the city's electronics factories combined efforts to produce over half the communications equipment utilized by the U.S. military during the war.

This rush of production activity set Chicago in continuous and fast-paced motion, causing far-reaching changes in the usual arrangements and rhythms of family life. Companies that had laid off thousands of workers in the 1930s were now desperate for new hires to operate assembly lines around the clock. With the departure of so many fathers to battlefields overseas, the federal government looked to mothers to help fill the gap in the labor supply. Winning the "good war" was going to take the participation of even middle-aged mothers who had long given up on aspirations for a career, let alone one in the manufacturing sector. Exhorted by government-sponsored posters picturing a sturdy but comely Rosie the Riveter rolling up her blue denim shirt sleeve to expose a flexed bicep beneath the phrase "We Can Do It!," nearly four million homemakers entered the labor force during the war. For many of these women, the decision to start punching the clock reflected a sense of patriotic duty. For many more, however, it was an act of economic necessity. The Great Depression had ravaged savings accounts and living standards, and the allotment checks that were supposed to sustain the families of servicemen did not go nearly far enough. Yet even though working mothers were vital to the war mobilization and a boon to employers, who paid them 65 percent of what they paid male employees doing comparable work, social conservatives saw them as threatening cherished values of motherhood and female domesticity and ultimately placing the nation's youth in grave danger. One of the most strident critics of working mothers was director of the Federal Bureau of Investigation J. Edgar Hoover. Having rallied in the 1930s against the nefarious effects of gangster movies on the minds of youths, Hoover now turned to the problem of neglected children on the home front, arguing that "boys and girls" were the nation's "most priceless ... asset," and "their preservation [was] as important as any objective in this war."[5]

Concerns voiced by social conservatives about the sanctity of traditional gender roles quickly became subsumed by a more generalized sense of anxiety about the state of the nation's youth. With so many fathers away fighting the war and mothers increasingly entering the workforce, Americans worried about who was watching the children after school. A range of problems arising from this lack of supervision materialized in the mainstream press—from "latchkey children" locked alone in their homes to "victory girls" engaging in casual sexual adventures with soldiers out of a misplaced sense of patriotic duty, to juvenile delinquents carousing all night with street gangs. As a vital war producer and key stopover for servicemen travelling between the coasts, Chicago was touched by these trends as much as any city, and the local press reported on such issues as if they were, as Hoover believed, matters of national security. Criminologists urged police to crack down on the immoral activities of victory girls, who threatened to spread an epidemic of venereal disease through the ranks of servicemen, and to impose curfews in order to keep wild youths off the streets. One article on the "alarming" increase in the juvenile delinquency rate in the *Chicago Tribune* went so far as to claim that divorce and delinquency were "breaking up Chicago homes far faster than battle front casualties."[6]

Such hyperbole in one of Chicago's more sober newspapers suggests that the various incarnations of the youth problem taking the stage during World War II were more symbolic than real. Despite the public outcry about latchkey children, wild youths, and victory girls, the citywide juvenile delinquency epidemic that experts kept predicting never really materialized. Even the moderate rises in juvenile delinquency rates that were recorded in wartime Chicago could have merely reflected changes in law enforcement practices and data collection methods that occurred in response to the increasing perception of a juvenile delinquency problem.[7] Moreover, all the attention paid to the mothers who heeded Rosie the Riveter's call was somewhat exaggerated. In fact, while the labor force participation of women between the ages of 35 to 44 showed significant gains, the change was relatively minimal for women in the prime childbearing years of 20 to 34.

Rather than indicating actual behavioral changes among youths, the wartime delinquency crisis reflected uncertainties and anxieties linked to the realities of everyday life on the home front. Chicagoans, it should be remembered, received daily reminders of the sacrifices being made by soldiers. By the second half of 1943, as death tolls rose precipitously, hundreds of memorial plaques were hanging on street sign poles, and residents across the city were assembling in parks and on street corners to pay their tributes to fallen soldiers. Around this same time, moreover, the draft began to draw even more fathers and sons into service, creating more and more agonized mothers and guilt-plagued brothers. While such circumstances characterized cities across the nation, the intensity of Chicago's war mobilization campaign seemed particularly effective in reaching into communities and turning the force of neighborly scrutiny upon those failing to carry their load. How else to explain the city's national leadership in enlistments and war bond purchases? Mayor Kelly's management of Chicago's wartime labor force was so extensive that in January 1943 he organized a Noise Abatement Commission to ensure that war production workers were not awakened by unnecessary noises.

Yet as successful as Chicago's OCD had been in the first few years of the war, it could not prevent the malaise that spread throughout the city beginning around the summer of 1943. With factories running at full throttle day and night and a sizable segment of the labor force trying to adjust to eight-hour night shifts starting at 11:00 P.M., Chicago newspapers began to report on poorly attended civil defense meetings and waning interest in war bond and salvage drives. In addition, the class tensions that had been subsumed by civic boosterism and patriotism in the initial years of the war began to resurface—not at work but in the sphere of consumption, as working-class Chicagoans began to complain that their more wealthy neighbors were buying restricted commodities on the black market and hoarding them. Once again, much like the delinquency crisis of this same moment, it is difficult to know the extent to which the circumstances being reported by the press actually reflected shifts in consciousness and behavior. Such stories could have been placed on the desks of editors by a mayor's office worried about indiscipline and apathy in the ranks. That the OCD was thinking along these lines was revealed in February 1944, when it created the Committee for Patriotic Action to help pick up morale around the city, a move suggesting that the malaise being covered by the local media was palpable. In view of the physical and psychological conditions characterizing daily life on the home front— the gut-wrenching concern over loved ones overseas, the disruptions in lifestyles and household routines, the grinding work regimen, and the heightened sense of patriotic duty owed in view of those risking their lives for the country—it would have been surprising if Chicagoans had reacted in any other manner.

BLACK MIGRATION AND WHITE RESPONSE

Chicago was surely not alone in translating this social upheaval into concerns over its children. The wartime juvenile delinquency crisis was national in scope—a matter taken up by a U.S. Senate subcommittee chaired by Florida senator Claude Pepper in November 1943. That many of the testimonies before this subcommittee tended to place the blame for wayward youths on working mothers revealed the extent to which anxieties about children intermingled with uncertainties surrounding the new place of women in the workforce. Yet working women and wild children were not the only forces turning the world upside down during the war years. In fact, the hearings of the Pepper Committee were prompted, at least in part, by another situation that was threatening public safety and unity on the home front. The summer of 1943 had witnessed the explosion of major race riots in three key war production centers—Los Angeles, Detroit, and New York—and the outbreak of near riots in numerous other cities where the higher wages offered by war production employers had drawn hundreds of thousands of African American migrants from the rural South. Once again America's youths moved to the center of discussions about another wartime social problem.

However, in the case of America's race problem, as it presented itself to the country in 1943, the correlation with youths was not so abstract. The riots in Los Angeles, commonly referred to as the "Zoot Suit Riots," featured mobs of young white servicemen hunting down and beating Mexican and black youths clad in stylish, baggy zoot suits, which flaunted rationing restrictions on textiles and emblematized the affiliation of their wearers to a nightlife scene that valorized "kicks" over patriotic duty. In Detroit, zoot suiters and white teens clashed for weeks around the city before a skirmish between black and white youths in a crowded park ignited a three-day riot that resulted in thirty-four fatalities. And in New York, rumors surrounding a police bust gone wrong in a Harlem flophouse brought thousands of young blacks into the streets, with zoot suiters, according to many eyewitnesses, leading the way.[8]

The riots of the hot summer of 1943 were among the first spasms of a much broader and longer-lasting movement of white resistance to the massive flow of Southern black migrants to the urban North and West. Pushed from the South by the mechanization of cotton farming and the collapse of cotton prices on the world market in the 1930s, black migrants packed all they could carry and boarded trains heading to big war production cities like Los Angeles, Chicago, Detroit, Philadelphia, San Francisco, and New York. Believing they would find good jobs, better schools, and a friendlier racial climate, many migrants viewed such destinations as the "promised land." Referred to by historians as the "Second Great Migration," this demographic shift began in the early 1940s and continued through the 1960s, dramatically reconfiguring the landscape of American politics in the process. The estimated five million blacks relocating from the South to the North and West between 1940 and 1970 accomplished nothing short of urbanizing the vast majority of the black population, nationalizing the problem of race, transforming the cultural landscape of the urban North, and redefining party politics throughout the country.

In the postwar decades the Democratic Party would begin staking its electoral hopes on strategies that sought to align blacks, the white working class, and liberals behind federal programs that promised solutions to racial and social inequalities, and its Republican Party foe would increasingly rally its base behind values of individualism, color blindness, small government, and the free market in order to fend off the challenges of racial liberalism. On the local level, moreover, metropolitan politics would never be the same again. Big city mayors—those of Chicago perhaps most of all—would have to figure out the calculus of attracting black votes and losing white ones, and middle-class suburban residents would turn towards the politics of erecting barriers between themselves and inner-city blacks. The geographical and demographic swelling of black ghettos in the urban North between the 1940s and the 1970s paralleled their expansion in the American psyche. Blues, jazz, funk, soul, disco, hip hop, rap, gangs, drugs, prostitutes, riots, poverty, unemployment, welfare, immorality, fear, and hate circulated through dark ghettos that most Americans would increasingly view only through the prism of the mass media or through the windows of cars speeding safely above them on highway overpasses such as Chicago's Skyway, constructed between 1956 and 1958 to swiftly convey automobiles over communities like Greater Grand Crossing, whose black population would increase from 6 to 86 percent in a single decade as whites fled the advancing ghetto.

Edward Kelly was one of several Chicago mayors to tangle with the prickly politics of race within this shifting landscape, and his downfall would come, in part, because he underestimated just how intensely many white Chicagoans loathed the idea of having blacks as neighbors. In a somewhat ironic twist, while the city of Chicago would go on to have one of the more tumultuous and eventful histories of race relations in the two decades following the Second World War, it was spared a spectacular explosion of racial violence in the spring and summer of 1943—even though there was no lack of sparks to ignite the fuse. In May 1943, for instance, just about three weeks before the Los Angeles riots, two white police officers shot a sixteen-year-old black student several times in the back after he allegedly hurled rocks at them. If that was not enough, shortly after the incident the boy's father received a note threatening the same fate for him if he did not "keep his mouth shut" and move from his home in the South Side's Morgan Park neighborhood.[9] Days later, hundreds of angry citizens gathered to protest the boy's slaying but ended up heeding the pleas of a local black minister to refrain from violence. Then, just hours after the stories of race warfare in the Motor City had hit the streets of Chicago, police responded to a call from Hyde Park, where a mob of white youths armed with shovels, pick handles, and other weapons had taken to the streets in search of some blacks who had allegedly threatened them on their way to the beach.[10] A few days later, Horace Cayton observed that African Americans were "arming" themselves in case of rioting, and two social workers on the Near West Side reported that Mexican adolescents were discussing the riots and "waiting" for something to happen. Another community worker, a representative of the Hyde Park Neighborhood

House, remarked on the "changing attitude of white boys," noting that several of those he was in contact with had taken to carrying large knives on the streets and "expressing themselves as preparing for fights against Negroes."[11] Seemingly overnight, Chicago had a racial crisis on its hands. Mayor Kelly hastily moved to establish a high-level commission—the Mayor's Committee on Race Relations—to monitor racial flare-ups and advise ways of keeping the peace. The situation appeared so grave, in fact, that community leaders in several racially mixed areas urged their aldermen to make provisions for first aid stations and safety shelters.[12]

Such panicked responses stemmed in part from the dramatic, even anarchic way in which the Chicago press had depicted the situation in Detroit. To begin with, as news of the violence spread, Detroit officials could offer no explanation for its origins, other than a vague report of an interracial incident in a crowded recreation area on Belle Isle, a park on a patch of land in the middle of the Detroit River. The absence of a sense of causality contributed to the spread of a perception that what was being witnessed was the outbreak of race war, pure and simple: "a frenzy of homicidal mania, without rhyme or reason," as one writer for the *Detroit Free Press* referred to it.[13] This was the conclusion many Chicagoans most likely came to when they read in their own city's leading paper the quotes of riot victims, white and black, expressing shock at having been attacked by mobs for no apparent reason other than the color of their skin. Adding to the unease about the circumstances of the riot was the fact that it was by no means clear from the coverage which race had acted as provocateur. The following description is typical of the reportage Chicagoans received: "Groups of Negroes and of whites milled about on street corners in a wide section bordering the northeastern side of downtown Detroit and hurled bricks and stones at passing automobiles bearing members of the opposite race."[14] Such treatment left intact the perception that the aggression might have been initiated by members of Detroit's African American community, perhaps even in an organized fashion, an idea that had much deeper implications for racial attitudes in Chicago than if the riot were merely another case of white aggression and black response.[15]

In the end, however, the bomb planted in the summer of 1943 never blew, even if its ticking continued to be heard in the city for months, if not years. But if Kelly had managed to dodge a bullet in the summer of 1943, his troubles were just beginning. The events of the spring and summer of 1943 were revealing that, after more than a decade of relative calm along the color line, parks, schoolyards, beaches, streets, and neighborhoods were once again becoming battlegrounds in a war of attrition over the city's limited resources. The immediate cause of this renewal of hostilities was the arrival of some seventy thousand black migrants between 1940 and 1943—a roughly 25 percent increase in the city's black population. Further aggravating the situation was the halt on construction during the Great Depression, which left the city woefully lacking in proper housing for these new workers and their families. By the end of 1943 an acute housing shortage gripped the city, particularly within the Black Belt, where one study estimated that 375,000 inhabited an area suited for no more than 110,000. Addressing a meeting of realtors in July 1943, Chicago Housing Authority chairman Robert Taylor cited statistics indicating that the Second and Third Wards—the heart of the South Side black ghetto—were more densely populated than the slums of Calcutta.[16] And of course it did not take long for slumlords to recognize the opportunity a tight and racially stratified housing market offered them. Ensuing rent gouging practices left black migrants with few alternatives but to pay far too much for poorly maintained apartments within the Black Belt and a number of other pockets of black residence scattered around the West and South Sides. Faced with such conditions, migrants began seeking more affordable housing at the edges of neighborhoods where they were less than welcome, if not openly detested.

In wartime Chicago, with factories desperate for bodies to operate machines, the housing dilemma faced by blacks became a pressing problem for a mayor who was desperately trying to keep money flowing into the city and war goods flowing out. The situation was so critical that a 1943 government study predicted that Chicago would need an additional 375,000 new workers by the end of the year. Unlike Detroit, however, where the first reflexes of white backlash revealed themselves at the point of production in a series of hate strikes by auto workers protesting the insertion of blacks into all-white production departments, similar demonstrations by white workers in Chicago were isolated. In fact, the Federal Employment Practices Commission (FEPC), a watchdog agency created by President Roosevelt after A. Philip Randolph threatened a massive March on Washington to protest discrimination in the war industries, met with fairly strong success in its efforts to integrate Chicago workplaces. The relative calm on Chicago's factory floors while whites were walking off the job in Detroit is not easy to explain with any certainty. One factor could have been the success of CIO campaigns during the 1930s to bring white and black workers together in a range of interracial recreational activities—bowling competitions, basketball leagues, and picnics, for example—that encouraged workers to form bonds of solidarity off the job.[17] However, such programs had been tried in Detroit as well, and from the subsequent pattern of violence that broke out in spaces of leisure in both cities, it seems evident that white participation in these activities was largely forced, artificial, and ephemeral. Rather, what made the difference between Detroit and Chicago were Mayor Kelly's strong alliances with all of the forces capable of maintaining the status quo: labor unions, organized crime, and the black political machine. While union leaders were certainly on board with Kelly on the need to keep assembly lines moving, it helped that workers who had ideas of disrupting things might have to worry about some wiseguys showing up at their doors.[18]

Moreover, Kelly's role as kingmaker for the new Black South Side boss William Dawson, the former Second Ward alderman and Democratic committeeman whom Kelly had handpicked to fill the House seat vacated by Arthur Mitchell in 1942, also helped to keep a lid on things in the Black Metropolis. After defeating Oscar DePriest in 1934 to become the first African American elected to Congress as a Democrat, Mitchell had remained fiercely loyal to President Roosevelt through his four terms in office, never pushing the president's reluctant hand on civil rights. But he had fallen out of favor with the Kelly-Nash machine when he had sued the Chicago-based Rock Island and Pacific Railroad for forcing him to sit in a segregated Pullman car on a trip to Arkansas in 1937. Dawson, on the other, owed everything he had to Kelly, who had handed him control of the Second Ward by helping to make him congressman and committeeman. Using his control over the police and his leverage with organized crime syndicates, Kelly provided protection to the black South Side policy cartel, which poured cash into Dawson's war chest. Dawson's gratitude to Kelly had helped him garner 57 percent of the black vote in the mayoral election of 1939 and 54 percent in 1943.

Blacks in Chicago were no doubt linked to the political machine in ways they were not in many other cities, and Kelly's protection of the black syndicates meant that black Chicagoans generally had fewer occasions to be angry with the police for bringing down the boot. All this was important to Kelly's effective stewardship of the war mobilization because, as Detroit's wartime troubles were revealing, African Americans were hardly passive bystanders in the racial conflicts and work stoppages that were holding up war production. Black workers in Detroit had carried out wildcat strikes to protest the racism of coworkers and the discriminatory practices of employers and had on several occasions aggressively confronted white picketers trying to deny them their rights. In Detroit, in particular, these early forms of civil rights activism in the workplace had a lot to do with gains blacks had made through several racially progressive union locals of the United Auto Workers (UAW). In particular, the Communist-influenced UAW Local 600, which during the war years represented over eighty thousand autoworkers at Ford's colossal River Rouge Plant, placed blacks in leadership positions, pursued a program of grassroots collective action against racial discrimination, and strongly promoted ideals of racial equality. With tens of thousands of black workers among its members, Local 600 became a driving force for civil rights activism in Detroit. Black workers radicalized by the local had wives, brothers, sisters, daughters, sons, cousins, and friends, and its spirit of militancy quickly fanned out into the black community, inspiring a will to fight back that explains a great deal about why Detroit's massive riot of 1943 came to pass.

While Mayor Kelly had nothing like UAW Local 600 to deal with, there were other sources of black rebelliousness that were forcing his hand in ways that would get him into trouble with white voters. A new assertiveness had taken hold of black communities throughout the urban North during World War II as black veterans returned from the war to find they had risked their lives for a country that still treated them like second-class citizens. The *Pittsburgh Courier,* one of the nation's most widely circulating black newspapers, provided a slogan for this sentiment with its 1942 Double-V campaign: victory over fascism abroad and over racism at home. Chicago's own black daily, the *Defender,* added its voice to the Double-V chorus, and it was not long before African Americans in Chicago were wearing Double-V pins and even cutting the letter *V* into their hair.

In addition to this new spirit of militancy taking shape around the idea of black servicemen's unrequited sacrifices, the zoot suiter represented another strain of street-smart rebelliousness that was crystallizing within the youth subcultures of black ghettos of the urban North and West. The zoot suit was unequivocally antipatriotic: not only did it brazenly disregard rationing restrictions on clothing materials, but in a moment when everyone was supposed to be making sacrifices, it symbolized an ethos of self-indulgence. Zoot suits belonged to the milieu of big commercial dancehalls, like the famed Savoy in New York or the Pershing or Parkway in Chicago, where jitterbugs swung, flipped, and gyrated to fashionable dances like the lindy hop and partied into the early morning hours. Yet if this was a world where getting one's kicks was a primary motivation, it would be mistaken to think of its habitués as apolitical. Malcolm X, known as Malcolm Little in his younger

FIGURE 6. Zoot suiters at the Savoy Ballroom in 1941. Photo by Russell Lee. Courtesy of the Library of Congress.

days, wore a zoot suit when he went out to the jazz clubs and pool halls at night, and, as historian Robin Kelley has argued, even though he later renounced this as part of the profligate lifestyle he was trying to leave behind after his conversion to Islam, he surely had understood the political meaning of covering his body with such a loaded symbol during the war years.[19]

The zoot suiter, to be sure, represented a very different message than that conveyed by the figure of the black soldier, and proud veterans and insolent hipsters did not always see eye to eye, but the new civil rights consciousness circulating through black communities nonetheless formed powerful bonds of solidarity between these two elements of the community. Such was the case, to be sure, in the Harlem riot, which saw zoot suiters taking to the streets in violent protest after hearing that a black serviceman has been shot by a police officer after attempting to defend a black woman who was being roughed up during an arrest at the Braddock Hotel. After conducting a series of interviews with riot participants, one social psychologist found the zoot suiter so central to the uprising in Harlem that he spoke of a generalized "zoot effect." Capturing the way many of the young Harlem rioters viewed their uprising against the police were the words of one riot participant, who, after reflecting on a savage beating police administered to one of his peers, warned: "Do not attempt to fuck with me."[20]

The zoot suiter was all about a new posture of defiance that was sweeping through northern black ghettos—defiance to the police and to whites trying to stand between African Americans and their civil rights. This form of defiance became accentuated in the months following the hot summer of 1943, when everyone in the nation knew that it was open season on zoot suiters. Continuing to wear a zoot suit was, in a sense, an overt provocation—one part machismo, one part racial pride—directed at white toughs out on the streets, a double-down on a dare that was becoming increasingly dangerous in view of the white youth gangs increasingly gathering along the color line. In the face of such dangers, black youths in Chicago remained undaunted, continuing to strut their stuff in these flamboyant outfits in the months following the riots of 1943. Just several weeks after the incident in Harlem, for example, a nearly half-page ad in the *Defender* told jitterbugs to "wear your zoot suit" to the "Zoot Suit Dance" at the Parkway Ballroom on 45th and South Parkway Avenue, where a prize would be given to the "zootiest."[21]

The zoot suiter and the milieu of teenage gangs to which he belonged kept authorities on edge throughout 1944 and 1945. Many officials serving on the newly formed Mayor's Commission on Human Relations (an updated version of the Mayor's Committee on Race Relations) were convinced that if a riot were to break out, it would be ignited from friction between black and white teenage gangs. The Chicago Police Department thus made great efforts to monitor hot spots throughout the city where black and white youths regularly crossed paths. In July 1945, for example, a special police patrol was stationed in the Woodlawn district, at the busy intersection of 63rd and Cottage Grove, after reports that black and white jitterbugs were tangling in the streets around the Pershing ballroom.[22] What such incidents were revealing was that Chicago had become an unavoidably interracial city during the war. The war years represented the first chapter in a new phase of ghettoization that in two decades would add to the city's vastly expanded South Side ghetto a massive West Side swath, over a mile wide in parts and stretching all the way to the city's western limits. But this outcome was far from self-evident for white residents on the ground in the mid-1940s. With the sorry state of housing conditions in the Black Belt, many black migrants began settling at the edges of white neighborhoods and in other racially mixed areas where small numbers of black families already lived. Moreover, even in areas of the city in which the residential color line was absolute, where white hostility was too coordinated and too fierce for blacks to dare taking up residence, blacks and whites inescapably crossed paths at lakefront beaches, in shopping and nightlife districts, in parks, and on buses and streetcars.

Marxist theorist Raymond Williams coined the term *structure of feeling* to describe a dominant sensibility about lived experience that circulates through the culture of everyday life of a specific generation at a specific time and place.[23] For the generation of African Americans who had migrated from the Jim Crow South to the "promised land" of the urban North during the war, the zoot suiter and the black serviceman were the most potent embodiments of a broader structure of feeling of betrayal and injustice that shaped the new spirit of resistance to racial oppression. The collective sense that a limit had been reached—that enough was enough—permeated black Chicago like an acrid smell, the scent of which continuously reminded blacks of what was at stake in the insults they faced in their daily interactions with whites. Recalling his experiences as a young man living in New Jersey and working in defense plants during the war, James Baldwin claimed that was when he "first contracted some dread, chronic disease, the unfailing symptom of which [was] a kind of blind fever, a pounding in the skull and fire in the bowels." Baldwin explained that he picked up this "disease" while experiencing racial indignities at "bars, bowling alleys, diners, places to live."[24] His affliction eventually caused him to put his life on the line in order to take a forceful stand against a restaurant that refused to serve him—the kind of act that was occurring much more frequently after the riots in the summer of 1943.

While most black Chicagoans were not nearly as daring as Baldwin, never left home in a zoot suit, and did not serve in the American military, they were captivated by the same anger and by the same will to not back down in the face of intimidation—a situation that, in the context of the severe housing shortage in wartime Chicago, translated into a will to live where they chose. However, the zoot suiter, the black serviceman, and the ordinary black resident who had reached the end of his patience had analogues on the other side of the color line. Standing opposite them was the white gang tough ready for a fight, the white veteran angry about heroically risking his life for his nation only to return to find strange black faces in his neighborhood, and all of the ordinary white residents who, like the blacks they so feared, were beginning to feel themselves to be victims. Even though 1945 brought news of an impending victory in the war, Chicagoans were certainly not looking into the future with great optimism. Employers and economists alike were predicting that the loss of war contracts would lead to recession and massive layoffs, and as white workers viewed increasing numbers of blacks joining them on factory floors, the usual fears of blacks undercutting wages and stealing jobs were exchanged in taverns and on street corners. It has often been the tendency of Americans to view racial others as simultaneously lazy and so hardworking that they are willing to labor for pitiful wages, and this was one such time.

Yet to view the racism of white Chicagoans in such economizing terms gives a somewhat distorted impression of what lay at the core of their racial fear and contempt. Many working-class whites did, of course, envision blacks as undermining their class position and their standard of living. This was an idea whose origins stretched back to earlier decades, when bosses employed blacks as scabs to break strikes in the stockyards and steel mills, and real estate agents began using panic-peddling tactics to get whites to sell their homes on the cheap for fear of losing their property values when the neighborhood turned black. Such circumstances give us reason to invest in a notion of white racism as a tool created and exploited by the ruling class in the process of accumulating capital—in the idea articulated by W. E. B. Du Bois in 1935 that white workers enjoyed a "psychological wage" related to their whiteness, which caused them to accept low standards of living and poor working conditions because of their self-proclaimed sense of racial superiority to blacks.[25] According to such reasoning, a steelworker might have remained satisfied with wages that were clearly too low for the work he was performing, precisely because both his wages and his job category were superior to those of African American workers. This, we might conclude, is why whites joined together in factory hate strikes and why employers resisted promoting blacks and integrating departments—not for fear of causing racial disturbances among workers but of jeopardizing a tool that helped them exploit their workforce. And yet in wartime Chicago, racial barriers on the factory floor seemed to crumble relatively easily whereas those in the neighborhoods became increasingly fortified. In other words, white racism, as it manifested itself in wartime Chicago, was less about work than it was about family, community, and neighborhood.

Hence, while white workers in Chicago at times invoked fears of black competition for jobs, they seemed much more actively invested in the threat that blacks and their culture posed to their families and, ultimately, to their way of life. Stories that told of blacks moving into white neighborhoods or arriving at white schools were very frequently followed in the next breath by rumors of robberies and rapes, which, at times, spread so quickly that city authorities eventually established hotlines to try to quell them. Telling in this sense was the extent to which interracial rape rumors circulated around a series of 1945 hate strikes carried out by white students protesting small increases in black enrollment. In one school, for example, the visit of two police officers looking for an escaped juvenile delinquent led to wild rumors that two black students had raped a white girl. Some female students interviewed claimed, "We girls are afraid to go anywhere alone."[26]

Social workers and other observers of the race relations scene remarked that white residents, adults and youths alike, often described blacks as immoral, smelly, and syphilitic, a situation that was certainly not improved by the black domination of the city's commercial sex industry. One social worker on the near northwest side, for example, reported that when the boys he supervised were not talking about girls, they were making remarks like "niggers smell," "ninety percent . . . are syphylletic [sic]," and "Negroes should keep their place which is shining shoes and cleaning toilets."[27] The manifestations of such ill feelings became particularly apparent in the summer heat. An African American boy swimming too close to whites in Lake Michigan had provoked the 1919 race riot, so one can only imagine the anxiety aroused by the idea of blacks plunging their bared bodies into municipal swimming pools, which were preciously scarce resources in the sweltering heat and intense humidity that normally enveloped Chicago in July and August. New Deal public works spending had led to the construction of municipal pools in many U.S. cities in the 1930s, thereby democratizing access to what was previously an elite privilege. Yet, in Chicago, as in many other cities and towns, the power of white racism confounded the hopes of New Deal idealists and planning visionaries, making these new resources into flashpoints for racial incidents in the 1940s and beyond.[28]

What was thus becoming clear after the summer of 1943 was that white racism was increasingly running up against an immovable force: the black will to fight back. By 1944, Mayor Kelly found himself wedged uncomfortably between these two counterforces. His wartime race relations management strategy had helped Chicago avoid the worst, but it did little to stop the urban guerrilla warfare that was breaking out in the streets. Indicative of where things were heading was an incident that occurred early in 1944, when several youths from an Italian neighborhood around the Armour Square area entered the Little Zion Baptist Church on Wells Street and began stoning black congregants as they prayed. Obviously accustomed to such acts, the assistant pastor at the church had a loaded pistol within easy reach, and he managed to shoot and wound one of the assailants—a situation that had people in the neighborhood talking about a mob of Italians returning that night to burn the church down.[29] A police detail prevented more trouble on this occasion, but arson attacks against black homes under the cover of night mounted in this area in the months to follow.

In addition to such events, black leaders began to pressure the city to do something about the severe lack of housing for black war workers. The New Deal's Public Works Administration had bankrolled the construction of four new housing projects in Chicago in the mid-1930s, but only one—the Ida B. Wells Homes—was intended for black occupancy. Part of the problem stemmed from the federal government's "neighborhood composition rule," which prevented federal housing projects from changing the racial composition of the neighborhoods in which they were constructed. Bound by this rule, the Chicago Housing Authority (CHA), formed in 1937 to oversee the city's housing projects, steered black projects into black ghetto areas, white projects into white neighborhoods, and avoided the city's racially mixed areas altogether for fear of provoking racial conflict. When the CHA had attempted to house a substantial number of black workers in the Frances Cabrini Homes in the North Side Sicilian Little Hell District, skirmishes between neighborhood Italians and new black residents culminated in a near-riot after gunshots were fired into a black apartment. The CHA thus bowed to the forces of grassroots resistance, a policy that both reinforced the boundaries around the ghetto and did little to change the housing emergency for African Americans—a problem that was only going to become further exacerbated as increasing numbers of black veterans began returning home to find they had no place to live.[30]

This was the situation facing Mayor Kelly as the war was winding down in 1945. Hailing from the rugged streets of Bridgeport, where Irish gangs had been ruthlessly patrolling the color line to the east since at least the early 1900s, Kelly was no stranger to the dynamics of grassroots racism that were preventing him from solving the city's pressing housing problem. However, at the time of the 1919 race riot, when Bridgeport's Hamburg Athletic Club was leading raids into the Black Belt, Kelly had long graduated from his education on the Bridgeport streets. In fact, he was from a previous generation that had come of age before the city's black ghetto had taken full form, and, somewhat surprisingly, he seemed to have risen through the ranks of the Cook County Democratic Party machine—an organization full of racist athletic-club types and politicos who had cut their teeth decrying Big Bill

Thompson's "nigger-loving" ways—with certain ideas about racial justice intact. Then, as a loyal New Dealer, who had garnered a huge majority of Chicago's votes for F. D. R. in the 1936 presidential election, he apparently caught some inspiration from the democratizing winds blowing out of Washington. While most machine cadres harbored an open contempt for self-righteous reformers and the know-it-all university types from Hyde Park that gave them intellectual cover, Kelly had chosen Elizabeth Wood as the first executive director of the CHA, a woman—this in itself, a bold decision—who had been a caseworker for a progressive charitable organization while taking classes at the University of Chicago's School of Social Service Administration. Wood was clearly coming out of a tradition of social work and sociological research among whose primary objectives was to show that immigrant slums and black ghettos were caused not by the racial defects of their inhabitants but rather by racism and structural poverty.

Thus, when the time came for Kelly to take a stand on the question of open housing, he broke ranks with both the Cook County Democratic Party machine and its base. Initially, it was not so much what he did, but rather what he said. Kelly pledged repeatedly to guarantee the availability of housing to blacks throughout the city, and proclaimed that as long as he was mayor, any person would be allowed to live where he wanted to so long as he could afford it. This was not exactly music to the ears of South Side whites then digging into trenches to resist racial integration. People began referring to swimming pools monopolized by blacks as "Kelly's inkwells," and the Democratic Party brass began worrying about the upcoming election in 1947. Into the situation stepped Jacob "Jack" Arvey, who was elevated in 1946 to chairman of the Cook Country Democratic Party—a post Kelly had occupied after Nash's death in 1943. Arvey was a Jew and, as such, a relative outsider in Chicago politics, but his ability to deliver votes for the party—often at margins of nine to one—propelled him through the ranks of the Nash-Kelly machine. Kelly was in political hot water for a number of scandals, ranging from his failure to deliver adequate garbage collection services despite higher taxes to his tolerance of organized crime, to rampant police corruption. Arvey was thus brought in, fresh from his stint in the World War II Pacific theater, to do damage control, and he started by deploying his people to poll Chicagoans outside movie theaters and by telephone. When the results were tallied, Arvey found that despite all the scandals in play, what Chicagoans were most concerned about was the housing issue. As Arvey recalled later: "Well, we were solid with the Jews, we could see, and better than even with the Negroes, but everywhere else—the Poles, the Irish even, the Germans—we were in trouble. 'Him?' they'd say, 'Are you kidding? We'd sooner vote for a Chinaman.'"[31] After over two thousand angry whites battled police and destroyed property—in other words, rioted—to prevent the CHA from moving blacks into temporary housing constructed near the Chicago Municipal Airport on the Far Southwest Side, Kelly's situation became untenable.

And so Edward J. Kelly, under the strong advice of Arvey and the Democratic machine, did not seek reelection in 1947. Chosen to replace him was businessman-reformer Martin H. Kennelly, another one of Bridgeport's sons, who had made his fortune in the moving and storage business. Yet the leadership of the Democratic machine was dreaming if it thought that Chicago's race problem would follow Kelly out of politics. The pitched battles between angry mobs of white residents and police out by the airport would pale in comparison to what was in store for the city in the coming decades. Those increasingly joining the ranks to fight in these battles were largely immigrants and the children of immigrants—Italians, Poles, Slavs, Czechs, Hungarians, Jews, and Greeks, among others—who had themselves been the targets of racially charged aggression by the Irish, Germans, Scandinavians, and Anglos, and sometimes still were. But the nationalist fervor of the war, combined with the demographic sea change that the Second Great Migration had brought about, began the process of gathering all of these groups under one big happy umbrella of whiteness. White Americans of all origins had come together to oppose the Germans and the Japanese on battlefields overseas, and they had joined forces to oppose black invasion at home, in each case helping to make a more universal white identity that would play a key role in American politics in the years to come. This story was far from over—words like "polack," "wop," "mick," "kraut," "kike," and "hunky" could still be heard wherever white ethnics mixed, and, on the "white" side of the color line, bonds of ethnic solidarity were still as powerful as bonds of racial solidarity. But as black migrants from the South continued to pour into the city in the postwar years, whiteness was clearly gaining traction on the ground.

DEVIL'S MUSIC

Since 1934, when the *Chicago Defender* began sponsoring the mayor of Bronzeville election, the event had been allowing black Chicagoans to take stock of who they were and who they wanted to be. Bronzeville's mayor, of course, had no formal political power, but he served as the symbolic embodiment of the larger black community—a cultural icon of sorts, but one you might bump into on the streets.[32] During the war years, as black Chicago took on its more militant bent, mayoral candidates used their moment on the stage to speak out on political issues, such as housing problems and police misconduct. Even though the mayoral election could not avoid being somehow political in its implicit assertion of autonomy and representation within a city in which blacks were hardly getting their fair share of either, it was generally understood that the affair was to be, above all, a festive celebration of local black culture and community. Yet to speak of *a* black culture and *a* black community in 1940s Chicago is to simplify what was, in fact, a very complicated and often contentious interplay of different cultures and communities defined by class, regional origins, and lifestyle. The very name Bronzeville that these elections popularized was coined by cosmetics magnate Anthony Overton, a man who designed products for middle-class blacks seeking to lighten their skin, and the elections were publicized by a newspaper that spilled a great deal of ink trying to teach lower-class southern migrants how to "act northern." Southern migrants, in fact, had shouldered the blame for much of what was wrong with "the race" since the 1920s. Their arrival in Chicago, to be sure, had created a profitable market for a whole new generation of black entrepreneurs, but these same uneducated country folk—usually one generation removed from slavery and, in middle-class eyes, displaying unsavory predilections for liquor, the policy wheel, hot music, old-time religion, and jitterbugging—also threatened the self-image of the city's black middle class, which measured its status, to some extent, in terms of the approbation white society bestowed on it.

And these were only a handful of the numerous ways that made migrants disrespectable in the eyes of middling "old settler" African Americans. Their storefront churches and the jackleg preachers who shouted in them, their way of "jive talking" about "cats" and "kicks," their zoot-suit-wearing sons, their late-night revelry and loose sexual morals, their brawling and boisterous behavior, their sidewalk barbecues, fried catfish and chicken shacks, and taste for pig's intestines—all this, in the eyes of many middle-class black Chicagoans, signalled the recrudescence of a backwards-looking southern culture that was giving the race a bad name. Southern foodways, in particular, were at that time much too close to be nostalgic or comforting, as they would be some two decades later, when many African Americans would fetishize collard greens, cornbread, black-eyed peas, smoked spareribs, and fried chicken as "soul food" capable of liberating them from spiritual oppression.[33] Moreover, aspersions cast at migrants for setting back racial progress were not the stuff of hushed conversations behind closed doors; they were right out there in the open for everyone to hear, pronounced from sanctified pulpits and in the sanctimonious columns of the black press. Chicago was no Mississippi, but poor migrants understood very well that they occupied the bottom rung on the social ladder of the Black Metropolis.

Which explains why the election of R. H. Harris as mayor of Bronzeville in 1945 signified to the southern migrants who had been pouring into the city since the outbreak of the war that they had finally arrived. Southern-born blacks had of course been crowned mayor in previous elections, but most had been raised in Chicago and were well-established members of the community by the time of their election. By contrast, Harris was a relatively recent migrant from Texas, and although his silky-smooth falsetto singing in one of Chicago's most beloved gospel quartets, the Soul Stirrers, and his ownership of a successful Bronzeville business, Five Soul Stirrers Cleaners, seemed to distinguish him from the typical wartime migrant, Harris's election nonetheless signified that southern culture had captured the heart of Bronzeville. And it was no wonder it had. At war's end, migrants outnumbered "native" African Americans born and/or raised in Chicago before the First Great Migration by almost eight to one. And this numerical majority was translating into economic influence. By 1947, migrants owned thirteen out of every fourteen businesses in black Chicago. This was the same year that the rising number of barbecue joints warranted the creation of their own heading in the city's business directory for the first time. The smoky smells of southern barbecue, moreover, intermingled with the pounding sounds of southern blues music—country, Memphis, boogie-woogie, jump, big band—coming out of jukeboxes and radios across black Chicago. Respectable middle-class elements called it "devil's music," but this was a minority view, as was clearly suggested by the victory of local celebrity disc jockey Al Benson in the 1948 mayor of Bronzeville election. Benson, like Harris, was part entertainer, part entrepreneur—a mix of qualities that appealed to southern migrants—but he was much more country than Harris was. A storefront preacher before becoming the most popular disc jockey at black radio station WGES, Benson's folksy radio persona was matched by his preference for the blues over the more respectable gospel music. For lower-class migrants, the Mississippi-born Benson was surely one of *them,* and he had made it by staying true to his roots.

Hence, despite perceptions among some middle-class residents that migrants were lazy and shiftless, they were clearly "getting ahead." In fact, black median income in the city rose to nearly twice the national average for blacks by 1950, and remained higher than that of every other city except Detroit throughout the 1950s. Historian Adam Green has referred to such circumstances to argue that scholars and other observers of Bronzeville have largely overlooked and, in a sense, underestimated the grand importance of what was really transpiring there in the 1940s and early 1950s. Chicago, which Richard Wright once referred to as "the known city," has usually been viewed in the context of the local and the everyday—as a place where blacks got on better than elsewhere, where they got decent jobs, established local institutions, and seized a small but not insignificant measure of political power. Migrants have fit into this story as well; these rural folk, we have learned, encountered some difficulties but, in the end, were able to shed their agricultural orientations for the more rigid factory work regime and effectively adjust to life in the modern metropolis. What these angles of vision have obscured, however, is the extent to which Chicago moved to the very center of black life in the United States, becoming the driving force behind new feelings of national fellowship and racial community among African Americans that would provide the foundations for the civil rights movements of the 1950s and 1960s. Chicago in the first postwar decade, not Harlem in the 1920s, Green argues, hosted the quintessential moment of black modernity. It was the vital site of cultural production for a range of media and cultural forms that allowed blacks throughout the nation to feel they shared a common destiny and belonged to a community that spanned space and time. It was in Chicago that a savvy publishing entrepreneur named John Johnson Jr. saw the need for *Ebony* magazine, a black version of *Life* that presented "the happier side of Negro life" alongside perspectives on "the race question." It was in Chicago that the nation's only black newswire, the Associated Negro Press, and its most widely circulating black newspaper, the *Defender,* shaped the news content of blacks throughout the nation. And it was in Chicago that a cohort of virtuoso migrant musicians from the Deep South, with the help of two Polish immigrant club owners, electrified and amplified the bare-bones, roots sounds of the Delta, added a more elaborate rhythm section and a second guitar to the arrangements, and brought to market the internationally renowned Chicago blues sound.[34]

Encountering the blues scene in Chicago today, it is hard to imagine that the wailing harmonica solos, the bent and sliding guitar notes, the roaring

vocals, and the sparse lyrics that were signatures of this music once constituted the dominant soundtrack for life in the Black Metropolis—that jukeboxes in corner bars around the city belted out the gravelly voice of Muddy
Waters singing such classics as "I Can't Be Satisfied" and "Hoochie Coochie
Man." In the 1940s and 1950s, Bronzeville and the rest of black Chicago was
teeming with slick blues venues—the Club DeLisa, the Rhumboogie, Joe's
DeLuxe, the 708, and Silvio's, to name but a few; now, the blues can, with
some rare exceptions, only be heard outside of black neighborhoods, in areas
where white tourists, suburbanites in for a night out on the town, and college
students gather. The blues clubs of today—House of Blues, Chicago
B.L.U.E.S. Bar, and Buddy Guy's Legends—are theme-park-like affairs that
seek to offer white folks an "authentic" blues experience; T-shirts and other
merchandise are, of course, on sale as you enter, and all of the clubs are, as the
reviews on their websites seek to assure potential visitors, "friendly." Even the
storied Checkerboard Lounge, which was one of Bronzeville's last legitimate
blues clubs, moved from 43rd Street to Hyde Park in 2005, opening near the
University of Chicago in a space where the fitness club Women's Workout
World used to be. Yet, while white folks today constitute the principal consumers of the blues experience and the blues itself has become what Claude
Lévi-Strauss referred to as a "floating signifier," a cultural form unhinged
from its original context and meaning, the blues did not sell out or die, as
some purists would argue, but rather passed into other forms that became
more commercially viable in black communities beginning in the 1960s—
soul, Motown, funk, and eventually hip hop and rap.

Market forces made the blues into a museum piece, but these same market
forces were what made the Chicago blues sound innovative and viable in the
first place. A great many of the blues legends that came North to Chicago
from Mississippi and Louisiana in the 1930s and 1940s—Big Bill Broonzy,
Memphis Minnie, Muddy Waters, Howlin' Wolf, Little Walter, and Sonny
Boy Williamson—were, like the vast majority of migrants, trying to improve
their lives. If talented blues musicians could scrape together an existence in
the South, northern cities like Chicago and Detroit offered scores of clubs to
play in, black-appeal radio stations with renowned disc jockeys, record labels
that could transform recording sessions into national hits, and bigger pay-
checks. Yet all these things were contingent on reaching bigger and bigger
audiences, which especially after 1949, when *Billboard* magazine replaced the
industry term *race music* with *rhythm & blues,* included whites as well. What
has been largely overlooked in most accounts of the early blues scene in

Chicago is the importance of what Adam Green refers to as an "entrepreneurial ethos" among the performers, producers, and disc jockeys who made Chicago the place to be for blues musicians.[35] It all came together in 1948 when Muddy Waters recorded his first single for Chess Records, a label launched by two Jewish immigrants from Poland, Leonard and Phil Chess, who, as owners of the 708 club and the Macomba Lounge, looked to record the performers that were electrifying increasingly larger crowds in their establishments. The Chess brothers were smart enough to bring in polished bluesman Willie Dixon, whose impressive songwriting and production capabilities helped Waters record a long list of hit records for Chess throughout the 1950s, making the label a major force in the industry. With Dixon working behind the scenes, Chess would soon become the bridge between the blues and rock 'n' roll, recording Chuck Berry's early crossover hits "Maybellene," "Roll Over Beethoven," "Johnny B. Goode," and "Rock and Roll Music" between 1955 and 1958.

With Berry's "Maybellene" climbing to number five on *Billboard*'s Hot 100 chart, 1955 was a momentous year for Chess and for the blues in general, which seemed on the verge of dramatic crossover success. Yet it was also the year that country-and-western singer Bill Haley's whitened R & B single "Rock Around the Clock" catapulted to number one, that RCA Victor signed Elvis Presley to a record contract, that Rosa Parks's refusal to give up her bus seat sparked the Montgomery Bus boycott, and that the Supreme Court ordered the South to start desegregating its schools "with all deliberate speed." While a number of bluesmen have sought to disabuse Americans of the idea that the blues is only about anger and sorrow, the undeniable association between the blues and the black southern experience became a bitter pill for whites to swallow as images of virulent southern racism circulated in the mass media, and northern cities like Chicago increasingly began to take stock of their own racial problem. Crossover hits would continue for black R & B performers in the years to come, and a talented second generation of Chicago blues musicians—Buddy Guy, Otis Rush, Koko Taylor—would make its mark, but the rise of white rock and the changing racial landscape would reduce the blues to a niche market by the mid-1960s.

The eclipse of the blues by white rock 'n' roll in the late 1950s is a story filled with allegations of appropriation and exploitation. Phil and Leonard Chess may have had little to do, at least directly, with the theft of the black blues sound by the Elvis-propelled rock 'n' roll industry, but their image as patrons of the blues scene was tarnished by a slew of lawsuits filed against them in the 1970s by many of their headliners claiming they were swindled. Willie Dixon had serious problems working with the Chess brothers, and, as legend has it, Muddy Waters was once seen on a ladder painting the ceiling of the Chess studio.[36] Interviewed about such controversies in a PBS documentary on the blues in 2003, Leonard Chess's son Marshall, who worked as an executive producer with the Rolling Stones in the 1970s, described Chess's talented bluesmen as children interested only in Cadillacs and womanizing, further fanning the flames of rancor surrounding the Chess "success" story.[37]

Regardless of the racist overtones of such assertions, they touch on a fundamental truth about the Chicago blues scene, which is that the Chess brothers, Willie Dixon, Muddy Waters, and most of the label's other performers were entrepreneurs as well as artists. While blues romantics like to idealize the live blues performances of the 1940s and 1950s as utopic moments when musicians spoke from their souls through the medium of the blues—and, no doubt, they often did—the truth is that most blues artists in Chicago in the late 1940s and early 1950s were moving "with all deliberate speed" away from the stage and into the studio. And who could blame them? On the club stage they could reach hundreds; in the studio they could reach hundreds of thousands, if not millions. For musicians raised in abject rural poverty in the Deep South, the financial payoff that such popularity could bring was hardly beside the point. Though there was more to it than this. Blues musicians also understood that while black writers and artists—those in the more socially accepted fields—could gain some recognition for their accomplishments from white intellectuals and black power elites alike, neither white nor black society would bestow this kind of social and artistic value on black blues musicians, at least not yet. Instructive here is the case of Eric Dolphy, the sublime saxophonist, bass clarinetist, and flautist, who dreamed of being a classical musician but was forced into jazz because that was what black youths did in 1940s Los Angeles. In this situation where black blues musicians could not strive for artistic capital, commercial approval was all that was left, and when it came from white audiences as well, so much the better. This is why Louis Jordan, who spent a great deal of time performing in Chicago in the 1940s and who was one of the earliest blues musicians to achieve crossover success, boasted frequently about all the money he made from white audiences, and why Muddy Waters brought the house down playing in front of East Coast preppies at the prestigious Newport Jazz Festival in 1960.

And in some sense, this spirit of entrepreneurialism is what distinguished Chicago from the other major center of black cultural expression, Harlem.

As blues musicians in Chicago were trying to bring their music to wider audiences, jazz musicians in Harlem were moving in a somewhat different direction. At after-hours clubs like Minton's Playhouse and Monroe's Uptown, black jazzmen like Charlie Parker, Dizzy Gillespie, Thelonious Monk, and Coleman Hawkins invented a new jazz form, bebop, which, in its technical sophistication, fast tempo, and instrumental virtuosity, represented a turning away from the marketplace and from the white audience that had so eagerly consumed the swing music of the 1930s. Jam sessions were small, unstructured, and often consisted mostly of musicians themselves, many of whom took turns on the stage. This was not music one could dance to, and white audiences found it discordant, edgy, and nervous, which, on some level, was the point. Bebop connected on an aesthetic level to the new spirit of racial militancy that was sweeping through much of the urban North during the 1940s, but it also represented an attempt by black musicians to create a cultural form so opaque that it resisted both commercialization and critical denigration by white society.[38] In the process, they created an art form that lacked popular appeal among average blacks as well. By the late 1940s, bebop's practitioners were venturing into more commercial projects in order to make a living, but the avant-gardist spirit remained in the Harlem music scene for decades to come. Such circumstances meant that from the 1940s through the mid-1960s, the years of the blues, soul, and Motown, New York would take a back seat to Chicago and Detroit, where southern culture cross-fertilized a northern spirit of "getting ahead" to produce the music that touched African Americans across the nation.[39]

THE ROAD TO SEGREGATION

Viewing the Englewood neighborhood on Chicago's South Side today, it is difficult to imagine that it once sat at the crossroads of progress. In the 1920s and 1930s, its respectable turn-of-the-century brick two-flats and single-family bungalows housed middle-class workers of Irish and German descent, many of whom held jobs in the stockyards to the north. Its shopping district at Halsted and 63rd was one of the city's busiest, and thousands of elevated trains, streetcars, and suburban commuter trains serviced the neighborhood every day. Many of those who could afford to live in this neighborhood had the unions to thank for raising their wages, and loyalty to a union was surpassed only by loyalty to one of the area's ten Catholic parishes, whose pastors were frequently heard urging their parishioners to support union campaigns. A good many of the Irish Catholics in the area were also, no doubt, beneficiaries of the Irish control over the city's political machine and the wealth of patronage resources it had to spread around.

Cut to turn-of-the-twenty-first-century Englewood: a neighborhood chopped up by vacant lots strewn with rubbish and debris, where cryptic gang graffiti was splattered on countless boarded-up homes and businesses, where the only white faces were those of policemen and other civil servants, where the unemployment rate was triple the national average, and where a never-ending turf war between some of Chicago's most notorious street gangs—the Gangster Disciples, the Black Disciples, and the Black P-Stones— bestowed upon the neighborhood the ignominious claim of having the highest crime rate in the city, which ranked it near the top of the list of highest in the country. In 1991, eighty-one murders were committed in this one corner of the city in just four months. Most people in the United States live their entire lives without hearing a live gunshot pierce the night; in the Englewood of recent years, they have been almost nightly occurrences.

Englewood is a poster child for what historians refer to as the "urban crisis" that overwhelmed many northern industrial cities in the postwar decades.[40] In Detroit, the crisis spread like a cancer throughout the entire city, creating an impoverished black core ringed by more prosperous white middle-class suburbs; in Chicago the crisis was quarantined, contained within broad swaths of the black South and West Sides. One of the great intellectual challenges of the past few decades has been explaining how this transpired, how the roughly twenty-year period between the end of World War II and the turbulent race riots of the mid-1960s came to produce, in the famous words of the Kerner Commission studying the riots, "two societies, one black, one white—separate but unequal." The position Americans take on this question inevitably determines, in part, whether they fall on the conservative or liberal side of the ideological fence. Conservatives tend to privilege explanations that reflect cultural racism (such as "blacks live in poor ghettos because their culture is dysfunctional and therefore they underachieve"), free market rationalities (such as "blacks and whites have simply chosen to live in their own separate neighborhoods, as is their right to do so"), or some combination of the two (such as "blacks and whites have chosen to live apart because of irreconcilable cultural differences").[41] Liberals, on the other hand, have historically referred to the power of racial discrimination in housing, education, and employment, and, to a lesser extent, to economic circumstances and policies that have eroded inner-city employment bases while promoting suburban growth. Although most reputable historians of the postwar American city are more likely to be liberal than conservative in their outlook, they have offered different interpretations of the causes and origins of the urban crisis. Until somewhat recently, the dominant view was that the struggle for racial integration was lost as a result of the ghetto riots and black power consciousness of the 1960s. Such circumstances, the story goes, allowed the Republican Party to stoke white middle-class fears to provoke a broad-based backlash against racial liberalism that enabled it to capture the White House in 1968.[42] To be sure, many of those middle-class whites who imagined themselves within the ranks of the "silent majority" Nixon claimed to represent were scratching their heads and wondering: "Why should my hard-earned money be used to support people who burn their own neighborhoods and who hate white people?"

Yet such accounts are of little use in trying to make sense of a place like Englewood, which had already been transformed from a thriving white middle-class neighborhood to a distressed black ghetto by the time of the Watts rebellion of 1965—the first major uprising of the black power era. Englewood's story suggests that the origins of the urban crisis can be found way back in the 1940s and 1950s, when, faced with the prospect of racial integration, whites formed neighborhood associations and unruly mobs to oppose it with all the means at their disposal, including sometimes lethal terrorist tactics.[43] Any assessment of what went so horribly wrong in Englewood, for example, cannot avoid considering such events as the Peoria Street riot of 1949, when crowds as large as seven thousand or more gathered to vent their anger at what they wrongly believed was a black family moving into a home at 56th and Peoria. African Americans, had, in fact, been spotted entering the premises at this address, but their presence had nothing to do with real estate transactions. Rather, they had come to the home of Aaron Bindman that night for an informal labor union meeting and celebration. In a moment filled with tragic irony that speaks volumes about the decline of the U.S. labor movement in the postwar years, Bindman, an officer of the International Longshoremen's and Warehousemen's Union, attempted to no avail to use his union credentials to win over the angry crowd at his doorstep. His appeals to working-class solidarity only poured fuel on the fire, eliciting shouts of "Kike!" "Lynch the niggers!" and "Communists!"[44] Here, in the streets of Englewood, the sanctity of whiteness trumped any appeals to the class struggle, especially when issued from the lips of someone like Bindman—a Jew and thus an outsider in a part of Englewood that was home to the nearly four thousand Irish Catholic members of Visitation Parish. Although pastors of this and other Englewood parishes had once used their authority to promote the unions, they now rallied their flocks to protect the parish against racial invasion and white flight. Fear fermented into anger as residents heard rumors of friends and neighbors planning to move away. Homeowners worried about falling property values, longtime renters worried about having to cut ties with the parish, and those unable to move so easily worried about being left behind as the area morphed into a black ghetto. All this angst was focused on the two-story flat at 56th and Peoria that November night. If blacks could move here, most of those in the crowd reasoned, the neighborhood was lost. These were the circumstances that turned otherwise law-abiding citizens into rioters along Chicago's color line in the postwar years.

What was happening in Englewood was hardly unique to Chicago. The Peoria Street riot was one of the more serious events in what historians now consider to have been a broad-based wave of grassroots activism against racial integration throughout the industrial Midwest in the postwar years. Between 1944 and 1946, some fifty homes in Chicago were firebombed, stoned, or otherwise vandalized, usually in hit-and-run fashion under the cover of night, resulting in the deaths of three of their occupants.[45] These acts were most often perpetrated by teenagers running with street gangs. The movement of white resistance taking shape was a family affair, with mothers and children not infrequently seen on the front lines. But young men in their teens and twenties—a generation that had come of age after the great labor struggles of the 1930s—most commonly constituted the core of the racist mobs. Out of twenty-nine local residents arrested during the Peoria Street riot, for example, all were male and only one did not fall between the ages of seventeen and twenty-five.[46] It was this element of the mob that began pursuing bolder tactics of resistance in the late 1940s.[47] Hence, in August 1947, as crowds of between 1,500 and 5,000 whites battled police around the Fernwood Park Homes housing project at 103rd and Halsted over the city's plan to move in black veterans, groups of marauding whites pulled blacks out of passing automobiles and streetcars to beat them up.[48] The following month teenage gangs attacked numerous black youths and incited hundreds of students at Wells High School on the Near Northwest Side to strike over the transfer of 60 blacks to their school, despite the fact that these additional students brought the total number of African Americans at Wells to a mere 130 out of a student body of 2,200.[49] In late July 1949, some two thousand

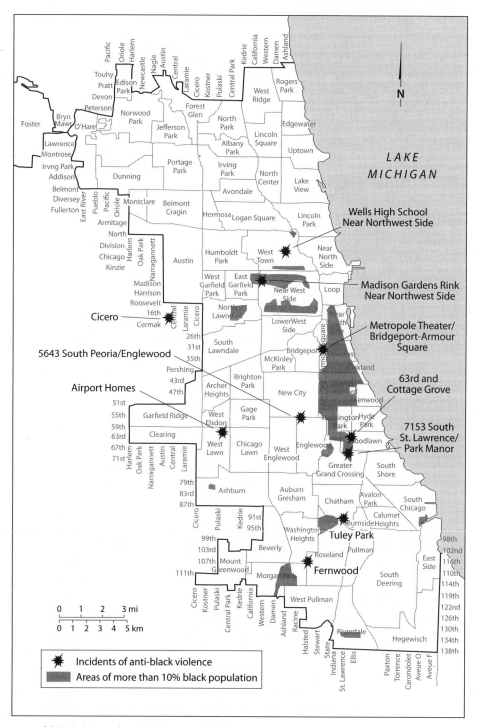

MAP 4. Major incidents of racial violence and the black population, 1946–1952.

incensed residents besieged a two-story building that had recently been purchased by a black teacher and his social worker wife at 7153 South St. Lawrence, around the southern edge of the Black Belt, burning mattresses and throwing stones at the house until daybreak.[50] And these were but a handful of the seemingly countless actions taken by whites to terrorize African Americans who dared to cross the color line.

Through such terrorist tactics white Chicagoans were able to stave off the advancing color line—if, in many cases, only temporarily—during a period when the Chicago Housing Authority possessed a leadership committed to promoting racial integration in the housing market. The Housing Act of 1949 made substantial federal funding available to municipalities for the purpose of building public housing, and the CHA, still under the direction of tireless liberal Elizabeth Wood, was ready with a list of proposed sites in white neighborhoods. Yet site after site met with dogged resistance from aldermen who understood all too well that allowing black housing into their wards would be committing political suicide. Since the city council had the power to veto any CHA project, Wood did not stand a chance without the support of the mayor. And, watching nervously as his base hurled insults at police fending off attacks against African Americans, Mayor Kennelly chose the path of least resistance, which was to refrain from taking on the city council's segregationist ways. Like most of the aldermen on the city council, the mayor had his ear to the ground, and the rumblings of white discontent began to sound like a freight train on a collision course with the mayor's office. Moreover, Kennelly's lack of resolve in backing the CHA against the city council was matched by his reluctance to deploy adequate police protection for the black residents targeted by racist mobs. Time and time again, human relations officials and other eyewitnesses criticized the police for insufficient manpower, incompetence, unwillingness to make arrests, and, perhaps most importantly, complicity with the mob. Kennelly scrambled to institute reforms, but complaints about the police continued. In the summer of 1953, for example, when yet another attempt by the CHA to integrate a housing project—the Trumbull Park Homes on Chicago's Far South Side— met with fierce neighborhood resistance, black tenants and outside observers once again criticized the police for failing to protect black tenants and sympathizing with their aggressors.[51]

Looking back upon this early chapter in the urban crisis, it is hard to avoid the conclusion that mob rule was allowed to shape a segregated future for Chicago while the city's leadership stood idly by. Not only would the CHA not pry open the housing market for African Americans, as Elizabeth Wood dreamed, but it would, in the years ahead, even become a lever of hyperghettoization.[52] With Wood resigning out of utter frustration in 1954 and the memories of the white housing riots of the 1940s and 1950s etched in the minds of the political establishment, the monstrous housing complexes built for black families in the 1950s and early 1960s would end up only in black ghetto areas or adjacent to preexisting projects on the city's South and West Sides. But the whites taking the streets in the Peoria Street riot and many of the other racial disturbances of these years won only a Pyrrhic victory. The dynamics of segregation in Chicago were as much about resistance as they were about flight.[53] The black population in Englewood increased from 11 percent in 1950 to 70 percent in 1960, as over 50,000 whites left the area. Those whites left behind, moreover, were hardly mixing with blacks; rather, they were preparing for their own departure. Ten years later Englewood was solidly black, along with many of the surrounding areas. Whites in Chicago, with astonishingly few exceptions, were unwilling to share their neighborhoods with African Americans, and with the federal government guaranteeing long-term, low-interest loans for veterans and other potential homeowners, they began heading for more leafy environs far from the color line. And Chicago was well on its way to becoming one of the most segregated cities in the nation.

FOUR

The Boss and the Black Belt

If, as historian Arnold Hirsch has claimed, the 1940s was an "era of hidden violence" along Chicago's color line, the race issue was clearly out of the closet by the early 1950s.[1] In fact, postwar Chicago-style racism made its dramatic worldwide debut in July 1951, when thousands of angry whites took to the streets in the suburb of Cicero to protest the settlement of a single black family there, overwhelming the town's police force and causing Illinois governor Adlai Stevenson to send in National Guard troops. Lying at the city's eastern limits, about seven miles away from the Loop, this tough, working-class town, which had once served as the Capone syndicate's base of operations, was not exactly Chicago. But it was close enough, and news of Chicago racism hit international newswires. More locally, the Cicero riot was something of a cause célèbre that witnessed several hundred and perhaps thousands of young men from Chicago pouring into the neighboring town in cars and on city buses to lend a hand to what one racist organization referred to as "the brave youth of Cicero."[2] Arnold Hirsch was the first historian to examine the arrest lists from the several nights of rioting in order to explain the motives of those who took to the streets in a frenzy of racial hatred. The Cicero rioters, he concluded, were largely residents of the neighborhood trying to protect their community from a racial invasion that they believed would destroy the very fabric of their lives. Yet Hirsch's analysis overlooks something very important that was transpiring in Cicero: the arrest records for the final few nights suggest that once news of the demonstration spread, it changed from a territorially based action to a much broader rally against integration that pulled in participants from West Side Chicago neighborhoods—some a considerable distance away from the scene at 6139 West 19th Street in Cicero.[3] The Cicero riot revealed that the more "hidden violence" of the previous

FIGURE 7. Young rioters brazenly confronting police in Cicero in July 1951. Photo from Ullstein Bild via Getty Images.

decade—the hit-and-run vandalism and nighttime raids, which, due to pressure from the mayor's office, had been kept off the front pages of the city's dailies—was by the end of the 1940s spreading throughout the city. Even though the events of Cicero were eye-opening for those outside Chicago, working-class ethnics and their black neighbors residing anywhere near the color line understood very well that this kind of thing was business as usual. Nonetheless, while African Americans in Chicago certainly did not lack events to reveal to them the racism they faced in their daily lives, the widespread media coverage given to the Cicero riot could only have emboldened the city's black leadership.

Moreover, there were other sources of black discontentment simmering in Chicago around this time. Mayor Kennelly's zeal for reform had begun to arouse cries of racial injustice in William Dawson's five black-majority wards. Although Dawson's political submachine had been critical to Kennelly's election in 1947, just as it had for Kelly in the two previous mayoral elections, the mayor began to break the unwritten rule that Dawson and his underling ward bosses should be given free rein over the illicit operations that had created a parallel underground economy in black Chicago. Two rackets in particular, policy wheels and jitney cabs, headlined Kennelly's crusade. Under the system Kennelly had inherited from his predecessor, the police were supposed to give a wink and then close their eyes to such activities, both of which provided thousands of jobs to ordinary black residents and substantial revenues to the black politicians that protected them. But within months after the election, different police details began making raids on South Side policy operations.

By the late 1940s, black Chicagoans began to view such actions as constituting racial injustices, especially as police officers proved to be showing much greater dedication in upholding the laws against policy and gypsy cabs than they did in defending the rights of innocent black citizens being attacked by racist mobs. In July 1946, for example, the Mayor's Commission on Human Relations reported several such cases of police negligence, including an officer who refused to arrest two vandals because he was off duty, a policeman asleep at his post, and another who "expressed opposition to guarding residences of Negroes."[4] Especially galling, in this sense, was the crackdown on the jitney cabs, a trade that had developed in the first place because white taxi companies generally refused to serve black neighborhoods. Moreover, the Capone gang had tried repeatedly in the 1920s and 1930s to take control of the South Side policy business, leaving Kennelly open to charges that he was backing a takeover of this lucrative source of black wealth by the white syndicates. To make matters worse, the mayor had continuously refused to give any credence to Dawson's arguments about why a harmless vice like policy should be left alone. "Our people can't afford to go to race tracks and private clubs," Dawson reportedly told the mayor, "so they get a little pleasure out of policy." In an episode that has become legendary in accounts of Dawson's storied career, the boss of black Chicago refused to talk to Kennelly until just before his reelection bid in 1951, when in a heated backroom meeting, Dawson blasted the mayor: "Who do you think you are? I bring in the votes. I elect *you*. *You* are not needed, but the votes are needed. I deliver the votes to you, but you won't talk to *me?*"[5]

However, if Dawson was voicing complaints that might have helped to fuel the growing sense of racial injustice in black Chicago, one would be mistaken to think of him as a civil rights activist. In his 1960 study *Negro Politics,* political scientist James Q. Wilson categorized black leaders of the pre–civil rights era as either those who promoted the "status" of the black community or those who fought for its "welfare." According to this scheme, the status-oriented leaders were the ones supporting objectives that uplifted the race by defending black rights, such as integration and equal educational and employment opportunities, while the welfare-oriented leaders focused on bread-and-butter issues that met the social needs of the black poor.[6] To say that Dawson, who was heard on a number of occasions comparing himself to Booker T. Washington, belonged to the latter camp does not adequately describe the situation. Not only did Dawson not fight for status issues, but his very position depended on the failure of those who did. Segregation had made Dawson, and he knew all too well that integration threatened to unmake him. Until 1948, when the Supreme Court's decision in *Shelley v. Kraemer* struck down the use of contracts between homeowners to prohibit sales or rentals to blacks and other perceived racial undesirables in the eyes of white residents, African Americans were largely relegated to the three main community areas that made up the Black Belt. If those championing racial integration were to carry the day, many of the votes underpinning the black submachine would be dispersed throughout the city, thereby deteriorating Dawson's base and the harvest of votes he could deliver to the Democratic machine. Dawson's fear of civil rights activism was so pronounced, in fact, that, when serving on the Civil Rights Section of John F. Kennedy's presidential campaign in 1960, he had tried to persuade the other members of the committee to drop the term *civil rights* from its name, arguing that the words might "offend our good southern friends."[7]

Yet Dawson could take some consolation in the fact that he did not face his dilemma alone. In fact, the whole Cook County Democratic Party machine depended on Dawson's ability to deliver votes. Even though by the early 1950s Chicago blacks had not abandoned the party of Lincoln to nearly the same extent that African Americans in the rest of the nation had since the 1936 presidential election, when some 76 percent had cast their vote for Franklin D. Roosevelt, Dawson's black submachine had nonetheless provided Democratic candidates with Black Belt majorities—albeit somewhat slim ones—that had ensured their victories in the elections of 1939, 1943, 1947, and 1951.[8] However, for the Democratic machine, civil rights agitation for integration represented a double-edged sword. Not only did it threaten to undermine the pivotal electoral advantage the Black Belt had been providing, but even more importantly, it held the potential to wreak political havoc in the machine's white working-class strongholds, causing many families to move to outlying Republican wards and to the suburbs and spreading feelings of animosity among those left behind. For the next few decades, two opposing forces—the black struggle for integration, equality, rights, and power on the one hand and a white reaction that historians have described as "defensive localism" and "reactionary populism" on the other—would shape a treacherous landscape for mayoral politics in the Windy City.[9] With the increasingly rights-conscious Black Belt holding the margin of victory, one could not afford to be viewed as soft on questions of racial justice; take too aggressive a stand though, and the fury of the white backlash threatened to make even the strongest of black votes irrelevant.

As early as 1954, the year the U.S. Supreme Court declared segregated schools to be unconstitutional in *Brown v. Board of Education of Topeka, Kansas,* these two counterforces of black struggle and white reaction were fighting it out in a small community of steelworkers in the southeast corner of Chicago. In the far-flung neighborhood of South Deering a set of two-story brick buildings constructed around grassy courtyards—the prototypes of the "garden apartment" public housing complexes built in the New Deal era—became, quite by chance, the city's test-case for racial integration. The affair began around the summer of 1953 when a Chicago Housing Authority official mistakenly granted an apartment in the Trumbull Park Homes project to a light-skinned black woman named Betty Howard. When, just days after moving in, Mrs. Howard was sighted with her darker-skinned husband, residents in the area launched a campaign of terrorism that forced the Howards to board up their windows and wait for police escorts every time they wanted to step outside their home. What amounted to an ongoing race riot continued for over a year, during which time embattled CHA director Elizabeth Wood took on the mob by moving ten other black families into Trumbull.

In an effort to understand what lay behind the intensity of South Deering racism, the American Civil Liberties Union enlisted a "spy" to hang out at local bars and parks and record the conversations he overheard, a move that unwittingly yielded some compelling documentation of the shadowy, everyday milieu of 1950s white reactionary populism. In the conspiratorial nightmares and daydreams of South Deering residents, we learn from these conversations, powerful Jews pulled the strings of the city's housing policies in order to promote intermarriage and exploit the real estate market, and it was the handful of Trumbull's harried black families, not the established white residents, who had the upper hand. "I heard there is an organization of smart niggers that use certain other niggers like this fellow Howard to move into a neighborhood, and this ruins the neighborhood," one patron at a local bar told the crowd one afternoon, "and then these smart ones with money come in and buy up the property at a low price and then sell to other niggers at a high price."[10] For many of the folks sharing such anxieties over beer and cigarettes, the *Brown* ruling was not so much about desegregating southern schools as it was about integrating their own neighborhoods. Here was an early glimpse of the now very familiar populist rhetorical style of turning the world upside down—to put "liberals" and minorities on top and average, white, middle-class taxpaying people on the bottom—that infused the conservative ascendancy in the postwar United States from Nixon's "silent majority" backlash to George W. Bush's triumphant alliance of neoconservatives and evangelical Christians. The heated barroom conversations of South Deering suggest that this sense of victimization at the hands of liberals was not merely spoon-fed by Republican politicians to their antiliberal constituents; rather, it was elemental to the everyday experience for many working-class whites in the metropolitan United States, and it was an emotion that crystallized most visibly in places where African Americans were mounting spirited challenges to their own victimization.

By the fall of 1954, the South Deering situation had been the subject of a nationally televised news broadcast and numerous articles in the *Chicago Defender,* and Elizabeth Wood had been forced out of her post. But Wood's ouster had done little to recoup the damage Kennelly had sustained over the situation. His failure to adequately protect blacks in Trumbull Park had made him the scourge of black Chicago, and yet his association with the whole affair was hardly reassuring to working-class whites living around the color line. More importantly, both his reform crusade and his falling out with Dawson had made him a persona non grata with the leadership of the Cook County Democratic machine, whose new chairman, Richard J. Daley, began maneuvering behind the scenes to replace him as the machine's candidate in the upcoming mayoral elections. In fact, not much maneuvering was required to get the job done. As chairman and thus "boss" of the machine, Daley controlled the selection of the "slating committee" responsible for recommending to the Cook County Democratic Central Committee all the candidates to run on the machine's ticket. Suffice to say that few were surprised when the Central Committee approved the slating committee's recommendation of Daley for mayor by a vote of 47–1, with Kennelly's campaign manager casting the lone dissenting vote.

Few people, if anyone, in the room that day could have sensed the historic significance of their choice. Few could have imagined that Daley would become *the* quintessential boss, that he would create the nation's most powerful political machine at a time when reformers were putting machines across the country to rest, that presidents would be indebted to him, and that it would take a heart attack to remove him from office twenty-one years later. Daley, to be sure, was ambitious, but by most accounts, he was hardly a visionary leader, and fortune more than anything else had placed him in a position to become the machine's mayoral candidate in 1955. Three years earlier a powerful South Side bloc within the party had appeared to have effectively opposed Daley's bid for party chairman, but in the midst of the selection process, Daley's leading opponent, Fourteenth Ward alderman Clarence Wagner, had perished in a car accident while on a fishing trip in Minnesota, and Daley prevailed after all.

Yet Daley's rapid ascent was not merely a matter of chance, even if chance had played a part. He was the right man for his time and place. Having grown up the son of a sheet-metal worker in a large Irish Catholic family in the working-class neighborhood of Bridgeport, where he continued to live after his election, Daley was intimately acquainted with the spirit of defensive localism that was developing across the city's Bungalow Belt and white working-class neighborhoods. Moreover, Daley was a rhetorical genius, a virtual savant in the art of appealing to the common people with his heavy Chicago accent and straight-talking style, while avoiding any easily discernable position on the issues. This skill had the astonishing effect of enabling a Bridgeport kid who had run with the famously racist Hamburger gang to capture the endorsement of none other than the *Chicago Defender,* which, in a front-page editorial, opined that he had "taken a firm and laudable stand" on civil rights issues.[11] In a hard-fought primary against Kennelly, who decided to try to go it alone after being dumped by the machine, Daley met his opponent's charges of bossism with classic populist retorts about being a man of the people in a struggle against the "big interests." But Daley best exhibited his talent for populist platitudes in his campaign against his Republican challenger, Robert Merriam.

A former Democrat from Chicago's liberal Fifth Ward, which included the campus of the prestigious University of Chicago and the surrounding Hyde Park neighborhood, home to a constituency that machine politicians referred to contemptuously as "lakefront liberals," the stately and well-spoken Merriam staked his campaign on the reform spirit sweeping across U.S. cities. But Merriam's WASP background and his social distance from most Chicagoans played right into Daley's hands. Faced again with allegations of bossism, Daley swore to voters that he would "follow the training [his] good

Irish mother" had given him. "If I am elected," he added, "I will embrace mercy, love, charity, and walk humbly with God." Moreover, when pushed on the thorny issue of public housing, Daley pronounced himself a proponent, but when asked where it should be built, he replied, "Let's not be arguing about where it's located." Similarly, in contrast to Merriam's very specific policy positions, Daley spoke repeatedly and vaguely about the need to protect the "neighborhoods"—"the backbone of the city," as he called them.[12] When I walk down the streets of my neighborhood," he assured his supporters, "I see the streets of every neighborhood." And sounding the old populist refrain, he promised that under his administration, "The sun will rise over all the Chicago neighborhoods instead of just State Street."[13]

In the end, however, Daley's populist rhetorical talents were mere icing on the cake. It was the machine, in all its organizational splendor, that pushed him over the top in what was a relatively close election by Chicago standards. The machine, as always, supplied Daley with a large financial edge and a veritable army of campaign workers, who, under the leadership of precinct captains, local fixers whose position depended on their ability to produce votes, pursued their objective through a range of illicit activities: from fraud to blackmail, to physical intimidation and worse. This was, of course, an old Chicago tradition. But what was somewhat new—and, in a sense, modern—about the machine's campaign tactics under Daley was the very deft exploitation of white racial fears. Commenting on this campaign years later, famed Chicago journalist Mike Royko claimed: "Even before the phrase 'white backlash' was coined, the machine knew how to use it."[14] And it knew how to use it in a manner that barely even jeopardized black votes—due to the long reach of the machine into neighborhoods, up doorsteps, and into the very living rooms and kitchens of potential voters. The machine's precinct captains could lean on scores of residents in their neighborhoods who were indebted to them for a job or any of a long list of political favors and services. This extensive network of loyal supporters enabled Daley to play a double game with the race issue.

Thus, while Daley avoided making any public statements that painted him as unsympathetic to the plight of black Chicagoans, his operatives were spreading the word behind the scenes that he was no friend to racial integration. This message was transmitted, in part, through a shameless smear campaign to stir up racial concerns about his opponent. Machine cadres, for example, circulated letters in white neighborhoods from a bogus organization called the American Negro Civic Association urging residents to vote for Merriam because he would make sure blacks found proper housing

FIGURE 8. Richard J. Daley celebrates his first mayoral election victory in 1955. Richard J. Daley Collection, RJD_04_01_0012_0002_025, University of Illinois at Chicago Library, Special Collections.

throughout the city. They also spread rumors that Merriam's first wife, who was born in France, was part black. Even though many people realized this was all pretty much a sham, they understood that the machine's involvement in such shenanigans meant that its candidate was no civil rights crusader. Not only were Daley and his people precocious in their understanding of backlash politics, but they were also ahead of their time in their use of "coded" language to appeal to angry white voters on racial issues without really saying anything specific that could raise the ire of black voters.

Hence, despite the endorsement of Chicago's largest newspapers, which gave Merriam's charges of corruption and bossism front-page exposure, Merriam amassed only 589,555 votes to Daley's 708,222. But the election was much closer than it looked. The candidates ran evenly in most of the city, with Daley's margin of victory lying in his overwhelming dominance in the machine's core wards—referred to by political commentators as the "automatic eleven." In the five black wards that Dawson controlled, Daley had garnered a nearly 50,000-vote margin; with the votes for him in several other black wards, the total black contribution to Daley's victory was a decisive 103,000 votes.[15]

Later that same year, African Americans in Montgomery, Alabama, most of whom had been disenfranchised by terror and administrative chicanery, would begin a powerful bus boycott that would help to launch a movement for civil rights aiming to renew American democracy. Southern blacks, with some help from the Supreme Court, were pushing themselves across a new threshold of modernity, pulling the nation along with them. And as Adam Green has argued, African Americans in Chicago were, in this very same moment, developing a new consciousness of their connection to a larger national black community that spanned both sides of the Mason-Dixon line—a bond soldered by the revelation of Chicago-native Emmett Till's brutal murder in rural Mississippi, where he had allegedly dared to flirt with a white woman while visiting relatives in August 1955; the experience of beholding the images of fourteen-year-old Till's mangled, bloated body, exposed sensationally in the pages of the Chicago-based black publication *Jet*, produced, according to Green, a "moment of simultaneity" between blacks all over the country that laid the foundations for the northern civil rights struggle in the 1960s.[16] Viewed in the light of these circumstances, the key role played by Chicago blacks in the election of Richard J. Daley appears an act of epic historical irony—even more so because Daley himself stood not for a return to the old order or even a maintenance of the status quo. Rather, the new mayor was a zealous modernizer. He would move almost immediately to upgrade Chicago's transportation infrastructure, make Chicago one of the first cities to fluoridate its water, and bring in a battalion of state-of-the-art street cleaners that enabled the city to remove ten thousand more tons of street dirt (the calculation of such a figure in itself suggests the logic of linear, scientific progress in operation). In Daley's Chicago, Bauhaus planners sponsored by modernist architectural trendsetter Ludwig Mies van der Rohe would design high-rise housing projects in an effort to provide more efficient housing for ghetto-dwelling blacks. Of course it was impossible for Chicago blacks to have known that they were helping to elect a man who would preside over the invention of the modern black hyperghetto, but it would not take long before they understood their place in the new order.

WRECKING MACHINE

To the untrained eye, it might seem contradictory that Richard J. Daley—a Democrat who had come of age politically in a moment when the Democratic

Party defined itself as the defender of society's disadvantaged—would manage a city that so clearly relegated African Americans to second-class citizenship. "My dad came out of the Roosevelt era and the Depression," Daley's son Richard M. Daley would later claim. "One person and one party made a difference in his life—that's what everybody forgot when they called my father and other people political bosses."[17] Although Richard J. Daley's legacy would be marked by his truculence in the face of civil rights protests, his "shoot-to-kill" order after rioters took to the streets in anger over Martin Luther King's assassination, his unabashed will to turn the full wrath of police repression against student demonstrators outside the 1968 Democratic National Convention, and his general unwillingness to alter the processes making Chicago the most segregated city in the United States, more recent accounts, many from people close to him and his son, have complicated Daley's place in the pantheon of backlash cranks. Daley, some have pointed out, initially preferred the construction of much more humane, four-story housing projects to the alienating high-rise complexes that would come to dominate large swaths of the city, and he even travelled to Washington on two occasions to plead, ultimately unsuccessfully, for the additional funding that would make this possible.[18] Some of Daley's apologists, moreover, have claimed that he genuinely believed he was acting as a New Deal liberal should when he authorized the expenditure of government funds to move blacks out of deteriorating slums and into new apartment buildings. Put such facts together with his close ties to liberal Democratic icons like John F. Kennedy and Lyndon B. Johnson, and Daley seems not so implausible as a New Deal–style Democrat after all.

Yet to understand Daley in these ideological terms is to completely misunderstand the Chicago machine system that gave meaning to his every move. In one of the most definitive studies of the Daley machine to date, sociologist and political insider Milton Rakove described the machine's raison d'être as "essentially nonideological." "Its primary demands on its members are," he claimed, "loyalty and political efficiency. In return, it carries out its obligations by providing its members with jobs, contacts, contracts, and its own 'social security' system."[19] While Daley would become renowned for his humorously botched phrases—one of the more colorful was "the police are not here to *create* disorder, they are here to *preserve* disorder"—much more emblematic of his political acumen was his oft-quoted maxim: "good government is good politics."

This idea more than any vague notion of liberalism, democracy, civic duty, or even human compassion guided Daley's decision to approve the construc-

FIGURE 9. Stateway Gardens at 35th and S. Federal, ca. 1958. Chicago Architectural Photographing Company. Chicago Photographic Collection, CPC_01_C_0282_006, University of Illinois at Chicago Library, Special Collections.

tion of two adjoining strips of high-rises—Stateway Gardens and the Robert Taylor Homes—that would together constitute the world's longest and largest housing project of its time. By the late 1950s, after the blueprints for these projects had been hashed out, one would have been hard-pressed to find anyone able to make a convincing argument that this seemingly endless, four-mile corridor of almost indistinguishable concrete slab structures, all occupied exclusively by blacks, would not create a ghetto far more sinister than the one it was replacing. But to build such structures was good government in Daley's eyes, because of the immense political benefits that would accrue from doing so. Not only would this housing "solution" be useful for steering clear of the thorny issue of racial integration, but also, thanks to Title I of the Housing Act of 1949, the federal government would be heavily subsidizing the work. In effect, a flow of capital would move through the mayor's office, where it would be magically transformed into patronage—the jobs and contracts that lubricated the machine and made it run. When Daley took office, the city of Chicago employed nearly 40,000 people. If, according to Rakove's estimate, each patronage job handed out translated into some ten votes from family members and friends, this meant that the Daley machine would enter each election with a lead of roughly 400,000 votes. But federally subsidized public works projects of the magnitude of those that built Chicago's numerous high-rise housing projects offered the possibility of expanding the machine's patronage resources even more while drawing very little from the city budget. For every hard hat on the job, for every light bulb and bolt, for every inspector and supervisor, the machine was expanding its base exponentially.

This patronage system had of course been fundamental to machine politics long before Daley had entered public life, but Daley's great coup lay in understanding the need to take the system to another level and to reconfigure it so that he held all the cards. Patronage, it must be remembered, was under threat in 1955. Reformers had gained the upper hand in many major U.S. cities, and, as was demonstrated by the favorable press coverage of both Kennelly and Merriam's anticorruption campaigns, even Chicago seemed ready for reform. More importantly, however, the city had entered a period of economic decline, which threatened to reduce the budget and with it the reservoir of patronage resources at the machine's disposal. Generous federal government programs providing subsidized long-term loans to veterans and other potential middle-class homeowners had sparked a massive migration to the suburbs, and Chicago, like many other cities, was witnessing the flight of people and jobs into the rapidly growing outlying areas, where the American dream of a home of one's own on a plot of green could be realized. What was happening to Chicago was part of a much larger story of deindustrialization and metropolitan sprawl that began sucking the life out of the urban core beginning in the late 1940s. The future was not broad shoulders and smokestacks but white collars and air-conditioned offices, a situation emblematized as early as 1955, when Chicago lost its claim as "hog butcher of the world" to the city of Omaha, Nebraska.[20] Yet the real estate and service activities that would eventually make the city prosperous again were, by the mid-1950s, far from being able to compensate for the declining manufacturing sector. When Daley took office, housing construction had come to a virtual standstill; only one major structure, the Prudential Building, had recently been added to the downtown skyline; retail sales at the swanky Loop department stores were falling fast; and real estate values in the downtown area had still not recovered from the 13 percent hit they had taken between 1939 and 1947.[21] Moreover, with the black ghetto converging on the Loop from the south, business leaders were bracing for the worst. The Chicago of Daley's first term was not at all the bustling, vibrant city it would become by the end of his second. It was more akin to the Chicago of Nelson Algren's gritty 1951 novel *City on the Make,* a landscape of sordid gin joints and dingy alleys peopled by stew bums, swindlers, crooked politicians, and gangsters. Being a part of this city was, Algren famously quipped, "like loving a woman with a broken nose."[22]

Chicago's new mayor took such insults personally. A poignant Daley anecdote, whether the stuff of legend or truth, captures the bare-knuckled intensity of his investment in the city's livelihood: the mayor once stopped his car so he could get out and, with his bodyguard looking on beside him, dispose of a piece of litter he had seen a pedestrian drop on the sidewalk. Yet for Daley, the goal of renewing Chicago was inextricably bound up with his own objective of holding on to power, and his political education told him that his hold on power was contingent on preserving and controlling the supply of patronage he could spread around. His first order of business was to bring patronage under his complete control in two ways that broke sharply with machine tradition. Despite promises to the contrary during his campaign, Daley refused to relinquish his position as Democratic Party chairman after being elected mayor. This not only handed him control of the party's campaign funds, which he could distribute to the different city wards through his ward committeemen, based on who was most loyal and deserving, but it also gave him decisive influence over the selection of the full slate of the party's candidates, including those for governor and both houses of the state and federal legislatures. These powers made every Democratic politician in the state beholden to Daley and thus ready to bend to his wishes. They also allowed Daley to become a player on the state and national stages, which could pay patronage dividends in some strange ways. For example, when Daley needed an increase in the city's sales tax to pay for his ambitious plan to hire thousands of new police officers, firefighters, and sanitation workers, he went downstate to negotiate with Republican governor William Stratton, the one man who could ensure the approval of the state legislature for such a measure. Rumor had it that Stratton's help came at a price: Daley's agreement to slate a lackluster candidate against him in the coming gubernatorial election. "Daley turned purple and pounded his fist when he later denied the rumor," wrote Mike Royko, "but he did indeed run a patsy against Stratton in 1956."[23]

Daley's second power play was to emasculate the city council, effectively reducing it to a rubber-stamp advisory board. This he did by forcing a number of procedural changes, the most important of which was transferring responsibility for formulating the city's annual budget from the city council into his own hands. This represented an enormous shift in the balance of power between the mayor and the city council, a change that was reinforced by Daley's elimination of the practice of requiring city council approval for any city contract over $2,500. Complementing such official changes were a number of tactics the new mayor pursued to limit the city council's informal powers. All of the aldermen sitting on the city council, for example, possessed the authority to bestow a range of favors on constituents, most of which came at a price. One of the most profitable of these favors was the issuance of permits to construct driveways; under Daley, requests for such permits would now need to pass through the mayor's office. The members of the city council were, of course, not happy about such restrictions on their power, but resistance was futile.

Daley may not have gotten away with such actions were he not also moving swiftly to make everyone with any financial clout in the city happy. The candidate who had run a populist campaign against the "big interests" quickly became the toast of State Street with a flurry of decisions that exhibited the progrowth ideology that would come to define the Daley era. What perhaps few expected of the kid who knew the summer stench of the stockyards was an unparalleled ability to draw massive amounts of both public and private funding to modernize and improve the city's infrastructure. Once again Daley was the man for his time and place. The Housing Acts of 1949 and 1954 had extended generous federal funds for local governments to buy land in blighted areas and then sell it off to private developers for public housing and nonresidential projects, such as universities and hospitals. While policy makers and lobbyists in Washington debated what forms of redevelopment should be prioritized and which populations should be targeted by "urban renewal"—with the business community cheering for the rehabilitation of downtown business districts and liberals arguing for better housing for the poor—the matter would largely be settled on the local level, where municipal governments put the federal money to work. In Daley's Chicago, the progrowth ideology was never in doubt, and all of the "trickle-down" arguments from the coalition of developers, bankers, and commercial interests that rallied merrily around their new mayor seemed like pipe dreams by the late 1960s, when black Chicago was engulfed by the flames of rebellion.

In this moment of black disillusionment about the unfulfilled promises of the civil rights movement, novelist James Baldwin provocatively referred to "urban renewal" as "Negro removal," a description that fits the case of Chicago particularly well. Indeed, when Daley pushed his plan for the Robert Taylor Homes through the city council in May 1956, it was not yet clear just how this and the numerous other ghetto high-rises being planned and constructed would fit into the overall scheme. In fact, these housing complexes were among a number of public works projects being pushed forward by the mayor during his first term in office. The city was going to get new skyscrapers in the Loop, new expressways that connected the suburbs to the downtown business district, new parking garages to accommodate the additional rush of commuters, the new $35 million McCormick Place convention center on Lake Michigan that would make the city "the convention capital" of the nation, a new and improved O'Hare Airport, new bridges and train crossings, new government buildings, new police stations, and a new University of Illinois campus. Daley was unleashing the growth machine and it promised to make everyone involved fat—bankers and lawyers, realtors and developers, contractors and suppliers, politicians and friends. And the State Street crowd was jubilant. The old retailers like Marshall Field's applauded the expressways and parking garages that would bring suburban shoppers safely and quickly downtown, and the top brass of the many *Fortune* 500 companies with headquarters in the Loop—in 1957 Chicago was second only to New York in housing corporate headquarters—saw a solution to the ghetto blight creeping northward from the South Side. The only inconveniences in this scheme were the human beings who remained after their neighborhoods were cleared away. What was to be done with them? Moreover, one could talk about holding off the ghetto, but what did this mean in a city that had seen its black population increase from 277,731 (8 percent of the total) in 1940 to 812,637 (23 percent of the total) in 1960? Here, alas, is where federally subsidized public housing fit into the big picture, and in a picture as black and white as Chicago's was, urban renewal did indeed mean just what Baldwin said it did: "Negro removal."

This was how a federal urban renewal program whose most idealistic framers viewed as capable of lifting up the urban poor, became, in Daley's Chicago, a powerful means for reinforcing inequalities of race and class. To be fair, Daley inherited rather than invented the city's growth machine; in fact, Chicago was a pioneer in early urban renewal efforts, lobbying the state legislature to pass the Blighted Areas Redevelopment Act and the Restoration Act of 1947, which granted it broad powers of eminent domain for acquiring large slum areas and selling them to developers, as well as state subsidies to sweeten the deal for investors. The legislation was largely the brainchild of a civic planning group called the Metropolitan Housing and Planning Council (MHPC), and in particular of two of its leading members—Chicago Title and Trust president Holman Pettibone and Marshall Field's executive Milton C. Mumford—both of whom favored a downtown approach to the city's redevelopment plan in order to stave off blight and reverse the trend of falling real estate values in the Loop. While downstate Republican legislators—many of them rural-based and hostile to anything that smacked of New Deal aid to urban blacks—were adamant that state funds would not be used to subsidize public housing for displaced residents of redevelopment projects, Pettibone and Mumford worked out a compromise that would create the Chicago Land Clearance Commission (CLCC) to deal with the housing of displaced residents. The idea was to bypass the Chicago Housing Authority and its nondiscriminatory tenant-selection policy. Pettibone hailed the legislation as "a pioneering combination of public authority and public funds with private initiative and private capital," but the public side of the partnership had clearly been given a subsidiary role.[24] By legislative sleight of hand, the capacity of public authorities to acquire and clear land and then sell it to private interests at below-market costs had come to be defined as a "public purpose."

By the end of the 1940s the city was using such powers to begin redeveloping the Near South Side neighborhoods around the Illinois Institute of Technology (IIT) and the Michael Reese Hospital. Working closely with real estate magnate and MHPC president Ferd Kramer, the city cleared hundreds of acres of slums to make room for two new middle-class housing complexes, Lake Meadows and Prairie Shores, which would end up raising rents around IIT and Michael Reese between 300 and 600 percent—an increase that priced out the vast majority of the mostly black residents who had been displaced.

This first foray into the new postwar frontier of urban renewal did not go so smoothly. Opposition to the Lake Meadows project crystallized soon after the announcement, with property owners filing suit in federal court to prevent the CLCC from taking their homes, and a group called the Property Conservation and Human Rights Committee of Chicago petitioning the federal government to withhold funds. Moreover, the uncertainties surrounding the situation of the thousands of black residents who would be displaced by the project caused considerable political fallout, prompting Third Ward alderman Archibald Carey Jr. to propose a city ordinance, backed by the Chicago Urban League and CORE, outlawing discrimination "where public aid is provided for housing units . . . even though such housing units are built with private funds." While the ordinance was, in the end, soundly defeated in the city council, it stirred up a rancorous debate, with Carey and other proponents of the measure evoking "negro removal" and comparing the treatment of blacks to that of Jews in Nazi Germany. Sensing the seriousness of the threat to Chicago's urban renewal plans, Mayor Kennelly, who normally observed a policy of nonintervention in legislative matters, appeared in person before the city council to speak against the ordinance.

Moreover, African Americans residing in the area around Lake Meadows were not the only ones to feel threatened. Late in 1950, with the bulldozers rumbling away, a range of community associations from a number of white South Side neighborhoods, some located several miles away from the Lake Meadows site, began agitating against the project for very different sorts of reasons. Leading the charge was a realtor from the Roseland community who argued that the rehousing of those displaced by the Lake Meadows project posed a "disastrous financial burden" to taxpayers while stoking fears about the "dispersal of the colored inhabitants . . . into outlying areas."[25] Adding to all this trouble and delay was more controversy surrounding the proposal to close a stretch of Cottage Grove Avenue, an idea that the Chicago Plan Commission pondered for several months before finally signing off. By 1950, the New York Life Insurance Company, the project's principal investor, was threatening to pull out, but Kennelly proved a capable fixer. Nearly two years later ground was finally broken.[26]

In the end, Lake Meadows was built, and the ultimate success of the project opened the way for a lot more of the same. Emerging out of the wrangling and controversy over Lake Meadows was a new modus operandi for the city's planning and development process. During this time the MHPC's downtown agenda prevailed over a range of Loop area interests who favored a very different approach to the future—one that sought to revitalize the neighborhoods surrounding the Loop rather than merely orienting their redevelopment around the priorities of Pettibone, Kramer, Mumford and the rest of the downtown business crowd. Standing opposed to the MHPC, for example, was the South Side Planning Board, an organization that represented a range of manufacturing, printing, and warehousing interests from 12th Street all the way down to 47th Street. Rather than the middle-class residential development favored by the downtown interests to house white-collar workers, provide downtown shoppers, and buffer the Loop against blight, the South Side Planning Board supported infrastructural improvements that would aid the expansion of Near South Side manufacturers, which would, in turn, provide a healthy job base for working-class South Side residents.

A similar campaign against the downtown agenda emerged on the Near West Side in 1949, when the Near West Side Planning Board, with the support of Twentieth Ward alderman Anthony Pistilli, successfully challenged the classification of a part of the neighborhood as blighted and put forward a redevelopment plan that sought to promote local manufacturing activities and to rehabilitate rather than clear existing structures. The back-and-forth between such neighborhood groups and downtown interests continued into 1954 with the announcement of the Fort Dearborn project, which was to involve the clearance of a 151-acre swath of land on the north bank of the Chicago River for the construction of five thousand private middle-income housing units and a $165 million civic center. Almost immediately Near North Side planning groups sprang into action, protesting the classification of the area as blighted and the effects the project would have on the local real estate market. However, just as things were getting unruly, with ordinary residents actually demanding a say in the planning process, Pettibone and Hughston McBain, chairman of the board of Marshall Field's, moved to build a new and more powerful coalition of downtown business interests, the Chicago Central Area Committee (CAC), that would ultimately save their day.[27]

And yet the CAC remained restrained in Mayor Kennelly's Chicago, where the city council actually possessed a legislative function and aldermen allied themselves with local planning groups looking to throw wrenches into the growth machine's plans. This would change under Daley's watch. Like Kennelly, Daley, despite all his blathering about defending the neighborhoods against State Street, believed that what was best for Ferd Kramer, Holman Pettibone, and Marshall Field was best for the machine. And he reconfigured city government accordingly. After taming the city council, Daley moved to sever it from the planning process with his creation in 1956 of the Department of City Planning, an agency that would be answerable to him rather than the city council. As a sign of how Daley conceived of the role of the Department of City Planning, he appointed Ira Bach, the former executive director of the CLCC who had worked closely with Pettibone on the Lake Meadows project, as its commissioner. During his years directing the CLCC, Bach had favored relying on the private housing market to rehouse working-class blacks displaced by clearance projects—a dubious notion in Chicago's segregated housing market—and expressed annoyance about the attempts of federal housing officials to obligate the city to formulate adequate and precisely detailed relocation plans. Taking over the tasks of planning and zoning, the Department of City Planning reduced the meddlesome Chicago Plan Commission into a purely advisory body. One of Daley's first directives to the department was to instruct it to work with the CAC on a new plan for downtown. The fruit of this collaboration was the 1958 Development Plan for the Central Area of Chicago.

With a board that included the heads of Illinois Central Railroad, United Airlines, Marshall Field & Company, and some of Chicago's largest banks, it was to nobody's surprise that the CAC would promote a plan for the downtown area that emphasized increased office development, more expressways and garages, a beautified riverfront, a downtown subway system, a transportation center, near-downtown housing for fifty thousand families, and a University of Illinois campus—all that was necessary for a downtown business district oriented around management, financial services, and retailing. The development plan represented a blueprint for deindustrialization that clearly prioritized real estate values and Loop retail activities over jobs and proper housing for the city's working class. The plan, the South Side Planning Board predicted, "will tend to drive business from the area to a section of the city where it can feel more secure."[28] Those who invested in such an eventuality made spectacular profits. During the first ten months of 1959, developers bankrolled eight major office and residential building projects with an overall price tag of $130 million, and between 1958 and 1963, construction activities around the Loop amounted to an impressive $662 million.[29] One notable victim was the vibrant printing sector housed within the industrial loft buildings around Printing House Row, an area the development plan had designated for "resident reuse." Between 1960 and 1970, land values here increased by $10 per square foot, after having remained virtually unchanged during the previous decade. Such speculation paved the way for the rapid loft conversion of the 1970s, and by the mid-1980s Printing House Row no longer contained a single firm to justify its name. The impact of such processes on the city's labor market was nothing less than spectacular. Between 1972 and 1983, Chicago lost some 131,000 manufacturing jobs, roughly 34 percent of its total manufacturing employment.[30]

If Daley had never once uttered the term *neoliberalism,* his willingness to hand over the planning of the city's future development to its business community suggests that he can be considered a kind of proto-neoliberal in a moment rarely characterized as belonging to the history of the neoliberal city. In fact, historians of the "neoliberal turn" have seldom traced its origins back into the 1950s and 1960s. For David Harvey, for example, the history of neo-liberalization in the United States begins in New York in the mid-1970s, when, in the midst of a severe budget crisis, a cabal of investment bankers bailed out the city and thereby seized control of its resources and municipal institutions in order to restructure the city according to their entrepreneurial agenda. The result, according to Harvey, was that "city business was increasingly conducted behind closed doors, and the democratic and representational content of local governance diminished."[31] But who could deny that a similar result had not already been achieved in Chicago some two decades earlier?

However, Daley's embrace of the downtown agenda and his moves to create a governance framework that silenced the grassroots and shifted the planning process into corporate boardrooms were not the only dynamics that were neoliberalizing the city during the 1950s. No less important were the kinds of governance criteria that the downtown business crowd were managing to inscribe within Chicago's governing institutions—a set of notions that aligned the public interest with their interest and that viewed the primary role of city government as a mechanism to unleash the forces of private enterprise. This phenomenon was hardly unique to Chicago. The protests emerging out of Chicago's neighborhoods against the downtown agenda reflected a broader struggle taking place in municipalities across the nation over the very definition of *blight*. Emerging out of the New Deal context, blight during the 1930s was largely synonymous with *slum* and thus with unsafe and unhealthy conditions of residential living. But by the early 1940s, as state legislatures moved to give legal grounding to the activities of redevelopment agencies, the meaning of *blight* increasingly began to take on a much more pecuniary character, with key criteria related primarily to proper and productive economic use.[32] Those pushing the downtown agenda in Chicago thus evaluated the public-private partnerships that would drive the city's planning and growth in terms of revenues generated rather than in terms of social benefits created. They generally considered social costs, if they considered them at all, as nuisances to be managed.

Indeed, if, as political theorist Wendy Brown has argued, the advance of neoliberalization has increasingly placed the state "in forthright and direct service to the economy" and reduced it to "an enterprise organized by market rationality," then the decade between the launch of the Lake Meadows project and the release of the 1958 Development Plan for the Central Area of Chicago was certainly a crucial one in Chicago's move towards a neoliberal future.[33] During this moment, for example, one of the city's most critical social needs institutions, the Chicago Housing Authority, was transformed from an agency whose mission was providing decent affordable housing to low-income families to what Ferd Kramer described at the time as "the critical key to freeing land for redevelopment by private enterprise."[34] The gutting of such an important institution was accomplished so easily because public housing in Chicago had been thoroughly racialized in the decade following the end of the Second World War, when Elizabeth Wood had tried to use it as a lever of racial integration. Public housing, in the minds of most, was about black people, and, the Carey Ordinance aside, these same people watched helplessly as Boss Dawson and the rest of their political leadership failed to raise much of a stir about the use of their constituents' tax revenues to finance the displacement of working-class African Americans living in the paths of the bulldozers.

But even though Daley possessed neoliberal sensibilities, the patronage game made him something of a quasi-Keynesian in spirit. Far from being ideologically driven by the notion of cutting budgets and reducing the state, the Daley machine was all about expanding municipal government and spending as much as possible—just as long as it was the federal government and private investors who were footing the bill. To be sure, the mayor's Keynesian side was devoid of any sort of vision of trickled-down social justice (and here is where the *quasi* becomes necessary); only the machine's faithful could share in the wealth, and the others could suffer for their stupidity for all he cared. Rather than social justice, Daley gave Chicagoans city services—cleaner streets, roads without potholes, more extensive police protection, better public transportation—even if such services varied widely according to which side of the color line you lived on. And he used signs, stickers, and highly publicized campaigns to make sure that nobody overlooked all that he was doing for the city.

However, if Daley was eager to entrust an alliance of business interests and technocrats with the task of planning Chicago's future, preserving the city's racial order was a job he would often take into his own hands. In reality, his business allies and their planners were mostly after the same thing he was, even if they often articulated their goals in coded, technical terms. In a 1958 urban renewal plan spearheaded by the University of Chicago, for example, the idea of demolishing hundreds of acres of mostly lower-income black housing between 47th Street and 59th Street in Hyde Park was justified in the name of developing a "compatible neighborhood" for the university. Similarly, the CAC's vision of the Loop's future lay in promoting middle-class residential communities around it, with the term *middle-class* serving as a euphemism for *white*. By the late 1950s there was a clear consensus among Chicago's most influential developers, realtors, and planners that the creation of white middle-class communities provided the best defense against the rising tide of ghetto blight. They were acting to protect valuable institutions and the value of the real estate around them, and in doing so they were doing the mayor's bidding, for increasing real estate values meant increasing revenue for the city, and revenue, of course, translated into patronage and power for the machine. This was the beginning of a new period in the history of the American city when the capital generated from the redevelopment of urban space increasingly replaced that derived from manufacturing activities. In the case of Chicago, in particular, the presence of an administration so wedded to this progrowth ideology has caused historians to debate the extent of Mayor Daley's part in this process, with some of the more persuasive studies arguing that the mayor's role was more that of "caretaker" than "creator."[35]

Certainly, broader structural forces were also driving the move towards a redevelopment approach that ended up privileging the interests of the downtown business elite over any goals of social justice, and Chicago's land use profiteers were not much different from other big city developers throughout the country in their haste to take advantage of their privileged role in municipal governance. But one would be mistaken to overlook the enormous power that Daley wielded over Chicago's urban renewal adventure. While developers and planners often hid behind technical language to draft plans that hinged on racial exclusion, the mayor exhibited a will to act boldly and ruthlessly to preserve the city's segregated racial order. It was a will, one could argue, that developed out of Daley's years of fighting with the Hamburgers on the front lines of a guerrilla war against racial invasion—a background that distinguished him from other big city mayors of the time. This did not mean that Daley did not choose his words carefully; he understood the civil rights awakening that was in motion, and he was very adept at leaving few public traces of his segregationist ways. And yet his actions spoke much louder than his words.

A prime example was his intervention into the plan to construct the new Dan Ryan Expressway, a badly needed highway that was to serve as a southern route out of the Loop. The Dan Ryan was one among several new highways radiating out of the Loop that the mayor was going to build—a project that created a massive public works boondoggle paid for with federal dollars provided by President Eisenhower's Interstate and Defense Highway Act of

1956. Few commuters taking the Dan Ryan today think much about the two sharp turns they are forced to make after crossing the Chicago River, but they are a remnant of the race war of position that was being fought in Chicago in the 1950s. These turns were not part of the original plan for the expressway, but after Daley saw that the proposed route would cut his childhood neighborhood of Bridgeport nearly in half, he ordered the planners to shift the road so that it would run right along Wentworth Avenue—the traditional boundary between white and black Chicago on the South Side that Daley's gang had defended with their fists. But protecting his beloved Bridgeport was only part of the story. Daley's intervention into the Dan Ryan's planning came less than a month after the city council had approved the Robert Taylor Homes, and, having just authorized the placement of several thousand black families along State Street, just three blocks east of Wentworth, the mayor was now moving to make sure those families and their black neighbors would keep to their side of the color line. With seven lanes in each direction, the Dan Ryan would form an impenetrable boundary. "It was the most formidable impediment short of an actual wall," wrote journalists Adam Cohen and Elizabeth Taylor, "that the city could have built to separate the white South Side from the Black Belt."[36]

Hence, if critics and even more neutral observers of urban renewal in the 1950s and 1960s often sounded like war reporters, throwing around terms like *demolition, no man's land, razed neighborhoods,* and *displaced people,* that was precisely because urban renewal *was* a form of warfare. Few people strolling by any of the vast areas cleared out by bulldozers could resist comparisons to the bombed-out European cities of the war years. Were similar events of this scale to take place today, references to "ethnic cleansing" would no doubt be rampant. The fact is that while urban renewal made victims and displaced persons out of immigrants and poor whites along with blacks, the front lines of this war were at the edges of the ghetto, and the fact that the ghetto lay so close to valued real estate called for extraordinary actions at times. In Chicago, the battle to hold the color line required brutal tactics, and Richard J. Daley proved to be the perfect battlefield commander, unflinching in the face of the injuries he was helping to inflict. But a battlefield commander is hardly the ideal person to handle the refugee crisis caused by his actions, which Daley, the builder of the city's most notorious high-rise housing projects and the numerous new police stations that went with them, was. When the dust had cleared, the city had obliterated a number of vibrant neighborhoods and destroyed more housing units than it had created.

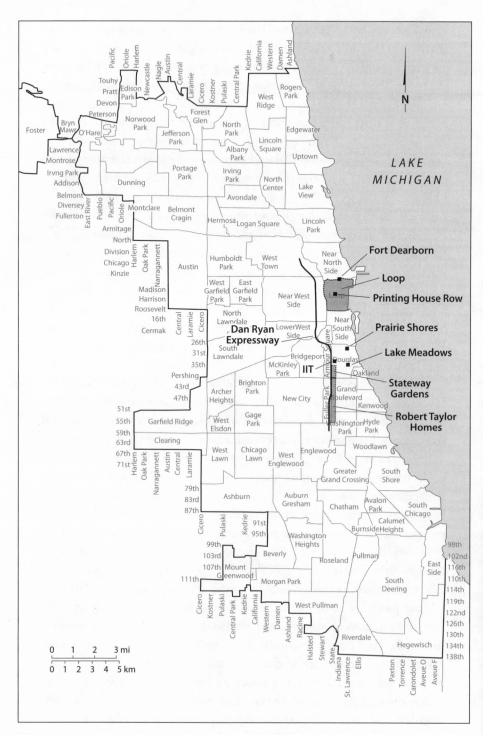

MAP 5. Downtown development and public housing in the 1950s.

The massive urban renewal projects of the 1950s and 1960s set Chicago on a whole new course. Deciding whether that course took the city towards a bright or dismal future depends on which Chicago you are talking about. The Chicago one sees when moving north on Michigan Avenue past Millennium Park and its Frank Gehry bandshell, across the river to the Magnificent Mile, swanky retail stores packed with eager shoppers as far as the eye can see, and then on to the ritzy brownstone-lined streets of the Gold Coast, Old Town, Lincoln Park, and Lakeview leads to one conclusion; an encounter with some of the grittier streets of the segregated West Side, where storefront churches and liquor stores are the most conspicuous signs of life in a landscape dominated by litter-strewn vacant lots and boarded-up buildings, leads to quite another. It is hard to imagine today that neighborhoods like North Lawndale and East Garfield Park, both of which lie just minutes west of the Loop, right off the Dwight D. Eisenhower Expressway, were thriving, middle-class districts when Mayor Daley began his first term in office. Yet that was when the fate of such neighborhoods was determined. In the late 1950s, Daley and his allies in the business community decided that these areas should lie on the other side of the barriers they were erecting to insulate the downtown business district from the rapidly expanding black ghetto. This decision was made, in fact, as these very same communities were in the process of becoming the blighted ghetto that everyone feared. In the 1950s, whites began to flee these areas as if they were escaping a flood or some other natural disaster, transforming the population from overwhelmingly white to predominantly black in the span of less than a decade. North Lawndale's demographic transformation was the most dramatic of all, shifting from 87 percent white to 91 percent black between 1950 and 1960. What was a middle-class mix of Jews, Poles, and Czechs became a lower-income black ghetto seemingly overnight, a movement of people that was quickly followed by a migration of viable businesses and decent jobs out of the area. Studying the structural conditions behind the social distress of young blacks in this area in the 1980s, then University of Chicago sociologist William Julius Wilson found, astonishingly, that while the area provided just one bank and one supermarket for a population of 66,000, it possessed no less than 99 bars and liquor stores and 48 lottery vendors.[37]

What was happening in North Lawndale resembled the situation in a number of areas south of the Loop as well, such as Woodlawn and Englewood, and the incredible rapidity with which such neighborhoods were transitioning from stable middle-class settings to depressed slums weighed heavily upon the minds of the business leaders and city officials who drafted Chicago's 1958 development plan. It weighed even more heavily upon the spirits of residents of these areas, who looked into the eyes of the young around them and saw frustration and disillusionment staring back. After happening upon a group of teens shooting pool during school hours one day in her South Side neighborhood, Pulitzer Prize–winning poet Gwendolyn Brooks reflected upon this precocious fatalism in her famed poem "We Real Cool," a short stanza that reads like an autobiographical epitaph concluding with the brutally simple words "We die soon."[38]

By 1960 African Americans constituted nearly a quarter of Chicago's population, and the migration of southern blacks into the city was showing no signs of letting up. In the face of such circumstances, downtown boosters looked to use as many physical and social barriers they could muster to insulate the central business district from the encroaching ghetto. Physical barriers included expressways, new government buildings and housing developments, and, perhaps most importantly, a new campus for the University of Illinois; social barriers would be constituted out of the new middle-class and upscale residential communities that would develop around these new structures. The objective was not only to keep the ghetto out but also to keep the exploding population of suburban commuters shopping and otherwise amusing themselves downtown. Race was never mentioned in the plan—the mayor himself ordered that it not be—but, in a city with such a negligible presence of upwardly mobile middle-class blacks, the idea of catering to the needs of middle-class residents, so often evoked in city planning discourse, was unambiguously segregationist.

This did not mean, though, that working-class whites escaped the bull-dozers unscathed. If Chicago was aspiring to be the most segregated city in the United States, the goal, at least by the early 1960s, had hardly been achieved in several areas north, northwest, and west of the Loop, where black neighborhoods lay close to communities of Puerto Ricans, Mexicans, Italians, and Poles. About seventy thousand blacks, for example, lived in the relatively integrated Near West Side neighborhood area, particularly in and around the Jane Addams Homes, Robert Brooks Homes, and Grace Abbott Homes projects, just a few blocks below Little Italy's main drag along Taylor Street. For the coalition of developers and downtown business interests behind Chicago's 1958 plan, this high crime and delinquency district, so perilously close to the Loop's lower western flank, was a force to be reckoned with. But in view of the relatively large scale required for the development of any kind of effective buffer between the gritty streets of the Near West Side and the suits and skyscrapers of the Loop, the solution to the problem would necessarily involve the destruction of the neighboring community, which consisted of a multiethnic mix of Italians, Greeks, Jews, Mexicans, blacks, and Puerto Ricans. To be sure, this neighborhood was hardly a model of ethnic pluralism—the Italians had long monopolized the area's political machinery, street gangs divided along racial and ethnic lines, many bars and restaurants were off limits to certain groups, and discriminatory practices by realtors and landlords meant that blacks and Puerto Ricans almost never lived in the same buildings as whites of European descent. And yet, if this neighborhood lacked cohesion and if its housing stock was a bit dilapidated, it was far from being a stagnant slum with little hope for the future. Storefronts were generally occupied, local associations were relatively numerous, and the area possessed a vibrant street life, replete with lemon ice vendors, Italian beef and sausage joints, and pizza parlors. In short, this area hardly fit the profile of a slum to be cleared at any cost, and yet it would be cleared anyhow, if not without a fight, so that the downtown business crowd could have its wish—a new branch of the University of Illinois to buffer the Loop against the swelling ghetto to its west.

Such circumstances explain why it would be here, between 1959 and 1962, that a scrappy movement of citizens would become the first real thorn in the side of the growth juggernaut. Some vocal resistance to urban renewal had manifested itself a year earlier, when the Hyde Park chapter of the NAACP had raised objections to the University of Chicago's plan to demolish more than 20 percent of the housing in an 855-acre stretch of land between 47th and 59th Street—a scheme that would have displaced thousands of black families, raised rents in the area, and effectively whitened the community (which is precisely what eventually happened). But the campaign had fizzled out when the Hyde Park chapter of the NAACP, under pressure from the Chicago NAACP's pro-machine leadership, pulled out.

On the Near West Side, however, the battle against urban renewal would take a very different course, with thousands of residents, mostly women, demonstrating in the streets holding signs emblazoned with such slogans as "Daley Is a Dictator."[39] The mobilization of the Near West Side's Harrison-Halsted Community Group in response to the city's intention to acquire 155 acres for the construction of a new university represented one of the first in a wave of similar protests that questioned the legitimacy of urban renewal plans that advanced the cause of downtown commercial development at the expense of working-class residents.[40] In the case of the site selection for Chicago's new campus, the subordination of neighborhood interests to those of the downtown business elite was particularly blatant because an earlier plan to locate the campus in the East Garfield Park area had elicited enthusiastic support from both university trustees and community leaders, who viewed the university as a bulwark against the area's transformation into a black ghetto. Here was an idea that seemed to fit a much more democratic conception of what should be at stake in urban renewal—democratic not only in the sense that it would have redistributed resources to the average residents of a neighborhood badly in need of help but also in its potential support for the cause of racial democracy. As the primary public university in the metropolitan Chicago area, the University of Illinois at Chicago (UIC) was destined to attract a racially diverse student body and staff, which made it the perfect cure for a community in the throes of rapid racial transition. But in the end, the pleas of Garfield Park and the protests of the Near West Side fell on deaf ears. As the Harrison-Halsted organization was filing last-ditch appeals to the city's plan, its leader, a housewife turned activist named Florence Scala, met with the mayor to ask that residents, many of them elderly, be allowed to remain in their homes until the appeals were ruled upon. Daley denied the request and began evictions the next day.

Yet if Mayor Daley ultimately brushed aside Scala's Harrison-Halsted organization without much trouble, the mobilization of Near West Side mothers embodied a new spirit of activism and a new will to frontally take on the sources of power behind the policies that were reshaping the city. In some sense, these angry moms rallying to preserve their families and their neighborhoods looked much like the mothers who had joined the ranks of racist mobs in years past for—to their minds—very similar reasons. In the protests against racial integration at both the Airport Homes and the Trumbull Homes, observers had noted with some surprise the very active participation of women, often with small children in tow. On both these occasions, much like numerous other such incidents around this time, protestors expressed not only hatred for their dark-skinned potential neighbors but also a populist-inflected anger against a city government that seemed to be conspiring against their families, their communities, and their property values. In challenging the machine's undemocratic manner of decision making, the Harrison-Halsted organization was also drawing upon another more progressive legacy of political activism that had taken root in Chicago with the pioneering efforts of community organizing virtuoso Saul Alinsky in the early 1940s.

The Harrison-Halsted organization was not the only grassroots organization challenging the Daley machine's growth agenda in this moment. About eight miles south of the UIC site, just to the east of the Dan Ryan, citizens in the black working-class area of Woodlawn were also coming together to oppose an urban renewal plan that threatened to wipe away their neighborhood to make way for another of the city's institutions of higher learning, the prestigious University of Chicago (UC). With the bulldozers plowing away in Hyde Park, the university's leadership, guided by fervent urban renewal advocate Julian Levi, devised another big urban renewal play that would further stabilize its environs by displacing lower-income black people. Initially constructed to hold the world's first Ferris wheel, a replica "street in Cairo," and a number of other carnival attractions for the 1893 World's Columbian Exposition, a one-block-wide grassy strip known as the Midway (originally called the Midway Plaisance) had been buffering the university from the ghetto streets of Woodlawn since the 1940s. But by the late 1950s complaints of muggings around the Midway were proliferating. Seeking to push the ghetto further from its pristine Gothic walls and manicured lawns, the university announced a new plan to convert a mile-long strip just south of the Midway into a new South Campus for the university. Thousands of black families would be evicted from their homes and, as usual, nobody was saying much about where they would end up, but the mayor could not have been more on board with the plan. Daley was convinced by Levi's argument that this was "the moment of truth" for the neighborhood—"the moment when assets and liabilities have to be cast up, when what is wrong and what is right has to be defined."[41] Due to Levi's lobbying efforts in Washington, moreover, Congress had passed new legislation in 1959 that gave the city enormous financial incentives for supporting such projects; if all went as planned, the university's spending on the South Campus project would generate an estimated $21 million in federal urban renewal credits that could be used anywhere within the city limits. In other words, the whole affair was looking a lot like a fait accompli.

The idea of organizing residents in Woodlawn to take on the University of Chicago and City Hall over this plan thus represented a David-versus-Goliath scenario. If no time was a good time to take on the Daley machine, now was worse than ever. By the start of 1961, the mayor seemed invincible. Not only had he won reelection two years earlier with a near-record 71 percent of the vote, but he had also played a critical role in winning the presidency for John F. Kennedy, the nation's first Catholic president, in 1960. In the tightest presidential election of the twentieth century Kennedy had carried the key swing state of Illinois by a mere 8,858 votes out of the 4,657,394 cast, but, with Daley getting out the vote in the machine's strongholds, he had amassed a 456,312-vote margin in Chicago. Allegations of improprieties and lawsuits followed, but such suspicions only boosted Daley's new political capital with the president—Daley was a kingmaker, and Kennedy would surely be taking his phone calls.

But Chicago had in its midst the kind of larger-than-life figure who relished this situation, and the story that was unraveling in Woodlawn in 1961 fit his larger agenda perfectly. Radical community organizer Saul Alinsky had already won accolades from progressives all over the country for his efforts in overcoming the intense ethnoracial conflicts that had divided residents living in the downtrodden, smelly neighborhoods around Chicago's stockyards in the early 1940s. With the moral support of the Archdiocese of Chicago in the form of renegade Bishop Bernard Sheil and the financial support of enlightened philanthropists like Marshall Field, Alinsky had led a bare-knuckle campaign to unify Poles, Lithuanians, Slovaks, Bohemians, and Mexicans within a grassroots democratic organization known as the Back of the Yards Neighborhood Council (BYNC). The immediate objectives were to fight against poor housing and health conditions, malnutrition, and juvenile delinquency, but the project fit into a much broader framework in Alinsky's eyes. "This organization," he had written during the BYNC's first days, "is founded for the purpose of uniting all of the organizations within the community . . . in order to promote the welfare of all residents . . . regardless of their race, color, or creed, so that they may all have the opportunity to find health, happiness and security through the democratic way of life."[42] Reflecting on the BYNC's impressive achievements on these fronts in the first years of its existence, the *Chicago Daily Times* referred to the organization as a "miracle of democracy," and New York's *Herald Tribune* claimed the spread of Alinsky's methods to other cities "may well mean the salvation of our way of life."[43] Moreover, these efforts at participatory democracy attracted the attention of the French Thomist philosopher Jacques Maritain, who struck up a close friendship with Alinsky during his wartime exile in the United States. It was Maritain, in fact, who convinced Alinsky to write his first book, *Reveille for Radicals,* which built upon his organizing experiences in the Back of the Yards to argue for the need for radicals throughout the country to form such "People's Organizations" and to present them with the strategies for doing so. Faced with the rise of fascism in Europe and the Nazi occupation of his country, Maritain saw Alinsky's work as a means of bringing about the democratic dream of people working out their own destiny. As Maritain argued in 1945, organizations like the BYNC could produce an "awakening to the elementary requirements of true political life," which would, in turn, lead individuals to experience "an internal moral awakening."[44]

By the late 1950s, however, such awakenings had been largely disrupted by the forces of everyday white racism. To be sure, Alinsky could take comfort in some remarkable achievements. The BYNC, for example, continued to win praise for its innovative housing revitalization program, which, among other things, fought blight by enabling potential homeowners to procure cheap credit from local lenders for rehabilitating old homes and constructing new ones on vacant lots. This was an impressive feat in view of the economic hardships facing the area after the decline of the meatpacking industry. But the racial issue threatened to undermine such successes. Even if Alinsky had managed to reduce the harassment of black packinghouse workers in the bars, stores, and parks around the stockyards, few black families from the expanding ghetto surrounding the stockyards area had been allowed to move into the community. In essence, "the democratic way of life" Alinsky had established in the Back of the Yards depended, in large part, on the exclusion of African Americans, a situation he deemed unacceptable.

Moreover, this failure was jeopardizing Alinsky's relationship with his major donor, the Archdiocese of Chicago, which had recently committed $118,000 to Alinsky's organizing network, the Industrial Areas Foundation. The archdiocese, much like its counterparts in other cities dealing with the arrival of large numbers of southern black migrants, was seeking a solution to the racial violence and white flight breaking apart its parishes. In Chicago, Catholic leaders like Cardinal Samuel Stritch (until his death in 1958) and his successor Cardinal Albert Meyer represented a more progressive wing within the Church's upper echelons that viewed a move towards interracialism as the best way of preserving endangered parishes. Yet this position often placed them at sharp odds with many of their clergymen at the parish level. In fact, what was beginning to scandalize the Church leadership, all the way up to the Vatican, was the active role that some priests were playing in rallying parishioners to collectively oppose—through at times violent forms of intimidation—the racial integration of their neighborhoods. Catholic parishes organized community life for many Chicagoans living around the color line. Young people went to parish schools and played on parish sports teams, parents participated in a range of parish social activities, and both young and old attended church on Sundays. Many parishioners envisioned the loss of their whole way of life if blacks breached the territorial boundaries of the parish. The archdiocese thus had a crisis on its hands, and it looked to a Jewish radical—the son of poor Russian immigrants who had made his way from the Jewish West Side to the University of Chicago—to find a solution.[45]

Woodlawn would not be Alinsky's first attempt at confronting the forces that were destabilizing the city's neighborhoods. In the late 1950s he had launched the Organization for a Southwest Community (OSC) on the predominantly Catholic Southwest Side, working with local pastors—Catholic and Protestant, white and black—on a number of schemes to stop the flow of white residents out of the area. Alinsky's efforts had brought about some impressive changes. The OSC confronted real estate agents that were spreading panic to make whites sell their homes below market value, forced city inspectors to prevent the illegal conversion of single-family homes, established credit schemes to enable residents to buy homes with lower down payments, and worked tirelessly on campaigns to convince homeowners they did not have to sell their homes just because blacks had moved in. It also worked as a liaison between community workers and the police to try to prevent racial violence between white and black youth gangs.[46] Alinsky even toyed with the idea of establishing quotas of black settlement to assure whites that racial integration would not necessarily mean community disintegration. Yet, despite winning over some of the most reluctant pastors to the cause, the OSC faced a relentless onslaught from the area's more reactionary elements, who labelled its staff members as "commies" and "nigger-lovers." By the end of 1960, the OSC was looking like a lost cause, and Alinsky had already begun preparing the ground for a new campaign in Woodlawn.

Part of Alinsky's genius was his ability to anticipate key shifts that were about to transform the political terrain. Back in the early 1940s, when many on the left were still rallying around the promises of organized labor after the heroic unionization struggles of the previous decade, Alinsky was already asserting that the labor movement had lost its progressive spirit, and that People's Organizations were needed to move beyond bread-and-butter issues and address the fundamental class injustices of monopoly capitalism. This view, no doubt, was informed by his understanding of how good union men could stand behind their black brothers on the assembly line and then come back home and stand behind the racist mobs attacking them in their neighborhoods. By 1947, the year the rabidly anticommunist Taft-Hartley Act effectively stripped labor unions of any strong ideological orientation, Alinsky's assessment of the labor movement looked prophetic. Now, as Alinsky began his first campaign to organize blacks, he seemed to understand that he was once again on the cutting edge of progressive politics. "The crucial history of race relations," he told his protégé Nicholas von Hoffman around this time, "would be written in the northern cities."[47] With the whole nation fixing its eyes on the civil rights battles of the South and most folks in the North thinking the "race problem" was located down there, this statement seemed somewhat far-fetched; several years later, by the mid-1960s, as ghetto riots were ripping apart the urban North and Martin Luther King was being stoned and jeered on Chicago's Southwest Side, it appeared self-evident. Yet again Alinsky understood where the next frontier of left politics lay and he rushed towards it with a great sense of urgency, the Catholic Church, ironically enough, behind him all the way.

That Alinsky was able to convince the Archdiocese of Chicago to come up with $150,000 over three years to fund his organizing efforts in a community that was just 5 percent Catholic and overwhelmingly black suggests just how dire the situation appeared in 1960. Church officials had voiced some muted opposition to the earlier Hyde Park plan from the standpoint that blacks displaced from the area around the university would end up seeking housing at the edges of nearby Catholic neighborhoods, provoking a wave of panic-selling and street-level violence that would further destabilize parishes already on the verge of collapse. The same kind of thinking was likely behind the archdiocese's sponsorship of the Woodlawn effort, though with the black population of the whole industrial Midwest on the rise, Catholic leaders were also beginning to think about some other benefits that would accrue from preventing viable middle-class black neighborhoods from turning into impoverished ghettos. The private Catholic school system, for example, was facing some potentially serious enrollment problems, and a new wave of pupils from respectable, black middle-class homes offered a potential solution. Thus, even before Alinsky had begun his work in Woodlawn, a visionary Catholic priest in the area had convinced Cardinal Meyer to force the principals of all six Catholic schools in Woodlawn to accept some black students. Questions of social justice were by no means absent from the archdiocese's agenda, but the money being put into Alinsky's hands also related to the Church's pressing need to establish a meaningful presence among the population that would dominate large sections of Chicago and the rest of the urban Midwest.

That need had already placed the archdiocese in opposition to its working-class base, and it was now on the verge of bringing it into direct conflict with City Hall and its proudly Catholic mayor, not to mention the city's most powerful institution of higher education. Alinsky had warned Meyer of this when he committed the money, but the cardinal was unflappable. However, what nobody in the archdiocese understood at the outset was just how radical things would get down in Woodlawn. To begin with, Alinsky's approach to organizing stopped short of nothing for the cause, and organizing a place like Woodlawn often required tactics that would raise eyebrows among the pious. The western part of Woodlawn was largely stable and middle class, but to the east, across Cottage Grove Avenue, was a run-down slum area filled with pot-smelling jazz clubs, gin-soaked bars, and greasy chicken shacks—a territory whose organization Alinsky conferred to his only black organizer, Bob Squires. "I knew every bookie, every whore, every policy runner, every cop, every bartender, waitress, store owner, restaurant owner," Squires later recalled. "We had chicken dinners, barbecues," Woodlawn's other organizer, Nicholas von Hoffman added; "we even had hookers running fund-raisers."[48]

Yet what turned out to be the organizing event that sparked what became a powerful grassroots movement in Woodlawn was when Alinsky's Temporary Woodlawn Organization (TWO) arranged for southern civil rights activists—Freedom Riders just out of the hospital after being brutally beaten by white mobs as they attempted to desegregate interstate bus lines—to speak to residents about the meaning of their own struggle. In a moment that would completely redefine what was going on in Woodlawn, the Freedom Riders led a jam-packed gymnasium at Woodlawn's St. Cyril's Church in a rousing version of the then little-known civil rights protest song "We Shall Overcome." Almost instantly, the residents who had joined up with TWO established a profound, emotionally charged connection to their brothers and sisters in the South. Woodlawn's precocious activists had achieved a sense of their own "historicity"—to borrow a term from sociologist Alain Touraine; they now perceived their involvement in TWO as inscribed within a much broader struggle that challenged the very foundations of their society, and the spread of this perception transformed TWO from a protest organization into a movement.[49]

Quite suddenly the campaign in Woodlawn caught fire. It began with a voter registration event that witnessed a breathtaking caravan of forty-six buses holding some 2,500 residents descending on City Hall—folks had never beheld such a thing in Chicago. Alinsky's people had, of course, notified the press in advance, and Alinsky himself had made sure that one bus packed full of nuns would be included in the procession in case the police were tempted to get rough. After that, TWO had the idea—once again inspired by the unfolding struggle to desegregate schools in the South—of capitalizing on the anger of Woodlawn residents about the atrocious condition of their schools, most of which were so overcrowded that they had instituted a double-shift system that caused horrible inconveniences for working parents. TWO activists, many of them mothers, barged into Chicago School Board meetings wearing black capes to symbolize the fact that they were mourning for the plight of their children, established "Truth Squads" to go to white schools and document with cameras the existence of empty classrooms, and carried out school boycotts that made the front pages of the Chicago dailies. Understanding how much the sight of mobs of black bodies stoked fear in middle-class whites, moreover, TWO organized protests against dishonest landlords in front of their stately homes (rather than in front of the buildings of their tenants) and threatened to bring hordes of black shoppers into downtown department stores if they did not begin hiring black employees.

Then, in July 1963, as the University of Chicago began to move forward on its South Campus plan, TWO mobilized another caravan of buses holding more than six hundred people to head down to City Hall to confront the mayor, with talented local minister and budding civil rights star Arthur Brazier as its spokesman. In this moment that predated "black power" discourse, Brazier's stern black face, which by now had appeared all over the Chicago newspapers, came to represent Woodlawn's determination to control its own community, which meant controlling the university's urban renewal project. The show of might worked. Faced with what was beginning to look like a rebellion in Woodlawn, until then one of the machine's more reliable districts, Daley conceded to TWO nearly everything it was demanding—that "no Great Wall of China" be built to restrict the access of Woodlawn residents to the Midway recreation area, that Woodlawn residents hold a majority on the citizens council that would oversee the area's redevelopment, and that TWO have the power to approve or reject the administrator named to direct any urban renewal plan. Saul Alinsky, Arthur Brazier, Nicholas von Hoffman, Bob Squires, and thousands of ordinary people in Woodlawn had won a landmark victory, effectively helping to launch a new era of civil rights struggle in Chicago.

FIVE

Civil Rights in the Multiracial City

WEST SIDE STORY

Few people felt the heat on Chicago's streets in the summer of 1963 as intensely as Frank Carney. The weather was typical for that time of year—unrelenting heat and humidity, with overnight lows that never dropped enough to cool things off before the blazing sun rose again. But for Carney, the supervisor of a regiment of youth workers on the city's Near West Side, the heat rose as much from the friction of clashing teenage bodies as it did from the pavement. Making his rounds of the neighborhood to gather information, Carney listened to stories about black and white youths throwing rocks at each other around the Holy Family Church on Roosevelt, tensions between Mexican and Italian gangs around 18th Street, Puerto Ricans and Italians scuffling at Little Italy's summer carnival, and Puerto Ricans attacking blacks around St. Jarlath's Church at the corner of Hermitage and Jackson. Speaking with the priests over at this church, Carney wondered to himself why Puerto Ricans who knew little of such racial antagonism in Puerto Rico would so readily pick it up here. After the interview, he decided to assign one of his youth workers to, as he noted in his report for the day, "cultivate a relationship with the Puerto Ricans who hang out on the corner of Jackson and Wolcott."[1] This was damage control—not nearly enough to change the situation—but it might keep a lid on things for a while.

Carney worked for the Chicago Youth Development Project (CYDP), a delinquency prevention and research program experimenting with a new approach to keeping youths out of trouble. Whereas most programs in the past had been based around the idea of drawing youths into local clubs and community associations by offering various recreational resources—sports facilities or halls for dances, for example—the CYDP was trying out a more aggressive strategy. What youth workers in previous delinquency initiatives had discovered was that the teens who were most in need of guidance kept away from the institutions that were attempting to serve them. The CYDP thus sought to move its "extension workers" out into the streets and parks to become acquainted with the more hardened youths; ideally the extension worker would be young and indigenous to the neighborhood—someone who had the kind of swagger and street cred that would enable him to win the respect of the youths he was trying to reach. However, Carney and his crew would very rapidly discover that the task of preventing juvenile delinquency was almost indistinguishable from that of managing the tense relations between the different ethnoracial groups sharing the streets, parks, snack joints, dance halls, and movie theaters of the multiethnic Near West Side.

Somewhat ironically, when the CYDP began operations out of its Near West Side "Outpost," as its staff referred to it, crowds were lining up at cinemas everywhere to see *West Side Story*—the Academy Award–winning film whose visions of white and brown street toughs pirouetting and jumping in the mean streets of a New York City slum made it the second highest grossing film of 1961. While the experience of dealing with the daily threat of homicidal violence in the real world of Chicago's Near West Side no doubt made CYDP's workers somewhat jaded about such glamorized renditions of violence, poverty, and racism, few could deny that the film's tale of hate and love between Puerto Rican and Italian youths bore some resemblance to the dramas they were encountering. Yet, if the enormous popularity of *West Side Story* had something to do with its dazzling choreography, electrifying Leonard Bernstein score, and Natalie Wood's stunning beauty, it also reflected a fascination with the nation's "troubled" younger generation. In fact, images of wild youths had filled the screens of American theaters since 1955, the year of such provocative films about delinquency as *The Blackboard Jungle* and *Rebel Without a Cause*. This was the same year in which Bill Haley and the Comets' *Rock Around the Clock* shot to the top of the pop charts, and RCA signaled rock 'n' roll's takeover of the popular music industry by signing Elvis Presley to a recording contract. The image of the dangerous teen was thereafter coupled with the menacing sounds of rock music droning in the background from some far-off jukebox or transistor radio.

Such trends had touched down in Chicago in July 1955 in the form of a media-induced panic about the subculture of deadly gang violence in the city's working-class districts. The defining event was a gang of toughs from

Bridgeport gunning down a teen in front of a snack joint, an incident that prompted the *Tribune* to run an investigative series on "youth gangs and the juvenile delinquency problem."[2] Several months later, after a fatal stabbing and vicious gang attack hit the papers in the span of three days, the *Daily News* reported that Chicago youths were increasingly falling under the influence of a "wolf-pack complex."[3] In response, the YMCA announced plans to infiltrate gangs with "secret agents," and Mayor Daley, who had expanded the ranks of the police department's juvenile bureau by nearly 50 percent since his recent election, urged stricter enforcement of the city curfew law while reassuring Chicagoans that "our young people are good."[4]

These events coincided with an epidemic of racial violence along Chicago's color line, and, while evidence of the leading role played by youths in the defense of neighborhood boundaries had been mounting since the war years, the local press marshaled the jargon of social psychology and popular beliefs about lower-class gangster pathology to explain the problem at hand. Juvenile delinquency, in this view, was merely the stuff of "grudge killings" and "gang feuds" perpetrated by young men afflicted by "gang complexes," "feelings of inadequacy," and "misguided bravado." Although James Dean's gripping portrayal of a troubled suburban teen in *Rebel* had demonstrated that delinquency could just as easily strike middle-class America, the delinquency issue in Chicago came across as it had in the past—as a manifestation of working-class life. The black press, on the other hand, had a very different perspective. When the *Chicago Defender* printed a front-page editorial entitled "Juvenile Terrorism Must Be Stopped" in the spring of 1957, its editors were referring not to gangland grudge killings but rather to a "wave of crimes and violence" that was, they claimed, "paralyzing social relations and hampering normal race relations."[5] The main incident prompting their call to Mayor Daley for a "citywide emergency committee" came in March 1957, when twelve teens belonging to a predominantly Polish Englewood-area gang known as the Rebels surrounded a seventeen-year-old African American named Alvin Palmer and one of their members landed a fatal blow to his head with a ball-peen hammer.

Palmer's slaying awakened the city to the gravity of its racial problem, and to the deep implication of its young within it. Startling to many was the utter banality of the whole affair. The Rebels were not killers—they were not even high school dropouts—but rather ordinary teens from the Back of the Yards area who had never been in any real trouble with the law before. And yet, despite the chilling senselessness of the Palmer murder, Chicago—its political leadership, its news media, and its citizens—was still far from any public reckoning of the simmering racial tensions in its streets or of any policy response to the conditions producing them. With most of the city turning its back on the interrelated problems of neighborhood transition and racial conflict, young men on both sides of the color line began taking things into their own hands and acting in ways that, in their collective and concerted nature, began to have some political implications. The summer after the Palmer murder, for example, several thousand white youths rioted in Calumet Park, not far from the Trumbull Park Homes on the city's Far South Side, in a demonstration against the use of the park by African Americans. Eyewitnesses reported rioters waving white flags or tying them to the radio antennas of their cars and singing racist chants. Police officials monitoring such events spoke of large street gangs rallying youths to the scene, and of white gangs from different parts of the city coordinating their actions.

While few at the time may have viewed such events as constituting anything resembling a social movement in the making, the task of explaining how a crowd of some seven thousand mostly young white men could have materialized so quickly moves us towards the kinds of theoretical perspectives offered by sociologists seeking to understand the structures and networks that mobilize large groups of people to action, and the cultures and identities that make individuals feel themselves to belong to the groups acting.[6] Here, in Chicago, youth gang subcultures had exploded throughout the city's working-class districts, replete with the black leather jackets, white T-shirts, slicked-back hairstyles, and spirit of nihilism that had become the signifiers of youth rebellion throughout the nation. But in the context of the city's shifting racial geography, the youthful angst and anger that circulated through these subcultures was directed as much at rival ethnoracial groups as it was at sources of adult authority. The gangs that had brought thousands of youths into Calumet Park had been organized to protect neighborhood boundaries, and they shared a common identity of whiteness that they ritualized with flags, banners, and racist songs. While no doubt unaware of it, these youths were the foot soldiers of a broader grassroots movement to defend white identity and privilege that was just starting to rise up as black demands for integration and equality were growing more vocal.

With every rock thrown and every insult shouted, the black will to resist grew stronger. The white youth movement that was crystallizing stood dialectically opposed to a black one feeding off the anger produced by the everyday indignities its members faced at the hands of white gangs and the police. Until somewhat recently, historians of the civil rights struggle in the urban

North have tended to overlook such dynamics because of a tendency to employ top-down perspectives that placed the actions of mass-based organizations and the pronouncements of great leaders at the center of the story. Even if some fine studies have contributed to changing that view over the past decade or so, most still view the history of the civil rights movement as beginning in the South in the mid-1950s under the aegis of Martin Luther King and the Southern Christian Leadership Conference (SCLC) and then moving north in the mid-1960s, where it was derailed by the allegedly destructive influences of the Black Panther Party and divisive Black Power leaders like Malcolm X, Stokely Carmichael, and H. Rap Brown.[7] Despite the best efforts of scholars, the collective memory of the civil rights struggle still thinks in tidy dualities—Martin and Malcolm, rights and power, nonviolence and violence, integration and separatism—that tend to oversimplify what was actually a very messy interplay of ideologies and organizations.

To be sure, Martin Luther King did move his people to Chicago in 1966 to take on the problem of northern de facto segregation—that much is true. But black youths in the city were hardly waiting around to be led; they were already organizing to defend their civil rights many years before their city became a key battleground in the nationwide mobilization for rights. Throughout the 1950s, groups of blacks youths—sometimes affiliated with gangs, sometimes just cliques of kids from the same block or school—frequently took on white aggressors attempting to prevent them from using parks, beaches, swimming pools, and streets. By the beginning of the next decade, such actions began to take more organized form. In July 1961, for example, some two thousand black youths participated in "wade-ins" organized by the local branch of the NAACP Youth Council at Rainbow Beach around 76th Street. Perhaps even more impressive than such demonstrations, however, were the much more frequent informal protest actions that characterized these years. A stunning example occurred in June 1962, when in the midst of a series of racist attacks against black students on the city's Near West Side, over one thousand African American students from Crane High School staged a remarkable march through the heart of Little Italy—a street normally off limits to blacks. While youth workers and scores of policemen were alerted to help prevent a riot from erupting, the youths walked in an orderly procession, school books in hands, without any sign of provocation towards the mainly white onlookers—a nonviolent demonstration that surely drew its inspiration from the courageous southern sit-ins that had recently been carried out by the young members of the Student Nonviolent

Coordinating Committee (SNCC). This event would not make it into the newspapers—the only reason we know it happened is because Frank Carney recorded it in his daily report log—but its assertion of black solidarity and resolve would certainly be remembered in the area for months to come.[8]

And yet as most of the city's youth workers knew all too well, things were not always so orderly out on Chicago's streets—far from it. Although young black Chicagoans were beginning to exhibit a growing awareness of their role in the broader struggle for civil rights, many youths nonetheless continued to live by codes of the street that were shaped by powerful structural conditions: periodic recessions that ravaged the labor market, massive urban renewal projects that tore up communities and displaced their inhabitants, and demographic forces of flight and migration that transformed the composition of neighborhoods with breathtaking rapidity. By the early 1960s, these circumstances had produced two broader interrelated trends that defined the street cultures of many working-class areas, especially those on the city's ethnoracially diverse West Side. The first was an escalation in the intensity and stakes of racial aggression that reflected both the increasing use of firearms and a dogged fixation on the presence of racial others. The second was the widespread emergence of fairly large (between fifty and one hundred members) ethnoracially defined street gangs—commonly referred to by youth workers as "fighting gangs"—whose principal function was to engage in potentially deadly combat against rival groups.

Chicago was not alone in this second development. Historians have documented similar trends in New York around the same period, showing how fighting-gang subcultures there developed within the context of deindustrialization, urban renewal, and racial marginalization. But according to one study of postwar New York, violence between opposing gangs was more about controlling territory than it was about ethnoracial conflict.[9] Certainly the protection of "turf" was also a driving force in Chicago, but here *turf* was usually a euphemism for *community*, and community was often defined in ethnoracial terms.[10] Geographers building upon the theoretical frameworks introduced by geographer Henri Lefebvre have drawn attention to the ways in which groups "produce" or define space through their everyday activities.[11] Youth gangs in Chicago had been principal actors in this process since at least the late nineteenth century, playing a key role in creating a patchwork of ethnoracial neighborhoods. And ethnoracial identities played a defining role in the politics of everyday life—in telling people who they were and where they stood—because, at least in part, these

FIGURE 10. White gang members standing watch on a Near Northwest Side corner as a youth worker looks nervously over his shoulder, ca. 1961. Courtesy of Lorine Hughes and James Short.

very identities were physically inscribed within the city's geography. Characterizing urban social movements in the 1960s and 1970s, sociologist Manuel Castells has observed that "when people find themselves unable to control the world, they simply shrink the world to the size of their community"—an idea that seems particularly well suited to understanding what fighting gangs were, on an instinctive level, trying to accomplish as they defended neighborhood boundaries amidst the racial and spatial turbulence of Chicago of this same era.[12]

But the forces that propelled young men impetuously into rumbles against enemies armed with lethal weapons like guns, knives, and bats went beyond ethnoracial pride and prejudice. The violent confrontations they provoked and joined also involved a search for respect and honor when such values were becoming harder to find in the workplace. Between 1955 and 1963, the Chicago metropolitan area lost some 131,000 jobs (or 22 percent) as the number of potential job seekers increased by some 300,000.[13] While this period is often considered to be one of national prosperity, Chicago employment figures indicate a slump-and-boom pattern of economic growth that tended to make the labor market precarious for young workers. Recessions struck the city especially hard in 1958 and 1961, causing sharp spikes in unemployment. Moreover, by the early 1960s Chicago was feeling the effects of the larger process of deindustrialization that was beginning to transform labor markets across the old steel belt of the urban Midwest.

One now needed a connection to land the kind of good union job on a factory floor that had provided the previous generation with a decent living and the sense of manliness that comes with working around heavy machines in the company of men; much more available to the generation coming of age in the 1960s were the low-wage, unskilled jobs being offered by hotels, restaurants, and retail stores. Making matters even worse, these labor market conditions coincided with massive clearance and renewal projects on the Near West and South Sides of the city to make way for the construction of giant public housing complexes, new medical facilities around the Cook County Hospital, and the new Chicago campus of the University of Illinois. Describing the Near West Side area in February 1961, Frank Carney offered a stark vision of the situation faced by area residents remaining there: "Many men are in evidence on the streets and street corners when it is warm enough. The emptiness of certain sections resulting from land clearance increases the generally depressing atmosphere." "It is impossible," he concluded, "to escape the feeling that the area is on its way out."[14]

In addition to industrial decline, labor market volatility, and the social dislocations caused by urban renewal, the forces of postwar racial migration heightened the uncertainties working-class youths felt and shaped their responses to the predicaments they faced. The ethnoracial demographics of the metropolitan United States would be transformed in the 1970s after the passage of the landmark Immigration and Nationality Act of 1965, when new family reunification entitlements would open the floodgates to immigration from Asia and Latin America. But Chicago stood apart from many other major cities in that migration flows from both the American South and Latin America had already been altering its racial geography back in the 1950s and 1960s. Constituting just over 14 percent of the city's population in 1950, the steady flow of African American migrants from the South increased their share of the population to over one quarter by 1962. Paralleling this steady black migration were the waves of Mexican and Puerto Rican immigrants in the 1950s and 1960s. After increasing some 43 percent between 1940 and 1950, the number of Mexicans in Chicago grew almost fivefold between 1950 and 1970 (from 24,000 to 108,000). In this same period, the city's overall Spanish-speaking population increased from 35,000 to 247,000, while the total population of the city dropped from 3,600,000 to 3,300,000.[15] These large migratory flows of Latin Americans complicate the idea, evoked most notably in Arnold Hirsch's classic study *Making the Second Ghetto,* that the 1950s was a moment of racial consolidation, the end of a long process of black ghettoization that reinforced the idea of a black-white binary racial order. While one could speak of a universally recognized "color line" separating black from white in previous decades, the situation had become much more complex by the early 1960s, especially on Chicago's West Side, which had become a mosaic of black, Puerto Rican, Mexican, and white neighborhoods. In this context whiteness and blackness seemed stable enough. African Americans knew they had few friends outside the boundaries of their neighborhoods, and although the Irish still muttered words like *guineas* and *greasers* when they crossed paths with Italians at late-night Polish sausage stands, by the end of the 1950s European Americans of all origins could feel secure in their identification with whiteness. The situation was quite different for Puerto Ricans and Mexicans, who were forced to navigate an unpredictable course between blackness and whiteness.

As recent newcomers to the city, Puerto Ricans, in particular, faced some of the most formidable challenges in their efforts to integrate into the city's housing and labor markets. While New York City was the primary destination for Puerto Ricans leaving the island for city life on the mainland in the 1930s and 1940s, by the early 1950s several small Puerto Rican communities were becoming visible to the north and west of the Loop, especially in Lincoln Park, Lakeview, the Near West Side, Woodlawn, and East and West Garfield Park.[16] By the early 1960s, however, the Puerto Rican population was consolidating into two main sectors of the city: the lower Lincoln Park neighborhood on the North Side and a large area to the Loop's northwest that stretched westward from the community area of West Town into the neighborhood of Humboldt Park, with its main drag along Division Street. Scholars seeking to explain the factors behind such swift internal migrations often refer to "push" and "pull" dynamics—the forces of racial discrimination that pushed migrants into certain areas and the cultural forces that pulled them towards people with whom they felt strong affinities. In reality, these two sides of the story are difficult to separate. While it is hardly surprising that Puerto Ricans arriving in Chicago in the 1950s and 1960s would gravitate towards areas where Spanish was spoken, where plantains could be easily procured to mash into the garlicky comfort food *mofongo,* and where friends and neighbors could share stories and reminiscences about the island, the flight *to* the familiar is often, in some sense, a flight *from* the unfamiliar. The development of a concentrated Puerto Rican barrio along Division Street in the mid-1960s said something about the new spirit of "Boricua" pride and solidarity circulating within the community, but it said just as much about the climate of racial hostility—the insults, the hard stares, and the acts of physical aggression—that Puerto Ricans dealt with on a daily basis. The decision of so many Puerto Ricans to opt for a home in the West Town/ Humboldt Park area during the 1960s suggested that, even after almost two decades in the city, few expected this climate to change.

Some Puerto Ricans relocating to the barrio during these years were displaced by urban renewal projects, particularly on the Near West Side, but many more were swept there by the currents of white flight, as entire neighborhoods on the West and South Sides transformed into black ghettos at breakneck speed. Puerto Ricans fled along with European Americans from their black neighbors, but they had quite different motivations. A good many Puerto Ricans, in fact, were Afro–Puerto Ricans whose ancestors had been brought to the island as slaves, and Chicagoans tended to identify them with African Americans. Reflecting on this situation, one Puerto Rican immigrant in Chicago recounted a story of being refused service at a bar on the grounds that he was black. When he responded that he was Puerto Rican, the bartender yelled back, "That's the same shit."[17] This incident was part of a larger process of "racialization" that forced Puerto Ricans to compete with blacks for housing in the lowest-rent neighborhoods and for work in the lowest-paying sectors of the labor market. Moreover, discriminatory practices by realtors and landlords relegated many of Chicago's Puerto Ricans to the fringes of black ghetto neighborhoods, where, in some cases, they very quickly found themselves serving as buffers between white and black.

Even if whites tolerated Puerto Ricans somewhat more than their black neighbors, a wave of vicious attacks against Puerto Ricans on the West Side in the mid-1950s left little doubt about which side of the color line most whites felt they belonged. In West Town, where Italian and Polish residents commonly referred to their Puerto Rican neighbors as "colored," a series of fatal arson fires struck low-rent buildings housing Puerto Ricans, and along the Near West Side's northern boundary, Italian and Mexican gangs led the resistance against Puerto Rican settlement with repeated beatings.[18] Such circumstances explain a great deal about why Puerto Ricans would close ranks by transforming a section of the famed Division Street into a vibrant barrio that would, by 1980, contain almost half the Puerto Ricans in the entire city. But Puerto Ricans moved not only to escape the antagonism of their white neighbors but also because they understood that their proximity to blacks—racially and spatially—had placed them in a precarious position.

Historian Robert Orsi's concept of a "strategy of alterity" provides an apt way to describe the Puerto Ricans' tendency to put distance between themselves and African Americans.[19] Nor was residential location the only tactic they pursued. According to a 1960 report on the city's Puerto Rican community conducted by the Chicago Commission on Human Relations (CCHR), dark-skinned Puerto Ricans adopted a range of behavioral tactics to mark themselves off from African Americans. "The dark Puerto Rican," the authors of this study concluded after hundreds of interviews, "develops unique defensive attitudes in order not to be taken for an American Negro; thus he will speak only a bare minimum of English, trying to convey the impression that he is a foreigner rather than a Negro."[20] But this tendency to use the Spanish language to distinguish themselves from blacks also pushed them closer to their Mexican neighbors, who, themselves, began to engage in their own strategies of alterity.

Mexicans, for their part, had also served as buffers between white and black in parts of the Near West Side as well as in the South Chicago community area around the Illinois Steel mill, and there is ample historical evidence that Mexican youths were active participants in the gang and mob attacks against blacks in these areas.[21] Yet Mexicans were second-class citizens in the society of whiteness, and, as such, were the targets of racial hate in the 1950s and 1960s. One poignant example of anti-Mexican aggression during these years occurred when a group of youths mistook a Native American family for Mexicans and repeatedly stoned their East Garfield

Park home, once leaving a note pinned to the door that read, "Ha Mex, get out of here"—signed by "the Whites."[22]

Such circumstances explain why, when Puerto Ricans were moving en masse into the West Town/Humboldt Park area, Mexicans were gravitating towards the Pilsen neighborhood between 18th Street and 22nd Street, which by the mid-1970s had become the unequivocal center of Chicago's Mexican community. Once again urban renewal played its part, with the construction of the new UIC campus essentially wiping out what had been a substantial and long-standing Near West Side Mexican community. For decades, Mexicans and Italians on the Near West Side had shared—if at times grudgingly—parks, streets, and community centers. Similarly, in the South Chicago area, the children of Polish and Mexican steelworkers mingled, played, flirted, and sometimes scrapped in the streets and schoolyards. Mexicans had arrived in Chicago in the early years of the twentieth century seeking work on the railroads and in the steel mills and packinghouses. Although they had earned the enmity of many when the bosses employed them as strikebreakers to break the organizing efforts of steelworkers, by the 1930s they had founded newspapers, tortilla factories, restaurants, bodegas, and Spanish-language newspapers. To be sure, they lived in ethnic enclaves—*colonias,* so to speak—but by the 1950s they were well on the path towards integration. However, the demographic shift around this time constituted a rather significant bump in the road. Established Mexicans quickly found themselves being reracialized by the arrival into their neighborhoods of both Puerto Ricans and Mexican immigrants who spoke little English and knew nothing of American ways. Although in 1957 Mexican faces were conspicuous amidst the mobs of youths rallying around white supremacy in Calumet Park, many Mexicans seemed less certain of their place in the ranks of whiteness in the following years—a situation revealed poignantly in the early 1970s when activists in Pilsen began using the term *la raza* to designate the Mexican community.

Indeed, just as a color changes in relation to which colors surround it, the racial identity of Mexicans seemed to change in a city with increasing numbers of African Americans, Puerto Ricans, and Mexicans themselves. In a matter of years, the ethnoracial identities that had taken shape along the interfaces between Puerto Rican, Mexican, black, and white would be called forth in the name of political movements demanding rights, equality, justice, and power. Those rallying behind these identities would, at times, look outside their communities to build bridges with others around universalistic notions of class justice—Chicago, after all, would be where the notion of a "rainbow coalition" was first imagined and tried. And yet, with Puerto Ricans packing into the Division Street barrio, Mexicans flowing into the *colonia* of Pilsen, the black population becoming increasingly ghettoized, and whites fleeing the city, the odds seemed long for any kind of reform coalition politics capable of unifying different ethnoracial groups behind a sense of shared class injustice. Although working-class whites, blacks, Puerto Ricans, and Mexicans would all be scarred by the injuries of class, the racially inflected circumstances of Chicago in the 1950s and 1960s would ensure that the cause would be perceived or felt in racial rather than class terms: that race would be, as Stuart Hall has written, "the modality through which class [was] lived."[23]

THE BIRMINGHAM OF THE NORTH

In late July 1963, the *Chicago Daily News* referred to the growing black mobilization for civil rights in Chicago as "a social revolution in our midst" and "a story without parallel in the history of our city."[24] Such pronouncements reflected, in part, events transpiring in the southern civil rights struggle. In particular, *Birmingham* was the word on the lips of blacks in Chicago and elsewhere that spring as the news media brought startling images of police turning attack dogs and high-pressure hoses on peacefully protesting men, women, and children, and Governor George Wallace declared he would "stand in the schoolhouse door" to prevent federally ordered integration at the University of Alabama. But Chicago's civil rights leaders were quick to bring their fight into the discursive space opened up by the situation in Birmingham, challenging the notion long held by the Daley machine and some middle-class blacks that such problems were endemic to the South and did not apply to Chicago's black community.

One could witness such processes in motion in early July, when Mayor Daley addressed NAACP delegates gathered in Chicago for their annual national convention. In classic fashion, Daley had arrived with a speech devoid of real substance, but when he proudly declared that there were "no ghettos in Chicago"—meaning that his administration did not view black neighborhoods in such negative terms—the head of the Illinois NAACP, Dr. Lucien Holman, blurted out, "We've had enough of this sort of foolishness." "Everybody knows there are ghettos here," he told a dumbfounded Daley, "and we've got more segregated schools than you've got in Alabama, Mississippi and Louisiana combined." Nor was this an isolated incident. A few days later, as Daley again addressed convention delegates and other black Chicagoans at the end of the July 4th "Emancipation Day" parade, his attempt to extend a friendly hand was once more met with derision. This time a crowd of about 150 protesters approached the platform shouting things like "Daley must go!" and "Down with ghettos!" Unable to complete his speech, Daley hurried off the stage, but his replacement, Reverend Joseph H. Jackson, minister of the South Side's 15,000-member Olivet Baptist Church, fared no better. Jackson, a political ally of Daley and an outspoken critic of the civil rights movement, was met with a chorus of jeers and boos before he even uttered a word. The situation deteriorated so much that police had to escort him out of the area amidst shouts of "Kill him!" and "Uncle Tom must go!" While Daley later dismissed the whole affair with his quip that the protest must have been set up by Republicans, it was clear that something very real was afoot in black Chicago.[25]

By the fall of 1963 the many hundreds of miles stretching between Birmingham and Chicago could no longer keep the cities apart in the minds of many black Chicagoans. Reporters for the *Chicago Defender* missed few opportunities to highlight the link, especially in their coverage of the unraveling struggle being waged by local civil rights groups and ordinary parents about the deplorable conditions of black schools throughout the city. When school superintendent Benjamin Willis stubbornly clung to the ideal of colorblindness in resisting demands for student transfers to alleviate the problem of overcrowding, the *Defender* referred to him as Chicago's own "Gov. Wallace standing in the doorway of an equal education for all Negro kids in the city."[26] Yet although the southern movement for civil rights lent African Americans in Chicago a sense of their own "historicity" as they organized to take on the status quo, such ideas were clearly secondary to the more immediate concerns—namely, the indignities and inequalities experienced by African American children in woefully inadequate schools.

Why the schools of black Chicago had fallen into such a sorry state by this time had a great deal to do with the city's inability or unwillingness to effectively accommodate the rapidly increasing black population. Problems began to arise in the 1950s when Chicago's overall population declined by almost 2 percent, but the number of African Americans living there increased by some 300,000, bringing the total to 812,637—nearly a quarter of the city's 3.5 million inhabitants. The increasing densification of black neighborhoods and the fact that newly arriving black families during these years tended to be quite a bit younger than the white families they were replacing further strained existing school facilities in black Chicago. At the Gregory School in the Garfield Park area of the West Side, for example, the student body rose from 2,115 in 1959 to 4,194 in 1961.[27] Citing the sanctity of the "neighborhood school" and the need to separate school policy decisions from city politics, Superintendent Willis responded to the problem of overcrowded black schools with an extensive double-shift program and trailer-like temporary classrooms—referred to by protesters as "Willis wagons."

While Willis had dictated that the school district not keep any "record of race, color or creed of any student or employee," several independent studies revealed the deep-rooted racial disparities that Willis's colorblind ideals and band-aid policies were attempting to cover up. A 1962 Urban League study, moreover, found that class sizes were 25 percent larger in black schools and expenditures per pupil were 33 percent lower.[28] Most African Americans, however, did not need such studies to confirm the injustices they confronted on a daily basis. Widespread disgust with the situation led first to the Chicago NAACP's Operation Transfer campaign to have black parents register their children in white schools, and after that failed, to a series of parent-led sit-ins in several black neighborhoods, including Woodlawn, where the Alinskyite TWO (The Woodlawn Organization) organized school boycotts and demonstrations against the use of mobile classrooms at a local elementary school. Capitalizing on these uprisings from below, the Chicago Urban League, TWO, the Chicago NAACP, and a number of other newly formed community groups forged an umbrella civil rights organization, the Coordinating Council of Community Organizations (CCCO), to carry on the fight.

By the summer of 1963 school protests had spread into several black communities on the South and West Sides, including the Englewood area, where parents joined activists from the Congress of Racial Equality (CORE) in a spirited effort to halt the installation of mobile classrooms. Laying their bodies down at the construction site at 73rd and Lowe, the Englewood demonstrators provoked police into hauling them off, a spectacle that offered a first glimpse of the militant Chicago movement that was beginning to come together that summer. Renowned comedian and activist Dick Gregory was among the more than one hundred protesters arrested,[29] some of whom broke with CORE's nonviolent philosophy by kicking and stoning police. The militancy that day spawned a range of grassroots civil rights organizations seeking to carry on the fight for better schools, including the Parents Council for Integrated Schools and the Chicago Area Friends of SNCC (CAFSNCC), and those familiar with the fiery rhetoric from the charismatic

Nation of Islam minister Malcolm X around this same time began to brace for some rough times ahead. So palpable was the anger of black protesters against the stonewalling tactics of Willis and the Daley machine that even after Chicagoans and the rest of the nation beheld what seemed like nonviolence's finest hour—the spectacle of more than two hundred thousand gathered in Washington that August to hear Martin Luther King evoke his "dream" of racial integration—organizer Bayard Rustin told the *Sun-Times* that the march marked not the end but rather the beginning of a campaign of "intensified nonviolence" in Chicago.[30]

While somewhat nebulous, Rustin's reference to intensified nonviolence was indicative of a tendency among civil rights leaders in this moment to stretch the concept of nonviolence to its breaking point—both rhetorically as well as through increasingly provocative protest actions. This was still some eight months prior to Malcolm X's popularization of the call to armed struggle in his famous speech "The Ballot or the Bullet," but many activists frustrated with the slow pace of progress were beginning to articulate tactics, ideas, and emotions that looked more and more like the ideological position Stokely Carmichael would describe as black power in June 1966. As historian Robert Self has argued, by paying too much attention to charismatic leaders like Malcolm X and Stokely Carmichael, most scholars have treated black power as a "distinct, even fatal, break with the civil rights movement," an interpretation that overlooks how much black power politics evolved gradually and logically out of the failure of integrationist approaches at the grassroots level.[31]

If by the hot summer of 1966 young African Americans shouting "black power" were rioting on the West Side and packing into halls to hear Stokely Carmichael speak, if they had begun to imagine complete control of their communities as the only form of political arrangement possible, that was because they had already run up against the unbending will of the machine. What was happening in 1966 was part of a longer story that had begun in 1963, just days after the March on Washington, when the Chicago Board of Education (CBOE) had raised the hopes of black Chicagoans by agreeing to an out-of-court settlement of a nearly two-year-old lawsuit filed by TWO charging racial segregation in the Chicago school system. In addition to agreeing to name a study group to come up with a racial head count and devise a plan to address racial inequalities, the CBOE had also adopted a rather symbolic transfer plan to permit a limited number of top students to switch to schools with honors programs when their own schools did not offer them. Yet even this cautious plan provoked virulent reactions in white neighborhoods around several of the schools on the transfer list, and Willis quickly caved in to this pressure, removing fifteen schools from the original list of twenty-four. When the CBOE ordered him to reinstate the schools, Willis refused, and then when faced with a court order to do so, he resigned. But in a surprising turn of events, the CBOE responded by voting not to accept his resignation, a move that received broad support among white residents on the city's Southwest Side.

This outrage—not just the CBOE's decision but also the emergence of Willis as a hero in the Bungalow Belt—provided the spark activists were looking for to consolidate the movement and take it to the citywide level. Two days later, Lawrence Landry, a University of Chicago graduate student and leader of CAFSNCC, called for a mass boycott of Chicago schools on October 22. On the day before the boycott, the CCCO published a list of thirteen demands in the *Chicago Daily News,* which included, among others, the removal of Willis as superintendent, the publication of a racial head count and inventory of classrooms, a "basic policy of integration of staff and students," the recomposition of the board of education, the publication of pupil achievement levels on standardized tests, and the request by Mayor Daley for federal emergency funds for remedial programs in all schools where test scores were revealed to be subpar.[32] Prior to the boycott, organizers were counting on the participation of between 30,000 and 75,000 students. When the day arrived, a stunning 225,000 answered the call to stay home from school.

To counter charges that students had merely taken the opportunity to skip school, boycott leaders set up "Freedom Schools" in churches and other neighborhood associations, where students sang freedom songs like "We Shall Overcome" and discussed civil rights issues. All students who attended Freedom Schools that day left with a Freedom Diploma. The lessons emphasized the contributions Africans Americans had made to the country's history, compared the boycott to the Boston Tea Party, and encouraged students to think of themselves as "writing another chapter in the freedom story." Landry had taken steps to make sure these classes were well attended, recruiting students to distribute thousands of informational leaflets in schools and churches throughout the city. The event was a smashing success. Chicago civil rights leaders had, in some sense, mobilized as many people as the March on Washington, and this success led to a series of similar boycotts in Boston, New York, Kansas City, Cleveland, Milwaukee, and other major cities. After several rounds of fruitless negotiations with school officials, the CCCO called for a second boycott on February 25, 1964, which, in comparison with the first boycott, was somewhat disappointing but nonetheless garnered the impressive participation of 175,000 students.

While generally appreciating the magnitude of what had been accomplished during these boycotts, most accounts view these events largely as failures. For one thing, the negotiations that followed the citywide boycotts failed to yield any substantial policy changes. For another, the coalitions of civil rights groups that staged these demonstrations were rife with tensions over strategy, and, in the course of the frustrating negotiations that followed them, the rifts between moderates and militants widened even further. This was particularly the case in Chicago, where within weeks after its triumphant first boycott, the CCCO was already in disarray. At the end of November it voted not to support a boycott of Loop stores called by CAFSNCC and then in mid-December Chicago CORE revealed that it would split into two chapters: a moderate West Side unit and a more militant South Side group. And yet, despite such divisions and despite the lack of tangible gains won by the anti-Willis demonstrations, a new style of organizing was in the making. An emerging class of homegrown militants had stepped onto the stage of the local civil rights struggle—people like Lawrence Landry, soon to be leader of the Chicago chapter of the ACT (not an acronym) organization, and Rose Simpson, head of the Parents Council for Integrated Schools. Defined as "militants" or "extremists" because of their anger over the intransigence of school and city officials and their belief in the need to counter it with more aggressive direct-action tactics, these new civil rights leaders also distinguished themselves by their vision of where to tap the potential lifeblood of the movement: in the streets of the poorest black neighborhoods in the city.

Activists like Landry who had taken on the machine frontally and had been mercilessly crushed, began to look to guerrilla tactics—albeit nonviolent ones if possible—to keep the struggle alive. And as with nearly all guerrilla campaigns, among the most eager recruits were the most precarious members of the community: the young and poor. In fact, black radical circles were discovering ghetto youths as the potential vanguard of black protest politics around this time. In an interview published in *Monthly Review* in May 1964, Malcolm X, whose autobiography would soon show how a young, small-time crook could grow into a heroic activist, declared that the "accent" in the struggle for black community control "is on youth . . . because the youth have less at stake in this corrupt system and therefore can look at it more objectively."[33] Several months later, Max Stanford, one of the founders of the radical Revolutionary Action Movement (RAM), published an article in which he argued that as opposed to bourgeois black youths, working-class gang youths offered a potential rich source of oppositional energy. "Gangs are the most dynamic force in the black community," he wrote. "Instead of fighting their brothers and sisters, they can be trained to fight 'Charlie.'"[34]

Landry had met with both Malcolm X and Stanford in the spring of 1964, and he had come back to Chicago with a new idea about how to fight "Charlie." While keeping up the pressure about the city's refusal to adequately address the deplorable conditions of black schools, Landry now sought to capitalize on a form of injustice that was immediately familiar to ghetto youths: the almost daily experience of being frisked, manhandled, insulted, and sometimes arrested for trumped-up infractions in their own neighborhoods. By the summer of 1964, police brutality had come to serve as a perfect focal point for the more aggressive program Landry's organization ACT was pursuing in Chicago for a number of reasons. For one thing, as groups like ACT and CORE sought to straddle the fence between a philosophy of nonviolence and increasingly popular calls for armed self-defense, direct-action protests against police brutality seemed to offer a way to strike back at the police without using violence. If being manhandled and hauled off by police did not exactly provide a triumphant sense of turning the tables on police power, at least it showed that demonstrators were not afraid to be subjected to such treatment. For another, focusing on the cops as aggressors turned the bodies and minds of youths towards the state and away from petty rivalries with other black gangs. Police brutality, especially when it involved a white officer and a black youth, was the ideal expression of the lack of control black residents possessed over their communities and their everyday lives—an issue that opened the way to a broader critique of race and state power that fit mobile classrooms and white beat cops into the same frame. Finally, this was a golden age for stirring up indignation about rough cops. Things were already bad in the late 1950s, when a federal investigation of the Chicago Police Department had led to the indictment of two West Side patrolmen for tying a black gang youth to a post and whipping him repeatedly with a belt, but the arrival of police chief Orlando Wilson in 1960 ushered in a new period of degenerating relations between the police and black communities.

An experienced police officer with a criminology degree from Berkeley, Wilson was brought in by Daley in the wake of a police corruption scandal to modernize and professionalize the Chicago Police Department. Wilson was supposed to produce immediate results to justify his ballooning budget, which led him to institute a controversial stop-and-frisk policy that had the logical effect of dramatically increasing confrontations between police and youths out on the streets in the early 1960s. Moreover, in 1961, Wilson issued the order that "gangs must be crushed" and established a Gang Intelligence Unit (GIU) to get the job done. Yet, perhaps the most important policy change Wilson ushered in was his effort to recruit black police officers. After just two years of his tenure, black officers in the Chicago Police Department had increased from 500 to 1,200, a change that was, on the surface, intended to improve relations between the CPD and black communities, but that actually may have helped facilitate the more aggressive policing tactics being employed by beat cops in black neighborhoods. Under Wilson's rule, notorious black officers like James "Gloves" Davis were given free rein on the streets in the early 1960s. Davis, who years later would participate in the raid that resulted in the death of Black Panther leader Fred Hampton, earned his nickname from his habit of wearing a black glove on his right hand when he administered beatings. In one particular incident, Davis was disciplined for pistol-whipping a youth, who was later awarded $4,800 in damages.

By the summer of 1965, Landry was rallying hundreds of youths to participate in demonstrations against police brutality in neighborhoods on the South and West Sides. In one protest in the West Garfield Park area, things got out of hand after a police officer had applied a chokehold and sprayed mace on an ACT demonstrator. Within just a few hours after the incident, some two thousand protesters carrying banners that read "Black People Must Control the Black Community" had assembled in front of the local police station to vent their anger by hurling rocks and bottles.[35] Once again police brutality against a young man had proven the spark that could ignite the kind of outrage that moved people to act with their feet. That very same day, CCCO leader Albert Raby had led an anti-Willis march of barely one hundred demonstrators from Grant Park into the South Side. Three marchers were arrested for blocking traffic at 64th Street and Cottage Grove Avenue, but, even with news of an upcoming meeting between the CCCO and Martin Luther King in the air, this march failed to muster much energy. What had happened in Garfield Park, on the other hand, had drawn thousands into the streets and had planted the seeds of rebellion.

Almost a month later, on August 13, as the fires of an uprising in the Watts area of Los Angeles—the first in a wave of large-scale civil disorders across urban America—blazed for a third day, this West Side neighborhood revealed what ACT's brand of direct-action tactics and consciousness-raising could yield. In a tragically poetic twist of fate, a speeding fire truck from a West Garfield Park fire station swerved out of control and knocked over a stop sign, which struck and killed a twenty-three-year-old African American woman. This all-white fire station in an all-black neighborhood had been the object of numerous ACT protests in the weeks leading up to the incident. The next night a youthful crowd of over three hundred battled with police, sparking off two days of rioting that caused some sixty injuries and over a hundred arrests. Occurring in the context of the devastating Watts riot, which began with a routine traffic stop gone awry and then continued with clashes between youth gangs and police, the struggle for community control between gangs and police took center stage in black Chicago. For leaders of the nonviolent movement, gangs would need to be reined in so as to allow direct-action protests to continue without the risk of urban disorders; for those who saw the need for more militant tactics, street gangs seemed like the perfect soldiers— if not leaders—in the battle for community control. Relegated to the role of community problems for many years, gangs appeared suddenly in the guises of social bandits and tragic victims of white oppression.

GANGBANGERS, MINISTERS, AND UNCLE TOMS

It was only a matter of time before gangs themselves began to recognize their part in the historic drama unfolding around them. In the wake of Chief Wilson's mandate to crush gangs in 1961, gang youths would have had difficulty envisioning themselves as anything other than social misfits, but the script began to change during the rush of civil rights activism that hit Chicago in 1963 and 1964. Reflecting on their turn towards political activism in the twilight of the age of civil rights, members of the Vice Lords, the West Side's most powerful gang during the mid-1960s, dated their awakening to the summer of 1964. The leaders of the Lords at that time—men in their twenties who had met in 1958 while serving sentences at the St. Charles reformatory (known on the streets as "Charlie Town")—claimed that what motivated their decision to "do something constructive" was a concern about the "younger dudes" in the gang. "The fellas looked around and saw how many had been killed, hurt, or sent to jail," they told their biographer, "and decided they didn't want the younger fellas coming up to go through the things they did and get bruises and wounds from gangfighting." To be sure, their idea of "doing something constructive" was by no means purely political or altruistic; influenced by increasingly fashionable black power ideas about the key role of black entrepreneurialism in uplifting African American communities, the Lords initially conceived of their turn away from gangbanging as an opportunity to "try to open some businesses." However, Watts had a dramatic impact on their thinking. "When the riots started in Watts in 1965," some Lords later claimed, "most people felt kind of proud because somebody could do something like that."[36]

Controlling a territory that extended into neighborhoods falling under ACT's influence in the summer of 1965, the Vice Lords began to see their role in the community in a somewhat different light. Although ACT's guidance made the Vice Lords a precocious case in the story of gang politicization, this story had hardly begun for them. Before any kind of political expression of black solidarity could take hold among Chicago's African American gangs, they had to relinquish, at least in part, the brutal struggle for supremacy and respect on the streets. Beginning in the spring of 1965, the city's largest and most fearsome fighting gangs—the Vice Lords and their West Side rivals the Egyptian Cobras, and the South Side's Blackstone Rangers and their enemies the Disciples—could think of little more than the imperative of expanding their ranks; their very survival depended on it. By the end of 1966, the Blackstone Rangers and Conservative Vice Lords were each rumored to command more than two thousand members, and their respective rivals—the Disciples and the Cobras—could likely count on the allegiances of between five hundred and one thousand members, which gave them just enough muscle to resist incorporation.

These gangs attained their stature through campaigns of forced recruitment, earning them the enmity of many in their communities. In areas like Woodlawn on the South Side and Lawndale on the West Side, where gangs were engaged in Darwinian fights to the finish, there were a good many youths who, whether through their own calculation or through pressure exerted by their parents, wanted little to do with this homicidal world. But gangs could not afford to lose unaffiliated youths to their rivals, and they could never be certain that a group of teens refusing to join them would not at some point run with their enemies. Under such circumstances bloodshed became commonplace in schoolyards and wherever else youths gathered, and Daley's public relations team made sure to use every gang incident to claim that gangs rather than the mayor's policies were to blame for the two main problems African Americans had been complaining about for years: defective schools and brutal cops. And although black parents generally understood that Daley was playing politics with his antigang offensive and that gangs were providing him with a convenient excuse to bring down the boot rather than investing more money, it was difficult for some to remain cool when their children's lives appeared to be at risk. In one particularly heated community meeting between parents and police in Woodlawn after the killing of a local Boy Scout, for example, an enraged crowd cheered enthusiastically when someone shouted, "To heck with getting accused of police brutality, let's use some force on these punks!"[37]

But to an increasing number of residents in certain black South and West Side neighborhoods around this time, gang members were also sons, nephews, cousins, and sometimes daughters and nieces. While the larger gangs around this time were overwhelmingly male, they usually encompassed female branches—the Vice Ladies, Cobraettes, and Rangerettes, to name some notable examples. And they almost always incorporated junior and sometimes "midget" divisions, a situation that was often disquieting for parents but that also indicated just how broadly representative of the surrounding community these organizations were. Moreover, the school protests and boycotts of previous years had revealed to numerous black Chicagoans that many of these gang youths had dropped out of school as a result of systemic discrimination; more and more residents thus began viewing the punishment they received from cops on the streets as further evidence of such problems. All these factors pushed gangs into the main currents of local politics in black Chicago, but even more important was the fact that the gospel of black power had created an enlightened and charismatic set of leaders who recognized larger goals than the mere accumulation of muscle on the streets and who viewed themselves as "organizing" or "building something" rather than just recruiting. These leaders, as in the case of the Vice Lords, tended to be older than most of the youths they were seeking to recruit—mentors, big brothers, sometimes even father figures—and they understood that rather than merely intimidate, their task was to organize, educate, and enlighten. They needed to convince youngsters to turn away from traditional conceptions of street respect and towards a mix of black power ideas related to racial unity, the struggle for civil rights, community control, and black entrepreneurialism.

A sign of the times was the adoption by both the Vice Lords and Blackstone Rangers of the term *nation* as part of their names—a potent symbol of the new meaning youths were attributing to membership in these gangs. "Their country is a Nation on no map," poet Gwendolyn Brooks mused about the Blackstone Rangers.[38] Yet nothing enhanced their credibility and status more than the close attention they were getting from top representatives of the SCLC, journalists, and even briefcase-carrying officials from Washington. Beginning in the summer of 1966, almost every major civil rights organization in Chicago wanted sit-downs with the Conservative Vice Lord and Blackstone Ranger Nations, and news of these meetings traveled fast around their neighborhoods. Already admired by teens and kids in the community for their swagger, this publicity made the leaders of these gangs into local heroes in the eyes of the younger generation. In Woodlawn, boys as young as eight and nine formed "Pee Wee Ranger" groups, and kids throughout the area could be heard shouting "Mighty, Mighty Blackstone!" in the playgrounds and schoolyards.[39] In Lawndale, young boys crowded around the Vice Lords as they stood on street corners and donned oversized berets like the ones worn by some of the Vice Lord "chiefs," as the gang's leaders were called.[40]

However, if the leaders of the nation gangs were already beginning to look like homegrown celebrities by the spring of 1966, nothing gave them that aura of greatness more than their sudden intimacy with Martin Luther King himself. With the landmark Civil Rights Act of 1964 and Voting Rights Act of 1965 now on the books, the SCLC turned to the problem of de facto segregation in the North, and, as fate and circumstance would have it, Chicago was to become the critical battleground for the SCLC's northern campaign. On some level, the choice was made by default after key black leaders in both Philadelphia and New York City had rebuked King while the CCCO under the guidance of Al Raby had been reaching out to him to help revive its flagging movement. Moreover, King had always been warmly received when he spoke in Chicago, and he felt—naively so, in hindsight—that Daley's complete dominance over the city's political machinery offered a unique opportunity. Daley's press secretary Earl Bush later observed, "King thought that if Daley would go before a microphone and say, 'Let there be no more discrimination,' there wouldn't be."[41]

King's advisers had tried to convince him that things were not going to be so easy. In one memorable meeting, according to an SCLC staffer, King kept running on about what he could do in Chicago while close advisor Bayard Rustin repeatedly interjected warnings like "You don't know what you are talking about. You don't know what Chicago is like. . . . You're going to get wiped out."[42] To be sure, Chicago posed some new problems for King. Unlike southern cities, Chicago possessed its own black political leadership in the figures of black submachine boss William Dawson and a group of black aldermen who received just enough patronage to buy out their potential opposition to Daley's brand of "plantation politics." Nicknamed the "silent six" by critics who claimed they could only speak in city council meetings when Daley's floor leader Thomas Keane allowed them to, this group consisted of William Campbell of the Twentieth Ward, Robert Miller of the Sixth Ward, William Harvey of the Second Ward, Ralph Metcalfe of the Third Ward, Claude Holman of the Fourth Ward, and Benjamin Lewis of the Twenty-Fourth Ward, until 1963, when he was found the night of his victory in the primary elections handcuffed to his desk with three bullet holes in his head and a cigarette burned down to his fingers. Lewis had apparently fallen out with both Daley and William Dawson over his piece of the ward pie; the moral of the story, one can be sure, was clear to the remaining "silent five." Daley's men in the so-called plantation wards had already been doing their very best to oppose the CCCO's school protest movement, and they would surely be no friend to King. Nobody missed the fact that King's integrationist "dreams" meant nightmares for black submachine politicians whose power depended upon the color lines keeping their constituents hemmed into their wards. And what was good for the black submachine was good for the machine itself.[43] Moreover, while King's southern campaign had received broad support from the black religious community, he could not expect the same in Chicago. By 1966 the machine's longtime ally Reverend Joseph H. Jackson was coming under increasing fire for his "Uncle Tom" opposition to the Chicago civil rights struggle, but he still presided over a South Side congregation of some 15,000 members. And then there was Nation of Islam leader Elijah Muhammad, who could claim thousands of black Muslim followers in Chicago and who, after promising his support to King, turned around and blasted him for selling blacks out to white America.

For King, all of these issues were secondary to what he considered to be the two major challenges ahead: getting average Chicagoans into the streets and keeping things calm. And he understood that Chicago's big gangs could make or break both of these objectives. Summer was approaching and after the riotous events in Watts and the near-riot in the Garfield Park area during the previous summer, the leaders of the Chicago Freedom Movement (CFM)—the name given to the new alliance between the SCLC and CCCO—feared that the outbreak of rioting might jeopardize their nonviolent campaign. Gangs, some believed, could not only be persuaded to refrain from rioting, but they might also be convinced to help keep the cool on their respective turfs. Moreover, the sheer numbers of youths loyal to these organizations made them useful to King's and Raby's objective of amassing an army of nonviolent protesters for a series of marches into Chicago's lily-white Southwest Side—even if including them came with the additional challenge of keeping them nonviolent.

Hence, in January 1966, just days after King's family had settled into their dilapidated slum apartment at 1550 South Hamlin Avenue in the West Side Lawndale neighborhood, King was already receiving a group of neighborhood kids who also happened to be Vice Lords. By spring, the campaign to win the hearts of the city's gangs to the nonviolent civil rights movement was in full swing. On May 9, key SCLC organizers James Bevel and Jesse Jackson held a "leadership conference" for over 250 Blackstone Rangers down in the Kenwood area, during which they led discussions on nonviolence after watching footage of rioting in Watts. Then, in the first week in June, the Chicago Freedom Movement's gang point men took their show to the West Side, where they organized meetings with the Vice Lords and Cobras.[44] After sending several members of the Vice Lords and Rangers on a trip to Mississippi to witness the southern civil rights campaign firsthand, the SCLC hosted over fifty gang leaders at the First Annual Gangs Convention, in the Sheraton Hotel downtown on the eve of the CFM's first big civil rights rally.[45]

The next day, however, when the Chicago Freedom Movement gathered its army at Soldier Field for a show of unity and strength, serious tensions between Chicago's black gangs and the CFM revealed themselves for all to see. Some two hundred Vice Lords, Blackstone Rangers, and Disciples occupied the center of the field, several waving a large white banner emblazoned with the words "Black Power"—a phrase that King openly detested. Then a scuffle ensued between some of the gang members and a few newsmen snapping photos, and several minutes later, without warning, the whole group abruptly marched out of the stadium. Afterwards it was learned that a gang member had apparently heard a high-ranking SCLC official insult the gangs, remarking something to the effect that they did not need them there because they would only cause trouble. Upon hearing about the affront, the leaders of the gangs gathered and decided they would all depart in unison on signal.[46] With CFM leaders predicting a crowd of 100,000, the turnout, estimated to be some 30,000, was already being spoken of as a disappointment; the gaping hole in the center of the crowd where the gangs used to be seemed to show why. For those close to the gang organizing effort, however, this incident came as no surprise. The nonviolent style of struggle had met with skepticism and outright criticism on the part of gang members from the beginning. On one occasion the Rangers ridiculed the idea of singing free-

FIGURE 11. Martin Luther King at Soldier Field, July 10, 1966. Chicago Urban League Records, CULR_04_0194_2204_4, University of Illinois at Chicago Library, Special Collections.

dom songs, causing the physically imposing SCLC organizer James Orange to shout back, "You think you're too bad to sing? Well I'm badder than all of you, so we're going to sing."[47] Perhaps most importantly, gang members could not stomach the idea of putting their necks on the line for nonviolent demonstrations whose impact was dubious at best. From the start, mainstream civil rights leaders asked them to be prepared to go to jail and take beatings for the cause, something that in the minds of many gang members offered little reward.[48] Longtime Vice Lord, Cupid, one of those who marched out of the Soldier Field rally, later explained: "I can't sing no brick off my motherfuckin' head. I just can't overcome. If a motherfucker hit you, knock that motherfucker down."[49]

The prevalence of such thinking among black gang members was revealed more strikingly just two days after the rally, when a massive rebellion shook the West Side. The explosion occurred after police responding to the theft of some ice creams from a broken-down truck at Throop and Roosevelt on the Near West Side manhandled a group of kids seeking refuge from a heat wave in the cool water of an open fire hydrant. There were several public swimming

FIGURE 12. Black power militants at Soldier Field, July 10, 1966. Photo by Ted Bell. Chicago Urban League Records, CULR_04_0092_0966_001, University of Illinois at Chicago Library, Special Collections.

pools in the vicinity, but all were off limits to blacks. Despite the efforts of community leaders from the local West Side Organization (WSO) to calm the angry crowd that began to form around the scene, things got out of control. That same night, Martin Luther King addressed a mass meeting at the nearby Shiloh Baptist Church, issuing a plea for nonviolence, but youthful members of the audience abruptly stormed back out onto the streets amidst shouts of "Black Power!" The next evening, a meeting between gang members, police officials, and civil rights leaders yielded similar results. When the SCLC's Andrew Young took the podium to make an appeal for nonviolence, a teenager in the audience immediately interrupted him, inviting his "black brothers . . . out on the street."[50] By the time a battalion of National Guardsmen had managed to restore order, the West Side riot had caused two deaths, over eighty injuries, and over $2 million in property damage. Mayor Daley exploited the situation by accusing CFM leaders of inciting violence among gangs, pointing to the SCLC's screening of films about Watts as proof. "Who makes a Molotov cocktail?" he asked at a press conference."

"Someone has to train the youngsters." Such ludicrous charges placed the CFM on the defensive, but what was perhaps even more disconcerting about the riot for civil rights leaders was that it had broken out spontaneously among youths unaffiliated with any of the city's notorious gangs. It seemed to reveal a general mood, not a plan. King and the SCLC, it appeared, were not reaching the younger generation of black Chicago.

Nonetheless, despite this falling out between the CFM and Chicago's elite gangs, when the time came to march into some of the city's most racist strongholds, at least some gang members were still willing to answer the call. The plan called for a series of "open-housing marches" into the Gage Park–Chicago Lawn–Marquette Park area of the Southwest Side, where, according to the 1960 census, only seven out of more than 100,000 residents were not white. The marches into Chicago Lawn and Gage Park got off to a bad start when angry white residents hurled rocks, bottles, and explosives at the hundreds of marchers and shouted "White Power!" and "Burn them like Jews!"[51] The SCLC-CCCO thus mustered up a larger group for the next big march through Marquette Park and Chicago Lawn on August 5. Among the group of some 1,400 gathered at the New Friendship Baptist Church before the march, according to a police operative from the Gang Intelligence Unit (GIU), more than 200 were members from a range of South and West Side gangs. Having sworn to observe the rules of nonviolent protest, they were there to serve as marshals for the march.[52] A number of Blackstone Rangers participating in the demonstration wore baseball gloves to catch bottles, bricks, and stones.[53] Despite their best efforts, however, they were no match for the thousands of whites who showered them with hate and debris, even fiercely battling with police to get at the demonstrators. Shouts of "Kill those niggers!" and "We want Martin Luther Coon" filled the air. A rock struck Martin Luther King in the head, opening a bloody gash, and he was far from the only casualty. So intense was the frenzied hatred directed at the marchers that King would tell a reporter from the *New York Times* that "the people of Mississippi ought to come to Chicago to learn how to hate."[54] Faced with this barrage of violence, much of it perpetrated by kids and young men of about their age, the gang members kept their word. As King recalled proudly after the march, "I remember walking with the Blackstone Rangers while bottles were flying from the sidelines, and I saw their noses being broken and blood flowing from their wounds; and I saw them continue and not retaliate, not one of them, with violence."[55]

In spite of this symbolic triumph, that bloody day in Marquette Park destroyed what little was left of the alliance between Chicago's gangs and the nonviolent movement. South Side gangs like the Rangers and Disciples had participated in the march because King had personally managed to patch up relations between the gangs and the CFM in the aftermath of the civil rights rally and West Side riot; on the other hand, relations were still tenuous with West Side gangs, which were noticeably absent from the event. The gangs that did come no doubt recognized the historic opportunity they had been handed. These gang youths had been marginalized in their communities, knowing only the glory of a world disparaged by many around them; the attention King and other civil rights leaders bestowed upon them inserted them into the flow of history itself. Ironically, however, this same consciousness empowered the gangs to the extent that they no longer needed the CFM, making them wary of being submerged in a movement directed by people they considered to be outsiders.

Moreover, the CFM's open-housing campaign was out of step with the main concerns of working-class black communities. No doubt touched by the explosion of black power notions of community control around this time, many young African Americans on the West Side could not understand the idea of sticking their necks out to march into a white, middle-class neighborhood where they would not want to live even if they could.[56] The Vice Lords, for example, seemed more receptive to organizations addressing immediate problems in their own neighborhood. For example, when the East Garfield Park Community Organization newsletter reported on July 25, 1966 that Vice Lord leader Duck (James) Harris had told the East Garfield Union to End Slums (EGUES) that "the Vice Lords have joined the movement to help organize the people," the "people" they were referring were their West Side neighbors.[57] While Martin Luther King had been instrumental in the founding of EGUES, the success of this organization hinged on its local focus. When EGUES brought slumlords to the negotiating table that summer, people were given the kind of direct taste of empowerment that was lacking in the CFM's nonviolent movement. Moreover, the SCLC was surely somewhat out of touch with the reality of many gang members. This much was clear early in the campaign, when, in an effort to spark the interest of the Rangers and Disciples, an SCLC representative had told a room full of high school dropouts that they would soon be able to attend classes at the prestigious Northwestern University.[58]

Any citywide movement would have run up against similar problems: these street gangs had developed within a logic that placed a premium on autonomy and the control of turf, and they followed a code by which one never allowed a physical attack to go unchallenged. Black power ideas of community control and self-defense were thus a much better fit with the consciousness and experience of gang youths. And as the SCLC-CCCO was leading hundreds of marchers into ambushes on the white Southwest Side, others in black Chicago were rallying around black power. At an ACT rally attended by West Side gang members on July 31, speakers referred to the beatings of civil rights leaders in Gage Park that day, advocating the use of violence to deal with such acts by "Whitey."[59] Just four days earlier, Stokely Carmichael, SNCC's field secretary, had spoken at a "black power rally," where he had urged blacks to regain control of their communities, even if it meant using violent means to do so. Such ideas filtered down into the ghetto through the words and deeds of a charismatic group of gang elites, whose reinterpretation of black power became the gospel of the streets.

While a good many of these leaders were men in their mid to late twenties who were able to use their street experience to garner the respect of teenagers, perhaps the most charismatic of them all was Ranger leader Jeff Fort. At just nineteen in 1966, Fort was already one of the most influential members of the Main 21 governing body that directed the many semiautonomous groups that composed the Blackstone Ranger Nation. Somewhat small in build, Fort's ability to capture the hearts and minds of teens on the South Side more than his ability to rumble elevated him through the ranks. Fort articulated a variant of black power ideology shaped to the context of black youths on the South Side. Reverend John Fry, the white pastor of the First Presbyterian Church of Woodlawn, which beginning in 1966 provided the Rangers with a space to organize and meet, captured one of Fort's greatest rhetorical moments in December 1966, during a key moment in the gang's turn to the politics of community control. After invoking images of ancient Africa and describing the advent of the slave trade, according to Fry, Fort whipped the "younger fellas" into a frenzy of excitement when he told them, "All the stud-yin' we do ain't gonna change one thing.... We gonna have our own gova-ment, the way our daddies did long time back.... They don't let us in their govament, we git our own."[60] Then, after speaking about getting roughed up by the police, Fort brought the house down when he declared, "That ain't right, cause WE'S ALL PRINCES," evoking the image of strong, beautiful princes with rings on their fingers and crowns on their heads. Fry relates that kids in Woodlawn spent the next several weeks scrawling variations of the word *prince* on walls all over the neighborhood until someone wrote out "Black P. Stone Rangers."

The leadership talents of Fort and other leaders—Lamar Bell and Eugene Hairston of the Rangers, David Barksdale and Nick Dorenzo of the Disciples, Bobby Gore and Alfonso Alford of the Vice Lords, among others—were too valuable to be overlooked. Their value derived not only from their ability to mobilize but also from their capacity to demobilize. Watts and then the outbreak of other urban disorders in the summer of 1966 had placed Great Society Democrats on the defensive. Ronald Reagan's backlash, law-and-order rhetoric had won him the 1966 gubernatorial election in California, and, with a presidential election looming in 1968, Johnson administration officials were looking for damage control as the summer of 1967 approached. Moreover, the Great Society project of investing in lower-income urban communities through its Community Action Program (CAP) and of ensuring the "maximum feasible participation" of local residents in the Community Action Agencies that administered CAP initiatives was put on the line with each outbreak of violence; to successfully incorporate gangs into the legitimate local power structure would have yielded the kind of win-win situation that political strategists dream of. And that gangs were useful to Washington suddenly made them useful to local organizations seeking federal funds for community development programs as well. As it hashed out the details of a youth program with officials from the Office of Economic Opportunity (OEO) in early 1967, TWO found Washington totally unbending on one major point: that the gangs themselves be given a substantial role. The result several months later was a $957,000 OEO grant for a revolutionary youth project that used the Woodlawn area's existing gang structure—the Blackstone Rangers and the Devil's Disciples—as the basis of a program to provide remedial education, recreation, vocational training, and job placement services to youths.[61] Inspired by their South Side rivals, the Vice Lords, with the help of a researcher who had met the gang's leaders when conducting a study on gang youths for the President's Council on Youth Opportunity, registered as a corporation in September 1967 and by early in 1968 had obtained a $15,000 grant from the Rockefeller Foundation and a matching grant from a private sector urban renewal campaign called Operation Bootstrap.[62]

The subsequent story of the involvement of the Rangers, Disciples, and Vice Lords in youth services and community improvement projects is as complicated as it is controversial. Several scholars and activists, most of them somehow associated firsthand with the organizations, have attempted to sort out some of the issues surrounding the scandals and legal proceedings that led to the termination of funding to such programs. For gang sympathizers, the argument is generally that Mayor Daley used the Gang Intelligence Unit (GIU) to actively harass, infiltrate, and subvert the gangs involved in these programs because their apparent success compromised his power on the black South and West Sides—areas of the city that had traditionally delivered a strong vote for the Daley machine.[63] Those who have made this argument have pointed to the fact that the reinforcement and reconfiguration of the GIU in 1967 occurred not coincidentally while TWO, the Rangers, and the Disciples awaited notification of funding from the OEO. They have also referred to the antimachine activities of the Rangers and Vice Lords, including their support of antimachine aldermanic candidates and their active promotion of a 1967 mayoral election boycott that dramatically reduced Daley's vote totals in what had been known as the plantation wards. They could have made even stronger cases had they had the benefit of seeing the GIU's files, which, as a result of a 1981 court decision in an ACLU lawsuit against the city's political surveillance activities, are now accessible to researchers. Despite the destruction of a large part of the files, what is left provides compelling evidence of the role the GIU played in sabotaging these programs. Readily apparent from a survey of the files is the fact that infiltrators were not only on hand to observe and dig up dirt; they were also there to plant the seeds of destruction in the already fragile alliances of gangs, community organizations, and black power groups.

Of particular interest to GIU operatives were any signs of cooperation between the different super gangs, as well as the developing links between the gangs and a range of black power groups—ACT, RAM, SNCC, the Afro-American Student Association, the Deacons of Defense, and later the Black Panthers. The surveillance, to be sure, went way beyond sniffing out possible criminal enterprises, and, even if the threat of a plot to foment urban disorders was somewhat credible during these years, the large body of GIU reports detailing the political and social activities of the Rangers, Disciples, and Vice Lords can hardly be explained away in this manner—as the city attempted to do. As John Hall Fish has argued, most observers, including a team of independent evaluators appointed by the federal government to examine the OEO grant program, tended to agree with the view of TWO's spokesman, the Reverend Arthur Brazier, that "The project was killed because the political establishment could not tolerate an independent community organization such as TWO receiving federal funds that were not controlled by the Establishment itself."[64] According to Fish, there were just too many interests in Chicago—the mayor, the police, and even the social services community—invested in the failure of TWO's program.[65]

While the most cynical detractors would paint their "positive results" as merely attempts to create smokescreens to distract from ongoing criminal activities, the list of achievements that can be credited to the Rangers and Disciples in a relatively short span of time is impressive: they staged a successful musical production, *Opportunity Please Knock,* under the direction of jazz pianist Oscar Brown, that played to sold-out audiences for six weekends; they helped calm near-riots in their territories on a number of occasions, including most notably after the assassination of Martin Luther King, when rioting broke out in many other areas of the city; the two gangs managed a truce during their involvement in the TWO program, and, according to the TWO evaluators, played a key role in significantly reducing the violent crime rate in the Third Police District; and their vocational training efforts led to the placement of between 83 and 107 of 634 trainees in jobs—results that the TWO evaluators qualified as equal to or better than most programs of this kind in the city.[66] Across town, in the Lawndale area, with much less funding but nearly as much police malevolence, the Vice Lords boasted an even more remarkable set of accomplishments, including a highly successful neighborhood clean-up campaign ("Where there was glass there will be grass"); a vocational training program funded by the Coalition for Youth Action and the U.S. Department of Labor; a Tenants' Rights Action Group that blocked forty-three evictions and relocated thirty-two families; two youth centers and an employment agency; an African heritage shop and snack restaurant; and an art gallery (Art and Soul). As in Woodlawn, moreover, such activities corresponded with a drop in violent crime.

The memory of these striking accomplishments has been deeply tarnished by the Daley administration, which declared its "war on gangs" in 1969, and by the sensationalistic media coverage of the hearings of Senator John McClellan's Permanent Subcommittee on Investigations of the Committee on Government Operations in the spring of 1968. Seeking to expose the shortcomings of the program, McClellan charged, among other things, that the OEO grant was a "payoff" for peace in black neighborhoods, that the Rangers had demanded kickbacks from trainees (who were paid a modest weekly stipend to attend job training programs), and that the gangs had used the program as a front to continue their criminal activities, which included murder, robbery, rape and extortion. Such allegations, while substantiated by the subcommittee's very dubious star witness, George "Watusi" Rose, a former Ranger warlord turned police informant, were enough for the OEO to pull the plug on the Youth Manpower Project. For their part, the Vice Lords continued on after 1968, but their image also suffered enormously from scores of highly publicized legal problems, including the controversial murder conviction of their talented leader Bobby Gore, who maintained his innocence until his death from lung disease in 2013. Typical of the ways in which the local press, especially the notoriously pro-Daley *Tribune,* exploited the legal problems of the Vice Lords and Rangers to arouse outrage about their community activities was the June 21, 1969 edition of the *Chicago Tribune,* which included a story about Vice Lord murder convictions beside another entitled "U.S. and Private Grants Pay Big Dividends to Street Gangs."[67]

However, while Gore may have been innocent of the charges against him, he candidly admitted that many in his gang were not as able as he was to trade their gangbanging ways for the roles of students, activists, or youth workers. In an interview conducted for a History Channel documentary on the Vice Lords, Gore argued that the GIU's success in sabotaging the efforts of the Vice Lords was made possible by the fact that members of his gang were continuing to commit murders, robberies, and rapes. "We screwed ourselves somewhat," Gore claimed, "because had it not been for guys doing dumb shit—excuse the expression—they wouldn't have had the excuse to pounce on us as they did."[68] Such observations suggest that the search for manhood and respect continued to push youths affiliated with these gangs into violent acts, and the gang leadership structure was not nearly strong enough to do much about it, especially as the GIU continued to target the most powerful gang leaders in a concerted strategy to cut off the heads of the nation gangs.

Yet black power consciousness, even if not for the overly simplistic reasons often offered by its detractors, also played a disruptive role in the struggle of ordinary black Chicagoans for their fair share of the pie. "Black Power," as Robert Self has argued, "was an extraordinarily plastic concept."[69] In the hands of people like Jeff Fort, it largely represented the continuation of the same logic of turf control that had organized black street gangs since the 1950s. The tragic irony of this form of black power ideology centered on local control is that while it directed street gangs onto the route of protest politics, it also limited how far down this road they could go. In particular, the idea of community control in the minds of street gangs already fixated on the boundaries of their turf made the project of uniting gangs a virtual impossibility. When Jeff Fort electrified his audience of young Rangers by telling them, "We gonna have our own govament," few in the room imagined the "we" to include Disciples or anyone else in the city, for that matter. Then there were problems arising from the emphasis that the black power movement placed on *power*. After being courted by nationally recognized civil rights leaders and then—in the cases of the Rangers, Vice Lords, and Disciples—being given the chance to earn income and praise by working to improve their communities, the thousands of youths affiliated with these gangs expected a piece of the action and there was not nearly enough to go around.

The story of how Chicago's most powerful street gangs joined the civil rights struggle but ultimately became disenchanted with its goals and methods of protest tells us a great deal about why King's northern campaign ultimately ended in failure. But there were other reasons why the open-housing "summit negotiation" that would take place between King and Daley in August 1966 would be referred to by West Side community leader Chester Robinson as "empty promises" and by Chicago CORE's Robert Lucas as "nothing but another promise on a piece of paper." Perhaps most importantly, the broader ideological context surrounding the Chicago civil rights theater had changed dramatically. When the struggle for civil rights arrived at the doorstep of white northerners, the well of northern sympathy that had seemed so deep in 1964 suddenly ran dry—a phenomenon reflected in polls after the open-housing marches revealing that whites blamed the marchers rather than the counterprotesters for the violence that ensued. Yet Daley had played an active part in bringing this about, a situation that King might have prevented had he not greatly underestimated Daley's ability as a political strategist as well as his will to resist the kinds of demands the CFM was making.

From the moment King had begun planning a Chicago campaign, Daley was devising ways to defuse the situation by creating shadow programs to counter every CFM initiative. "All of us, like Dr. King, are trying to eliminate slums," he announced early in January 1966, and from that point onward the objective in City Hall was not to take on the CFM but to give the impression of supporting its goals—albeit in a colorblind way that was nebulous enough not to stir up any anger in the Bungalow Belt. When, for example, Seventeenth Ward alderman Charles Chew, the first black city council member to oppose the machine, joined liberal lakefront alderman Leon Despres in sponsoring an open-housing bill, Daley made sure his own "fair housing" bill was passed in its place. And when the SCLC launched Operation Breadbasket, which, under the aggressive leadership of Jesse Jackson, put pressure on white-owned businesses in and around black neighborhoods to hire more African Americans, Daley responded with his own symbolic rendition of a minority recruitment program, which he ironically called Operation Lite (an acronym for "Leaders Information on Training and Employment"). Moreover, although King was an expert in exploiting the brutal police repression directed at civil rights protesters in the South, he would not have this same tactical resource in Chicago, where the police—under the direct orders of Daley—would not only not be fighting with black demonstrators, but they would actually be protecting them from unruly white mobs. Finally, King had never really had to deal with the stubborn opposition of local black leaders in the South as he did in Chicago. Indeed, Daley's ability to throw counterpunches depended on the political and religious support he could marshal in black Chicago. From the moment Lyndon B. Johnson's War on Poverty had through its concept of "maximum feasible participation" mandated that local people be put in charge of the antipoverty programs it was financing, Daley had been using all of his resources in black Chicago to make sure that those local people were his local people. And as soon as it became clear that King was not going to change the rules of the game—far from it—even some of the black leaders he thought he could count on turned against him. Alderman Charles Chew, for example, flipped from strident supporter of the CFM to active critic and was often seen driving around his ward in a white Rolls Royce in the months after the movement had died.[70]

Yet all these things aside, the fact is that King did not arrive at the summit negotiating table holding the bargaining chip he needed—a credible threat to paralyze the city with massive demonstrations—because he had failed to capture the hearts and minds of gang leaders and other young blacks who appeared ready to rise up. To be sure, Daley did not like what was transpiring in Chicago's Bungalow Belt, where, in the mayoral election of 1963, his support had dipped below 50 percent. The spectacle of angry white crowds numbering in the several thousands clashing with his policemen in the streets of their own neighborhoods to get at civil rights demonstrators was problematic to say the least. A radical spirit of antistatism was taking root on the Southwest Side—so radical, in fact, that the American Nazi Party had moved into the area and had begun organizing demonstrations that were attracting thousands of local youths. And yet, as bad as this situation looked, Daley knew that King could not muster the kind of mass participation he needed to really disrupt the city, and he knew that the support King had was waning rather than waxing in the wake of the open-housing marches. His intelligence operatives were reporting that even among the black Chicagoans who were least sympathetic to the machine and its black puppets, the nonviolent movement was failing to pick up momentum. And this allowed him to control the dialogue of the open-housing summit from the start, diverting blame from his administration onto the real estate industry, and then conceding only his word on a set of principles: the city would do more to enforce the open-housing ordinance of 1963, the CHA would try to build public housing units outside of the ghetto and limit buildings to eight stories, the Department of Urban Renewal would try to make sure that lending practices were not promoting segregation, the Chicago Real Estate Board would try harder to make realtors obey the law. These were mostly promises that would never really be kept, a fact that escaped much of the rank and file of the white anti-integration movement. Indeed, whites joined their black counterparts in complaining that Daley had sold them out—a sign of just how polarized the city had become in the twilight of the civil rights era.[71]

SIX

Violence in the Global City

1968

To many, the roughly two-year period that began with the toxic mob violence surrounding the open-housing marches and ended with the apocalyptic chaos that reigned in the streets outside the Democratic National Convention of 1968 represented the darkest of moments in Chicago's history. This was a time when American Nazi Party leader George Lincoln Rockwell, regaled in black boots and swastikas, drew admiring crowds of thousands of angry white youths in Marquette Park, when black youths on the West Side took to the streets in a riotous outburst of destruction while Mayor Daley told his police force to "shoot to kill . . . arsonists," and when Chicago cops savagely beat antiwar demonstrators during the convention, the air thick with choking teargas, nightsticks cracking bones, shouting "kill, kill, kill!" It was a time when political organizations with names like Black Panthers and Young Lords patrolled the streets in color-coded berets and military attire, when ordinary African Americans wore dashikis and spoke in a stylized language about "brothers" and "sisters," and when college students kept their hair long and greasy, dressed like factory workers or flower children, and swore they really believed the revolution was imminent. It was a time when politics was in the streets, out there for all to see. Many cities had some of this, but Chicago seemed to have it all, which, was, in part, why in 1968 Norman Mailer called it "perhaps . . . the last of the great American cities." In one of the more enigmatic passages of his masterful reportage for *Harper's* on the tumultuous events surrounding the Democratic National Convention in Chicago that year, Mailer mused that "only a great city provides honest spectacle, for that is the salvation of the schizophrenic soul."[1]

While what Mailer meant by "honest spectacle" is a matter of interpretation, he may have been contrasting Chicago's gritty, kick-in-the-face feel—captured by the blood and entrails on the floors of its packinghouses, its beefy mayor, and the very visceral beatings its police force doled out to those who dared oppose him—to the kind of dishonest spectacle being disseminated by the advertising industry that, according to Guy Debord's 1967 work *The Society of the Spectacle,* was distancing people from both "authentic" experience as well as from each other. It was not difficult to see traces of Debord's ideas on a range of student groups in the United States, who, after years of seemingly futile marches and administration-building occupations against the war in Vietnam, began to look for new methods of combat that would change the traditional endgame of student demonstrators being beaten and hauled away by the authorities. The Youth International Party (commonly referred to as the "Yippies") was the most high profile group to use alternative forms of association and expression—high-concept pranks and political theater in the streets—to bring about transformations in consciousness, but the whole countercultural student movement was moving in this direction. This was not a movement that had a great deal to do with Chicago, whose campuses never mustered very much newsworthy activism during the peak years of student protest. The national bases of the student movement and of the counterculture were San Francisco, Berkeley, New York City, and a number of midwestern college towns like Ann Arbor, Michigan, and Madison, Wisconsin. A courageous group of politicos belonging to the Students for a Democratic Society (SDS) had launched the ambitious Economic Research and Action Project (ERAP) in 1964 to organize working-class whites in Chicago's tough Uptown neighborhood on the North Side, but the initiative had largely failed to accomplish anything lasting. The "city of the big shoulders" was resistant to the idealism and countercultural ethos of the student movement. The only university of any national prestige within the city limits had been building walls around itself for years, and the city's tradition of radicalism was far too rooted in a jaded, Old Left, workerist vision of the world to embrace the faddish existential critique circulating around the New Left in the late 1960s. And then there was the racial divide, which, as black power consciousness surged throughout the ghetto, was becoming wider by the minute. With good reason the white middle-class SDS cadres that started Chicago's ERAP chose to knock on doors in largely white Uptown rather than in the heart of the West Side ghetto.

During the high times of student activism and countercultural expression in the United States, Chicago's hippie scene thus remained undeniably sedate, confined to a relatively small area around Wells Street in the Near North Side's Old Town neighborhood, where white flight and undesirable commercial activity had made the area affordable for self-styled bohemian types. Here one could find a handful of head shops, record stores, coffee shops, and music clubs. The national chain Crate and Barrel got its start in this neighborhood around this time, finding an eager clientele of the young and disenchanted in need of affordable home furnishings imported from Asia, India, and Europe to help them escape the painful conformity of American consumer culture. The community had its own newspaper, *The Chicago Seed,* and with the national headquarters of SDS just down in the Loop, there was enough activity to keep things interesting. Yet Chicago was clearly a "second city" for hipsters; considering the city's size and its role as the only real refuge for alienated youths and other social misfits looking to escape the suffocating conformity of the suburbs and small towns of Ohio, Indiana, Michigan, and Wisconsin, it is surprising how few folk artists, writers, and activists hailing from Chicago made it on to the national stage. Chicago's Old Town hippie scene was swallowed into the mainstream before it produced anything to distinguish it. "The aimless young and suburbanites swarm all over this area on weekends," Studs Terkel mused in his 1967 book *Division Street America.* "It has the spirit of a twentieth century carnival, in which commerce overwhelms joy."[2] So it is ironic that beginning in the spring of 1968, Chicago became the destination for a generation of young radicals looking to vent their anger against the Democratic Party's stubborn support of the escalating war in Vietnam, and it is even more ironic that beginning in the fall of 1968, when the show was over, it became the place that Americans would associate with the countercultural excesses and confrontational street politics of the antiwar movement and of the New Left in general.

Chicago was an unwilling participant in the denouement of the student movement, so unwilling that its very reluctance became a crucial element in the plot—a primary reason why the antiwar protest around the Democratic National Convention would be interpreted across the nation as the last gasp of a dying movement. One can argue with good reason that the poor turnout of protesters doomed the Chicago campaign of 1968. The National Mobilization Committee to End the War (MOBE), under the leadership of movement veterans Rennie Davis and Dave Dellinger, had begun organizing for the convention more than ten months in advance, but they made a fatal error of expecting crowds in the hundreds of thousands, numbers that would have overwhelmed the capacity of the forces of order to contain them. Their optimism was based largely on the idea that students from all over the country would pour into Chicago for the event, but they did not come, in part, because of all the rumors about the dangerous tactics being plotted on both sides of the barricades and, in part, because of the multiple fractures dividing the New Left. Their hopes for a momentous show of opposition were also based on the expectation that a number of local protest organizations in black, brown, and white Chicago would participate, as well as students from the city's colleges and high schools. Regardless of how many itinerant hippies and politicos from out of state made it to town, a city of Chicago's size could have very well gone it alone.

But when nominating night finally arrived and the movement got a chance to see itself massed in Grant Park awaiting orders to march (in which direction was a matter of debate), it was clear that the movement culture that the Yippies and MOBE had attempted to put together had failed to take root in the city of Chicago. In the days leading up to the convention the Yippies had planned a series of stunts and events to try to attract fellow travelers. They had arrived with a two-hundred-pound pig named Pigassus, whom they declared their Democratic candidate for president, they had circulated ribald rumors about dosing the city's water supply with psychedelic drugs and recruiting an elite corps of handsome Yippies to seduce the wives and daughters of delegates, and they had planned a "Festival of Life" in Lincoln Park featuring the hip Detroit rock band MC5. Yet, even if the media found the Yippies good for a few laughs and, more importantly, for selling some newspapers, the whole campaign failed to spark much interest in the city. Almost one year later to the day, Woodstock would attract some five hundred thousand participants; most estimates of the crowd at the Festival of Life top out at five thousand. To be sure, many probably stayed away from the Sunday afternoon event because of the wild happenings of the previous nights, when the police had used teargas and brutal tactics to clear Lincoln Park of the thousands intending to use it as a campground. Organizers had been requesting that the city waive its park curfew rules in order to give protesters a place to sleep, but the city had equivocated and ultimately rejected the demand. The request of the Festival of Life organizers to drive a flatbed truck into Lincoln Park to provide a stage for MC5 had also been refused, so only a few hundred in the audience could actually see the band, a situation that led to pushing and flaring tempers. When the organizers attempted to bring the truck in anyway and were stopped by the police, things got out of hand once again, with police roughing up protesters and the concert being called off. That night the police again used teargas and nightsticks to clear the park, with protesters retreating to the surrounding streets to wreak havoc.[3]

Many of the more than ten thousand demonstrators who made it to the afternoon rally in Grant Park before the big night of the convention, when the Democratic Party was going to name Hubert Humphrey as its nominee, were ex-combatants in this war of attrition. The crowd gathered here for what would turn out to be the final act of the drama included the more clean-cut supporters of the antiwar candidacy of Minnesota senator Eugene McCarthy; the scraggly, sleep-deprived, nervy demonstrators from the Lincoln Park battles; and a host of high-profile intellectuals such as Norman Mailer, William Burroughs, and Jean Genet. Organizers had been warned that they would not be allowed to get anywhere near the convention proceedings at the International Amphitheater, but police intelligence had learned they were going to try to make the four-mile walk anyway. Bolstered by some seven thousand National Guard troops outfitted with bayonet-tipped rifles, teargas masks, and jeeps mounted with barbed wire, the Chicago police once again moved into the crowd with astonishing speed and indiscriminate violence.

What happened next inarguably played a role in changing the course of American political history—if not in the way one might have expected at the time. After the police had dispersed the crowd in Grant Park, a mass of marchers re-formed at the intersection of Balbo and Michigan Avenue, where the media had set up fixed cameras to cover the delegates leaving their rooms at the Conrad Hilton, and that was when things got utterly and spectacularly ugly. A battalion of blue-helmeted policemen rushed the crowd, and, with no attempt whatsoever to distinguish marchers from onlookers, began smashing heads, legs, and arms. Piecing together a number of eyewitness accounts, historian David Farber describes the scene:

> A police lieutenant sprayed Mace indiscriminately at a crowd watching the street battle. Policemen pushed a small group of bystanders and peaceful protesters through a large plate glass window and then attacked the bleeding and dazed victims as they lay among the glass shards. Policemen on three-wheeled motorcycles, one of them screaming, "Wahoo!" ran people over.[4]

In the midst of it all, people started spontaneously chanting, "The whole world is watching, the whole world is watching." The delegates, however, did not have to wait the ninety minutes it took for the networks to get the images to television screens. Looking down from his fourth floor room at the Hilton, Senator George McGovern reportedly said, "Do you see what those sons of bitches are doing to those kids down there?" Hours later, on the floor of the amphitheater, Connecticut senator Abraham Ribicoff—a man not known for his oratorical flair—used his nominating speech for McGovern to tell the convention, "With George McGovern we wouldn't have Gestapo tactics on the streets of Chicago," a comment that provoked Daley and his entourage to jump up and shout a litany of barroom obscenities whose precise nature is still a matter of debate. Some close by heard the mayor shout, "Fuck you, you Jew-son-of-a-bitch!"—a phrase that lip-readers not employed by the city of Chicago would corroborate from the video footage of the outburst. Supporters of the mayor would later claim he had called Ribicoff a "faker," and during the convention's final session the next day, he made sure to pack the amphitheater with machine diehards who were under orders to engage in rousing choruses of "We love Daley!" Yet, regardless of what the mayor had said and regardless of the show of adoration he had orchestrated, Daley appeared to be in trouble for the second time in five months.

Chicago had been awarded the convention, in part, because it had avoided civil unrest in the summer of 1967, when ghetto riots raged in Detroit and New Haven, and Daley was seen as a man who knew how to keep a lid on things. Even before the summer, Daley's tough talk on law and order, combined with the growing realization among working-class whites that the open-housing summit had hardly been the catastrophe that hardcore anti-integrationists had feared, had enabled Daley to regain the support he had lost in the Bungalow Belt. The result was a staggering landslide election victory that saw the Boss capturing 73 percent of the overall vote and winning all fifty wards. Even after breaking the promises he had made to Martin Luther King at the summit, Daley had run strongly in the black wards, taking nearly 84 percent of the vote. The mayor seemed as invincible as ever, and many within Chicago's homegrown left began half-seriously pondering guerrilla warfare. But then in April, he seemed to have gone much too far in his reaction to widespread rioting on the West Side following King's assassination in Memphis. After Daley had publicly excoriated new police chief James Conlisk for not following his orders to "shoot to kill any arsonist . . . and to maim or cripple anyone looting," even some of the machine's loyal black aldermen spoke up against him. After the damage and destruction of the West Side riot—hundreds of arrests, eleven deaths, thousands homeless, and a twenty-eight-block stretch of West Madison Street burned—it was no longer possible to claim that Daley had managed to appease black Chicago with all the money he had garnered from the federal government's antipoverty programs.

The riot, which broke out after mobs of West Side youths went from high school to high school, disrupting classes and urging students out into the streets, revealed the extent to which the West Side's working-class black population remained marginalized in Daley's Chicago despite the best intentions of the federal government's antipoverty programs. As was the case for the federal urban renewal initiatives of the 1950s, the Daley machine had hijacked Chicago's Community Action Program, which had expressly sought to bypass the machine by placing power directly into the hands of neighborhood people. Black communities would have their representatives—this, after all, was the law—but Daley made sure that their representatives would also be *his* representatives and that the black man running the whole program, Deton Brooks, was *his* black man. By the spring of 1967, the situation prompted a Senate subcommittee to look into allegations that Daley was not adhering to the spirit of "maximum feasible participation" required by the law. But Senator Robert Kennedy, who needed Daley's support for his presidential run (which would end nearly three weeks later with Kennedy's assassination), defended the mayor, and when riots ripped through New Haven and Detroit, it was hard to find a liberal in Washington who would support the idea of empowering black ghetto communities.

By the summer of 1967, newspapers across the country were painting every urban disorder and inflammatory black power declaration as evidence of the failure of Lyndon B. Johnson's War on Poverty and of liberalism in general, and few pursued this polemic more zealously than Chicago's own *Tribune*. If, as longtime Chicago columnist Mike Royko has argued, Daley was a "white backlash" mayor years before anyone was even using the term, one could extend this observation to the city that had been so strongly supporting him since his election in 1955.[5] Not only was Chicago—despite its Democratic stripes—in the vanguard of the white backlash that decisively captured the American political center with the election of Richard Nixon to the presidency in 1968, but the city itself had been the main stage upon which the dramas of a surging reactionary populism played out before the eyes of the nation. It was in Chicago that the black struggle for equality ran into the wall of white homeowners' rights during the open-housing marches; it was in Chicago that one of the cornerstones of Great Society liberalism—the idea of redistributing power and resources downward to neighborhood people—was shattered by a Senate subcommittee investigating a gang called the Blackstone Rangers for embezzling federal funds; it was in Chicago that a big-city mayor told his police force to shoot at young African Americans for stealing transistor radios and to, in effect, summarily execute black arson suspects; and it was in Chicago that battalions of policemen bloodied and teargassed college kids, hippies, members of the media, and innocent bystanders in front of the whole world. And finally, it was in Chicago that most of the mainstream media and much of the population cheered the mayor's campaign of repression every step of the way as liberals throughout the nation were decrying it.

What was transpiring in Chicago defined the "backlash" structure of feeling and reactionary politics that had taken hold of the country's political culture by the middle of 1967—and has not relinquished its hold ever since. Students of modern American conservatism usually recognize Richard Nixon as one of the key architects of this approach. Campaigning and taking office in a media landscape inhabited by gun-toting black militants, flag-burning student radicals, bra-burning feminists, and liberated gays and drag queens, Nixon claimed to be representing the "silent majority" of law-abiding, hard-working, patriotic Americans whose voices had been silenced by the clamor of extremists in the streets. And yet, if Nixon was the one who actually uttered the clever phrases, he was taking his cues from Richard J. Daley, who, unlike Nixon, was a pure product of the backlash. Although some scholars have highlighted the importance of hard-core segregationist George Wallace's surprising northern success in the 1968 presidential primaries, which, according to some, pushed Nixon and the Republican Party towards a "southern strategy" that instrumentalized racial fears in order to lock up the South forever, it was Daley—a northern Democrat no less—who revealed the prescription for backlash politics moving forward.[6] It was Daley who showed the nation that most people were bothered more by rioting blacks than by mayors who ordered the use of lethal force to stop them, and that most people identified less with antiwar protesters than with the police officers beating them with nightsticks.[7] Facing reporters after the convention, the straight-talking mayor defended the actions of his police force by referring to the nasty insults that antiwar protesters hurled at the police and repeatedly asking, "What would you do?" When anyone mentioned antiwar protesters, he would ask, "What programs do they have?" and "What do they want?" Apparently these were the same questions being posed by Americans throughout the nation. Thus, it was of little consequence that Daley was being slammed in the *New York Times, Washington Post,* and many other major northern media outlets and that a federally appointed investigative commission had blamed the police for the violence at the convention and condemned the mayor for failing to reprimand them for it. By the fall of 1969, a *Newsweek* poll revealed that 84 percent of white Americans felt that college demonstrators were being treated "too leniently" and that 85 percent felt the same way about black militants.[8] Daley had played a critical role in making the backlash, and now it was making him a living legend.

BESIEGED BY LAW AND ORDER

Chicago was thus a backlash city years before anything looking like a backlash had spread across the metropolitan United States, and as such, it was an ill-fated choice for the site of the antiwar movement's last-ditch battle. The massive scale of Chicago's black migration in the 1940s and 1950s, which multiplied the color lines throughout the city as well as the border wars that came with them, certainly played an important role in producing its precocious backlash sensibilities. Such circumstances shaped a siege mentality long before the urban disorders of the mid-1960s had normalized such thinking in most major U.S. cities, and this siege mentality created an insatiable appetite for law enforcement and an aversion to the intervention of city government in any other form, especially when it involved constructing housing for the poor. Even the illustrious University of Chicago, which, with so many liberal luminaries on its faculty, could have provided a powerful bulwark against backlash sensibilities, was seized by this siege mentality. This had not always been the case. The Chicago School sociologists were great leaders in the intellectual struggle against racial theories of black and immigrant poverty, and their students were not infrequently arrested while defending blacks against white mobs in the 1940s and 1950s. Saul Alinsky had enrolled here to study archaeology, but after spending four years in UC classrooms had set out to work as a community organizer. But by the time he returned to Hyde Park in 1960 to defend the people of neighboring Woodlawn, his alma mater had switched sides, aligning its interests with the machine and thus becoming his adversary in his fight for social and racial justice.

UC chancellor Lawrence Kimpton, the man who had helped broker the real estate coup that was going to cleanse the area around the university of thousands of working-class black families, it is worth mentioning, was the same man who in 1958 had intervened to forbid the university's literary magazine, the *Chicago Review,* from publishing the works of Beat writers Jack Kerouac and William S. Burroughs. Kimpton was thus clearly not keen on allowing the University of Chicago to reach out into the community and become a refuge from the backlash, a role that universities at times played in the late 1950s and 1960s. But more important to Chicago becoming a full-fledged backlash city so early was the enormous power of the Daley machine in co-opting, blackmailing, infiltrating, and, when all else failed, using brute force to stifle any potential opposition to itself and its friends.

In fact, such practices predated Daley's rule. Starting in the 1930s, Chicago had become, according to historian Frank Donner, "the national capital of police repression," a reputation that went far beyond the Memorial Day Massacre of 1937.[9] The Chicago Police Department's "Red Squad" was rooting out Communists and using intimidation to subvert the labor movement throughout the 1930s and 1940s. The success of these efforts was revealed by the quiescence of its unions during World War II, while its industrial neighbor to the east, Detroit, was a hotbed of labor agitation. But the Red Squad's purview did not stop at the workplace; it extended into any organization engaged in political activities. "Issues dealing with labor, wages, working hours, strikes, peace, housing, education, social welfare, race, religion, disarmament, and anti-militarization" were all named as sources of "subversive activities" by the Chicago Red Squad's Lieutenant Frank J. Heimoski in a 1963 speech to a national conference of police intelligence officers: in other words, in the paranoid minds of Red Squad operatives, the very idea of politics itself, when practiced by any person or group not directly affiliated with the Cook County Democratic Party, was subversive. "Our job," Heimoski claimed, "is to detect these elements and their contemplated activity and alert proper authorities."[10]

The extent to which the Chicago Police Department's Red Squad stunted the development of a political and cultural infrastructure for the left in Chicago is one of the great untold stories of American history.[11] In 1960, the CPD claimed it had intelligence files on 117,000 local individuals and some 14,000 organizations nationwide, most of which were destroyed after the ACLU and a coalition of local civic and religious groups called the Alliance to End Repression successfully sued it for improper police intelligence activities. The files that survived the shredder, however, were more than adequate to show how aggressively the Red Squad had, through illegal surveillance and infiltration, intimidated, harassed, and effectively neutralized individuals and organizations who dared to think outside the box.

Police repression was thus a deeply established tradition in Chicago in the decades leading up to the great progressive challenges of the mid-1960s. It was as emblematic of the city as the ivy-covered red brick walls at Wrigley Field. But the technologies and methods of repression reached a whole other level during the turbulent years of the 1960s. To keep up with the rapid proliferation of political organizations and individuals with multiple and shifting affiliations, the Red Squad developed a sophisticated cross-referencing system, and to counter the development of threats to the machine's power in black, Puerto Rican, and Mexican neighborhoods, it deployed an army of undercover operatives to engage not only in intelligence activities but also in tactics of subversion. The Red Squad left no stone unturned. There were even files on the Old Town School of Folk Music, and no small number of them either. But the organizations and activists that drew the most attention were those attempting to build bridges across different racial and ethnic communities, and it is here one can detect a mayoral agenda at work, even if the purge of documents would later cover most of its traces.

The Daley machine had expertly maintained its power by the logic of divide and rule and by fostering a political culture in which the substance of politics consisted of nonideological, neighborhood-level struggles for shares of the patronage pie. Anything that disrupted this status quo set off alarms in City Hall. In the months leading up to the convention, for example, the buzz in the Red Squad revolved around the potential for a concerted mobilization of white middle-class students and ghetto blacks affiliated with super-gangs and black power groups—a potential demonstration of cross-class and cross-racial solidarity that would have created a public relations problem for Mayor Daley. Thus, this was not only a matter of police intelligence but also one of special operations. Chicago cops blanketed the South and West Sides, rounding up gang leaders and warning them that they would pay a heavy price if they were seen anywhere near the convention, while undercover police operatives sought to stir up racial tensions among both black power and student groups.

In fact, the Red Squad was a big beneficiary of the FBI's COINTELPRO (Counterintelligence Program), a holdover from the rabid anticommunism of the 1950s, which funneled manpower and resources to a number of major American cities to help them "expose, disrupt, misdirect, discredit, or otherwise neutralize" organizations and individuals viewed as posing threats to national security and social order. FBI chief J. Edgar Hoover believed, much like Mayor Daley, that black power organizations were worthy of special attention, and nothing caused more consternation at FBI headquarters than when these organizations began to make alliances and develop their bases.

A bright, charismatic young activist named Fred Hampton, who assumed the leadership of the Illinois Black Panther Party in 1968, found himself on COINTELPRO's high priority list around this time. An electric orator and savvy organizer, Chairman Fred, as he was known within his entourage, had shown great promise by organizing hundreds of youths in the suburbs west of Chicago for the NAACP Youth Council. "Power to the people" was his mantra, and as chairman of the Illinois Panthers, the twenty-one-year-old Hampton quickly began forging ties with activists all over the city—black, white, and Puerto Rican. Hampton was in good company for this mission; among the leaders of the Illinois Panthers were several talented activists, including future congressman (and eventual mayoral candidate) Bobby Rush—the man who in 2000 would deal Barack Obama his first crushing defeat in electoral politics.

Understanding that it suited the needs of the Daley machine to keep these communities in competition with each other for resources and power, Hampton set out in 1969 to assemble what he referred to as a "rainbow coalition" that brought his Illinois Panthers together with the Young Lords, a Puerto Rican street gang turned political organization under the talented leadership of Jose "Cha-Cha" Jimenez, and the Young Patriots, an enlightened group of working-class whites, many of whom were the children of poor white southern migrants who had settled in a "hillbilly" section of the North Side Uptown neighborhood in the 1940s and 1950s. Their fathers had rallied around Confederate flags, but the radical currents circulating through Chicago in the 1960s had turned these Dixie sons into homegrown Marxists with a nuanced understanding of the interplay between race and class. These were strange and exciting times indeed. And even though the Black Panthers, Young Lords and Young Patriots were, as young idealists who dared to extend their hands across racial lines, not exactly mainstream elements of their communities, this astonishing alignment held the potential of establishing a power bloc that brought together the West Side ghetto, the Near North Side Puerto Rican barrios of Humboldt Park and Lincoln Park, and the white working-class sections of the Far North Side neighborhoods of Uptown, Edgewater, and Rogers Park.

Moreover, in an effort to get Chicago's more powerful gangs behind his project to bring power to the people, Hampton had also made inroads into the Main 21, the governing body of the federation of neighborhood gangs that now constituted the mighty Blackstone Rangers. Many felt that if the Rangers committed to the cause, the Vice Lords and the Gangster Disciples would follow, and the Daley administration would be facing the dreaded alliance of supergangs it had feared for years. However, there was still some work to be done to make this happen. Hampton's efforts to recruit in Ranger territory, for example, had led to the shooting of a Panther and then a heated sit-down with Jeff Fort that culminated in threats and dozens of Rangers bursting into the room with guns drawn. The Rangers were hostile to any encroachments on their turf, no matter how well intentioned. Yet, Hampton was allowed to walk out of that meeting alive, and in view of his charisma and determination, nobody in City Hall could be too sure that he would not be able to eventually get through to the headstrong Ranger leadership. The twenty-one-year-old was, by the winter of 1969, quite likely the most dangerous man in Chicago, and, as such, he was high up on J. Edgar Hoover's list of the most dangerous men in the United States.

One can only imagine Hampton's frustration about the refusal of his brothers in the Blackstone Rangers to accept that neither he nor their brothers in the Disciples were the enemies. What he would never know was how much this mistrust had been sown by informants and infiltrators executing stratagems issued from high up in the FBI. The Rangers were trying to make the transition to community activists, but they still lived by the codes of the streets, which told them that threats to their power and pride could not go unanswered, so it was all too easy for FBI and Red Squad operatives to plant all kinds of rumors and doubts in their heads. The Panthers, on the other hand, were less susceptible to such subterfuges; this was a group that furnished new members with readings lists that included works by Karl Marx and Frantz Fanon. Stopping Fred Hampton would thus require a different approach.

On December 4, 1969, just before dawn, a heavily armed tactical police unit under the command of state's attorney Edward Hanrahan burst into the West Side apartment at 2337 W. Monroe Street where Hampton and several other Panthers lived and shot nearly one hundred rounds of ammunition at anything that moved or slept. When the guns fell silent, Hampton and fellow Panther Mark Clark lay dead and four other Panthers had been seriously wounded. Hampton had been shot in the head at point-blank range, execution style, while lying in his bed. Ostensibly, the police were there to serve a search warrant for illegal weapons and things got out of hand, but evidence from the crime scene strongly suggested political assassination. The police displayed a pile of weapons that "six or seven" Panthers had allegedly used to fire upon them, a story that was predictably backed up by the city's investigation into the affair. But a federal grand jury report of the incident issued on May 15, 1970, was highly critical of the city's handling of the autopsies and ballistics tests, which, according to the report, concealed the fact that Hampton was shot in the head from above and falsified indisputable ballistics evidence indicating that only one of ninety-nine bullets fired could not be traced to police guns. The report revealed hardly anything that most people did not already know, except perhaps the extent to which the machine and its hired guns could act with nearly complete impunity. As is often the case in Chicago, utter desperation about the impossibility of challenging the political order gave way to jaded sarcasm. Mike Royko, who, incidentally, was highly critical of the Black Panthers, remarked in response to Hanrahan's comment that the police had "miraculously" escaped injury: "Indeed it does appear that miracles occurred. The Panthers' bullets must have dissolved in the air before they hit anybody or anything. Either that or the Panthers were shooting in the wrong direction—namely, at themselves."[12]

Further evidence would surface in the years to come that would shed even more light on the circumstances surrounding Hampton's murder, and, for that matter, on the entire history of the left during its most pivotal moment on the political stage in the last half century. Reflections on why the left seemed to implode in 1968, opening the door for the backlash and the subsequent conservative ascendency, have often emphasized ideological factors that weakened its ability to rally people behind a coherent, unifying reform project. Some, like SDS veteran and prominent sociologist Todd Gitlin, point to the New Left's abandonment of liberalism and move to extremist politics, while other, more reactionary commentators lampoon those who took to the streets in the 1960s as drugged-out or sex-crazed freaks driven by senseless rebellion against a society that had bestowed them with only privileges and opportunities. Another interpretation points to the idea that the rise of identity politics in the 1960s splintered the left into so many solipsistic, identity-centered projects—black power, brown power, yellow power, feminism, radical feminism, gay liberation, and so on—that it was no longer possible to build a progressive movement out of blocs that had everything to gain by joining forces against the status quo.[13]

Largely understated in most accounts of the period is the story of state-sponsored repression, which, as Fred Hampton's murder so dramatically demonstrates, took the form of a highly sophisticated campaign of countersubversion involving the close cooperation of federal and local authorities. Chicago cops harbored a palpable hostility towards the Black Panthers because they had the audacity to stand up to them with lethal weapons, and Mayor Daley wanted them neutralized because of their increasingly popular breakfast programs in black Chicago and their coalition-building efforts throughout the city. But the FBI, which, like the Daley administration, wanted to see the gangs continue to kill each other off, played a critical role in ultimately closing the book on Hampton and the Illinois Panthers. It was the FBI that had enlisted the help of William O'Neal, who would become the Brutus in Fred Hampton's very brief life on the political stage. A car thief by trade who had agreed to go undercover to avoid doing hard time, O'Neal was so convincing that by the winter of 1969 he was put in charge of security for the Illinois Panthers. In a story fit for Hollywood, O'Neal furnished the Chicago police with a detailed floor plan of Hampton's apartment and, according to his own confession, slipped a powerful barbiturate into Hampton's drinks the night before the raid, which explains why the normally agile Hampton never made it out of his bed during the raid. O'Neal, who was just eighteen at the time, spent the next sixteen years in a witness protection program, after which he returned to Chicago a broken man. In 1990, in the early hours of Martin Luther King Day, O'Neal's gut-wrenching guilt finally pushed him to try to make his peace with Chairman Fred by fatally throwing himself in front of a speeding car on the Eisenhower Expressway.[14]

While there is no easy way to assess the impact that such countersubversive activities had on left politics nationwide, the evidence from Chicago is weighty, to say the least. Hampton's murder was certainly the most dramatic case—the incident that threatened to blow the cover off the whole enterprise—but one would be hard-pressed to find a single political figure on Chicago's left who did not feel the heat in the 1960s and early 1970s. In Chicago things got hot enough to, as COINTELPRO intended, "expose, disrupt, misdirect, discredit, or otherwise neutralize" a generation of activists, some of whom would spend significant stretches of their adult lives in prison on charges they denied.

Although we will never know the entire truth, in view of what Fred Hampton's murder reveals about the lengths authorities were willing to go in their war on the left, it hardly takes a stretch of imagination to believe that the FBI and CPD would also engage in an extensive campaign of frame-ups. Just three weeks before the raid on the Panthers, Vice Lord leader Bobby Gore, one of the main forces behind the West Side gang's successful turn towards political activism, was arrested for a murder he maintained he did not commit until his death. Around the same time, State's Attorney Hanrahan managed to get eighteen indictments (mostly for easily contrived charges of assault and battery on police) against Jose Jimenez in the span of six weeks, an offensive that coincided with Jimenez's efforts to mobilize the Young Lords against a redevelopment plan in Lincoln Park that would lead to the displacement of thousands of Puerto Rican residents. This was just a few months after United Methodist pastor Bruce Johnson, who had provided his Chicago People's Church as headquarters for the Young Lords, was viciously stabbed to death in his Lincoln Park home, along with his wife, Eugenia. While we may never know for sure the truth about such incidents, the pieces seem to fit together.

What the events of 1969 tell us is that the brutality on display at the Democratic Convention of 1968 was far from aberrant; it was merely the spectacular coming out of a systematic, banal campaign of political violence that flourished in the new national backlash context of the post-1968 years. Some New Left leaders felt there was something to be gained by flushing this campaign out into the open for "the whole world" to see, but such hopes ultimately proved to be naive. Writing in this precise moment and with the unfolding Chicago story clearly in mind, Hannah Arendt warned in her essay *On Violence* that "since violence always needs justification, an escalation of the violence in the streets may bring about a truly racist ideology to justify it, in which case violence and riots may disappear from the streets and be transformed into the invisible terror of a police state."[15] This was a fairly accurate way to view what was transpiring in Chicago in the years following the convention. The war on gangs declared by Mayor Daley and his right-hand man Edward Hanrahan in the spring of 1969 represented the symbiotic relationship of racist ideology and police terror; notions of ghetto pathology reduced all black youths to gang members, and, as gang members, youths were thus deemed incapable of anything other than criminal behavior. This, in turn, justified a merciless wave of police repression, which, by criminalizing youths out on the streets, served to prove the point that all black youths were gang members, and all gang members were criminals. Once again, Chicago was in the vanguard of conservative politics. A little more than a decade later, during the Reagan administration's War on Drugs in the 1980s, municipalities all over the country would seize upon similar antigang offensives to garner federal funds for law enforcement initiatives and win over fearful white middle-class voters.[16]

And yet, if, as Arendt claimed, violence could destroy power, it was not the only force that was working against the project of bringing "power to the people." The politics of identity was a double-edged sword for the left in Chicago during this epic moment. The streets of Chicago had always been the place where young people constructed, performed, and negotiated the meanings of their ethnoracial identities—in rituals of play, war, and love. By the early 1960s, during the high times of the civil rights era, these rituals took on an increasingly perceptible political feeling; with the circulation of images and ideas associated with the struggles of young blacks in the South against forms of discrimination at school and in venues of commercial leisure, kids out on the streets defending their communities and their identities began to see themselves as political actors, and local activists were quick to capitalize on this to get people out on the streets for more formal political causes. British sociologist Paul Gilroy has observed that "collective identities spoken through race, community and locality are, for all their spontaneity, powerful means to co-ordinate actions and create solidarity," a situation that by the end of the 1960s had made a fetish out of the city's most visible ethnoracial identities.[17]

The spiritual, magical, salvational qualities that people attributed to these identities pushed them out into the streets of their neighborhoods to engage in quasi-religious rituals of collective identification. Some of the violence between gangs around this time loosely fit this description, as did uprisings against the police, which could very quickly turn into potent demonstrations of community pride. Such was the case in the often overlooked Division Street riot of 1966, when the Puerto Rican barrio in Humboldt Park seemed to discover its sense of self as it took to the streets to protest the shooting of a local youth by a policeman breaking up a gang scuffle. This was also the context that gave rise to the Chicago mural movement of the early 1970s, which saw aspiring artists in black, Puerto Rican, and Mexican neighborhoods spreading broad swaths of bright paint over drab walls to create vivid scenes of everyday community life that harkened back to the New Deal–era murals influenced by artists like Diego Rivera. The "community mural movement," as it has come to be known, began in black Chicago before spreading, most notably, to New York, Boston, Philadelphia, and St. Louis. More precisely, it began with the once-famous *Wall of Respect* at 43rd and Langley—a kind of Mount Rushmore for the black community—which included the faces of fifty black writers, musicians, and political leaders considered to be "black heroes" by the fifteen artists who collaborated on the project in 1967. The *Wall* became a meeting point for black power groups around Bronzeville

FIGURE 13. The *Wall of Respect,* a site of frequent gatherings in the late 1960s. Photo by Robert Abbott Sengstacke/Getty Images.

and the Kenwood area, a place where the maxims of Malcolm X, Stokely Carmichael, and H. Rap Brown (Martin Luther King's head was conspicuously absent from the *Wall*) filled the air, and in 1969 and 1970 it became a rallying point for its own sake, as the city devised an urban renewal plan that would have meant the *Wall*'s demolition. However, a fire "of unknown origins" rather than urban renewal ultimately destroyed the *Wall* in 1971, but by then one of its principal creators, William Walker, had already met up with some Mexican and Puerto Rican artists to form the Chicago Mural Group—a multiracial artists' cooperative that sought to fill the urban landscape with billboards displaying racial and social injustices. One of the finest examples of the work of this collective can be seen today in the Humboldt Park barrio at the corner of LeMoyne and Rockwell, where the mural *Breaking the Chains* covers the wall of a well-maintained three-story walk-up. Painted by John Pitman Weber, the cofounder of the Chicago Mural Group, along with a number of Puerto Rican residents, the mural depicts black, brown, and white hands breaking chains and reaching up towards the sun.[18]

Such celebrations of "race, community, and locality" created a level of political engagement by average people in the context of everyday Chicago life that has seldom been approached since. The problem was that the same primordial feelings and attachments that were bringing people into the streets were also reinforcing a logic of ethnoracial difference—a logic already embedded within the city's ethnoracially balkanized social geography—that made the development of powerful multiracial coalitions a nearly impossible task. We will never know how far Chairman Fred might have taken his "rainbow coalition," but we do know that, at the time of his death, such notions had, for the most part, captured the hearts and souls of only an avant garde fringe of activists, intellectuals, and artists.

More indicative of how the politics of identity were shaping grassroots progressive politics was the student-led movement to reform Chicago's high schools in the spring and fall of 1968—one of the last of its kind. Emerging out of a general spirit of discontent about the sorry state of Chicago schools, this movement took the form of two parallel mobilizations—one black and one Latino—from its very first days. Ironically, black and Latino students had similar complaints regarding the Chicago Board of Education's refusal to recognize their cultural identity and deal with the discrimination they faced at the hands of white teachers, but their demands never found common ground. White students, for their part, largely stood on the sidelines when they were not actively, even violently, opposing their fellow black and Latino students. Harrison High School, located on the 2800 block of West 24th Street, along the border between the Near West Side and Pilsen, found itself in the center of things. The leaders of the militant black student organization the New Breed went to school at Harrison, and the most vocal Latino student organization, a group that included famed Mexican activist Rudy Lozano, also formed here. Harrison was one of the only schools in the city at that time that mixed significant numbers of blacks, Mexicans, Puerto Ricans, and whites, so it could have served as a stunning example of multiracial cooperation against the machine. But this was not to be. The black, Mexican, Puerto Rican, and white youths at Harrison had come of age in a street culture that placed a premium on defending the boundaries of their ethnoracial communities against outsiders, and these were hard habits to break. If, as Paul Ricoeur has argued, the self achieves identity and meaning through the detour to the other, this process, in the context of Chicago politics, had profound consequences.[19] In the end, the board of education had little reason not to accede to the demands of black and Latino students. And so Superintendent James Redmond pledged to extend the half-year Afro-American history course being offered in thirty-six high schools to a whole year, to purchase new textbooks that "placed greater emphasis upon contributions of minority groups," to pursue "efforts to achieve a racial integration of staff throughout the system," and to strengthen relations with parent-teacher associations (PTAs) and student groups.[20] The board of education had effectively institutionalized the politics of identity, a situation that did little to change the fact that public school system was heading straight towards the precipice.

SKYSCRAPERS, MARTINIS, AND FUTURES

Perhaps more than any other city in the United States, Chicago today captures with stark clarity the contrast between wealth and poverty that American-style free-market capitalism produced over the long twentieth century. What makes the contrast so vivid is the spatial proximity of the two extremes. In Chicago, one can board an "L" train amidst the bustling avenues of the Loop business district, where an army of chauffeurs, valets, and doormen expedite business executives through revolving doors and into the stately lobbies of firms whose influence stretches to the far corners of the world, and minutes later be looking down from the elevated tracks at the hyperghetto, where boarded-up buildings and litter-strewn vacant lots mark a land that time forgot. In some areas of the hyperghetto, the main signs of commercial activity are hand-to-hand drug sales, liquor stores, and currency exchanges, where those without proper bank accounts can cash checks and pay utility bills for hefty fees. The only institutions competing with liquor stores for customers in need of medicine for the soul are storefront churches.

Chicago's hyperghettos are not so different from ghetto neighborhoods in several of the other midwestern and northeastern cities that constitute the American Rust Belt, and they share a similar story of deindustrialization, urban decline, and white flight that reshaped much of the northern metropolitan United States in the postwar decades. Between 1947 and 1982, factory employment in Chicago dropped from 688,000 to 277,000 (59 percent), a period that also witnessed a steep decline in Chicago's middle- and upper-income families—some 30 percent between 1960 and 1980 alone. Between 1947 and 1982, moreover, Chicago's share of the metropolitan-area job market dropped from 70.6 percent to 34.2 percent, a decrease that was due not only to the loss of manufacturing work in the city but also to the increase in suburban jobs.[21] Some of these losses of jobs and people were associated with the suburbanization that the federal government had set in motion with a range of subsidies that placed homeownership within the reach of middle-class citizens who before the 1940s could have only dreamed of owning a home. The 1960s and 1970s saw the rapid growth of Chicago's posh North Shore railroad suburbs, as well as the suburbs of DuPage County to the west.

Already by the end of the 1960s, these processes had caused Chicago to lose its place as "second city" to Los Angeles, whose population of 10 million easily surpassed the 7.8 million inhabitants in its greater metropolitan area. But things took a sharp turn for the worse in the 1970s, when, within a national economy disrupted by oil shocks and stagflation, Chicago lost 15 percent of its retail stores, 25 percent of its factories, and 14 percent of its jobs, and Chicago families experienced a 10 percent fall in real income.[22] Moreover, while per capita personal income did still rise during this decade, the pace lagged behind Detroit, Milwaukee, Cleveland, and St. Louis, and by 1981 it was just 4 percent above the national average (whereas in 1965 it had been 30 percent higher than the national average).[23] The devastation wrought during these years was made visible by the 1980 census, which indicated that ten of the country's sixteen poorest neighborhoods were in black Chicago. If times were hard in the 1970s, black Chicagoans bore the brunt. Between 1963 and 1977, when the city as a whole lost 29 percent of its jobs, black Chicago's drop was 46 percent.[24]

Yet it is misleading to think of this decade and the turbulent years leading up to it as a period of doom and decline. By the early 1970s, one could behold in the Chicago sky a number of majestic steel and glass structures stretching towards the clouds—symbols of a city on the rise. Between 1968 and 1975, work was completed on five of the ten tallest buildings that would define the contours of Chicago's skyline at the end of the twentieth century: the John Hancock Center (1968), the Chase Tower (1969), the Standard Oil Building (1972), the Sears Tower (1973), and Water Tower Place (1975), along with what was at the time the tallest residential building in the world, Lake Point Tower (1968).[25] Just when the action on the streets was at its hottest, the city, with the help of the internationally renowned architectural firm Skidmore, Owings & Merrill, was doing all it could to move its precious white-collar professionals into secure, air-conditioned cubicles in the sky. If the 1920s witnessed the first great vertical move of American cities, a second wave of skyscraper construction occurred in the late 1960s and 1970s, when work was completed on a number of the buildings that would become the well-recognized landmarks of the country's great urban centers—the World Trade Towers in New York City, the Transamerica Pyramid in San Francisco, the John Hancock Building in Boston, and the Sears Tower in Chicago.[26]

FIGURE 14. The Chicago skyline looking north from the South Loop lakefront, 1974. C. William Brubaker. C. William Brubaker Collection, bru005_11_oF, University of Illinois at Chicago Library, Special Collections.

At first glance, the timing of this skyscraper boom may seem rather enigmatic. Normally, such capital-intensive projects thrive in relatively risk-free market circumstances, and, while credit had been lined up and ground had been broken on some of these buildings a few years prior to the global economic doldrums that followed the Arab-Israeli War and OPEC oil embargo of 1973, the U.S. economy had already been showing signs of instability by 1966, when corporate productivity and profitability began to decline, provoking a credit crunch in 1966 and 1967. With increasing competition from Japan, Western Europe, and a number of newly industrializing countries, the U.S.-dominated international economic order that had been established by the 1945 Bretton Woods agreement broke apart at the end of 1971, and with it, its system of fixed exchange rates that tied currencies all over the world to the gold-backed U.S. dollar. These were thus precarious times to be investing in large-scale infrastructural projects whose success depended on strong economic growth. New York City was facing bankruptcy and Chicago's financial condition was hardly rock solid. In 1971 the stockyards closed down for good and the steel mills were on the verge of a significant decline. Moreover, Illinois was struck with a sharp drop in defense contracts in the 1960s and 1970s, another factor that weighed heavily upon the local economy. By the end of the 1970s, the credit-rating agency Moody's downgraded Chicago's bond rating, and the school system was facing a major budget shortfall. And yet, despite all this, the buildings kept moving skyward.

As the old industrial order was crumbling, a new economic order was already rapidly taking shape, and Chicago was vying for a central place within it. Scholars like David Harvey and Saskia Sassen have described this moment as one of deep structural transformation for the world economy, as the postwar framework of Fordism and state managerial Keynesianism collapsed and out of its remains emerged a new system characterized by more flexible labor arrangements and new sectors of production based on the provision of specialized financial services for an increasingly globalized economy.[27] For Sassen, in particular, such momentous changes would have major consequences for a group of new "global cities" that would take on strategically critical roles "as highly concentrated command points in the organization of the world economy" and "key locations for finance and for specialized service firms."[28] FIRE (finance, insurance, and real estate) activities would come to dominate the new "producer services" orientation of these global cities, along with marketing, advertising, employment, and legal services. The rise of these new service industries, in turn, would have a powerful impact on urban form, especially on the spatial layout of downtown business districts. Although many observers of the urban scene at the time believed that recent advances in telecommunications technologies would make high-density business districts obsolete, a very different scenario came to pass; the internationalization of corporate operations instead transformed the cores of global cities into dense concentrations of service providers capable of exercising centralizing functions over sprawling commercial activities.

The consequences for Chicago—once the "city of the big shoulders" and "hog butcher to the world"—were nothing short of spectacular. By 1980, Chicago's central business district, which covered just 3.5 percent of the city's total surface area, accounted for roughly 40 percent of the city's property taxes. Moreover, while the city as a whole lost nearly one-quarter of a million jobs during the 1970s, white-collar employment in the Loop rose at a respectable pace. In effect, Chicago was turning the corner towards its future as the nation's third-ranking global city, with a (4.2 percent) share of the total national employment in producer services that placed it close behind Los Angeles (with 4.6 percent) and far ahead of fourth-place Houston (with 1.7 percent).[29] In the insurance sector, it was second only to New York—a position symbolized by the black fortress-like tower that Skidmore, Owings &

Merrill designed for its developer and tenant, the John Hancock Mutual Life Insurance Company. At one hundred stories and 344 meters, it was at the time of its completion the tallest building in the world outside Manhattan, and, although credit problems halted its construction in 1967, it was ready to serve as a backdrop to the combat that reigned in the streets during the summer of 1968. This was, in part, its function, even if few involved in its construction would have thought of it in this way at the time.

Guy Debord seized upon the notion of "spectacle" in 1967 because it was elemental to the epic struggle that was transpiring in this pivotal moment in the history of capitalism. "The period from 1965 to 1973 was one in which the inability of Fordism and Keynesianism to contain the inherent contradictions of capitalism became more and more apparent," David Harvey has argued.[30] In the United States a range of protest movements had made the streets and neighborhoods of American cities into spectacles of this crisis, notably during Chicago's Democratic National Convention of 1968. As ineffectual as the Yippies may have seemed to many, they helped hijack the Daley administration's attempt to create a spectacle of prestige and power and to transform it into one of ignominy, violence, and disorder. This posed a potential threat to the city's livelihood in a moment when its political leadership was trying to project an image of order and progress to all the investment capital beginning to fly around the globe.

To understand the stakes, one needed only to cast a sidelong glance at Detroit, where the spectacle of rioting and black power anger prevailed in the years after the 1967 riot, a situation from which the city never recovered. Thereafter, the name *Detroit*—previously known as the "arsenal of democracy" and the "Motor City"—evoked images of burning ghettos and middle-class whites taking target practice in the suburb of Dearborn, preparing for the race war to come. That the city was never able to counteract this spectacle explains a great deal about why Detroit failed to keep either its white middle class or the companies they worked for within its limits, and why it would never attract enough service firms to make it into a global city. Chicago, on the other hand, had as much ugly spectacle as Detroit to contend with, but it seemed able to repel the stigma of each seemingly disastrous episode with astonishing ease. Chicago made it through the late 1960s and 1970s with its sense of civic pride intact, even if its civic pride had become an exclusively white feeling. But even to maintain the civic pride of the white middle class was a feat during this period of urban decline and white flight, when the American dream lay beyond the noisy, polluted urban landscape in the leafy outlying suburbs, and Chicago's ability to accomplish this owed a lot to its mayor. Every time the city seemed on the verge of falling apart, Chicagoans rallied around their mayor. And their mayor seemed to understand just what needed to be done to take his city into the global age.

Daley was ferociously proud of his city, and his pride was infectious, but the resilience of Chicago's civic spirit was due to the fact that it was embedded within the city's physical environment. Between 1960 and 1965, Chicago became the kind of city that middle-class whites could feel good about living and working in, and Daley played a key role in making this happen. In fact, he was merely following the blueprints of the 1958 "Development Plan for the Central Area of Chicago," which had singled out for "special emphasis ... the needs of the middle-income groups who wish to live in areas close to the heart of the City."[31] In the context of 1958, the phrase *middle-income groups* meant white people, and the "needs" being referred to were luxury housing and the kinds of leisure and retail resources that would keep these people happy. The idea being voiced by Loop business leaders, especially retailers and developers, was that the central business district was in danger of being overrun with black pedestrians and shoppers and desperately needed an infusion of white middle-class residents. Developer Arthur Rubloff, a major player in the transformation of Chicago's Near North Side, captured this view perfectly when he famously remarked, "I'll tell you what's wrong with the Loop, it's people's conception of it. And the conception they have about it is one word—*black*. B-L-A-C-K. Black."[32]

Rubloff, who, at the time of his death in 1986 possessed a wardrobe that included one hundred hand-tailored suits, forty cashmere coats, five hundred silk ties, one hundred pairs of shoes, and fifteen tuxedos, had been eyeing the area north of the Loop since 1947, when he had coined the term *Magnificent Mile* to capture his vision for a major upscale commercial strip to be built along North Michigan Avenue, from the Chicago River to the ritzy Gold Coast neighborhood. In 1960 Daley moved to make Rubloff's dream into reality when he cleared the way for a massive redevelopment project to the southwest of the Gold Coast, using $10 million of federal grant money to acquire and bulldoze a sixteen-acre strip bounded by North Avenue and LaSalle, Clark, and Division Streets. Of course the city made a call for tenders on the project, but, predictably, the Rubloff Company landed the contract with its plan for a $40 million middle-class housing development, complete with town houses, high-rises, swimming pools, tennis courts, and playgrounds. The development would be named Carl Sandburg Village— after, ironically enough, the poet who had so brilliantly evoked the hopes and frustrations of the kind of working-class people the project would be displacing. The overwhelmingly white middle-class Sandburg Village made the area a lot less diverse, replacing a sizable community of Puerto Ricans and the small Japanese "Little Tokyo" neighborhood around Clark and Division, but that was precisely the point. The city now had its barrier protecting the Gold Coast from the Cabrini-Green housing project, and the Loop, along with its Magnificent Mile extension, had a vital infusion of white middle-class residents and shoppers. And this was only the beginning.

Around the time that bulldozers were making way for Sandburg Village, builders were breaking ground at the other end of the Magnificent Mile on Marina City—a $36 million residential complex consisting of twin corncob-shaped, sixty-five-story towers on the north bank of the Chicago River at State Street. Advertised as a "city within a city" with such built-in amenities as a marina, a gymnasium, a movie theater, a swimming pool, an ice rink, a bowling alley, restaurants and bars, a parfumerie, and a gourmet shop with "items gathered from all over the world," Marina City was a monument to the slick, sophisticated urban lifestyle that Madison Avenue was concocting in the mid-1960s to sell everything from automobiles to hi-fi stereos.[33] The idea was a smashing success. Marina City's nine hundred apartments were fully rented before the building even opened in 1965, providing the Loop with another concentration of solid middle-class residents on its northern border and thousands of shoppers perched at the southern edge of the rapidly developing Magnificent Mile. And once again it was Daley who worked behind the scenes to close the deal. In fact, the whole thing was a classic machine boondoggle, with the city selling the riverfront property at a considerable discount off its market value to CHA board chairman Charles Swibel, who then procured financing from the Janitors International Union, whose president, William McFetridge, was a close friend of Daley.[34]

The same year Marina City was completed, work began on Lake Point Tower, another utopian "city within a city" development that would further guarantee that the Near North Side would be filled with well-to-do white professionals into the foreseeable future. Overlooking Navy Pier just north of the mouth of the Chicago River, this two-hundred-meter-high, black undulating glass tower was designed by two students of Mies van der Rohe who were inspired by his 1922 design for a glass-curtained skyscraper in Berlin. In addition to offering truly breathtaking views of both city and lake, residents there enjoyed their own two-and-a-half-acre park that included a playground, swimming pool, duck pond, and waterfalls.

FIGURE 15. Daley, the builder, ca. 1958. Richard J. Daley Collection, RJD_04_01_0040_0005_0122, University of Illinois at Chicago Library, Special Collections.

Carl Sandburg Village, Marina City, Lake Point Tower, and the swanky stores opening up on North Michigan Avenue represented the new corporate image of white-collar Chicago and the suave lifestyle of urban consumerism and indulgent leisure that came with it. Every day at 5:15 P.M. the bartender at the Marina City bar rang a bell signalling that customers could claim 5-cent refills. Chicago was quickly redefining itself as a city that knew how to swing—a public relations coup that owed a lot to Frank Sinatra's popularization of the song "My Kind of Town (Chicago Is)" in 1964 and Hugh Hefner's opening the first Playboy Club on Walton Street in the heart of the Gold Coast. During its first three months in 1961, Hefner's club attracted 132,000 guests; by the end of the year, it had 106,000 members, each one possessing a metal key topped with *Playboy*'s trademark bunny head. An astonishing number of people were thus flashing bunny keys around the city, and, even if a good many were out-of-towners who frequented the club when in town on business, the implications were the same. Chicago was a corporate city on the make, and this had profound consequences for its public culture and for its politics.

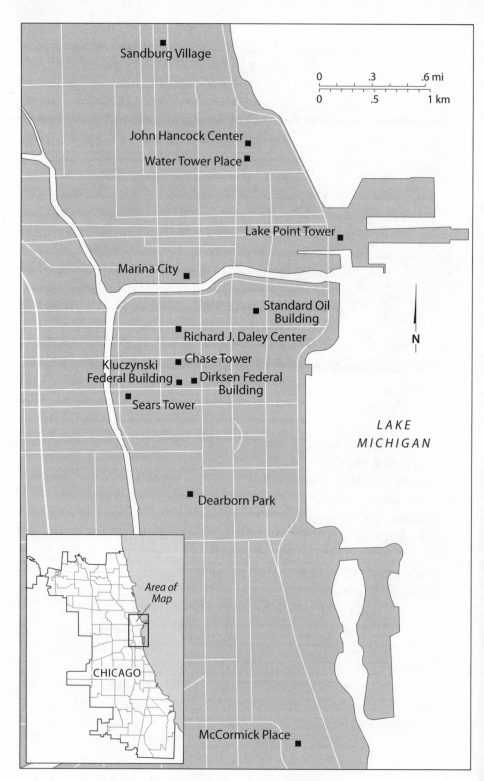

Sandburg Village

0   .3   .6 mi

0   .5   1 km

John Hancock Center

Water Tower Place

Lake Point Tower

Marina City

Standard Oil
Building

Richard J. Daley Center

Kluczynski
Federal Building   Chase Tower

Dirksen Federal
Building

Sears Tower

N

LAKE
MICHIGAN

Dearborn Park

Area of
Map

CHICAGO

McCormick Place

MAP 6. Major Loop building projects, 1963–1977.

Symbolic of the broader cultural change under way was *Playboy Magazine*'s 1965 move into the thirty-seven-story art deco Palmolive Building, replacing, ironically, toothpaste- and soap-maker, Colgate-Palmolive-Peet. With its prominent location behind the famed Drake Hotel at Lake Shore Drive's sharp Oak Street Beach bend, the prestigious 1929 building became a billboard for *Playboy*, whose name was spelled out on its top floor with nine-foot-high illuminated letters. *Playboy* was on the rise—in 1972 an estimated one-quarter of all American college men bought the magazine every month—and its genesis in Chicago was critical to its mass appeal. It was further testament to the fact that the cultural essence of Chicago was not to be found in coffeehouses and folk clubs but rather in the bars and nightclubs on the Gold Coast's Rush Street strip, where many of the top jazz and blues performers played and got paid. This explains why in 1969, the Weathermen, an SDS splinter group advocating violent tactics to shake the country out of its self-satisfied stupor, attacked nightclubs on Rush Street in the infamous "Days of Rage" riot; such radicals understood, if perhaps only subconsciously, that these nightclubs were somehow as emblematic of the capitalist order they were opposing as banks and military contractors.

Although Chicago earned its credentials in the 1960s as a city that could play, it would soon come to be known as "the city that works." The description, first used in a 1971 *Newsweek* article lauding Mayor Daley's ability to create an efficient infrastructure for business and everyday urban life when other cities were floundering, conveyed a double meaning: that Chicagoans worked hard and that their mayor made the city work efficiently for them. "But it is a demonstrable fact," *Newsweek* reported, "that Chicago is that most wondrous of exceptions—a major American city that actually works."[35] The phrase began appearing in local newspapers by 1972, and then in the *Washington Post* and *New York Times* in 1974 and 1975. Chicago had defined its brand, so much so that by the time Mayor Daley died of a heart attack in office in 1976, the phrase was run at the top of his obituary in newspapers nationwide. Yet the nickname was not merely the result of some kind of brilliant public relations campaign. Chicago became "the city that works" by the early 1970s in part because while other cities were dealing with crumbling infrastructures and deficient services in the midst of a generalized fiscal crisis, it had already managed to upgrade—often with the use of other people's money—its transportation and municipal infrastructures.

By the end of 1960, Mayor Daley had overseen the completion of the badly needed Northwest Expressway (renamed the John F. Kennedy Expressway in

1963) out to O'Hare International Airport, most of which had been paid for with federal highway funds, and by 1970 the Blue Line of the "L" was conveying commuters out to the airport on its median strip. In 1961, moreover, O'Hare got a $120 million makeover financed without a penny of taxpayer money; Daley had driven a hard bargain and forced the airlines themselves to put up a forty-year bond to pay for the project, which helped make O'Hare the busiest airport in the world. And many of those arriving in Chicago would be there to attend a convention at Chicago's new McCormick Place convention center. Then, in 1964, work was completed on a spectacular modernist federal government complex at Jackson and Dearborn, designed by Mies van der Rohe in the International Style, consisting of the thirty-story Dirksen Federal Building, the forty-five-story Kluczynski Federal Building, and a United States Post Office station around a spacious plaza. Once again, Daley had marshalled considerable federal funding to get the work done.

The following year was the occasion for another ribbon-cutting ceremony, when the city opened its magnificent new Chicago Civic Center (renamed the Richard J. Daley Center in 1976) between Randolph and Washington, across from City Hall. Yet another International Style skyscraper with an expansive modernist plaza, the center, which would house the county court system along with office space for both the city and county governments, was constructed with a special steel that was designed to rust, giving the building its distinctive red and brown color. Two years later, in 1967, Pablo Picasso completed a fifteen-meter-high, 162-ton cubist sculpture, made of the same material as the building it fronted and paid for with grants from local charitable foundations, to adorn the Civic Center plaza. When asked to approve the choice of Picasso for the project, Mayor Daley allegedly replied, "If you gentlemen think he's the greatest, that's what we want for Chicago, and you go ahead." The "Chicago Picasso" was the first of a series of high-profile works of art that would bring a sense of worldliness to downtown Chicago. This was important for a city trying to cast off its image as blue-collar and obtuse. In 1974 the Federal Plaza got its own artistic landmark—Alexander Calder's 16-meter-high, red steel *Flamingo*.

The Loop thus morphed into a vision of modernity, efficiency, and prestige at the very moment when American corporations were seeking to project these same attributes, and thus feared getting trapped within decaying cities stigmatized by high crime rates and racial tensions. Hence, with companies looking to the inviting suburban environs of Cook and DuPage Counties, where the McDonald's Corporation would move its Loop headquarters and open its

Hamburger University training center in 1971, Daley was able to make a viable case that Chicago was a good place to do business. But even with elegant Miesian skyscrapers, internationally recognized artworks, state-of-the-art residential developments, a burgeoning shopping district, a first-rate airport, and a highway network that enabled Loop professionals to make the daily commute from the desirable towns to the west and north, the mayor was working against strong forces pulling towards greener suburban pastures. DuPage County's labor force doubled during the 1970s, and its population grew by 34 percent as numerous research facilities and corporate headquarters joined McDonald's, AT&T, and Amoco along Route 5. During this same period Cook County's "golden corridor" of high-tech companies quickly formed to the northwest, with Motorola, Pfizer, Honeywell, Western Electric, and Northrup Defense Systems setting up operations along the Northwest Tollway by O'Hare. Similar suburban high-tech corridors were taking shape in many of the nation's metropolitan areas, a phenomenon that sucked tax dollars out of inner cities at time when they were most in need.[36] In Chicago, Mayor Daley approved an 18 percent increase in property taxes in 1971, but this was not nearly enough to offset the loss in tax revenues from the flight of residents and businesses. In 1970, property taxes funded 39 percent of the city's budget; by the end of the decade this figure had dropped to 27 percent.[37]

Such circumstances required extraordinary measures, and Mayor Daley, "the builder," as some referred to him, worked tirelessly behind the scenes to close deals, get tall buildings constructed, and keep major corporations within the city. In 1964, he expedited the sale of a piece of land owned by the city so that work could begin on the First National Bank Building (now called the Chase Tower), a sixty-story curved granite building that opened in 1969 on Madison Street, between Dearborn and Clark.[38] In fact, 1969 was a banner year for the Loop, with the opening of eight new buildings that provided an additional 4.6 million square feet of office space. It was also the year that work began on the city's next tallest building, the $100 million, eighty-three-story Standard Oil Building, the result of another successful campaign by the mayor. Daley had moved quickly to arrange the company's purchase of vacant land just north of Grant Park after being informed by Standard Oil's chairman, John Swearingen, that the company had outgrown its South Michigan Avenue headquarters and was looking to move elsewhere. Around this same time, Daley also heard that Sears, Roebuck and Co., the largest retailer in the world, was considering new headquarters in the suburbs, and again went to work on preventing this from happening. After a sit-down with

Daley, Sears's chairman, Gordon Metcalf, announced plans for constructing the world's tallest skyscraper just west of the Loop. The only problem was that the parcel it wanted was bisected by a segment of Quincy Street. Faced with this dilemma, Daley ordered the city council to hastily authorize transferring ownership of the street to Sears for a very low price, and to make the deal even sweeter, he assured Metcalf that the city would cover the costs of relocating water and sewer lines for the new building. The offer was accepted: when the Sears Tower opened its doors in 1974, Chicago possessed a skyscraper that reached higher than the World Trade Center towers. Not only did this give Chicago a new symbol of prestige, but the $150 million it took to build the tower would also irrigate the local economy, and thousands of white-collar jobs, along with a good many of the professionals who worked them, would remain within the city.

In Metcalf, Daley now had a powerful ally in his quest to fortify the Loop—a job that was seemingly never finished. Thus, as workers were still welding girders on to the Sears Tower, Metcalf was already spearheading— along with Donald M. Graham, CEO of Continental Illinois National Bank and Trust, and Thomas G. Ayers, president of Commonwealth Edison Company—the ambitious Dearborn Park project to transform six hundred acres of blighted railroad yards in back of the old Dearborn Station on Polk Street into a mixed-income development that would house 120,000 people. The idea was part of the Chicago 21 Plan, which was drafted in 1973 by the quasi-public Chicago Central Area Committee, with the assistance of Skidmore, Owings & Merrill. Like the 1958 plan before it, Chicago 21 focused on the need to make the central business district attractive to middle- and upper-class residents through the development of upscale housing, playgrounds, parks, and high-quality retail resources. After all of the recent development on the North Side, the CCAC viewed this need as most pressing on the southern edge of the Loop, where the Sears Tower rose out of the ground like a hulking black sentinel.[39]

In the minds of the business leaders who had collaborated on Chicago 21, this was the soft underbelly of the Loop, exposed to the dagger of black poverty jutting up from the north end of the "State Street corridor." Dearborn Park would provide the South Loop with the "protection" it needed, and Daley was of course on board with the plan, guaranteeing the city would bankroll the project's eventual infrastructure requirements. So, in a striking example of the new face of unrestrained corporate power in Chicago, a group of downtown business executives formed the Chicago 21 Corporation and raised $14 million in investment capital to acquire land and build a massive "mixed-income" housing development on the Near South Side. There was no hiding the fact that Dearborn Park was intended to serve as a barrier between the poor blacks of the Near South Side and the suits and ties of the South Loop—the apartment buildings all faced inward, the parks would be fenced off and reserved for residents only, and all the streets running north-south within the development were cul-de-sacs.[40] As for the "mixed-income" aspect of the project, the Chicago 21 Corporation planned on reserving one building for low-income, subsidized housing, but it would be for the elderly rather than for families.

Even if its founder and boss was not alive to see it, Dearborn Park suggested that the Daley machine seemed to have finally achieved what it had been aspiring towards since the late 1950s—a system that produced patronage capital without any of the bothersome politics that usually comes with it. Dearborn Park would bring in a handsome sum in annual tax revenues for the city, and some serious injustices had been committed in its development: minority-owned contractors had been left out, and, given the project's design, it was difficult to deny the allegations made by various black community groups that it was, in the words of the *Chicago Defender*, "a white-only fortress to protect the financial district from blacks."[41] And yet the city was in a position to collect on the financial advantages of the project without having to deal with any of this negative political fallout. In fact, the fallout was not "political" per se because the project was a seemingly private venture, and the notion of private accountability had yet to be incorporated into the idioms and tactics of oppositional politics in the neoliberal city.

While, as this chapter has shown, the divisive tendencies of the politics of identity played an important role in undercutting the reformist challenges of the late 1960s, the story would be incomplete without a consideration of how the new neoliberal political order of the global city disoriented the forces of reform and transformed the battleground of political confrontation. Suggestive in this sense was a 1978 *Defender* editorial on the Dearborn Park issue that began by asking, "What is the obligation of the private sector toward solving racial inequality? Is financial profit the sole criterion for determining action or inaction? Should banks and independent retailers and manufacturers be required to solve the problems they helped to create?" In the text that followed, not a single elected or appointed city official was named as accountable, and the only political response to be recommended, if the "bankers, retailers, and manufacturers" did not live up to their "sense of social responsibility," was a consumer boycott.[42] The role of this privately driven development in reinforcing racial inequalities thus represented an early example of a phenomenon that sociologist Lawrence Bobo has referred to as "laissez-faire racism": a system in which "modern racial inequality relies on the market and informal racial bias to re-create and in some instances sharply worsen, structured racial inequality."[43] The incoherent and ultimately weak response of the black community in the face of this situation was symptomatic of the power of the neoliberal order to depoliticize the very forces that were reinforcing racial and social inequalities in the city.[44]

Moreover, since Dearborn Park was not financed with federal funds, opposition could not even rally around the affirmative action requirements established by Lyndon B. Johnson's Executive Order No. 11246.[45] Such mobilizations for greater minority representation in the city's construction workforce had occurred in 1969 and 1970, when the Coalition of United Community Action (CUCA), an umbrella organization including Jesse Jackson's Operation Breadbasket and some sixty other black community groups, forced work stoppages at several Loop construction sites to demand more blacks be admitted into the overwhelmingly white Chicago Building Trades unions. Marshalling the brawn of the three most fearsome street gangs—the Vice Lords, Blackstone Rangers, and Black Gangster Disciples—CUCA managed to shut down several sites, forcing the city to agree to the 1970 Chicago Plan to integrate the city's construction industry.[46] Yet, as the Dearborn Park controversy revealed, the solution was far from satisfactory, and with an increasing number of smaller firms getting into the construction business—contractors who did not do enough government-sponsored business to be covered by affirmative action requirements—it would become increasingly harder for blacks to press their claims for more employment opportunities. Moreover, with the pullback of federal funds from the construction market, minority-owned businesses were in the process of losing their legal basis for demanding their rightful share of the pie.

Although Daley began to lose support in minority communities around this time, the persisting lack of financial clout in black and Latino Chicago by the early 1970s prevented this rancor from ever loosening Daley's hold on power. The presence of strong minority-owned businesses in black, Mexican, and Puerto Rican communities could have helped bring the kind of employment opportunities, political capital, and leadership that would offer an alternative to the meager patronage resources the Daley machine was funneling to them to buy out just enough support. But during the 1970s, Mexican and Puerto Rican Chicago had not yet arrived, and black Chicago was moving in the other direction, with some of its older former centers of commercial activity turning into ghost towns and new ones slow to develop. Revolution was for radicals; bread and butter drove politics in the Windy City. And all the investment capital that was flowing into Chicago was not buttering much bread outside the Loop and its surrounding middle-class residential neighborhoods. Few working-class Chicagoans were qualified for the highly skilled jobs in the rapidly growing FIRE sectors, and while there was plenty to go around in the booming construction sector, the machine and the unions had already fixed the game so as to exclude those most in need of the work. By the time Daley died of a heart attack at the age of 74, the patronage model of machine politics he had championed for more than two decades seemed to have become as natural a feature of the world around him as the air he breathed. There was still work to be done in order to keep the city clean, safe, and ready for business, but the corporations were driving things now, and why would anyone raise any objections to what they were doing for the city?

Ironically, it was at this very moment, when its opposition seemed at its weakest, that the traditional machine system finally began to fall apart. Although Daley had coasted to victories in his final two mayoral elections in 1971 and 1975, his final half-decade in office was ridden with headaches, defeats and scandals. First, due to the 1969 ruling of a federal court in the *Gautreaux* case, which found the Chicago Housing Authority guilty of discriminating against blacks for decades in the location of housing projects, the city, it seemed, would now have to abandon its practice of building low-income housing in African American neighborhoods. Then, another federal court decision threw a wrench into the cogs of the machine when the U.S. Supreme Court upheld a lower court's ruling in the *Shakman* case that average city workers could not be fired based on their political affiliations. Beginning around this time, moreover, a series of corruption scandals revealed in sensational fashion the extent to which the machine had been misallocating and at times stealing public funds. In 1972 an investigation by the *Chicago Tribune* into the city's use of its $53 million antipoverty grant from the federal government's Model Cities program found that nearly half of the money was being spent on bogus administrative costs that lined the pockets of machine cronies. The following year, a story broke in the local press proving that the city had offered a contract worth nearly $3 million dollars to an Evanston insurance firm after Daley's son John had joined it, and then in 1974 Daley's longtime right-hand man on the city council, Tom Keane, was convicted of using his political influence to purchase parcels of tax-delinquent land and then sell them back to the city at above-market prices. The police department was not spared from the blowup. In 1973, Police Superintendent Conlisk announced his resignation amidst two sets of allegations: the first involving a number of his officers shaking down tavern owners and the second, and more serious, revolving around complaints that Chicago policemen were guilty of a pattern of physical and verbal abuse against blacks. To make matters worse, this latter criticism came from former Black Belt machine loyalist Ralph Metcalfe, who, after winning William Dawson's vacated seat in the U.S. Congress, began distancing himself from Daley. Each day seemed to bring a new scandal. And yet, through it all, deals kept getting made, buildings kept getting built, and Daley kept getting elected.

Although Richard J. Daley would have felt out of his element in discussions about telecommunications capacities, subcontracting, or the vagaries of global financial markets, his patronage instincts told him that what was good for John Hancock, Chase, and Sears was good for Chicago, and what was good for Chicago was good for him and his friends. Daley gazed at the conservative backlash he had helped create and understood that it meant that the well of federal government resources was about to run dry, especially after Democrats had given up the White House. And he knew from experience that Chicagoans, like Americans elsewhere, were getting increasingly irritable about paying their taxes; in 1962, he had seen voters reject his $66 million city bond issue because they did not want to pay higher property taxes to fund urban renewal and improve the city's sewer system. The new sponsors of tax revenues and patronage capital were the transnational corporations whose headquarters were bursting into the skyline, and his early understanding of the fact that he needed to do all in his power to make sure they did not leave his proud city once again made Daley the right man for his time and place. He had been unwittingly greasing the wheels of neoliberalization every step of the way—turning over the job of charting the city's future to a cabal of developers and businessmen in the 1950s, working tirelessly to create an urban environment and business infrastructure that would attract private capital downtown while many of the city's working-class neighborhoods decayed throughout the 1960s, and using generous public subsidies to keep that capital within the Loop in the early 1970s. Municipal governance during these decades had become progressively unhinged from any notion of the public interest and increasingly aligned with the interests of corporate capital, which, for Daley, were synonymous with the interests of all Chicagoans. Daley's unwitting genius not only told him what needed to be done but also how to get it done in the new age of globalization. Back in the 1950s when Daley was sinking tax dollars into new technologies to sweep the streets and sidewalks of the dingy, downtrodden Loop, he seemed somewhat compulsive; now, it all seemed to make perfect sense. Daley's patronage instincts led him to the idea that attracting private capital was the new game to win, and his near-obsessive concern about Chicago's image gave him the right idea of how to win it. In an age when the telecommunications industry was rapidly making place, in a geographical sense, less important, it was necessary for cities to brand themselves as good places to do business, and part of this branding involved projecting to the world an image of a city on the rise—a city that people were proud to be part of. And a city on the rise was certainly not a city in the throes of fiscal crisis, which Chicago, in some sense, really was in the 1970s, even if nobody seemed to know it. And nobody knew it, Chicago journalist David Bernstein has revealed, because Daley's finance people were using a number of "budgetary gimmicks" to hide mounting deficits. They had the city borrowing to pay off past debts and then using the new funds for operating expenses rather than for debt repayment, all in the name of keeping up the appearance of financial health.[47] Yet again, Daley was on the cutting edge—this time of the debt-financed modus operandi and accounting sophistry of the future.

But as gifted as Daley was at making his city a highly competitive player in the new global economy, other factors that had little to do with the machine conspired in Chicago's favor in the 1970s. An outgrowth of the city's historical role as the financial, marketing, and insurance center of the Midwest agro-industrial complex was its development of long-standing markets in agricultural commodities futures—namely, the Chicago Board of Trade (CBOT) and the Chicago Mercantile Exchange (known as the Merc, or CME).[48] For farmers worried about fluctuating crop prices, futures contracts traded on these markets offered a guarantee that they could sell their harvest at a fixed price within a designated window of time in the future; these futures contracts were also attractive to speculators gambling on commodity price changes. For most of the 1960s, Chicago's commodities exchanges experienced some difficulties as a result of stock market declines and a lack of investor interest in contracts for commodities like pork bellies, Idaho potatoes, lumber, and shrimp. But things changed dramatically in

1969, when commodity trading had its most active year in the history of the exchanges, and then again in 1972, when the CME introduced the first futures market in foreign currencies. The idea was the brainchild of none other than Milton Friedman, a founding member of the famed Chicago School of economics at the University of Chicago, which, in the early 1970s, was engaged in replacing Keynesianism with monetarism—a theory that correlated unemployment and inflation rates to changes in the supply of money. Monetary policy, Friedman argued, could have prevented the Great Depression, and it was now the only prudent way to ensure economic growth while stabilizing inflation. Around the same time he was educating the famed "Chicago Boys" on how to bring such free market magic to Chile, Friedman accepted a consulting deal from the CME to investigate the possibility of doing business in foreign currency futures. Having determined that the end of the Bretton Woods system in 1971 would bring about an enormous need for a futures market in which increasingly volatile currency valuations could be hedged so as to minimize risk, Friedman recommended that the CME take the lead in establishing this exchange in Chicago.[49] The CME took his advice to the bank, extending the idea to gold futures in 1974, Treasury bills in 1976, and Standard & Poor's stock index futures in 1982. Meanwhile, the CBOT was carving out its own niche in protecting investors against increasingly sharp fluctuations in interest rates by offering futures on mortgage-backed certificates in 1975 and U.S. Treasury bonds in 1977.

The combined effect of these exchanges on Chicago's financial sector was staggering. In 1972, for example, the CME recorded $66.1 billion worth of transactions and the CBOT tallied $123 billion worth, and each day the two exchanges combined made margin deposits of well over $300 million into Chicago banks. "Can we fully evaluate what this means for Chicago?" asked Leo Melamed, chairman of the CME, before an audience of Chicago management professionals in 1973.[50] But the answer was not forthcoming—in part because nobody really knew the answer, and in part because most sensed that the truth behind the answer was hardly comforting. The previous year, the first one after the closing of the stockyards, 48 million head of cattle worth some $20 billion were exchanged on the CME with scarcely a single cow turd dropping on Chicago soil. In the 1970s, sublime sums of money began traveling to Chicago from all over the world as figures and codes transmitted through telecommunications pipelines into the control centers of skyscrapers, but like the millions of phantom cattle being herded through the city, all this wealth never left a trace in large swaths of the black South and

West Sides. Meanwhile, as Milton Friedman sat in his office in Hyde Park concocting the ideological justifications that would naturalize all of this, he was seldom out of earshot of the wailing sirens in the neighboring Woodlawn ghetto, just across the Midway, where unemployment and homicide rates were rising much faster than the stock indexes.

THE BLACK MESSIAH IN "BEIRUT ON THE LAKE"

Some very odd things were happening in Chicago in March 1983. In a city that had not elected a Republican mayor for fifty-six years, in a city in which Republicans occupied a starring role, along with Jews and blacks as the butt of barroom jokes in some white working-class precincts, Democrats were volunteering in droves to work in the Republican mayoral campaign. The first sure sign that Chicago had been turned upside-down came during the annual St. Patrick's Day parade, an event that traditionally served as a ritualistic reaffirmation of the bonds of solidarity and loyalty that held the Democratic Party together. Each year the city colored the Chicago River fluorescent green with gallons of dye, and the machine's leading figures paraded by the party's rank and file wearing green ribbons and leprechaun hats; in election years, as this one was, the parade took on an even greater significance, with the party using the occasion to showcase its ticket. But 1983 was a year that broke with precedent in a number of ways. First, the Democratic Party's mayoral candidate, Harold Washington, who had recently prevailed in a hard-fought primary, did not march at the front of the procession, as was tradition, and when he arrived before the heart of the crowd, one heard not the usual enthusiastic applause but an intermingling of hushed tones and deflated, seemingly forced cheers. Then, in a truly strange state of affairs, the same crowd greeted the Republican mayoral candidate, Bernard Epton—an anti-machine reformer, a rich guy, a Jew, a resident of Hyde Park, a graduate of the University of Chicago, a composite of all of the qualities that should have rankled the sensibilities of South Side Irish machine loyalists—with a rousing show of support. In one episode later reported in the *Chicago Tribune,* a woman called out to Epton and when he turned to look, she opened her coat to reveal a bright green shirt emblazoned with the phrase, "Vote Right, Vote White."[51]

What had upset the natural order in Chicago was the fact that a black man born and raised in Bronzeville—a former member of the Illinois House and Senate who had managed to get himself elected to the U.S. House of Representatives in 1981—was, in all likelihood, going to be elected Chicago's next mayor. Normally, the Democratic primary *was* the mayoral election, with the general election a mere technicality, and Harold Washington began preparing his transition team soon after his startling victory in a three-way race against the incumbent mayor Jane Byrne and the future mayor Richard M. Daley. The Chicago political scene had already been shaken up in 1979 when Byrne had upset Richard J. Daley's successor, Michael Bilandic, to become Chicago's first female mayor and the first in any major U.S. city. This was a tremendous feat in an era still touched by the contentious feminist challenges of the 1960s and 1970s; Illinois, it should be pointed out, was one of the fifteen states that had refused to ratify the Equal Rights Amendment. Yet Byrne's gender was never really a major issue. By contrast, faced with the possibility of a black man in the top office at City Hall, white Chicago, with the exception of the Lakefront liberal wards around Hyde Park, became gripped by racist hysteria. Addressing a Byrne rally on the Northwest Side days before the primary, Edward Vrdolyak—Tenth Ward alderman, chairman of the Democratic Central Committee, and close advisor to Jane Byrne—summed it up in one of the more notorious public expressions of unabashed racism outside the Jim Crow South: "A vote for Daley is a vote for Washington. It's a two-person race. It would be the worst day in the history of Chicago if your candidate . . . was not elected. It's a racial thing. Don't kid yourself. I'm calling on you to save your city, to save your precinct. We're fighting to keep the city the way it is."[52] Because of Vrdolyak's stature, this was big news, but Vrdolyak and many Chicagoans seemed puzzled when his remarks became material for political scandal; for weeks such expressions had been circulating around street corners, taverns, precinct headquarters, and kitchen tables in much of white Chicago—especially on the city's Northwest and Southwest Sides.[53]

And yet, although Vrdolyak's remark was indicative of a broader wave of racial hate that would wash over white Chicago in the months to come, it also may have blown the election for Byrne. This might seem like a curious conclusion in view of the fact that this was Chicago and this was the Reagan era, when Republican politicians, North and South, made convenient use of popular notions of black cultural dysfunction and ghetto pathology to justify their cries for welfare reform. Moreover, Chicago, in particular, had a special role to play in the antiwelfare backlash. Perhaps the most conspicuous catchphrase echoing through the attack on the welfare state during the 1980s was

"Chicago welfare queen," an image Ronald Reagan had conjured up during his 1976 presidential campaign. The Chicago welfare queen, according to Reagan's hyperbolic tale, had cheated the federal government out of hundreds of thousands of dollars by having illegitimate children and creating multiple aliases. While Reagan never mentioned explicitly that the woman in his sordid tale was African American, he did specify that she lived on Chicago's South Side, a detail whose significance was missed by few. This was typical of the rampant coded or ventriloquized cultural racism during these years. By the mid-1980s, universities and corporations alike were instituting cultural sensitivity training programs, and even conservatives, who were increasingly appealing to values of colorblindness, meritocracy, and free market individualism, were beginning to understand that racism made them look bad. Furthermore, to confront the demands of minority groups for race-conscious policies, many conservatives had taken to minimizing the presence of racial discrimination. If racism could be eliminated as a cause for poverty, then one could only conclude that some combination of cultural deficiencies, individual failings, and the negative effects of the welfare system itself were to blame for the ghettos and barrios that persisted in American cities.[54] There was thus much to be gained in planting culturally racist notions in the minds of middle-class whites angry about their taxes, but the trick was to do it without opening oneself up to charges of racism. This was why the overt forms of racism that ran wild in Chicago around Harold Washington's rise ended up working to his advantage by shocking outside observers, turning the stomachs of just enough white liberals, and erasing much of Byrne's remaining support within the black community.

This last effect was perhaps the most critical of all, for it was the astonishing mobilization of the black community that ultimately pushed Washington over the top. Black organizers conducted an aggressive registration campaign that had added over one hundred thousand black voters, enabling Washington to capture a startling 84.7 percent of the black vote, which constituted 92.1 percent of his total citywide. In view of the machine's patronage leverage in black Chicago and the reluctance of many longtime residents to believe in the electability of a black candidate, this was a remarkable feat.[55] In fact, it was common knowledge among political insiders that the machine owned a certain percentage of the black vote, regardless of the candidates vying for election. Famed Chicago campaign manager Don Rose, who had helped Jane Byrne take black votes away from the machine in 1977, estimated the figure to be 20 percent. "This is the vote," Rose joked, "the machine

FIGURE 16. The carnival atmosphere of the Harold Washington campaign. Photo by Jacques M. Chenet/CORBIS/Corbis via Getty Images.

would deliver for a George Wallace against Martin Luther King."[56] But against Washington, Byrne had garnered the support of a mere 8 percent of registered black voters. The Washington campaign had accomplished this, according to historian and political consultant William Grimshaw, by developing a "carnival" and "movement" atmosphere that helped transform its candidate into a "messiah."[57] Some of this was orchestrated by Washington's skilled campaign manager and Chicago civil rights veteran Al Raby, but the real magic was in the movement's more spontaneous moments, when street rallies pulled thousands of observers off sidewalks and into swirling, singing, dancing masses, and groups of young people swept through neighborhoods chanting "Harold, Harold, Harold" and knocking on random doors to urge people to vote. It all came together just days before the primary, when more than twelve thousand supporters defied a driving snowstorm and packed into UIC's basketball arena for an electrifying two-hour rally. Days later, after the votes were tallied, Washington had garnered 37 percent to Byrne's 33 percent and Daley's 30 percent.

But after a raucous victory party, all the carnival jubilation began to ferment into consternation when Washington's supporters began to realize that, unlike in past years, the Democratic machine was not going to marshal its forces for this particular candidate, and victory in the general election was far from assured. In fact, at first there was a great deal of confusion among the Democratic Party's committeemen. In the immediate aftermath of the primary, Vrdolyak told the press that the party would give its full support to the Democratic candidate, and longtime alderman Vito Marzullo, the boss of Little Italy and the Near West Side since 1953, declared Washington "the Mayor of Chicago."[58] Then the defections began. Before the end of February, Alderman Aloysius Majerczyk, whose ward encompassed the Polish neighborhoods around the McKinley Park area to the north of the old stockyards, had announced his support for Epton. Referring to the "message of racial pride" his constituents had been giving him, Majerczyk told the *Tribune*, "We're against open housing in my ward, and we always have been."[59] Indicative of just how much Washington's candidacy was galvanizing whites of all ethnic stripes, Majerczyk's endorsement of Epton was quickly seconded by Ivan Rittenberg, alderman of the traditionally Jewish Fortieth Ward on the far North Side. Days later, the *Tribune* was reporting that Epton's campaign headquarters in Irish Bridgeport was being overwhelmed by Democratic volunteers, and that in the heavily Italian and Polish neighborhoods of the Northwest Side, buttons reading "Italians for Eptonini" and "Polish for Eptonski" were being passed around.[60] Irish, Polish, Jewish, Italian—these were groups that had quarreled almost incessantly over power, place, and resources since before the turn of the century. Certainly ethnic ties had progressively attenuated in the postwar decades, but it was hard to deny that business relations, real estate dealings, and friendships still tended to work best when the parties involved were of the same ethnic ilk. This was a situation, moreover, that the machine system had promoted with its divide-and-rule style of governance. It is therefore somewhat ironic that many of the Democrats who defected to the Republican camp justified their decision by claiming that Epton would be somehow better at uniting the city. In fact, whites in the city had never been as unified as they were in the spring of 1983, except perhaps in the months after Chicago's own Jack Johnson became the first black boxer in history to win the heavyweight crown, and the call sounded across the nation for the "Great White Hope" who could beat Johnson and thereby restore the supremacy of the white race. Epton was regarded as the next great white hope. Outside of a handful of Lakefront liberal and racially mixed wards, the only question for Democratic committeemen was whether to openly oppose Washington or to remain publicly neutral while working behind the scenes against him.

However, to say that race was the only issue for many Democratic defectors would be misleading. There is reason to believe that had Washington not run an uncompromising antimachine campaign, a good many committeemen and aldermen who ended up endorsing Epton would have grudgingly supported him instead. In fact, Washington was something of a machine insider. After earning a law degree at Northwestern University, where he was the only African American in his graduating class, he had worked for Third Ward alderman Ralph Metcalfe between 1951 and 1965, a time when Metcalfe was still cozy with Daley. Although some hoped that this political experience would make him come around and play ball with the machine, Washington never backed off his promise to rid the city of a system that he claimed perpetuated "outdated politics and pie-in-the-sky financing," while providing "fat consultant contracts for a few politically connected firms and jobs for a few patronage workers."[61] He was therefore a threat to the aldermen and committeemen, whose power rested in their ability to lubricate their precincts with patronage. If, as Milton Rakove had observed, the men who dominated the Chicago machine were, above all else, "practical, pragmatic, parochial, and nonideological," then the color of Washington's skin should have made little difference.[62] But it did—alas, it did.

Why it did, however, had to do more with culture than ideology, and it had less to do with machine cadres than with ordinary Chicagoans infusing the normally staid conduct of mayoral politics with a new energy, anger, and urgency. When Rakove wrote his scathing indictment of the machine in the early 1970s, the system he was attacking was still working to keep the city's political culture impervious to the ideological challenges of the era—liberalism, democracy, conservatism, you name it. Its ability to do this with such efficacy had allowed it to outlast all the other big city machines by decades. But what Rakove could not see as he was completing his manuscript was the role that grassroots cultural struggles would play in the coming years. By the early 1980s, the national political landscape was increasingly characterized by seemingly irreconcilable conflicts over cultural issues and moral values. Abortion rights, censorship of obscenity, and gay rights constituted the first wave of "culture wars" to grip the country. But beginning in the early 1970s, a new set of cultural issues revolving around the lingering questions of racial segregation and inequality had moved into the political sphere, as white Americans debated policies like busing and affirmative action and responded to minority claims for greater cultural respect and recognition in institutions of higher learning.

Such issues did not seem to translate into what one might call "politics" in Chicago. Aldermen like Vito Marzullo and Roman Pucinski, the "leader of Chicago Polonia" since 1959, knew little, if anything, about the politics of recognition and "political correctness"; politics to them was filling potholes, fixing parking tickets, and doling out jobs and contracts to key constituents. However, whether they knew it or not, the cultural politics of race was overtaking them, even if it would not remove them from power. One of the first things they learned was that they would have to watch what they said much more than before. One of the signs that Chicago was merging to a greater extent with mainstream political culture were the many allegations of racism that were flying around the city's newspapers. While many of these charges were, of course, warranted, some white Chicagoans began complaining that black leaders were construing as "racist" any opposition to Washington. In the face of such allegations, the Epton campaign and its supporters began throwing around charges of "reverse racism," claiming that the blacks accusing them of racism were, in fact, the racists, not them. These were sentiments that would be increasingly heard on college campuses in the coming years, as minority groups pressed their demands for greater cultural recognition and conservatives decried the censorship and factionalism of "political correctness," but such circumstances had seldom been witnessed in big city politics.

In retrospect, it now seems clear that Chicago was in 1983 staging one of the first major dramas of the new era of culturized politics, when all that separated whites from blacks—space, wealth, ideology—would be reduced to ethnocultural factors. By the 1980s a politics of resentment was clearly taking hold on both sides of the color line across the United States. Blacks were resentful about all the unfulfilled promises of the civil rights era, and whites about what they perceived as the stubborn refusal of blacks to let the race issue drop after the civil rights victories of the 1960s. But white resentment, in particular, went beyond this. White resentment, as Chicago '83 demonstrated, was not only articulated in cultural terms, it was about culture itself. As whites in Chicago gazed at the expressions of cultural pride and solidarity on display in Washington's messianic movement, they understood, on a palpable level, that blacks possessed something they lacked. As one Epton supporter so poignantly lamented about the dilemma of opposing Washington, "We're racist, and he has cultural pride."[63]

Such expressions of cultural envy and resentment explain a great deal about the violence that was entering Chicago's mayoral election around this time. Even if most operatives within the machine still tended to view the stakes of the election in terms of controlling political power and patronage, the groundswell of opposition to Washington was taking the whole affair into an entirely new realm. What was behind the bitter racial hatred exploding into public life in Chicago resembled, on some level, Slavoj Zizek's description of the dynamics underlying the ethnoracial tensions that tore the Balkans apart in the late 1980s and 1990s. Critical to Zizek's perspective is the idea that what drove the nationalist fears of ethnoracial others were imagined "thefts of enjoyment"—the idea that racial others threatened to take away the dominant group's "way of life."[64] This seems an apt way to explain what was transpiring as more and more Chicagoans were articulating the feeling that defeating Washington in the election was a matter of "saving" their neighborhoods and their city—a sentiment Epton sought to capitalize on by choosing the incendiary campaign slogan "Epton, before it's too late." Epton of course denied the phrase had any racial implications, insisting it related to the city's impending fiscal crisis, but this was disingenuous. Epton understood very well that in the eyes of many white Chicagoans, a victory by Washington meant the loss of their city as they knew it. Not only did they fear that blacks would finally get their rightful share of the patronage pie, but for many whites, a city run by blacks would be a city of immorality, corruption, and danger, where public culture would become synonymous with some nightmarish vision of the black nationalist ghetto. Under such conditions, racism ran wild throughout the city in the most virulent forms, seemingly unrestrained by any codes of propriety or civility.

The first sign that things were getting out of control occurred on Palm Sunday, March 27. Washington and former vice president Walter Mondale had planned to attend religious services at St. Pascal's Catholic Church on the Northwest Side, but when they arrived, they discovered "NIGGER DIE" painted on a church door. Later, upon leaving the church, the two were mobbed by hundreds of frenzied Epton supporters screaming racial epithets and other insults. Around this same time, a number of racially vicious flyers began circulating in many white neighborhoods. One suggested facetiously that if Washington won, the name of the city would be changed to "Chicongo" and that the city's official police insignia would include images of a watermelon slice and a rack of ribs; another joked that Washington would place basketball hoops on the Chicago Picasso and rename the CTA "Soul Train."[65] While Epton of course stayed clear of such low tactics, he nonetheless engaged in a smear campaign loaded with thinly veiled cultural racism, all the while accusing blacks and the local media of playing the race card. Understanding the propensity of whites to buy into "welfare queen" notions of black corruption and criminality, Epton exploited some minor legal problems in Washington's past to impugn his integrity. Washington, it was true, had been in legal trouble in 1972 for failing to file income tax returns, and in 1970 he had his law license suspended for billing a client for services he did not perform, but the amounts of money in question in both instances were insignificant. In a city like Chicago, where corruption was more the rule than the exception, such attacks against a white candidate would have been laughable. Of course Epton never said anything racist per se, but he knew where his comments would lead. By the time Chicagoans cast their votes, Washington had been forced to publicly defend himself against the baseless charge that he had been convicted for child molestation.

However, once again, on the eve of the election as in the primary, the expression of such ugly racism actually worked in Washington's favor. In what was the closest mayoral election in Chicago since 1919, Washington managed to prevail by just 46,250 votes out of a total of 1.29 million. The event was one of not just national but international importance. Black mayors had headed major American cities since 1973, when Tom Bradley was elected in Los Angeles, Coleman Young in Detroit, and Maynard Jackson in Atlanta, but this was Chicago—the city with the second largest black population in the United States, where the saga of black struggle was particularly well known. Moreover, it was an event of great significance for the black diaspora—of lesser magnitude, of course, but not unlike the election of Barack Obama as president in 2008. Indeed, Washington's election was made possible by a breathtaking show of black solidarity and, as such, was a source of inspiration for blacks all over the world. As in the primary, African Americans had turned out in record numbers and voted almost unanimously for Washington, while his opponent had captured an overwhelming share (87.6 percent) of the white vote.

Washington had once again garnered his strongest white support in the Lakefront wards, where roughly one in four whites voted for him. The main difference, however, was that Latinos had moved into his camp in decisive fashion. While Washington had captured a small percentage of Puerto Rican and Mexican votes in the primary, he had outrun Epton among Latinos at a rate of roughly 4 to 1.[66] A major reason for this shift was the fact that since few Latinos believed in Washington's chances in the primary, many found it prudent to go with their best bet for patronage down the line. But there is also good reason to believe that Latinos were responding, at least in part, to both the vitriolic racism that exploded onto the political scene as well as Washington's promises to make Chicago a fairer city. Nonetheless, the black-Latino alliance that crystallized during the general election had not sprung up overnight but was the product of a somewhat long process of negotiation and cooperation that grew out of the civil rights challenges of the 1960s. Glimpses of it had been seen in 1966, when black civil rights activists tried reaching out to Puerto Ricans after the Division Street barrio riot of that year; in 1968, when black and Latino high school students mobilized to change their schools to better suit their needs; and in 1969, when the Young Lords and Black Panthers joined forces to try to bring about a "rainbow coalition." Although these efforts had not been enough to overcome the legacies of intergroup conflict and divisive politics by the end of the 1960s, veterans from these struggles continued to carry forward the project of a multiracial struggle for justice and equality during the 1970s and early 1980s.

Black and Latino activists were thus joining forces on the grassroots level to tackle a range of issues related to high unemployment, diminishing welfare entitlements, poor housing, and low voter registration into the early 1980s, when the tide turned quickly against minority interests on both the federal and local levels. Nationally, the Reagan Revolution's antiwelfare crusade provoked a new wave of grassroots activism in black and Latino communities feeling targeted by its coded cultural racism. But even more important was the local situation, where Jane Byrne's apparent antimachine challenge had quickly turned into a big disappointment for minority groups. Byrne had snuck into the mayor's office by promising to root out the "cabal of evil men" she claimed had betrayed Daley's legacy and by having the extremely good fortune of delivering her message of machine inefficiency during a massive snowstorm that crippled the city's infrastructure for weeks in January 1979. In one instance, Mayor Bilandic closed several CTA stations in order to improve service without realizing that all of these stations served black communities, a situation that paid dividends for Byrne on election day, when her 45,000-vote edge among blacks allowed her to prevail in a tight race.

Once in office, however, relations between the mayor and Chicago's black leadership became strained. It did not help her case that she publicly supported President Reagan's policies when blacks across the nation were voicing sharp criticism of them. But even more destructive to her support in the black community was her replacement of several high-level black officials in the Chicago Housing Authority and on the Chicago Board of Education with whites. Then, as she was fending off charges of perpetuating the old "plantation politics" of the past, Byrne poured fuel on the fire by using her political funds to make cash contributions to black churches and to distribute small Christmas trees and hams in low-income black communities—gestures that vocal black community activist Lu Palmer criticized as "patronizing." Finally, with her support among blacks dwindling and talk of a mayoral run by Richard M. Daley increasing, Byrne made yet another political miscue when she and her husband enlisted a brigade of bodyguards and moved into the notoriously crime-ridden Cabrini-Green Housing Project. The stunt was intended to publicize Byrne's commitment to fighting gang violence and crime in black communities, but once again the mayor looked insensitive and out of touch with African American concerns—a point that was hammered home during an Easter celebration in front of Cabrini-Green, when a group of protesters led by fiery community activist Marion Nzinga Stamps confronted the mayor with shouts of "We need jobs, not eggs," and bodyguards wrestled one protester to the ground amidst shouts of "Assassin!"[67]

The new movement for black empowerment that would sweep Harold Washington into office the following year first took form within this context. Looking for a way to strike back at Byrne, Jesse Jackson and other black community leaders came up with the idea of organizing a boycott of the city's annual summer musical festival, ChicagoFest, an event Byrne used to showcase her role in promoting a vibrant social life for the entire city. After taking office, Byrne had renamed the event "Mayor Jane M. Byrne's ChicagoFest" to make sure everyone got the message, and her name was prominently displayed on the seemingly countless posters for the event throughout the city. In 1982, Byrne had authorized big money to bring in the popular black performer Stevie Wonder, who, upon hearing about the boycott, promptly agreed to cancel and forfeit his pay. Attendance and revenues dropped dramatically as a result, but, more importantly, blacks had won a symbolic victory.

A new sense of energy and purpose began to circulate within black Chicago, and from there it spilled over into Puerto Rican and Mexican communities. Quick to capitalize on this new movement spirit, for example, was People Organized for Welfare and Employment Rights (POWER), a coalition of sixteen black and Latino community organizations that had just launched a massive voter registration campaign. While Chicago's Latinos felt some resentment about all of the attention being paid to black injustices—Latinos, it must remembered, had even more reason than blacks to protest their second-class status in city government—a group of activists in both

Puerto Rican and Mexican Chicago began to take inspiration from the new sense of militancy that was emerging on the South and West Sides. Thus, by the time Harold Washington was beginning to look like a credible candidate, veteran community organizers like Cha-Cha Jimenez and Rudy Lozano were eager to sign on to his campaign and begin convincing reluctant Puerto Rican and Mexican voters that a Washington victory would mean expanded opportunities for Latinos as well. It was Jimenez who introduced Harold Washington in front of a crowd of tens of thousands of Puerto Ricans in the first event of the city's new program of "neighborhood festivals," put together to demonstrate Mayor Washington's commitment to including all ethnoracial groups within his administration, when the new mayor assured the appreciative crowd of Puerto Ricans that they would finally get their rightful share of power and resources.

But not even three months later, Washington was under fire for not keeping his promises to Latinos. The first attacks came from Mexican members of Washington's transition team, after the mayor passed over a qualified Mexican American candidate, Matt Rodriguez, for the position of police superintendent. Some of the criticism seemed to develop out of a sense that Mexicans were being given a back seat to the city's somewhat smaller Puerto Rican population—a feeling that had the president of the Mexican-American Organization of the Democratic Party of Cook County, Arturo Velasquez, reminding Washington that the "Hispanic community" is a generic term for numerous Spanish-speaking groups.[68] Before long, Puerto Ricans as well were complaining about unfulfilled promises. In October 1983, Reverend Jorge Morales, a leading activist in the Humboldt Park barrio area and the spokesman for a group known as the Commission on Latino Affairs, complained about the lack of Latinos appointed to key positions.[69] This was merely the latest in a series of problems between Puerto Ricans and the mayor. Even more troubling for Washington was the decision by Miguel Santiago, the newly elected alderman of the heavily Puerto Rican Thirty-First Ward, to side with "the Eddies"—Edward Vrdolyak and Edward Burke—and twenty-six other white alderman in the "council wars," which saw a unified bloc of white city councilmen (with the exception of Santiago) opposing the mayor's every move over the next three years. Santiago justified his decision by claiming that Washington was interested in helping only the "right minorities" and by arguing that he had failed to give Latino businesses their fair share of the contracts associated with the new project to expand O'Hare. But this was more politics than truth; in actuality, Latino businesses had obtained nearly 10 percent of the contracts at O'Hare compared with just under 14 percent for the much larger black population. Yet, Santiago's ability to play this game revealed how fragile Washington's rainbow coalition actually was.[70]

While the notorious council wars would come to characterize the Washington era, earning the city the nickname Beirut on the Lake, too much attention to the legislative battles of these years gives the misleading impression that the factionalism that reigned during Washington's term was merely a matter of whites versus blacks. [71] The fact was that the politics of identity that had emerged out of the progressive challenges of the 1960s still cast a large shadow over the city's political culture. If Washington was not reaching out enough to Latinos, it was in part because he was somewhat beholden to a vocal group of black nationalists who opposed any gesture of cooperation with whites and who saw no reason why, with Washington in the mayor's office, blacks should not behave precisely as the Irish had for much of the city's history. Upon arriving in Chicago in 1985 to take a job as a community organizer, Barack Obama was immediately awestruck by what Washington had accomplished, but he was also deeply dismayed by what he viewed as the destructive black nationalist sensibilities that produced "a Hobbesian world where distrust was a given and loyalties extended from family to mosque to the black race."[72] Even Jesse Jackson, the man who would market the idea of a rainbow coalition on the national political stage during his Democratic presidential primary runs in 1984 and 1988, had never had particularly good relations with either liberal whites or Latinos in Chicago. He had made a point of provoking Jews by calling Israeli prime minister Menachem Begin a "terrorist"; his organization Operation PUSH had never reached out meaningfully to Latinos; and in the late 1970s he had been publicly attacked by Latino leaders for entering into negotiations over a school desegregation plan without inviting Latinos to the table. Jackson may have fought beside Martin Luther King for racial integration and thus was certainly no separatist, but his actions were symptomatic of a widespread reluctance among Chicago's black political leadership to leave behind the cultural nationalism of the civil rights era.

Yet such inclinations were hardly restricted to the black community. A similar situation was also unfolding in Puerto Rican Chicago in the early 1980s, when a number of activists turned away from organizing working-class Puerto Ricans to fight against the injustices they faced in their everyday lives and towards the project of an independent Puerto Rican homeland. The

Young Lords had already begun mobilizing behind Puerto Rican independence in the 1970s, but by the early 1980s a radical organization called the Fuerzas Armadas para la Liberacion Nacional (FALN) was leading this struggle. When, in the mid-1980s, thirteen residents of the Humboldt Park barrio were sentenced to long prison terms for conspiracy to overthrow the U.S. government, it was clear that the independence movement was opening up cleavages in Puerto Rican Chicago between those invested in such nationalist dreams and those looking to carve out a decent living in the barrio.[73] This nationalist project, moreover, reinforced cultural nationalist tendencies that drove a wedge into potential alliances between Puerto Ricans and Mexicans, who, themselves, began to imbue their communities with a strong racialized sense of Mexican cultural identity beginning in the early 1970s. Despite some significant cooperation between Mexicans and Puerto Ricans based on appeals to "Latinismo"—the mixed-Latino-majority Fourth Congressional District, for example, elected the first Latino congressman from the Midwest in 1992—the trend was towards separation. The situation had degenerated so much by 1995 that both Puerto Rican and Mexican activists began calling for the breakup of the shared congressional district their predecessors had struggled to create on the grounds that they were racially distinct groups with only a language in common.[74]

All this explains why the so-called rainbow coalition of blacks, Latinos, and progressive whites that had so spectacularly vanquished the old guard in 1983 seemed to vanish after November 1987, when Harold Washington died tragically of a heart attack while sitting at his desk in City Hall. While news of the mayor's sudden death shocked the black community, nobody who knew him well was very surprised. The sixty-five-year-old Washington had been a longtime heavy smoker before quitting the habit during his campaign, and after giving up cigarettes he began quickly gaining weight with his steady diet of greasy food. According to staffers, the mayor would eat a healthy lunch and then wolf down a triple cheeseburger and French fries for an afternoon snack. According to the Cook County medical examiner, he was one hundred pounds overweight when he died. Moreover, Washington's constant wrangling with Vrdolyak and the "Vrdolyak 29" bloc no doubt raised his blood pressure. The conflict between the two had gotten so rancorous at times that it had even led to physical threats made on the city council floor.

Regardless of the mayor's combativeness, the Vrdolyak 29 bloc had the upper hand for the first three years of his term, voting down most of his attempts to reduce the city's deficit and controlling the key committees, like

Zoning and Finance, through which much of the city's power and resources flowed. While the twenty-eight white and one Puerto Rican aldermen that made up this bloc were largely fighting to keep the old patronage system intact, they did not hesitate to mobilize their constituents with racial appeals—as, for example, when they argued that white middle-income communities should get their fair share of federal Community Development block grant funds, which were legally designated to go to low-income neighborhoods.[75] Bosses in Chicago had always dominated their city councils, but now the shoe was on the other foot. Despite such difficulties, however, Mayor Washington could claim some accomplishments. He officially outlawed patronage hiring and firing, created a freedom of information act that opened city government up to public scrutiny, promoted the economic development and infrastructural improvement of all of the city's fifty wards, and, the complaints of some disgruntled Latinos aside, had managed to hire far more Latinos, blacks, and women than any mayor before him. He also became the first mayor in Chicago's history to embrace the issue of gay rights by creating the Mayor's Committee on Gay and Lesbian Issues (COGLI), which selected its members through a community-based process.[76] And yet all this was not nearly enough to build the kind of movement culture that it would have taken to overcome the legacy of intergroup conflict and install a durable "rainbow" coalition capable of moving the goal of a fair and open city forward after Washington's death. A reform revolution of this kind would have required a deeper cultural transformation.

There is reason to believe that such a transformation was in the works when Washington slumped over his desk on the day before Thanksgiving in 1987. By the start of 1986, the city had seemed to be turning the corner on its racial troubles. The first sign came from its vaunted football team, the Bears, which possessed a broad base of support that extended across racial lines. The Chicago Bears of 1985 were arguably one of the greatest football teams of all time, and as they coasted towards a victory in the Super Bowl in late January 1986, some of the team's black and white stars recorded a facetious rap video called the "Super Bowl Shuffle"—a symbolic expression of racial harmony that was not lost on the team's massive following. Soon after that came the break the city needed to free itself from its legislative straitjacket. A federal judge ruled that Mayor Byrne's redrawing of the Chicago ward map had violated the voting rights of blacks and Latinos and ordered that the boundaries of seven wards then controlled by the Vrdolyak 29 be redrawn and new elections be held to elect aldermen for them. Four pro-Washington candidates—two blacks and two Latinos—prevailed in these elections, creating a 25–25 split in the city council with the mayor casting the tie-breaking vote. One of the Latino aldermen joining Washington's bloc, moreover, was the talented Luis Gutiérrez, a future United States congressman who was outspoken about his alliance with black reformers, shunning the idea of forming a "Latino bloc" with two pro-Vrdolyak aldermen.[77] And the other pro-Washington Latino alderman, Jesús "Chuy" García, who represented the heavily Mexican ward surrounding Pilsen, was voicing similar support for the reform revolution. Washington's momentum carried into the 1987 mayoral election, when he gained an indisputable multiracial mandate by soundly defeating Jane Byrne in the Democratic primary and Vrdolyak in the general election, each time with over 53 percent of the vote.[78] Even better still, the election also saw Miguel Santiago losing his aldermanic seat to a pro-Washington lawyer named Raymond Figueroa. Meanwhile, Washington's endorsement of gay rights was strengthening his support in North Side lakefront neighborhoods, bringing new white voters into his base. "It's Harold's Council Now," the front-page headline in the *Chicago Sun-Times* read. Black alderman Timothy Evans promptly replaced Edward Burke as floor leader, and the new city council quickly passed an ethics ordinance and a tenant's bill of rights. The future seemed wide open. Washington had always joked that he planned to occupy the mayor's office for twenty years, and now that idea did not seem so far-fetched.

But just several months later, the "Washington bloc" and its progressive brand of politics was finished for good. Somewhat ironically, the fatal fault line lay not between black and Latino aldermen but rather between reform-minded black aldermen and the black machine loyalists who had supported Washington out of necessity rather than choice. In fact, in the city council vote to determine which of the two black candidates—the Washington bloc's choice, Timothy Evans, or the opposition bloc's choice, Eugene Sawyer—would finish out Washington's term, the four Latino aldermen (including the independent, Juan Soliz) backed Evans as the rightful successor to Washington's reform project. Yet it was not enough. Although some of the old, compromised councilmen from the plantation politics days had been ousted and a new generation of committed reformers like former Black Panther Bobby Rush and civil rights activist Dorothy Tillman had arrived, the mayor had never thought it necessary to try to clean out the remaining handful of old Daley loyalists from the middling black wards—Eugene

Sawyer, Wilson Frost, and John Stroger. Now they cut a deal with three wavering black alderman and most of what remained of the Vrdolyak 29 to pull together enough votes to make Sawyer the next mayor.

A young Barack Obama had gone to City Hall that frigid December night to join thousands of other dazed African Americans who felt that their presence might somehow help to avert the ending to the story that was beginning to seem destined. He had watched the crowd wave dollars bills at Sawyer and shout "Sellout" and "Uncle Tom," and he had left after midnight, several hours before the final vote, with a sinking feeling that "the fleshy men in double-breasted suits," as he referred to them, would seize the day. Walking across the Daley plaza to his car, he gazed with a sense of bitter irony upon a handmade sign that read "HIS SPIRIT LIVES ON."[79]

Obama had been working on the far South Side of Chicago since 1985 as a community organizer for the Calumet Community Religious Conference (CCRC), a grassroots Alinskyite organization that was attempting to bring together churches, labor unions, and other community organizations to give working-class blacks, whites, and Latinos greater leverage in solving the problems of high unemployment, poor housing conditions, inadequate schools, and violent crime. In the Alinskyite way, Obama's job was to interview folks, listen to their complaints, and figure out ways to use the data he collected to formulate strategies of mobilization. He conducted much of this work in the Altgeld Gardens housing project, a horribly maintained set of two-story brick buildings located next to the chemical waters of the Calumet River and just across the street from a sewage treatment plant that blanketed the area with putrid odors when the wind was blowing in the wrong direction. The residents of Altgeld were casualties of the sharp contraction of the city's steel and manufacturing sectors in the 1970s and 1980s, a situation that had largely unfolded outside the purview of city politics. No mayoral candidate had ever promised to save production jobs; the forces that had led to the collapse of steel and manufacturing in Chicago were located in Washington and in the corporate command centers of global cities. But Chicago could play a role in lessening the blow of plant closings by providing better services and better schools and promoting development and investment that would lead to the creation of the kinds of jobs that former production workers could fill. In his work for the CRCC, Obama was trying to make this happen, and by the end of his nearly three years as a community organizer he could claim some modest victories.

And yet by the time that Harold Washington died, Obama had submitted his application to Harvard Law School and was eagerly awaiting the admissions decision. Indeed, his experience as a community organizer told him what he probably already suspected, which was that he would be more useful to the people of Altgeld Gardens from a high position *within* the system. Much has been made about the political education Obama took from his first stay in Chicago in the mid-1980s and of the influence of the Harold Washington era on his ambitions. To be sure, Obama was inspired by Washington's ability to unite blacks, Latinos, and whites in a city where this had seemed impossible just years before, and he admired the fact that the mayor had accomplished this while gaining the support of big business, stabilizing the city's financial situation, and restoring its Moody's bond rating. However, what might have been most important to Obama, even if he was not entirely conscious of it at the time, was his perspective on all that did not happen with a dedicated reformer like Washington in power. He saw at the grassroots level that Washington's ascendency had little impact on mending the fractures between blacks, Latinos, and whites in low-income neighborhoods, and that even with a mayor committed to spreading resources throughout the city, very little seemed to be changing in the material conditions of life for the people he had gotten to know in the working-class neighborhoods of the Pullman and Roseland areas.[80]

A cruel twist of fate has left us with only speculation about what might have been had Washington's heart not given out in 1987. Washington was one among a new generation of black politicians elected mayor in the 1970s and 1980s, but as scholars like Adolph Reed Jr. have argued, most of them arrived to find that the prize they had struggled so hard to possess had been emptied of value.[81] Their hands were tied by budget shortfalls, the drying up of federal funds, and a neoliberal order that required them to cater ceaselessly to the demands of developers and business elites to maintain the flow of tax revenue. Even if he would continue to hold on to the dream of one day sitting in the mayor's office as he moved to Cambridge to begin his studies at Harvard in the fall of 1988, Obama's years in Harold Washington's Chicago had certainly dampened his idealism about what could be accomplished on the municipal level. He left Chicago with a new understanding of the extent to which the "the fleshy men in double-breasted suits" ran things—a revelation that probably made him start thinking seriously about ways of taking his mission to another level. And yet, upon reading Obama's rather terse account of Harold Washington's impact on Chicago politics in *Dreams from my Father,* it is hard not to feel that young Obama had missed something essential.[82] Somewhat curiously he made little mention of one of the key principles at the core of Washington's reform "revolution": a commitment to community participation in formulating and implementing public policy. So devoted was Washington to this goal that he had even opened up the city budget-making process to public scrutiny and input—a move that reveals just how radically Washington's approach to governance had departed from the machine tradition.

SEVEN

A City of Two Tales

HEAT, HIGH SCHOOLS, AND INEQUALITY

On Thursday, July 13, 1995, the temperature in Chicago rose to a stifling 106 degrees, but it was actually much hotter than that. Meteorologists reported that the more critical heat index, which measures the temperature a person actually feels, could reach as high as 120 degrees. Chicago's numerous brick apartment buildings transformed into ovens, roads buckled and cracked, city workers sprayed bridges to keep them from locking up, power outages left some fifty thousand residents without electricity for days, and a number of neighborhoods lost water pressure as a result of the many fire hydrants being opened by folks desperate for relief from the heat. In the hottest hours of the day, Chicagoans crowded into air-conditioned movie theaters and department stores or headed to the lakefront to wade into the cool water. But after sundown those without air conditioners or without the power to run them faced sleepless nights in sweltering apartments. On Friday, July 14, the heat index surpassed 100 degrees for the third consecutive day, and, since the human body can withstand such temperatures for only about 48 hours, thousands of city residents began to require medical attention, and more than one hundred died of heat-related causes.

With reports of rising death tolls and complaints of power and water problems multiplying, the mayor faced reporters about the situation for the first time that afternoon. Much like his father, Richard M. Daley was famous for bungling phrases or for seeming obtuse and insensitive. And since his election in 1989, he had almost always seemed annoyed when members of the media dared to question him.[1] "It's very hot, but let's not blow it out of proportion," he blurted. "Yes, we go to extremes in Chicago, and that's why people like Chicago—we go to extremes."[2] But by the end of the weekend, as the heat wave continued and stories of strained emergency services and a city morgue overwhelmed by dead bodies circulated throughout the local media, the mayor began to regret having taken such a dismissive tone and went into political damage-control mode. It was a blizzard, after all, that had sunk Mayor Bilandic not so long ago. A press conference was set up on Monday, and this time the mayor appeared alongside his health commissioner, Sheila Lyne; his human services commissioner, David Alvarez; his fire commissioner, Raymond Orozco; and his police superintendent, Matt Rodriguez. Despite the fact that Chicago newspapers had been warning of the grave dangers posed by the heat wave as early as July 12, the mayor argued that the city had been initially unaware of the gravity of the situation, but had then acted assertively and effectively. Then, in an effort to deflect blame, he railed at power company Commonwealth Edison for its inept response and threatened an investigation. Perhaps the most telling moment of the press conference came when Fire Commissioner Orozco stepped in front of the microphone and proceeded to redirect blame for heat-related fatalities onto the victims themselves. "We're talking about people who die because they neglect themselves," he claimed. "We did everything possible," he added, "but some people didn't even want to open their doors to us."[3] When temperatures finally dropped to more tolerable levels, an estimated 739 Chicagoans had died as a result of the heat wave—more than twice the number that perished in the Great Chicago Fire of 1871.[4]

Like the flood of 2005 that destroyed much of New Orleans during Hurricane Katrina, the 1995 Chicago heat wave has been remembered as a "natural disaster," an idea that obscures the policies and social values that left certain residents—mostly the poor and the elderly—overexposed to the deadly possibilities of the elements. Just as thousands of lives in New Orleans would likely have been spared had the federal government invested more money in the city's levee system and had the local government made serious efforts to evacuate its less mobile residents, hundreds of those who perished in the Chicago heat would have survived had the city responded more effectively to those in need, and, perhaps even more importantly, had years of social neglect not left residents of the black West and South Sides in such precarious circumstances. In his brilliant "social autopsy" of the Chicago heat wave, sociologist Eric Klinenberg found that the much higher incidence of heat-related deaths in black ghetto areas was caused by a "dangerous ecology of abandoned buildings, open spaces, commercial depletion, violent crime, degraded infrastructure, low population density, and family dispersion," which tended to undermine community life and to isolate elderly black residents.[5] In neighborhoods like North Lawndale, for example, where in 1995 there was about one violent crime for every ten residents, many old people remained in their overheated homes out of fear of being victimized on the streets. And such fears were far from groundless. Even though the heat wave produced a moderate drop in crime around the city, the Chicago Police Department nonetheless recorded 134 narcotics arrests, 50 assaults, and 2 homicides in the North Lawndale district for just that week.[6]

As the preceding chapters have shown, such conditions were shaped by a series of policies implemented between the 1950s and 1980s that tenaciously directed investment capital towards the Loop, reinforced the segregated spatial order of the city, and turned away from the critical challenge of stemming the flight of people and jobs out of Chicago's expanding ghetto. The consequences of such policies were clear in the North Lawndale neighborhood, where the population dropped from over 120,000 in 1960 to just over 40,000 in 2000, a decline that was hastened in the late 1960s and 1970s in particular, when International Harvester closed its factory there (in 1969) and Sears moved its headquarters out of the neighborhood and into the Sears Tower downtown. Back in those years, as Daley Sr. courted Sears CEO Gordon Metcalf, little thought was paid to the people of North Lawndale that Sears was leaving behind. The same had been true more than a decade earlier, when Boss Daley had rejected a proposal to build the city's University of Illinois campus in neighboring East Garfield Park, a move that would have helped to stabilize the economy and real estate market of a large swath of the West Side.

But, if a long history of neglect had made neighborhoods like North Lawndale and Woodlawn the kinds of places that were relatively easy to die in for young and old alike, more immediate circumstances also played a large part in the tragic story of the heat wave—circumstances that revealed a great deal about the direction Chicago was heading under Mayor Richard M. Daley's stewardship in the 1990s. While it is easy to point to the extraordinary conditions brought about by the heat wave—"Let's be realistic, no one realized the deaths of that high occurrence would take place," Daley had told the press—Klinenberg's "social autopsy" reveals that it was, above all, the city's approach to urban service provision that had made it unable to respond to the situation at hand. Under Daley, Chicago city government had become what Klinenberg refers to as an "entrepreneurial state" characterized by deregulation, fiscal austerity, unprecedented outsourcing of services to private organizations in the name of cost-cutting, the promotion of market solutions to public problems, and the guiding assumption that residents should be treated as individual consumers of city services.[7]

In the broiling Chicago heat, such practices became life-or-death issues for those without the means or capacity to fend for themselves. Directives from City Hall to reorganize, streamline, and outsource key emergency and social services hindered the city's capacity to locate and respond rapidly to those in need, and Daley's celebrated Chicago Alternative Policing Strategy (CAPS) program, which had been launched the year before with federal funding via the Violent Crime Control and Law Enforcement Act, failed miserably to deliver the kinds of services it was designed for. CAPS was intended to restructure police work so that beat officers became intimately familiar with the communities they patrolled, thus enabling them to take on roles beyond simple law enforcement—as neighborhood organizers, community leaders, and liaisons to social service providers and city agencies. As idealistic as this might have sounded, it was also a strategy for maintaining low-cost social service provision in a period when federal and state funding for welfare programs was drying up; since the end of Lyndon B. Johnson's War on Poverty, Republicans had been crusading for cost-cutting welfare reform, a project that President Clinton effectively completed when he signed the Personal Responsibility and Work Opportunity Reconciliation Act of 1996.

The orientation of police officers towards the field of social work was symptomatic of such national trends and symbolized how degraded the very meaning of social support had become after decades of antiwelfare rhetoric. It was also emblematic of a wave of urban revanchism—a demonization, criminalization, and disciplining of the poor—that geographer Neil Smith has compared to the Parisian elite's treatment of the laboring classes in late nineteenth-century France.[8] The police officers themselves resented being cast as "soft services" providers, and their reluctance to fill these roles made them ineffective in doing the kind of legwork it would have taken to save the lives of the many elderly residents who died in the Chicago heat.[9] And yet, when the time came to analyze how the system had failed the poor and elderly who had perished, the knee-jerk response by officials like Fire Commissioner Orozco was to blame the victims. This was no slip of the tongue. Orozco's reaction reflected racially infused, neoliberal notions that had been circulating within circles of urban governing elites for years— racially infused in their manner of linking up with time-worn ideas of dysfunctional ghetto culture; neoliberal in their tendency to privatize and individualize issues that in the past had been viewed as public or social in nature.[10]

Scholars have described the ideas and policy approaches that had such lethal consequences during the Chicago heat wave as characteristic of a broad shift to "neoliberal" modes of urban governance in cities all over the world beginning in the 1980s.[11] That is to say, Richard M. Daley's style of governing was part of a larger historical transformation that was hastened on the international level by the programs of Ronald Reagan, Margaret Thatcher, and Helmut Kohl to restructure the state so as to promote unfettered free trade, reduce both taxes and public costs, and privatize property, services, and social support systems. However, even though Daley most likely never even uttered the word *neoliberalism,* it would be mistaken to overlook the role he played in encouraging the hegemony of this rationality in municipal governing circles. Chicago became the poster child for such policies during Daley's twenty-two years as the city's "CEO," the title those in his entourage fittingly bestowed on him, when he guided the transformation of Chicago from a cash-strapped Beirut on the Lake into a bustling global city and world-class tourist destination. By the end of his first full term in office, Daley had turned a $105 million budget deficit into a surplus by reducing the city payroll, reorganizing City Hall, and raising water and sewer rates. During Daley's more than two decades in office, Chicago added more private sector jobs than Los Angeles and Boston combined; its crime rates generally dropped; its high school standardized test scores and graduation rates climbed; its population grew; its real estate market flourished; and the city became number one in the nation in green roofs, square footage of convention space, and annual domestic business-travel visitors.

The list of such successes goes on and on, and, when taken alongside the remarkable feat of being reelected five times without ever breaking a sweat, it is hard not to conclude that Richard M. Daley was, in many respects, the "greatest" mayor of his generation. Edward Rendell, a two-term mayor of Philadelphia in the 1990s before becoming governor of Pennsylvania in 2003, went so far as to call Daley "the best mayor in the history of the country."[12] One can thus be sure that Daley's policies were the buzz among municipal officials at both the U.S. Conference of Mayors and the National League of Cities. Although there is perhaps no better sign of the truly national scope of Daley's influence than the number of officials and advisors he appointed who went on to walk the carpeted halls of President Barack Obama's White House. Arne Duncan, who was Daley's CEO of Chicago Public Schools between 2001 and 2009 served as the United States secretary of education; Valerie Jarrett, Daley's chief of staff, became one of President Obama's closest advisors; David Axelrod, Daley's chief campaign strategist and advisor for nearly twenty years, served as the White House senior advisor for Obama's critical first three years in office; Rahm Emanuel, who headed Daley's fundraising efforts for his first successful mayoral run, was Obama's White House chief of staff before becoming the mayor of Chicago in 2011; even First Lady Michelle Obama, worked for two years in Daley's City Hall as an assistant to the mayor and as a planning official. Moreover, while never formally a member of Daley's administration, William Daley, the mayor's youngest brother, took over the role of White House chief of staff when Emanuel left to run his mayoral campaign. In view of all the links between Daley's City Hall and Obama's White House, it would be hard to argue that the political sensibilities that suffused the Chicago success story of the 1990s and first decade of the twenty-first century did not shape the Obama administration in significant ways.

And yet Obama was never comfortable with this idea. For example, when asked during a 2003 interview with *Chicago Tribune* reporter David Mendell if he thought it would have been a better idea to spend hundreds of millions of dollars on Chicago's poorest neighborhoods rather than on the construction of Millennium Park in the Loop, Obama, at the time an Illinois state senator planning a U.S. Senate run, responded, "If I told you how I really felt, I'd be committing political suicide right here in front of you."[13] Whether due to sheer political expediency or to Obama's increasingly pragmatic orientation, such ambivalence about Daley's policies seemed to resolve itself by the time he set his sights on the White House. But Obama's reluctance to embrace the Daley mystique in 2003 reflected perhaps his rather privileged glimpse into the underside of the Chicago success story. In 2002, for example, Chicago's 647 homicides made it the murder capital of the country, and two of its highest-profile murders that year occurred in the North Kenwood–Oakland area of Obama's own Thirteenth Senate District, where a brick-wielding mob of youths had beaten two men to death after their van had lost control and struck a group of young women sitting on a porch.[14]

This was merely one in a series of brutal murders perpetrated in Chicago's black ghetto neighborhoods that received national exposure in the first decade of the twenty-first century, each incident reminding white Chicagoans of the other world they sped through in the sealed safety of their automobiles on the Dan Ryan, the Skyway, and the Congress Expressway, or else in an "L" train rattling westward or southward from the Loop. During Congressman Bobby Rush's highly ineffective 1999 mayoral primary run, which culminated in his crushing defeat by Daley by a 73–27 margin, the former Black Panther had tried to arouse the ire of blacks and liberals alike by evoking the idea that there were, in fact, two Chicagos: "One Chicago is symbolized by flower pots and Ferris wheels and good jobs and communities where police respect the citizens," Rush had claimed, making reference to Daley's massive program to beautify the city's tourist areas and his $250 million renovation of the Navy Pier lakefront recreation and entertainment area, with its 150-foot-high Ferris wheel. "The second Chicago is still plagued by a lack of jobs, poor schools and police less tolerant of youths who dress and talk differently than they do."[15] If this message posed little threat to the seemingly invincible Daley and his Chicago success story on the citywide stage, it no doubt played a role in Rush's reelection to the House of Representatives the following year, when he collected twice as many votes as his challenger in the Democratic Primary—an ambitious state senator named Barack Obama.

When the figures from the 2000 census appeared, few could take issue with the veracity of Rush's claim. According to the new census data, Chicago had managed to retain its middle class during the 1990s; its median household income had grown at a rate that was twice the national average; and overall poverty had modestly declined—all of which seemed to confirm the triumphant image of Chicago as a leading global city and tourist destination, up there in the top tier with the likes of New York, Los Angeles, San Francisco, and Boston. But the data from the "second Chicago" offered a very different vision. The census readings related to black Chicago and to its astonishing disparity from white Chicago showed a city more statistically akin to the nation's most distressed urban centers: Baltimore, Newark, St. Louis, New Orleans, and Detroit. While the median household income for whites and Latinos in Chicago was $49,000 and $37,000, respectively, it was just $29,000 for blacks, and only 13 percent of black adults held bachelor's degrees, compared to 42 percent of whites.[16] Such disparities helped to explain why Chicago's 50.2 percent employment rate for black males over the age of sixteen put it just barely above New Orleans and St. Louis and well behind Baltimore (54.4) and Newark (54.2). Moreover, Chicago topped all other major metropolitan areas for its percentage of black residents having no access to telephone service (7.2), with Detroit a somewhat distant second. Perhaps most tellingly, African Americans were just 19 percent of the overall population of the Chicago metropolitan area but 43 percent of the popula-

FIGURE 17. The other Chicago: view north along S. Dearborn Street towards the Robert Taylor Homes on E. 54th St. in 1998. Photo by Camilo José Vergara. Reprinted with permission.

tion living below the poverty line, figures that placed the city ahead of every one of the fifteen largest metropolitan areas except for St. Louis in this statistical measure.[17]

Such figures tell only part of the story. They say little, for example, about the street culture and underground economy that so powerfully shaped the life chances of a generation of youths coming of age in the second Chicago. One of the major consequences of the festering poverty was the development in the late 1980s and 1990s of a Hobbesian world of ruthless street gangs engaged in a battle to the finish for control of the lucrative crack cocaine trade that exploded across the American urban landscape in the second half of the 1980s. By the early 1990s, several of the city's mightiest gangs—the Gangster Disciples, Vice Lords, Saints, and Latin Kings, among others—had set up elaborate centralized, hierarchical organizations to administer crack distribution in their respective territories. The business approach they came to adopt resembled the franchise model of the fast-food restaurants that were quickly becoming the only sources of nourishment in their communities: gang leadership distributed product to a number of competing "crews" within the general organization, each of which controled its sales methods and wages so as to maximize its profits after paying "dues" and "street taxes" to the central leadership. The arrangements amounted to a neoliberalism of the streets. Researchers studying the underground drug economy of this moment even observed subcontracting schemes, in which one gang leased a building or street corner to another for the purposes of drug trafficking within its territory. Since crack was normally distributed in small quantities with low purchase costs, the business tended to be labor intensive, requiring countless hand-to-hand transactions and numerous foot soldiers to make the sales, watch for police, keep track of the money, and, when need be, engage in turf battles. Even though estimates of total drug trafficking revenues in the city of Chicago ranged from $500 million to $1 billion, investigative journalists and ethnographers alike determined that the many thousands of foot soldiers—mostly teenagers pursuing hip-hop video dreams laden with Mercedes Benzes and Cadillac Escalades, gold chain necklaces, swimming pools, and shapely women—earned wages just a bit above those offered at McDonald's and KFC.[18]

Yet, despite the disadvantageous risk-reward ratio associated with entry-level work in a crew, gangs were incorporating—if not by financial inducements, then by force and intimidation—increasing numbers of young men into their ranks. In 2006, a Chicago Crime Commission study estimated that some 125,000 youths—more than a quarter of the total number of students within the entire Chicago public school system—belonged to between seventy and one hundred gangs within the city, a sharp rise from the previous count of 70,000 gang members in 2000.[19] It was this trend more than anything else that accounted for Chicago's top rankings among the nation's ten largest cities in rates for both violent crime and homicide. Between 1992 and 2004, the share of murders within the city that were "gang-motivated" rose from 15 percent to more than 35 percent, while the average age of the victims of gang-motivated homicides dropped significantly.[20] During the 2008–2009 school year, a record forty-three Chicago public school students became the victims of gang-related murders, a situation that gained national attention in September 2009 after the brutal murder of sixteen-year-old Derrion Albert, a solid student who had managed to stay clear of gang activities. The Albert affair attracted national and even international coverage through a mobile-phone video of his savage beating during a wild street fight between opposing neighborhood gangs in the far South Side Roseland area—one from around Fenger High School, where Albert had been an honor student, and one from the Altgeld Gardens Housing Project, where Barack Obama had worked as a community organizer in mid-1980s.[21] The video shows Albert, who had apparently walked into the fracas by chance, knocked to the ground by a youth swinging a long wooden board and then bludgeoned and stomped on repeatedly by several others, amidst the screams of female onlookers, who eventually tried to drag the boy to safety.

This scene of unspeakable horror belies or at least complicates the idea, heard in urban policy circles beginning in the late 1990s, that the Chicago Public Schools (CPS) under Mayor Daley's management had become what President Clinton referred to in 1998 as "a model for the nation." Once dubbed the "worst in the nation" by President George Bush's secretary of education William Bennett in 1987, Chicago's schools had been, by many accounts, transformed after 1995, when the Illinois state legislature handed complete control of the CPS over to Mayor Daley. With Gerry Chico as the president of the CPS and Paul Vallas its CEO, the Daley administration implemented a sweeping corporate-style reform that imposed centralized authority over the elected, neighborhood-based Local School Councils (LSCs) established during the Washington years, created a range of special schools and programs, and, perhaps most importantly, ushered in an unforgiving system of accountability based on student performance on annual standardized tests.[22] It was precisely the kind of model that the Bush administration looked to when it designed its No Child Left Behind program, which, after being legislated by Congress in 2001, required all government-run schools receiving federal funding to administer a statewide standardized test in order to evaluate performance. Any school failing to achieve acceptable results after a number of years faced a range of "corrective actions," from curriculum and staff changes to major restructuring measures, including subcontracting its administration to a private company. Several years after its inception, Chicago's program appeared to show some significant results. Between 1995 and 2005, the graduation rate increased from under 42 percent to 51 percent, which moved Chicago from the lower ranks into the middle of the pack of the nation's big cities.[23] Moreover, between 2004 and 2009, the rate of CPS graduates enrolling in college rose from 43.5 to 54.4 percent, a jump that more than tripled the 3.4 percent rise nationally.[24]

And yet such signs of progress pointed to the creation of a multitiered educational system rather than any wholesale improvement. If the Chicago school reforms of the mid-1990s had played a role in increasing the percentage of high school graduates heading off to higher education, they had done little to diminish the city's sizable share of the country's most troubled high schools. According to high school rankings compiled in a 2009 study based on standardized test scores, Chicago possessed seventeen of the one hundred worst performing schools in the United States. New York, by contrast had three, and Philadelphia and San Francisco one each.[25] With only 4 percent of its students proficient in math and 9 percent proficient in reading, Derrion Albert's school, Fenger, was twenty-fourth from the bottom—a situation that helps explain the scene that Albert walked into in September that year. Indeed, while an array of "college prep" magnet schools, charter schools, and high school International Baccalaureate programs had raised the educational bar for many middle-class Chicagoans, such new opportunities remained far out of reach for the vast majority of students.[26] In working-class black and Latino areas of the city, access to the kind of public education that can qualify students for advanced degree programs was scarce. To take but one example, out of the total 11,915 spots available in the city's nine selective college prep high schools in 2011, schools located in low-income black and Latino neighborhoods outside the North Side or immediate Loop vicinity provided only 2,670. And, while students were of course eligible to apply to schools outside their neighborhoods, if they could handle the long commutes, low-income students, who made up some 85 percent of the total student population in the CPS, constituted only about one-third of the enrollments in these North Side and Loop area schools that year.[27] In effect, then, Mayor Daley's celebrated reforms created a system of winners and losers, with the winners living predominantly in white, middle-class, and some gentrifying neighborhoods, and the losers concentrated in low-income black and Latino neighborhoods south and west of the Loop, where according to a 2003 report by the Center for Labor Market Studies, black males were six times more likely than their white counterparts elsewhere in the city to be out of school and unemployed.[28]

Certainly, the allure of the gangs and the absence of promising employment opportunities for young men in the ghettos and barrios loomed large in any explanation for this disparity. But there was also reason to believe that school policies implemented during Daley's aggressive drive to boost test scores and hold schools accountable for poor performance played a role in pushing young men into the precarious place between school and work. A number of studies conducted between 2000 and 2003 revealed dramatic increases in school suspensions for minor nonviolent infractions. Between 1999 and 2000, for example, suspensions jumped from 21,000 to nearly 37,000, with students of color receiving the vast majority of them. Increasing suspensions, moreover, also meant more expulsions, with African Americans, according to a report published by the social service agency Hull House, being three times more likely than whites or Latinos to be expelled.[29]

These strategies of weeding out the students identified as bringing down the numbers gave way in 2006 to a new policy under Daley's Renaissance 2010 plan to close some eighty poorly performing schools over four years and replace them with one hundred privately run charter or contract schools, whose teachers were not required to be certified by the state, received lower salaries, and were barred from joining the Chicago Teachers Union. This discovery of charter schools as the panacea for the city's failing public education system represented the same logic of neoliberalization that was shaping the city's approach to social services provision. Driving this scheme was none other than the Commercial Club, which constituted a committee of high-powered captains of industry and finance under the chairmanship of Exelon Corporation CEO John W. Rowe—including the chairman of the board of McDonald's Corporation and the CEO of the Chicago Board Options Exchange—to design a private-sector answer to Chicago's school problems. The report issued by this Education Committee of the Civic Committee of the Commercial Club was aptly named *Left Behind.* Journalist Rick Perlstein revealed that it "deployed the word 'data' forty-five times, 'score,' 'scored,' or 'scoring' 60 times—and 'test,' 'tested,' and 'testing,' or 'exam' and 'examination,' some 1.47573 times per page."[30] Within a year, Daley was moving on the Renaissance 2010 charter school initiative. Overseen by Arne Duncan, CEO of the CPS at the time, the implementation of Renaissance 2010 met fierce resistance from many LSCs objecting to the disruptions and violence caused by the often-precipitous school closures. In the initial phase of the plan, for example, a series of school closures on the South Side led to student transfers to neighboring areas, which, in turn, caused sharp spikes in gang violence. Community concerns like these, however, were clearly secondary to the objectives of raising scores and cutting costs. Further suggestive of the neoliberal rationality that infused the plan was a 2007 speech made by CPS president Rufus Williams in front of the Chicago City Club, a group of civic and business leaders, in which he compared the idea of LSCs running schools to a chain of hotels being managed by "those who sleep in the hotels."[31]

Such policies—suspensions, expulsions, closures, and the dampening of local participation in the decision-making process—were components of a public relations campaign to manufacture evidence of progress resolving problems that had opened the city to widespread criticism in the 1980s and early 1990s, when a series of teachers' strikes and parent-led community protests raised awareness about gang violence and of the lack of funding for necessary school improvements and salary increases. But they also spoke once again to the revanchist spirit of neoliberal governance that fed off the hard-edged antiwelfare, law-and-order rhetoric coming out of Washington during this same period. This was an approach and an ethos that circulated among policy makers in cities across the United States, but that saw perhaps its clear-est expression in Richard M. Daley's Chicago success story. One of the pio-neering innovations brought about by Daley's overhaul of the system in 1995 was the establishment of three military high schools as well as the dramatic expansion of military programs in numerous high schools and middle schools.[32] Predominantly enrolling blacks and to a lesser extent Latinos, these military high schools, which used military-style forms of punishment for violations of school rules, achieved graduation rates and test scores that placed them in the top ranks of the schools available to working-class blacks and Latinos. But they were also living monuments to the idea that what was amiss in Chicago's schools had more to do with the cultural shortcomings of black and Latino students than with the structural inequalities of the school system itself. All it takes is some military-style discipline, the argument went, to make things right.

A similar kind of rationale infused the move to orient the academic evalua-tion process around a standardized test. Yet, while Chicago school officials never missed a chance to remind people that all students in Chicago were evaluated by the same test—the "Iowa Tests"—and thus held to the same standards, the test in practice exacerbated already existing disparities between the city's most elite schools, which were disproportionately middle class and white, and its lowest-achieving ones, which were overwhelmingly working-class black and Latino. In schools where scores were lowest, classroom time was dominated by lessons geared more towards test preparation than intellectual development. One researcher who sat in on classes in several such schools observed teachers making extensive use of materials on test-taking strategies, training students for hours on filling in multiple-choice bubbles, and having them recite slogans such as "three B's in a row, no, no, no."[33] Understandably, such conditions contributed to higher dropout rates and disciplinary problems in poorly performing schools, whereas in schools with little risk of failure, teachers faced fewer test-related constraints and could more effectively orient their lessons to the interests and intellectual needs of their students.

In view of such glaring inequalities, it was becoming difficult to argue that Chicago's school system represented a model to be emulated. And yet, while fewer and fewer observers seemed willing to make this case, some of the key ingredients in its so-called success story—the replacement of failing neighborhood schools with charter schools and the emphasis on standardized testing—were incorporated into President Obama's education policy. Such circumstances beg the question of how, considering Chicago's disproportionate share of the worst performing schools in the nation and its high rate of student homicides, the CPS had ever stopped being seen, as George H. W. Bush's secretary of education William Bennett once referred to it, as the nation's worst.

And how was it that the dire situation in the vast majority of black and Latino high schools did not stir up more opposition to Mayor Daley within these communities. Even when faced with an established black politician from the South Side like Bobby Rush—someone who, as a U.S. congressman, had earned political capital both locally and nationally—Daley still managed to capture around half of the black vote. Among Latinos, moreover, Daley's support was so strong throughout his more than two decades in office that not a single Latino politician ever dared to make a serious run against him. These are questions that must be explored on a number of levels, and though this particular study has attempted to delineate a set of experiences that were somehow specific to the inhabitants of the 234 square miles of urban space that lie in the northernmost part of the state of Illinois, it is important to recall that Daley's Chicago was embedded within a national political context that played a critical role in shaping the meaning of the circumstances transpiring within its borders. In other words, how working-class blacks and Latinos viewed their situation related, in part, to ideological currents that blew into the city from elsewhere—through their television sets, radios and stereos, computer screens, and telephones.

And what they increasingly saw and heard beginning in the late 1980s and continuing through the 1990s were images, stories, diatribes, polemics, and anecdotes that described the problems in their schools and neighborhoods as consequences of cultural deficiencies—of dysfunctional family situations and debased moral values—rather than as the by-products of economic marginalization and racial discrimination. Moreover, these were messages purveyed not merely by the right flank of the Republican Party. The antiwelfare crusade that began during the Reagan years had gained so much momentum that by the mid-1990s it had captured the nation's entire political center. It was a Democratic president, Bill Clinton, in fact, who signed the famous 1996 Welfare Reform Act (officially known as the Personal Responsibility and Work Opportunity Reconciliation Act), which, as he proclaimed, "end[ed] welfare as we know it," a move that followed his active sponsorship of the largest federal crime bill (the Violent Crime Control and Law Enforcement Act) in U.S. history. With the Republicans under the leadership of Newt Gingrich regaining both houses of Congress in the 1994 midterm elections, Clinton sought to steal their fire by keeping pace with their calls for a tougher approach to law enforcement and an end to a welfare system that had destroyed values of "personal responsibility" and hard work. The two pieces of legislation amounted to a continuation of the Reagan Revolution's dramatic shift of federal funds from social spending to law enforcement—a trend that played a leading role in increasing the kinds of racial disparities in Chicago that had been so glaringly revealed by the 2000 census.[34] And yet in the national discussion about the persistence of such racial inequalities, notions of "personal responsibility" and cultural deficiencies took center stage, pushing to the margins analyses focusing on the forces of racial discrimination.

Making matters worse was the fact that some of the most prominent voices arguing for a cultural interpretation of black inner-city poverty came from a number of black intellectuals who had themselves risen out of such conditions—scholars like Shelby Steele and Thomas Sowell of Stanford's conservative Hoover Institute and the University of Chicago's famed sociologist William Julius Wilson.[35] That Wilson, a self-proclaimed "social democrat" favoring aggressive Great Society–style intervention in the urban labor market, found himself grouped with strident conservatives like Steele and Sowell was a sign of just how compelling the culture-of-poverty argument was to Americans in the late 1980s and 1990s. Wilson's primary objective in both his landmark 1978 book *The Declining Significance of Race* and in his 1987 study *The Truly Disadvantaged* was to argue for class-based social policies that were better adapted to the specific circumstances of poverty faced by a black underclass trapped in spatially and socially isolated ghettos with poor schools and scarce job opportunities.[36] But by making the corollary argument that fighting racial discrimination was no longer as necessary as it had been in the past, he left himself open to charges that he was minimizing racism as a cause of ghetto poverty, and in delineating the distinct conditions of black underclass poverty—single-parent families, juvenile delinquency, academic failure, the lack of positive role models, and the breakdown of community institutions—he seemed to some observers to be straying too far on to the well-worn ground of culture-of-poverty pathologies. Wilson, who served as an informal advisor to Bill Clinton during his first term and as a consultant to Mayor Daley, appeared to be telling Democrats to move past the kind of divisive race-based policies (for example, affirmative action) that had caused the defection of white middle-class moderates from the party since the late 1960s. Conservatives, for their part, were thrilled by Wilson's apparent minimization of racism. Of course they were distorting his argument, and Wilson himself cried foul in a number of high-profile interviews, but the fact remained that a Chicago-based, black social democrat with impeccable academic credentials who had been raised by a single mother on welfare had signed his name to an award-winning book entitled *The Declining Significance of Race.*

MANAGING THE MARGINALIZED

The views of prominent black conservative scholars like Steele and Sowell and of somewhat misunderstood liberals like Wilson were less consequential to ordinary Chicagoans of color than the more popular ideological currents and political movements circulating through their neighborhoods. In the early 1990s, Chicago was at the center of what was then and still is the largest single mass mobilization in the black community since the era of civil rights—the Million Man March on Washington, DC, in 1995. Organized by Chicago-based Nation of Islam (NOI) leader Minister Louis Farrakhan, the march was called in an effort to "convey to the world a vastly different picture of the Black male" during a moment when law-and-order politicians and the culture industries alike were painting black youths as gangsters and drug dealers.[37] The idea for the march took shape shortly after the Republican takeover of Congress, and march organizers sought to use the mobilization to register black voters for the next elections and draw attention to issues facing black communities. Yet such political projects were subsumed by the overriding messages of personal responsibility, self-help, and spiritual atonement. In effect, ordinary African Americans were being told to mobilize collectively against racism but that the real path to their salvation was not political but rather spiritual and, above all, personal.

This package of ideas had been assembled on Chicago's South Side, in the Nation of Islam's headquarters at 7351 South Stony Island Avenue, where, since the mid-1980s, Farrakhan had been drawing increasingly large audiences to his mosque to hear elaborate rants sprinkled with anti-Semitism, homophobia, and a range of conspiracy theories. Nor was this recipe unique. About twenty blocks southwest of NOI headquarters, Reverend Jeremiah Wright had been touching on some similar themes—if in less sensationalist and provocative terms—in sermons from the pulpit of Trinity United Church of Christ. By the early 1990s Wright's charisma had enabled him to amass a congregation of several thousand members—University of Chicago law professor Barack Obama and his wife, Michelle, among them. To be sure, Obama and many of his fellow congregants at Trinity would have been loath to think of themselves as somehow associated with the NOI, but it was hard to deny that Wright and Farrakhan belonged to the same context. It was not by chance, for example, that the two South Side religious leaders shared the stage at the Million Man March. But while Wright was rapidly becoming a powerful local figure, presiding over a congregation of more than six thousand by the time he retired in 2008, Farrakhan was moving into the national spotlight. By the early 1990s, the Nation of Islam's membership was increasing nationwide, Farrakhan's outrageous declarations about Jews and UFOs were making tabloid headlines, and a number of enormously popular rap artists, such as Public Enemy, Ice Cube, and X-Clan were incorporating excerpts of the NOI leader's speeches into gold- and platinum-selling albums. And yet rap and the NOI made rather strange bedfellows. If a new generation of West Coast "gangsta rappers," like NWA (Niggas With Attitude) and Ice Cube, had offered some penetrating critiques of what the Reagan Revolution's vision of law and order had meant for a generation of black ghetto youths, by the time of the Million Man March, the images of criminality, violence, sexism, and immorality purveyed by rap music and videos had become a big part of the problem that the movement's organizers were seeking to address. "By the summer of 1993 gangsta rap had been reduced to 'nihilism for nihilism's sake,'" writes historian Robin D. G. Kelley, and this sense of nihilism—much like the message of personal responsibility that stood dialectically opposed to it—only provided further confirmation for those claiming that black inner-city poverty was a cultural rather a structural issue.[38] *Nihilism, dysfunction,* and *pathology* were the terms that defined the problem of black underclass poverty throughout the 1990s and into the early years of the twenty-first century. That even the eminent radical black activist and philosopher Cornel West would peer into the heart of the black ghetto and see a world of "nihilism," as he did in his classic 1994 *Race Matters,* reflected a profound loss of faith in the political system among working-class blacks and their leaders across urban America.[39]

But in Chicago, in particular, where voter turnout was reaching new lows and mayoral elections were considered local jokes, the pessimism about the possibility of political solutions to the problems people faced in their daily lives was especially pronounced—a situation that seemed all too apparent during Bobby Rush's uninspiring campaign of 1999. There were glimmers of hope from time to time, as when blacks turned out in 1993 to help elect the first black woman to the U.S. Senate, Carol Moseley Braun. However this was state and not local politics, and Moseley Braun was, in some sense, a gift from Daley, who not only endorsed her but also convinced many of his deep-pocketed donors to throw their financial support behind her as well. This was, in part, payback for services already rendered; in 1989, as a member of the U.S. House of Representatives, Moseley Braun had given her own endorsement to Daley, a deed she repeated in 1995.[40]

Another moment of political possibility, moreover, appeared to be developing in the months leading up to the 1995 aldermanic elections, when, out of the deepest reaches of apparent black underclass nihilism—the impoverished neighborhoods around the Robert Taylor Homes in Chicago's Third Ward—an insurgent poor people's movement crystallized around the candidacy of former Gangster Disciple (GD) Wallace "Gator" Bradley. The financing, manpower, and guidance behind Bradley's campaign came from a political organization called 21st Century Vote, which Gangster Disciple kingpin Larry Hoover had launched in 1990 from a high security federal prison while serving a sentence of 150 to 200 years for murder. Hoover was running with the GDs in the late 1960s, when some of Chicago's most fearsome gangs were trying to transform into political organizations, but his own personal awakening came not on the streets of Englewood but in a number of prisons, where he earned his GED and remade the Gangster Disciples into a political organization he called Growth and Development. While critics would maintain that Hoover's turn to politics was a cover for his continuing leadership of the GDs' massive drug trafficking enterprise, a taped telephone conversation between Hoover and Vice Lord leader Willie Lloyd in 1992 revealed an ambitious plan to mobilize "the poor people" around the housing projects, including the "dope fiends and wineys," in order to take the aldermanic seat from Daley-backed Dorothy Tillman. In 1993, the organization moved into a second-floor office above an abandoned storefront in Englewood and promptly organized thousands of youths to march on City Hall to prevent the closing of some neighborhood health clinics and help settle a teacher's strike; a year later, 21st Century Vote had registered several thousand voters and had raised well over $100,000 from mostly small donations. Yet, although Bradley was able to get national attention by forcing a runoff with Tillman, African Americans in the Third Ward were not ready to believe that gangbangers could become community leaders, and the thousands of Gangster Disciples who hit the streets for Bradley only seemed to make matters worse. Bradley lost badly in the general election, and 21st Century Vote faded into insignificance.[41]

The story of Larry Hoover and 21st Century Vote provides some insight into how Mayor Daley could have presided over the two Chicagos while arousing so little agitation from those living in the subaltern one, the Chicago of litter-strewn vacant lots, boarded-up buildings tagged with gang symbols, impossibly high unemployment, and gunshots piercing the night. If the term *machine* does not do justice to the sophisticated mechanisms of social control that characterized the administration of Richard M. Daley, countersubversive tactics that resembled those from the glory days of Richard J. Daley's machine were certainly called to service in response to Gator Bradley's challenge. The police turned up the heat on the Gangster Disciples in the days before the election with roundups and other forms of harassment, and from the beginning the Chicago press seemed much too zealous in its demonization of Hoover. Prior to one of Hoover's parole hearings, for example, a *Tribune* editorial argued, "Hoover is a leader, all right. He helped lead neighborhoods down a self-destructive road of murder, drug abuse and despair. His release would undermine the authority of law-abiding folks who lead by example, yet don't get a parade of politicians to sing their praises." Whether City Hall had played a role in the *Tribune*'s crusade against Hoover we will never know for sure, but we do know that city officials came to every parole hearing to insist that Hoover was still the gangster he had always been.[42] However, Hoover and his ragtag band of lumpenproletariat was all too easy for Daley to contain. Harder to explain was Daley's role in anesthetizing the injuries of the city's other half and paralyzing any forces of political opposition amidst a series of scandals, any one of which might have been enough to bring another mayor to his knees.

In late 1995, just months after the Daley administration had displayed its callous attitude towards the poor during the heat wave, a massive FBI sting known as Operation Silver Shovel revealed a culture of rampant corruption within Daley's City Hall, including bribes for city contracts, fraud, money laundering, drug trafficking, and organized crime activity. The more than 1,100 wiretap recordings made during this operation showed that everyone around Daley seemed to be on the take, and these were hardly victimless crimes. Chicago residents, whose property taxes were on the rise in the 1990s, had for years been paying what amounted to a "contract corruption" tax, and minority-owned contractors, which had enjoyed an affirmative action program put in place during the Washington years, were no longer seeing their rightful 24 percent share of the city's construction business because of a range of fraudulent practices. In one of the worst cases, James M. Duff, one of the heads of a reputed organized crime family and a big financial supporter of Daley, had convinced an African American employee to pose as majority owner of one of his waste management companies in order to win a contract intended for minority-owned businesses.[43]

During this time, moreover, a series of investigations began to uncover a hideous pattern of police torture at the city's South Side Area 2 police station, where, it was later determined, 137 African American men were tortured into confessions on the orders of police lieutenant Jon Burge between 1972 and 1991. Detainees had reportedly had plastic bags placed over their heads, guns shoved in their mouths, and electrical shocks and cigarette burns administered to their ears, nostrils, chests, and genitals. Daley was not mayor while most of this was going on, but as Cook County state's attorney in the early 1980s, he had been informed of such practices by reliable sources and had refused to launch an inquiry. Based in part on the revelations of these coerced confessions, Illinois governor George Ryan halted all executions in the state of Illinois in 2000, and three years later commuted the death sentences of 167 prisoners on Illinois's death row while pardoning four death row inmates tortured at the Area 2 station. Ryan's bold moves, however, did little to change the killing going on in the streets. In 2001 and then again 2003, Chicago made headlines as the "murder capital" of the United States, registering more homicides than the significantly more populous cities of New York and Los Angeles.

In January 2004, City Hall was ensconced in scandal once again, when the *Chicago Sun-Times* discovered serious improprieties in the city's $40-million-per-year Hired Truck Program. Trucking companies with ties to both organized crime and high-ranking city officials were being awarded lucrative contracts for doing little or no work, and while nothing could be directly pinned on Daley, there was too much circumstantial evidence to dismiss. Some 25 percent, or $47.8 million, of all Hired Truck money went to companies from Daley's Eleventh Ward power base, companies in the program had contributed more than $100,000 combined to Daley's campaigns, and Daley's brother John had underwritten insurance policies for a handful of them.[44] As federal prosecutors continued on with the Hired Truck scandal, evidence surfaced that Victor Reyes, a close Daley advisor and head of the powerful Hispanic Democratic Organization (HDO), had rigged hiring and promotion exams to reward city workers, including members of the HDO, for their political activities on behalf of Daley and other candidates.

All this to say that between 1995 and 2005, there was almost never a moment in Chicago when the city did not seem, at least in the eyes of its mostly black and Latino low-income residents, to be a place of monumental injustice—where big businessmen, mobsters, and people with personal ties to the Daley family and its close friends got fat, while poor blacks and Latinos were being gunned down on street corners and tortured in the back rooms of police stations. Even if one could ignore the litany of corruption scandals that appeared in the pages of the dailies and utter, "That's just the way it is," Chicago slapped the have-nots in the face every time they ventured near the Loop. A simple drive north on Lakeshore Drive took one through the Chicago of clean, tree-lined streets, marinas full of shiny white pleasure boats, well-manicured green park spaces, tidy beaches with volleyball nets fronting a sparkling blue Lake Michigan, rapidly rising real estate values, and neighborhoods with names befitting the class of people living there: the Gold Coast, Lincoln Park, and Lakeview. The many thousands of residents in the Cabrini-Green Homes, a quadrant of mid- and high-rise block-like structures with fenced-in balconies, where the Gangster Disciples ran a drug trafficking operation that earned them an estimated $3 million per year before its demolition in 2010 and 2011, were just a short walk away from the upscale Gold Coast neighborhood. William Julius Wilson made an important point when he emphasized the social *and* spatial isolation of the black poor in Chicago, but one should not take this idea too far: African Americans in the city understood quite well how the other half lived. But even though poor people of color regularly confronted such "savage inequalities,"[45] they showed little interest in addressing them by investing in the electoral process. In the mayoral election of 2007, for example, overall voter turnout was just over 30 percent, with 70 percent of blacks and 80 percent of Latinos casting their votes for Richard M. Daley. In 1989, by contrast, Daley had garnered under 10 percent of the black vote.

So what accounted for the lack of opposition to Daley among blacks and Latinos and his virtual invincibility at the polls over his more than two decades in office? Some of the explanation brings us back into the cogs of the political machine he inherited from his father. The tactics City Hall deployed against Gator Bradley, as well as the various illegal schemes that created both jobs and lucrative contracts for Daley supporters, reveal the workings of a political machine that resembled the one run by Richard J. Daley in the 1960s and 1970s. Also similar was the absolute authority Richard M. Daley wielded over his city council, which came in part from a 1978 law giving the mayor the power to fill city council vacancies. By 2002, he had appointed one-third of the members of the city council, which may help explain why he did not have to use his veto power even once between 1989 and 2005. As political scientist Dick Simpson's research has found, two-thirds of the members of the city council voted with the mayor 90–100 percent of the time.[46] These aldermen stood with Daley because, as in the old days, the mayor controlled a spigot of patronage funds for irrigating their wards. But even if the Hired Truck scandal seemed to indicate that, in spite of the *Shakman* decree, a system of jobs for political supporters was still in operation, what really moved things during the Richard M. Daley era was "pinstripe patronage"— contracts for lawyers, consultants, and various other service providers, as well as enormous infrastructural subsidies and preferential policies for the developers who erected the city's office buildings and retail centers, as well as for the companies who filled them. It was in this area in particular that Richard M. Daley's patronage machine represented something of a paradigm shift from that of his father. Pinstripe patronage, in the high times of the global-city era, was not about demanding small donations from thousands of loyalists and giving out contracts to put new toilets in City Hall but rather about attracting five- and six-figure campaign donations from multimillionaires in exchange for seven- and eight-figure contracts, new tax loopholes, and a range of lucrative subsidies. Even in his very first campaign, in 1989, Daley had amassed an unprecedented $7 million in donations, with some 30 percent coming from just 1 percent of his contributors. Moreover, in addition to traditional support from contractors and construction unions, some two-thirds of Daley's donations came from law firms (like the famous Sidley & Austin, where Barack Obama met his wife, Michelle Robinson), banks, commodities and stock traders, businesses, and consulting firms enmeshed in the global economy.[47]

Moreover, if Richard J. Daley had used some accounting tricks to veil the city's financial situation, his son took this practice to another level of sophistication. Critical to Richard M. Daley's pinstripe patronage juggernaut, for example, was his tax increment financing (TIF) program, a labyrinthine public financing method that he used to create a virtual "shadow budget" of over $500 million—about one-sixth of the city's total budget—to fund large development projects, infrastructural improvements, and beautification efforts.[48] The original idea behind TIFs, which began to be increasingly adopted in municipalities across the nation in the 1980s with the drying up of federal urban renewal funds and sharp reductions in federal development grants, was to create a mechanism that would channel capital towards improvements in distressed or blighted areas where development might not otherwise occur.[49] In a typical TIF program, property tax revenues in excess of the amounts determined to be needed within a certain geographical area are allocated to a special discretionary fund for "public" projects. The thinking is that these projects, in turn, will theoretically improve the area and thus lead to increased tax revenues that will replenish the TIF fund and likely add to it in following years. Yet like so many other progressive-minded policy approaches that arrived in postwar Chicago, the problem with Chicago's TIF program was that City Hall took the money and ran away from the progressive goals attached to it, and it did so behind closed doors. In fact, TIFs, by nature, are ill-suited to socially progressive ends—the construction of affordable housing or the creation of middle-class jobs—because of their adherence to a commercial logic contingent upon sharp increases in property values.[50] Making matters worse in Chicago was the way in which Mayor Richard M. Daley incorporated the TIF system into his pinstripe patronage machine. While TIF projects involving private companies had to be approved by a city council vote and thereby made public, the large portion of funds used for neighborhood improvements—new schools, sidewalk and street repaving, and the upgrading of park and recreation facilities, for example—were not subject to public scrutiny, allowing them to be used as patronage rewards to distribute among aldermen loyal to the Daley machine.

This lack of transparency enabled the creation of a public funding system that reinforced inequalities rather than ameliorating them, a situation that remained largely obscured until Ben Joravsky, a journalist for Chicago's leading alternative newspaper, the *Chicago Reader*, managed to get his hands on some internal TIF documents. According to Joravsky's investigative work, TIFs skimmed $1 billion in property taxes off the city's revenues between 2003 and 2006.[51] Indicative of how unevenly this money was spread across the city, in 2007 the downtown LaSalle/Central TIF district added some $19 million in revenues while the Roseland/Michigan TIF district—the area often referred to as "the hundreds," where Derrion Albert was murdered— brought in a mere $707,000.[52] Moreover, in 2009, a year in which Daley announced the need to eliminate jobs and cut back services because of a $500 million budget deficit linked to the country's financial crisis, the city council voted in favor of allocating $35 million from the LaSalle/Central TIF district to subsidize the move of United Airlines into seven floors of the Willis Tower.[53] City officials justified the offer by arguing that United's presence in the Willis Tower, in addition to solving the embarrassing problem of vacant floors in Chicago's most prestigious skyscraper, would bring some 2,500 jobs to the city. This was a far better deal for the city as a whole than the $56 million in public subsidies paid to Boeing in 2001, when it moved its headquarters from Seattle to Chicago, bringing some 450 jobs with it.[54]

As the enormous subsidies offered to Boeing and United reveal, the maintenance of Chicago's image as a high-flying global city was a top priority for the Daley administration. In this sense, Daley was no different from his homologue in New York City, Rudolph Giuliani, who in December 1998 offered the New York Stock Exchange a historically unprecedented $900 million in cash along with a package of tax breaks and other subsidies to prevent its move across the river to New Jersey. Next to this, the money spent on Boeing and United seemed more than reasonable, and the addition of these high-profile corporations helped to offset the psychological blows of losing Amoco, Ameritech, and Inland Steel to corporate takeovers. City officials provided further justification by repeatedly referring to the rosy estimates of certain economists about the "multiplier effects" of having all these highly paid white-collar workers around the downtown area. During the United affair, for example, Second Ward alderman Robert Fioretti, whose jurisdiction stretches from the bustling Loop westward into the depressed area around East Garfield Park, argued that the airline's employees would spend an average of $6,700 in the downtown area—on, presumably, martinis, steaks, athletic club memberships, and a range of elite services. But the multiplier effects of this consumption stopped well short of Fioretti's constituents on the black West Side, where the challenge was to lure low-cost food retailers in order to combat the problem of "food deserts"—large areas in which residents have little or no access to healthy food sources.

This area of the city had been devastated in 2003, when just to the west of it, in West Garfield Park, candy maker Brach's Confections, Inc., closed a factory that provided more than a thousand jobs. With one of its signature items, Candy Corn, a nauseatingly sweet, waxy-textured corn-kernel facsimile commonly eaten by children around Halloween, Brach's did little to boost Chicago's global-city credentials, so Daley was unwilling to offer more than $10 million to try to retain its one thousand jobs—not nearly enough to dissuade the company from moving its operations into Mexico. Ironically, this was about the same amount City Hall would draw from the Northwest Industrial Corridor TIF five years later at the request of a developer seeking to convert the abandoned Brach's factory into a warehouse and distribution center, which, according to the developer's own estimate, would provide just seventy-five permanent jobs.[55] The project would, however, eventually pay for itself in future income tax revenue, much of which would find its way back into the Northwest Industrial TIF, where it would be spent, of course, at the discretion of City Hall.[56]

That more than $10 million was allocated to a project that promised to create just seventy-five jobs in an area whose 17.3 percent unemployment rate ranked among the highest in the city in 2007 and whose principal high schools, Marshall and Austin, reported attendance rates around 50 percent revealed that Chicago's TIF program had become almost entirely unhinged from any reasonable notion of the public interest. And yet much of what made the city's financing system patently unjust occurred under the radar. Unlike the machine of old, which was out on the streets taking bribes, pouring drinks, handing out turkeys, and dispatching thugs to make sure people voted "early and often," Richard M. Daley's well-oiled machine seemed to hum silently beneath the city. There were of course corruption scandals enough to raise eyebrows now and then, but it could be argued that these scandals, in the end, overshadowed and even legitimated the quasi-legal policies that were redistributing public capital upwards. That is to say, Operation Silver Shovel, the Hired Truck scandal, and many of the other tales of cronyism that made it into the dailies created a deeply flawed perception of Richard M. Daley's "machine." Mid-level city officials consorting with gangsters and taking middle-class bribes, private trucks idling in parking lots at a rate of $50 per hour, strings pulled to arrange jobs for political supporters—these scandals hardly scratched the surface of what was really going on with Chicago's finances. They made Richard M. Daley's administration look too much like Richard J. Daley's machine, an idea that obscured how much the scale of injustice had changed since the early 1990s. And even if the TIF program enabled City Hall to veil some of its dealings, the details of the majority of expenditures were out there for everyone to see, provided they wanted to make the effort to do so.

But until the months before the mayoral election of 2007, when the whole country was reeling from the blow of the subprime mortgage crisis, few political organizations were willing to take on either the global city agenda or the neoliberal municipal policies that were imposing austerity on the poor and shifting so much of Chicago's tax revenues to business interests downtown and elsewhere throughout the city. This was in part because, viewed from the perspective of its thriving downtown and surrounding areas, Chicago looked like a city that was clearly moving in the right direction. Mayor Daley had invested massively in both beautification initiatives and the upgrading of tourist attractions, especially around the downtown lakefront area, making Chicago a first-tier destination for both business travelers and tourists. In terms of beautification, City Hall pushed through a new landscape ordinance in 1999 that put more trees on sidewalks, more flower beds on the medians of avenues, more planters in commercial districts, and obligated developers and builders to incorporate aesthetically pleasing landscaping into their designs. Mayor Daley's drive to beautify the city was so consuming that after visiting Paris, he ordered the installation of lights on the city's bridges and skyscrapers in order to give Chicago a Paris-by-night feel.

His efforts to improve the city's tourism infrastructure were nothing short of staggering: In 1991, a new baseball park for the White Sox opened thanks, in part, to $81 million of city financing. Between 1992 and 1994, City Hall kicked in some $35 million in infrastructural costs for the construction of the United Center, the new home for the Chicago Bulls professional basketball team. In 1995, it allocated $250 million for the renovation of Navy Pier. In 1996 it completed a $675 million expansion of McCormick Place, giving the city the most square footage of convention space in the nation. In 1998 it spent $110 million to reconfigure Lake Shore Drive in order to create a "Museum Campus" that gathered Soldier Field (the stadium of the Chicago Bears), the Shedd Aquarium, the Field Museum of Natural History, and Adler Planetarium on one massive green space by the lake. In 2003 it financed a $680 million renovation of Soldier Field. In 2004 it inaugurated the $475 million ($200 million of which came from private donations) Millennium Park, a spectacular twenty-five-acre green space bordering the Chicago Art Institute to the north and Grant Park to the west that includes the three-story polished stainless steel bean-shaped *Cloud Gate* sculpture, the fifty-foot-high interactive glass brick *Crown Fountain,* a 2.5-acre flower garden, a large outdoor ice skating rink, a 1,500-seat performing arts theater, numerous spaces for art expositions, and its centerpiece, a state-of-the-art outdoor music pavilion crowned with a spectacular stainless steel bandshell designed by Frank Gehry.[57] In 2005, the Federal Aviation Administration approved an estimated $6 billion plan by the city to expand O'Hare Airport's capacity by 60 percent. And in 2007, Chicago opened yet another addition to McCormick Place, the $850 million McCormick Place West building.[58]

All this was of course part of the global-city agenda laid out by the mayor's planning advisors in the 2002 Chicago Central Area Plan, which called for a downtown district of revitalized green spaces, promenades, and waterfront attractions. "Chicago," the plan asserted, "will retain its role as one of the world's great crossroads cities, attracting businesses, residents, and visitors internationally... Its Central Area will be a preeminent international meeting place, easily accessible from major destinations around the globe via expanded O'Hare International and Midway Airports."[59] What was taking shape so spectacularly along Chicago's lakefront was part of a larger trend of urban revitalization that grew out of the convergence of the new economy of tourism and the global-city agenda. One result was the development of what political scientist Dennis Judd refers to as a "tourist bubble"—an upscale commercial district in which "tourist and entertainment facilities coexist in a symbiotic relationship with downtown corporate towers."[60] All one needed to do was to take a long stroll down Michigan Avenue from the area around the John Hancock Center and the Water Tower Place shopping center all the way across the Chicago River to Millenium Park to understand Judd's point. In this tourist-friendly swath of the city, restaurants, shopping centers, cafés, and bars catered to both tourists and daytime professionals. And yet there was much more to the overall plan than this. Chicago's massive capital investments in its tourism and business services infrastructure during the 1990s, which helped make it the top business traveler destination and the fourth for overall domestic travel by 2002, were part of a larger strategy to assure economic growth in an era of advancing deindustrialization. According to one study, travel-generated spending increased the city's sales tax revenues from $54 million in 1989 to $145 million in 1999. By 2007 domestic and international travelers to Chicago were spending more than $11 billion annually, a sum that contributed over $217 million in local tax revenues and generated some 130,000 jobs.[61]

This infusion of capital helped to offset the loss of about 100,000 jobs in the manufacturing sector between 1986 and 2000, and a good number of the new service jobs created went to the residents of the working-class black and Latino communities most affected by the forces of deindustrialization.[62] This was a process that Daley's school reform program promoted through its creation of several Education-to-Career Academies (ETCs), vocational high schools offering nonacademic concentrations in key areas of the tourist services sector such as secretarial sciences and hospitality management. Such structures of employment opportunity warn against taking too far the idea of an impenetrable barrier between the downtown business district and the other Chicago where low-income blacks and Latinos live. Every morning, thousands of people from these communities commuted into the Loop and its surrounding areas to work in office buildings, restaurants, hotels, bars, cafés, retail stores, and a range of tourist venues. To be sure, the service jobs they performed, on average, paid much less than the manufacturing jobs they replaced; a study commissioned by the U.S. Department of Labor in 2001, for example, found that while the average annual salary for Cook County manufacturing workers was $40,840, service-sector workers took home a significantly lower $32,251, and retail workers earned just $17,045.[63] But these jobs helped to stave off the worst in the other Chicago, extending lifelines into Latino and black communities facing 20 percent unemployment rates. The political stability prevailing in Chicago between 1989 and 2006 would have been unthinkable without the fantastic growth in tourist and business-traveler spending, which dipped sharply after the World Trade Center attacks of September 11, 2001 but then quickly rebounded after 2002.

In addition, at least some of the billions of dollars that City Hall poured into its infrastructural projects in the late 1990s and early years of the twenty-first century found its way into black and Latino communities—another reason why Daley's electoral coalition held together so well. While African Americans and Latinos never received their rightful shares of city business, Daley was careful to spread just enough patronage into these communities to preempt charges of racism. During his first decade in office, for example, blacks, who constituted around 36 percent of the population and 40 percent of the city council membership, represented about 33 percent of the municipal labor force, and black-owned companies secured between 10 and 12 percent of city contracts. Latinos, by comparison, who constituted 28 percent of the population but held just 11 percent of the city's jobs and procured 14 percent of its contracts, seemed to have fared rather poorly. But these numbers represented enormous gains from the Harold Washington years, when they procured a mere 4 percent of city contracts and 5 percent of city jobs.[64] And when complaints about such arrangements arose, as they did especially in some quarters of black Chicago, those responding to them were likely to be high-ranking blacks and Latinos within Daley's cabinet.

Political scientist Larry Bennett has argued that one of the main pillars of Daley's approach to governance was "elite social inclusivity."[65] Unlike his father, for whom, in the oft-quoted words of his press secretary Frank Sullivan, "affirmative action was nine Irishmen and a Swede," Richard M. Daley was the first white mayor in Chicago to appoint significant numbers of blacks, Latinos, and Asians to high-profile positions in his administration. This was an objective the mayor had pursued since his first days in office, when the *Chicago Tribune* declared a "rainbow cabinet" had been installed in City Hall.[66] By 2006, Daley's cabinet contained seven African Americans (17 percent), 24 whites (59 percent), 7 Latinos (17 percent) and 3 Asians (7 percent), with blacks and Latinos compensating for their relative underrepresentation by their presence in some highly visible posts. Daley's public relations savvy dictated that minority appointments be deployed strategically to those areas of city government most liable to come under public criticism from minority groups. His appointees for president of the Chicago Board of Education, for example, were always black or Latino, as were his human resources (or personnel) commissioners, and an African American served as his press secretary—the all-important face of his public relations apparatus—throughout Daley's twenty-two years in office.

What was being so brilliantly accomplished in all this—in the ward-level distribution of TIF funds for the benefit of local political leaders and business elites, in the parceling out of a quarter of the city's contracts to minority-owned business, in the maintenance of appropriate levels of minority employment in the city's workforce, and in the appointment of enough high-level minority officials to give blacks, Latinos, and even Asians the feeling of political representation—was what historian Michael Katz has termed "the management of marginalization."[67] Katz invokes the idea to help explain why U.S. cities witnessed relatively few outbreaks of collective "civil violence" between the 1970s and the first decade of the twenty-first century. He argues that in an American urban landscape in which the geographical boundaries of race were no longer being challenged—as they were during the Second Great Migration of African Americans from the 1940s through the 1970s—municipalities managed to dampen political opposition by "selectively incorporating" middling segments of economically marginalized communities with financial rewards and limited political powers while criminalizing and controlling the unincorporated.

Critical to this story of incorporation was the role played by minority elites claiming to represent group interests while brokering policies that were actually detrimental to lower-income members of their communities.[68] Mary Pattillo's penetrating study of the South Side North Kenwood–Oakland neighborhood in the 1990s has powerfully shown that a key dimension of the process of incorporation in Chicago was City Hall's deployment of a range of neoliberal policies—for example, the conversion of truly "public" high schools into selective "college prep" schools—to help promote gentrification.[69] The availability of high-quality educational opportunities was essential for attracting black middle-class professionals to the area and thereby boosting property values (as well as property tax revenues). Pattillo's work highlights how effective the Daley administration was at buying out the support of middle-class homeowners in black and Latino communities by convincing them that he was committed to "improving" their neighborhoods and raising their property values—whether through policing methods better adapted to community needs made possible by the CAPS program, beautification and infrastructural improvements underwritten with TIF funds, the creation of specialized charter and prep schools, or the demolition of crime-infested public housing projects that tainted the image of the neighborhood.

But there was more to the story than this. There was also a dimension that extended far beyond the city limits and that greatly surpassed City Hall's powers of persuasion. In accounting for the depoliticization of black and Latino communities, it is of course also necessary to consider how patterns of overactive consumption made possible by easy credit tended to mask growing inequalities. Blacks and Latinos with much lower incomes than middle-class whites were able to acquire some of the same class-status symbols—from Timberland boots to Ralph Lauren shirts to flat-screen televisions and video games—a situation that ended up sucking capital out of working-class minority neighborhoods. Credit card debt across the country, Katz reminds us, nearly tripled between 1999 and 2005, when some 84 percent of African American cardholders were carrying a balance (compared with 50 percent of whites).[70]

And then there was the frenzied consumption around professional sports, which in Chicago was especially pronounced at precisely the same time that Daley was restructuring the city's economy. The Chicago Bulls won an astounding six NBA championships between 1991 and 1998 behind the magical play of superstar Michael Jordan, and while we will never have a way to truly make sense of the political implications of this, it is realistic to think that the "hoop dreams" of a generation of young Chicagoans, not unlike the gangster dreams of rap videos, deflected attention from the injustices of the here and now.[71] As one sociological study of the impact of basketball on poor black youths has demonstrated, many teens clung desperately to the illusion that basketball could transport them out of the ghetto when the reality was that even winning a college scholarship was highly improbable.[72] Like the other narratives of personal failure circulating through black ghetto neighborhoods at the time—failure in school, failure to advance in the service-sector labor market, failure to climb the ranks of the gang hierarchy—the shattered dreams of basketball glory mostly left individuals blaming themselves rather than the surrounding conditions that made a long shot seem like the best option.

And yet ultimately what made Daley's machine function so smoothly, despite the glaring inequalities it exacerbated, was the economic prosperity that surrounded it and the flow of cash that lubricated its gears. Between 1989 and 2007, the year the subprime mortgage crisis caused the housing market to collapse nationwide, the United States experienced only two relatively minor and short-lived recessions—one between July 1990 and March 1991 and the other between March and November 2001. With the economy of tourism booming, real estate values surging upward, and the stock indexes rising, there was enough capital flowing into the city to make the system work. Moreover, Chicago's economy, labor market, and neighborhoods reaped enormous benefits from the massive wave of Mexican immigration in the 1990s, when Chicago's Mexican population increased by 50 percent and the number of Mexicans residing in Cook County jumped nearly 70 percent. Chicago managed to avoid the Rust Belt story of urban crisis in large part because Mexicans and other immigrants regenerated and repopulated some of its distressed neighborhoods, working service jobs, opening up businesses where boarded-up storefronts had once been, renting and buying apartments, and spending their hard-earned dollars in the local economy. A case in point was South Lawndale's Little Village neighborhood, whose population jumped from 62,821 in 1970 to 91,071 in 2000, with some 83 percent of the area's residents of "Hispanic" descent by 2010.[73]

But Chicago became a different place when faced with budget deficits in the hundreds of millions. Campaigning in the fall of 2006, Daley predicted a moderate $65 million shortfall for the fiscal year 2008, but after his election, with real estate values crashing, the actual figure came to $217 million, and the following year it rose to $470 million and then to $520 million in fiscal year 2010, when the mayor shocked everyone with the announcement that he would not be seeking a sixth full term. Daley seemed to have read the writing on the wall back in 2005, when he launched an aggressive privatization program to auction off some of the city's major assets for short-term gains. Although

Chicago was following New York's lead in making cash grants to high-profile corporations to advance its global agenda, it was clearly leading the way in using privatization schemes to raise capital. In 2005 City Hall signed a ninety-nine-year lease that gave the toll revenues of the Chicago Skyway to the Skyway Concession Company in exchange for $1.83 billion. The next year it signed another ninety-nine-year deal with a subsidiary of Morgan Stanley that handed over the revenue derived from the 9,100 parking spaces in the four underground parking garages beneath Grant and Millennium parks for $563 million in cash. Then, in 2008, Daley announced a $1.2 billion deal that leased out the city's 36,000 downtown parking meters for a period of seventy-five years—the first such privatized parking meter scheme in U.S. history. Finally, in 2009, the city made a bid to sell off Midway Airport for $2.5 billion, but the deal fell through when the buyers could not procure financing.

In the eyes of many economists and consumer advocacy groups, Chicago was on the bad end of all these deals, which were negotiated and concluded in a manner befitting a banana republic. Declining to issue calls for tenders, City Hall badly undersold its assets, and now Chicagoans looking to park their cars were at the mercy of private companies—and complaints about exorbitant fees and malfunctioning meters began to pile up.[74] But Chicagoans parking their cars were not the only ones being asked to tighten their belts in this moment of fiscal austerity. In 2007 the mayor announced the need for service cuts and fare hikes to keep the Chicago Transit Authority afloat, a burden that would have weighed most heavily upon low-paid service sector workers whose shifts fell outside banker's hours. In the end, Daley was able to avoid such measures by calling in a favor in the form of a $78 million bailout from Illinois governor Rod Blagojevich, who worked as an assistant prosecutor under Daley during his stint as state's attorney in the mid-1980s (and who was eventually removed from office and indicted by a federal court for trying to sell Barack Obama's vacated senate seat to the highest bidder). But this was merely a short-term fix, and for the first time in his career, Daley began to look vulnerable. After raising property taxes in 2007, he turned to scaling back services and trimming the payroll, including unionized city workers and teachers. Indicative of where the backlash against such actions was heading, alderman Patrick O'Connor of the Fortieth Ward raised eyebrows when he suggested dissolving the TIF districts and using the $1.2 billion in them to help solve the budget crisis.

This was the context within which City Hall put together its ultimately unsuccessful bid to host the 2016 Olympic Games—Daley's last-ditch effort to save Chicago's image in the midst of this financial distress. Apparently, the mayor was traveling in his limousine from the airport in Copenhagen when he heard the bad news, and one can only speculate about what was going through his mind at the time. This was a man who was used to getting his way; in 2003, for example, he had ordered city bulldozers to destroy the landing strip at Meigs Field, Chicago's small waterfront airport, because he was tired of hearing opposition to his plan to convert the airport into a park.[75] Making this defeat even more embarrassing was the fact that in an unprecedented move, President Barack Obama and First Lady Michelle Obama had personally traveled to Denmark to support Chicago's bid. When Daley announced he would not run again in September 2011, many pointed to the failed Olympics bid as the reason. Yet there was likely much more to it.

Chicago's political terrain had finally begun to shift dangerously under Daley's feet in mid-2006, when a grassroots movement spearheaded by a coalition of labor unions and community organizations managed to convince the city council to disregard the mayor's wishes and pass by a decisive vote of 35–14 a "big box living wage ordinance." The ordinance required large, profitable retailers with stores larger than 90,000 square feet to pay a wage of $10 per hour plus $3 in benefits to their employees—significantly above the $6.50 per hour minimum wage in the state of Illinois. Daley opposed the measure by arguing that it would steer big retailers like Wal-Mart and Target out of the city and into the suburbs, thus hurting low-income black communities badly in need of jobs and low-cost food retailers. He had used similar reasoning to oppose a living wage ordinance in the mid-1990s but then reversed direction in 1998 when he and his supporters on the city council saw the opportunity to exchange this minimum wage increase, which excluded employees of nonprofit organizations and contractors with fewer than twenty-five employees, for a significant hike in their own salaries. But this time there was no quid pro quo on the table and Daley dug his heels in, even going so far as to attack the largely white leadership of the Chicago Federation of Labor for racism. But the call for economic justice on behalf of the lowest-paid workers in the city carried the day; Daley's reverse race-baiting tactics were no match for the grassroots organizing activities of the Association of Community Organizations for Reform Now (ACORN) and Local 880 of the Service Employees International Union (SEIU), which had been mobilizing workers behind living wage ordinances since the mid-1990s. And even though Daley had won the battle by using the first and only veto of his mayoral career and then twisting the arms of enough aldermen to prevent an override, the marginalized began to seem much less marginal.

In 2007, for the first time in the Chicago Federation of Labor's modern history, the organization did not endorse an incumbent Chicago mayor in the municipal elections, instead spending some $3 million to challenge Mayor Daley's allies on the city council. Labor had been one of Daley's bread-and-butter constituencies, and even if the Building Trades Council would never leave his side, some of the major unions were leading a populist revolt against Daley's global agenda. Around the time the mayor was pondering another run in 2011, the Teamsters were incensed about Daley's use of non-union truck drivers; the leadership of the Chicago Teachers Union, which had been recently taken over by the militant Caucus of Rank and File Educators (CORE), began stepping up its fight against privatized charter schools; and the American Federation of State, County and Municipal Employees (AFSCME) was challenging Daley's plans to lay off thousands of city workers. And everyone was asking the same question: why not tap into the billions of dollars stashed away in the city's TIF funds?

Certainly, this groundswell of opposition owed something to the "Obama effect"—to the potent feelings of political possibility the election of this black president spread through the American left and through socially and economically marginalized urban communities across the country. On November 4, 2008, Barack Obama delivered his historic victory speech at Chicago's Grant Park, and one has to conclude that the hundreds of thousands of working-class black Chicagoans gathered there to witness the event believed him in their hearts when he told them "change has come to America." But for many blacks in Chicago the hope instilled by this victory was not nearly audacious enough to overcome a cancerous pessimism that had been spreading for decades. Not even three months after the celebration in Grant Park, political scientist Cathy Cohen, who was completing her fine study on the political lives of young African Americans in the United States, set up a focus group of black Chicagoans between the ages of 18 and 24. What she found was that even among people within this age group, who still had most of their lives ahead of them, the euphoria surrounding Obama's election was tempered with a strong dose of skepticism. "The young people in the room," Cohen observed, "were . . . quick to recenter the discussion about change away from the national level to city politics, where they hold little hope for any change . . . As far as the city of Chicago is concerned," one of her respondents told her, "most of the money and emphasis is being put on the more affluent . . . North Side neighborhoods, like the Wrigleyvilles and the Andersonvilles and Lincoln Park neighborhoods that have already been flourishing for years."[76]

CITY OF NEIGHBORHOODS ON THE MAKE

Of all the nicknames for Chicago, the one that seemed to be the most visible during Richard M. Daley's years in office was "City of Neighborhoods." This was somewhat odd in that it was the nickname whose origins were the most difficult to pin down. Sandburg gave us "City of Big Shoulders," Algren "City on the Make," proud New Yorkers "Second City," the national press corps "City that Works," and while the source of "Windy City" is still a matter of debate, one can find references to it in the Chicago press way back in the late 1850s. When City of Neighborhoods was referenced, on the other hand, it was always in the passive voice—as in "Chicago has often been called the City of Neighborhoods." Few, if any, scholars have attempted to establish the history of this appellation, and that is because it is a name that evolved gradually out of a number of sources. In terms of deep historical origins, it is hard to dissociate the whole City of Neighborhoods mythology from the project spearheaded by University of Chicago sociologist Ernest Burgess to divide the city into seventy-seven "community areas" in the 1920s. Then, during the reign of Richard J. Daley *neighborhood* gradually began to displace *community* in common parlance. Even as he was advancing policies that were pouring resources into the central business district and hanging many of the peripheral neighborhoods out to dry, the Boss's campaign rhetoric was filled with declarations of loyalty to the city's "neighborhoods." But it was during the Harold Washington years that the notion started to gain currency and legitimacy, when, for example, historians Dominic Pacyga and Ellen Skerrett chose to entitle their book *Chicago: City of Neighborhoods.*[77]

Chicago's identity as *a* city of neighborhoods was thus fairly well established when Richard M. Daley took the mayor's office, but it was during his reign that Chicago became *the* City of Neighborhoods. This was not only because Daley followed the lead of his father in lovingly employing the concept of "neighborhood" to charm working-class Chicagoans while he was betraying their interests, but also because he made Chicago's recognition as the City of Neighborhoods a matter of public policy. Whether it was installing eighteen-meter-high steel Puerto Rican flags at each end of Humboldt

Park's "Paseo Boricua" along Division Street, or cruising in a pink Cadillac on North Halsted Street—through the heart of the city's gay "Boystown" neighborhood—in the 1989 Gay Pride parade, or collaborating with black leaders in Bronzeville to better exploit the area's cultural heritage, or annually sponsoring some four hundred "neighborhood festivals ... showcasing the city's ethnic customs, music and food," Mayor Daley worked hard to maintain Chicago's reputation as the City of Neighborhoods.[78] Nor was this neighborhood motif merely window dressing for the larger neoliberal project. Rather, it was a core element of the global-city agenda, which hinged, in part, on the vitality of the new economy of tourism and on the city's ability to brand itself as a unique place to visit and live.

A prime example of how the City of Neighborhoods campaign fit into this project was the Chicago Neighborhood Tours program, which the Office of Tourism and Culture began operating in 1997 out of the Chicago Cultural Center downtown. Thirteen years later the City of Chicago was running tours of over thirty neighborhoods, each of which offered, according to the program's brochure, "a unique adventure in our exciting and diverse communities."[79] The Daley administration played an active part in marking and defining many of the city's different neighborhoods, dipping into ample funds made available through his $800 million "Neighborhoods Alive!" bond spending program in 1997 to put replicas of Greek temples in Greektown, twenty-three-foot-tall rainbow-striped metal pylons in the gay Lakeview neighborhood of Boystown, and, perhaps most importantly, ethnically flavored community centers throughout the city. Daley's drive to identify space was so determined that he went forward with his Boystown streetscape project despite a barrage of thousands of angry letters to the city council and a critical column in the *Tribune* that decried the equation of gayness with ethnicity. In the end, the mayor yielded to the pressure by toning down the original plan, but Boystown nonetheless got its $3.2 million renovation and its unmistakably gay-friendly pylons, which, according to the city, paid "tribute to the gay and lesbian community of Chicago and to the rainbow of diversity that has historically been the great strength of the Lakeview community."[80] Chicago thus became one of the first cities in the country to officially distinguish a gay neighborhood with such physical landmarks.

The strong role played by City Hall in advancing this kind of project seems to suggest once again the utility of Henri Lefebvre's work on the "production of space."[81] Developed out of a neo-Marxist framework, Lefebvre's notion of continual struggle over space between the state and capital, on the

FIGURE 18. Richard M. Daley marching in the annual South Chicago Mexican Independence Day parade. Kim Karpeles / Alamy Stock Photo.

one hand, and subordinate social groups, on the other, nonetheless needs some correctives to be effectively applied to Chicago's recent history. In the case of Boystown in the 1990s, where, as Timothy Stewart-Winter has argued, "queer clout was intertwined with pro-growth development policies," the story was ultimately one of incorporation rather than resistance to state power.[82] Moreover, as we have previously seen, efforts to identify neighborhood spaces as distinct ethnoracial communities have at times taken the form of turf battles between two different subordinate groups, and Lefebvre's Marxist framework is not well equipped for understanding such dynamics in multiethnic cities like Chicago, where blacks, Puerto Ricans, Mexicans, and working-class whites on the West Side were engaged in bitter battles over schools, parks, and neighborhood spaces—conflicts that ended up sorting these groups into a number of ethnoracially defined enclaves that still exist. This was the moment that witnessed Mexicans moving eagerly into Pilsen and Puerto Ricans into the Humboldt Park area—which is not to say that the "production" of these ethnoracially marked neighborhood spaces did not in some ways signify opposition to the state in the form of the Daley machine. After the 1966 barrio riot in Humboldt Park, Puerto Ricans marched along Division Street to demonstrate their right to live in their neighborhood without fear of police harassment, and in 1973 Mexicans in Pilsen, parents and students alike, organized a militant grassroots movement to pressure the board of education to provide them with their own community high school, which, quite symbolically, would take the name of reformist Mexican president Benito Juárez. And yet, although residents in these neighborhoods were certainly demanding their "right to the city," as Lefebvre referred to it, their demands were much more like appeals to a referee than challenges to the rules of the game. They were, in effect, objecting to the state treating them differently from some groups, or, even worse, treating them too much like others. Puerto Ricans taking to the streets against police brutality in Humboldt Park knew all too well that the police subjected mostly blacks to such abuse, and animating the Mexican uprising in Pilsen for a school of their own—for "La Raza," as activists at the time shouted—were years of simmering tensions between black and Mexican students at nearby Harrison High School.

Hence, even when Chicagoans seemed to have been directly engaged in struggles against city authorities, their actions were about much more than resistance to the city's drive to define and control spaces for the benefit of capital. The "right to the city" in Chicago in the 1960s and 1970s correlated closely with the politics of ethnocultural recognition, and this situation changed the story considerably from what Lefebvre was observing in Paris. Nor was City Hall particularly interested in opposing the kinds of ethnoracial boundaries being established. The machine had always made the most of Chicago's balkanized social geography, playing groups off each other and incorporating local elites to advance its objectives; after it became clear that the identity-based movements of the 1960s were not going to pose much of a threat to the order of things, it went about its business as usual. African Americans, for example, painted black fists and revolutionary slogans on ghetto walls, managed to place black nationalists in local positions of authority, and won the right to have black teachers teach their children about black history, but this did relatively little to change the overall calculus of power or to reshape city spaces in any significant way.

Despite these differences, Lefebvre's attention to how space is socially constructed is important for understanding some of the essential forces behind the making of Chicago's neighborhoods, especially during the Richard M. Daley era, when the city took on a new role of actually promoting the efforts of community leaders to define the identities of their neighborhoods. In a rapidly globalizing world, in which homogenous architectural styles and the proliferation of chain retailers (such as the Gap, Banana Republic, and Whole Foods), restaurants (such as McDonalds and Buca di Beppo), and coffee shops (such as Starbucks) were increasingly making a distinct sense of place a precious commodity, Chicago's diverse neighborhoods served as a strong selling point in attracting tourists and new residents. Support for the ethnoracial and lifestyle orientations (gay, bohemian, family, and so on) of different neighborhoods, moreover, distracted residents from bread-and-butter issues. The politics of neighborhood diversity became important in Chicago, it is important to emphasize, during the same moment when, according to Neil Smith, municipal administrations throughout the United States and much of the developed world were taking the scope and scale of gentrification to another level. Smith argues that around the mid-1980s a "third wave" of gentrification began to sweep through cities worldwide, when, in the context of deindustrialization, municipalities increasingly looked to the regeneration of urban space as a means of generating new tax-revenue streams.[83] Characterizing this shift were, among other things, a far more active role for the local state, the increasing autonomy of private capital in the development game, an underlying ethos of taking back the city for the middle class, and, in response to all this, the proliferation of local antigentrification movements.[84]

This last manifestation—the appearance of neighborhood movements defending the rights of low-income residents to affordable housing—seemed to signal the kind of class-based struggle over space Lefebvre described. But once again the politics of ethnoracial identity complicated the situation. In fact, despite appearing to be sensitive to the ethnoracial integrity of Chicago's neighborhoods, City Hall's myriad policies to promote gentrification tended, in practice, to undermine the goal of maintaining a diverse social geography. In a city in which nonwhites constituted a rather small segment of the middling class of homeowners, rising rental prices and property values invariably translated into increasing ethnoracial homogeneity. And these circumstances led at times to racially infused complaints likening gentrification to an invasion of white yuppies (or "young urban professionals")—a notion that ultimately worked to obscure the powerful logic of class division that was emerging at the urban grassroots in the high era of gentrification.

As Mary Pattillo has convincingly revealed in her study of the South Side neighborhood of North Kenwood–Oakland, even in predominantly black neighborhoods where bonds of ethnoracial solidarity were undeniably strong and where gentrification was largely being driven by black rather than white middle-class home buyers, community revitalization occured at the expense of low-income residents. Although the promoters of gentrification offered arguments that the poor would benefit from better schools and a more congenial atmosphere, Pattillo shows that this was often not the case. Poor, uneducated black parents were frequently unable to steer their kids through newly created selective schools, and, while crime rates did indeed descend as the middle-class population rose, low-income residents commonly encountered other forms of hostility directed at them from new homeowners anxious about threats to their property values. In North Kenwood–Oakland, for example, Pattillo observed middle-class residents seeking police intervention to put an end to the local custom of weekend barbecues in highly visible park spaces. The sight of working-class folks gathered around smoking barbecues was, for many of the new white-collar residents, an unbefitting image for an aspiring black middle-class neighborhood.[85]

While the "right to barbecue" may appear somewhat trivial in the overall scheme of things, it touches upon a critical development in the real story of neighborhood in Chicago. This conflict, in fact, represents merely one manifestation of the struggle increasingly pitting middle-class homeowners and local merchants against low-income renters to define neighborhood space in many of the city's ethnoracial communities. To be sure, fault lines of this nature had existed in Chicago's ethnoracial neighborhoods in the past. There was seldom one prevailing vision of what the neighborhood was or should be. For instance, even at the peak moment of ethnocultural awakening in both African American and Puerto Rican Chicago in the late 1960s, more moderate, assimilationist voices could be heard warning against the excesses of cultural nationalism. But during the "third wave" of gentrification some two decades later, when a powerful partnership between City Hall, private developers, and real estate promoters quickened the pace and scale of spatial transformation, the politics of neighborhood became increasingly polarized around opposing class interests within such communities. This was primarily because a real estate boom throughout much of the city translated into a bonanza for property owners and merchants ready to capitalize on the new class of clients. For example, in the West Town community area, a twelve-square-kilometer parallelogram northwest of the Loop encompassing some of Chicago's hottest real estate markets—Wicker Park, Bucktown, and the Ukrainian Village— average property prices rose by 83 percent and the median price for an apartment more than doubled in the 1990s.[86] The problem, however, was that low-income and elderly residents on fixed incomes realized few benefits from these gains. Rents rose in step with property prices, and more and more renters faced being pushed out of the neighborhood as property owners looked to convert rental units into high-yielding condominiums.

In many gentrifying neighborhoods, moreover, most of those being displaced tended to be Latinos and blacks while the vast majority of those replacing them overwhelmingly white. The case of West Town, where Latinos constituted nearly 60 percent of the population in 1990, was especially suggestive. By 1998, according to one study, white households in this area were the recipients of nearly 80 percent of the home loans granted, and Latino households received less than 10 percent.[87] This apparent "yuppie invasion" not only raised concerns among working-class residents about rising rents but also provoked a broader community reaction to the potential loss of the neighborhood's cultural identity. The response mingled feelings of ethnic pride with material concerns.

Although some businessmen had feared the negative consequences of fierce ethnoracial pride in the 1960s and 1970s, many local merchants in the West Town area, by the 1990s, had developed viable businesses providing goods and services to both an ethnic clientele as well as tourists seeking to sample local culture. Few neighborhoods exhibited this trend more than Pilsen, where Alderman Danny Solis led an aggressive campaign to market the area as a Mexican-themed tourist destination.[88] "My vision for Pilsen," Solis told the *Sun-Times* in 2003, "is to become the best Mexican-American community in the Midwest, where you can come, taste the food and experience the culture."[89] Ethnic commercial enterprises also played a role in maintaining the Puerto Rican community's claim to West Town's Humboldt Park district, where Puerto Rican businesses still dominated Division Street despite the fact that both African Americans and Mexicans had come to outnumber Puerto Ricans.[90] Yet even more important in preserving the Puerto Rican identity of the area were the numerous political and cultural associations clustered around the Paseo Boricua, including the vibrant Puerto Rican Cultural Center at 2739 West Division, whose work involved, according to its executive director, José E. Lopez, "recovering [the] community's historical memory as part of a holistic vision of development."[91] Elites in both Pilsen and Humboldt Park thus looked to exploit their neighborhood's cultural heritage, with somewhat differing results.

In Humboldt Park, such efforts helped the neighborhood retain its Puerto Rican flavor but did little to prevent the departure of Puerto Rican residents. Between 1990 and 2000, forces of white gentrification spilling over from the red-hot Wicker Park real estate market to the east caused the Puerto Rican population there to decline 23 percent—leading to some creative approaches. By the summer of 2006, for example, a group of local activists calling themselves the Puerto Rican Agenda began actively recruiting Puerto Rican professionals to buy homes in the area.[92] While a short-lived and ultimately unsuccessful experiment, this campaign was nonetheless suggestive of how the "third wave" of gentrification had reconfigured the struggle to produce ethnoracial community space in Chicago. Decades ago such struggles to identify community spaces were hard to separate from broader campaigns for social justice; in the Richard M. Daley era, the global-city agenda and the irrepressible push for gentrification transformed these very same identities into tools for branding, commerce, and accumulation.

There was perhaps no clearer testimony to this shift than the evolution of Danny Solis from militant activist for La Raza in the 1970s to Richard M. Daley's handpicked alderman and architect of Pilsen's theme-park marketing campaign in the mid-1990s. After being appointed in 1996 to fill the vacant aldermanic seat in the Twenty-Fifth Ward, which also included sections of Chinatown and Little Italy, Solis paved the way for a number of upscale housing developments, including, most notably, the controversial University Village—a massive middle- to upper-income housing development built on the land where the famous Maxwell Street flea market once stood. In addition to destroying a revered historical landmark, where blues greats like Bo Diddley, Junior Wells, and Little Walter played to admiring crowds of blacks and whites alike amidst the odors of grilling Polish sausages, University Village also spurred a wave of condominium development that caused median housing values in neighboring East Pilsen to rise as much as 548 percent in the 1990s.[93] While providing the University of Illinois–Chicago with much-needed housing and another middle-class buffer zone, such changes created significant hardships for Pilsen's low-income residents, and demands for affordable housing energized the campaigns of those who challenged Solis's seat. Nonetheless, Solis and his supporters in Pilsen's United Neighborhood Organization (UNO) remained unwavering in their support for new development. Founded by Solis in 1984, UNO viewed itself in its early days as modeled on the Saul Alinsky style of community organizing, but it remained somewhat silent about two of the most pressing issues for Pilsen's working-class residents: the need for more affordable housing and the high particulate and carbon dioxide emissions from the area's two coal plants.[94] Thus, while UNO's acronym was intended to connote its alliance with the larger Mexican community, its program inevitably advanced the interests of middle-class Mexicans at the expense of their working-class neighbors.

Appeals to ethnoracial solidarity also served those opposing the forces of gentrification in both Pilsen and Humboldt Park. For example, the Pilsen Alliance, a grassroots organization active in the fight for affordable housing and public oversight of rezoning decisions, tapped into the neighborhood's rich tradition of community murals to spread its message of social justice. This strategy of placing the community's Mexican identity at the center of its antigentrification campaign was revealed during Pilsen's annual Fiesta del Sol street festival, where the Alliance sold T-shirts emblazoned with the words "Pilsen Is Not For Sale."[95] In addition, Humboldt Park's many grassroots associations—the Latino United Community Housing Association (LUCHA), Communities United for Affordable Housing (CUFAH), the Near Northwest Neighborhood Network (NNNN), and the Puerto Rican Cultural Center's Participatory Democracy Project—engaged in similar tactics in voicing their demands for more affordable housing. Although the crowds that gathered at their rallies were usually multiethnic, Puerto Rican flags were often as conspicuous as signs reading "We Shall Not Be Moved."

Some of these same organizations were also active in the predominantly Latino Logan Square neighborhood just to the north, where gentrification advanced at a much faster pace than in Humboldt Park. Between 1996 and 2006, the median sale price for a single-family detached home in Logan Square jumped a remarkable 385 percent—a trend that was spurred more by the rehabilitation of its many beautiful Victorian greystone mansions than by new large-scale developments.[96] Once home to significant communities of Poles and Russian Jews, Logan Square had become a major port of entry for Mexicans, Puerto Ricans, and Cubans beginning in the late 1960s and by 2010 contained the largest population of Latinos in Chicago.[97] Yet this formidable presence of working-class Mexicans and Puerto Ricans did surprisingly little to slow down the rush of middle-class whites into Logan Square, where between 2000 and 2010 the non-Latino white population grew by 7,000 and the number of Latinos dropped by 16,000. Even a seemingly endless and at times homicidal battle for turf between such high-profile gangs as the Latin Kings, Maniac Latin Disciples, and Spanish Cobras failed to stop Logan Square's transformation. By 2010, the area boasted some of the city's most cutting-edge bars, coffee shops, and restaurants, including the famed Lula Cafe, where young hipsters could choose from such gastronomic creations as risotto with spiced rabbit, roasted morels, spinach, parmesan, and shaved foie gras.

Logan Square thus became a gentrification success story that replayed Wicker Park's dramatic conversion in the 1990s from a somewhat depopulated working-class Mexican enclave where the Latin Kings cultivated a lucrative drug-trafficking enterprise into a bastion of avant-garde artistic production and million-dollar Victorian mansions. Part of what made the change possible in both Logan Square and Wicker Park was the relatively unproduced nature of these neighborhoods. Without the psychologically imposing presence of the massive iron flags that marked off the Paseo Boricua, both Wicker Park and Logan Square were much easier for realtors and developers to market to white middle-class condo buyers. In other words, Wicker Park and Logan Square were more susceptible to white yuppie invasion because, unlike Humboldt Park or Pilsen, their spaces had never been produced to reflect a politicized sense of ethnoracial identity. Whites ended up moving into Logan Square rather than neighboring Humboldt Park in part because they were uncomfortable about living "between the flags" and in part because Humboldt Park's Puerto Rican heritage gave residents there a useful tool with which to mobilize against gentrification. Whereas a sense of exclusionary ethnic pride was inscribed within the geography and history of the Paseo Boricua—the iron flags, the barrio riot of 1966, and a militant Puerto Rican independence movement in the 1980s and 1990s[98]—Logan Square's brand of ethnic culture was alluring to white artists, musicians, and others looking for a lower-cost alternative to the increasingly homogeneous, high-priced North Side areas around Lakeview, Lincoln Park, Old Town, the Ukrainian Village, and Wicker Park, after it lost its "edge."

Logan Square, like Manhattan's Lower East Side (or "Loisaida" to the Puerto Rican residents who used to live there) in the 1980s, possessed an "edge": here Mexican vendors peddled *elotes* (grilled, spiced corn on the cob with mayonnaise) and tamarind popsicles in the streets, the remnants of broken piñatas littered the sidewalks, *banda* and mariachi music blared out of passing cars, and bursts of gunfire could be heard, at times, piercing the night.[99] Although white middle-class residents of course did not approve of the homicidal gunplay around them, gang warfare was nevertheless part of the larger package of qualities that branded the neighborhood as a place where alternative, artistic, and independently minded people lived. As Richard Lloyd's close ethnographic study of Wicker Park in the 1990s demonstrates, Chicago's bohemians and gentrification entrepreneurs tended to glamorize the danger of street life, often speaking nostalgically about it after gentrification had eliminated it. Their need to negotiate the dangers and cultural clashes that came with living in a largely working-class Mexican neighborhood shaped a "hipster aesthetic," influenced by the grunge style being popularized on the national stage, that included visible tattoos, secondhand clothes, and unkempt hair.[100] A similar austerity characterized Wicker Park's two signature hipster cafés in the 1990s, Earwax and Urbis Orbis. The edginess of the neighborhood—not to mention the low rents— attracted a bohemian crowd of artists, musicians, writers, and others employed in the culture industries. The arrival of such trendsetters made it much more attractive to middle-class white condo buyers, whose presence, in turn, attracted more upscale commercial establishments, thereby completing the gentrification process. Hence, by 2002 a chic fitness club called Cheetah Gym had opened in the space where cigarette-lipped hipsters used to drink coffee in Urbis Orbis.

Logan Square's new middle-class white residents constituted this second wave of gentrifiers, and they were engaged in producing the space around them to reflect their politics and lifestyle. The innovative cafés, bars, and restaurants that opened their doors to serve them were critical to this process. If earthy vegetarian fare and no frills coffee drinks were de rigueur at Earwax and Urbis Orbis, in twenty-first century Logan Square fresh-roasted coffee beans, organic baby vegetables, and Belgian-style microbrewed beer spiced with coriander and orange peel juxtaposed with pork tacos, rice and beans, and mofongo. As Logan Square hipsters and the commercial establishments they frequented sought to redefine the neighborhood, they engaged in a process that looked somewhat like what Dick Hebdige has termed bricolage—a blending of their own tastes and styles with seemingly dissonant elements from the working-class Latino culture around them.[101] Such acts of creative consumption even extended to one of the city's renowned culinary trademarks, the hot dog. Although in Chicago nondescript hot dog joints are ubiquitous, which rendered the standard hot-dog-and-french-fries meal undesirable to many hipsters, Logan Square residents lived not far from a hot dog restaurant, Hot Doug's, where they could find a Mexican-inflected sausage with chili-garlic mayonnaise and salsa jack cheese accompanied by fries cooked in duck fat. In Wicker Park, one of the hippest restaurants, star restauranteur Paul Kahan's Big Star, offered its hip clientele designer lamb, pork, and fish tacos, alongside an elaborate selection of bourbons, all consumed to a studied soundtrack of retro pop, country, and funk. Mexican service workers staffed the kitchen and takeout window, but around the bustling bar, the staff was mostly white and fashionable. Yet such examples should not give the impression that hipster bricolage on the gentrification frontier was only about replacing local culture or creating a parallel community. The hipster ethos in Chicago also celebrated an ability to adapt to the local scene, and this pushed white middle-class bohemians and professionals alike into indigenous bars and restaurants. In neighborhoods like Logan Square and the Ukrainian Village during the transitional 1990s, it was not uncommon to find corner bars with jukeboxes offering a selection of Polish polkas, Mexican banda, and a range of pop and indie rock.

But in advancing this idea of gentrification as a piecemeal, market-based process driven by individuals pursuing objectives of self-identification that slot them into distinct if at times overlapping communities, we risk overlooking a critical factor. A range of policies implemented by City Hall beginning in the early 1990s fueled gentrification every step of the way: the creation of TIFs throughout the city provided capital for costly infrastructural improvements and beautification efforts; the Renaissance 2010 school reform created schools acceptable to educated, middle-class homeowners; the CAPS program cultivated a police force responsive to homeowners' concerns about the "bad" behavior of their working-class neighbors; and perhaps most importantly, City Hall opened the floodgates to condominium development by allowing aldermen to control zoning changes within their respective wards with virtually no public oversight. While theoretically empowered to reject "upzoning" requests for the construction of large housing developments and commercial centers, the city council in practice acted as little more than a rubber stamp, vetoing a mere fifteen such petitions out of several thousand filed between 1997 and 2007. This meant enormous benefits for Chicago's aldermen, who enthusiastically traded their signatures on upzoning petitions for campaign contributions. In his first term on the city council, for example, only one other alderman approved more upzoning petitions than Wicker Park's (First Ward) Manuel Flores—a performance that explains why nearly a quarter of his $1.2 million in campaign donations came from contractors and developers and why Wicker Park emerged as one of the nation's most spectacular gentrification success stories.[102] Moreover, such practices ran up against little opposition because many of the local advisory bodies empowered to review rezoning requests were dominated by developers and contractors.

Chicago's rezoning system thus stacked the cards heavily in favor of gentrification during the 1990s and first decade of the twenty-first century. In

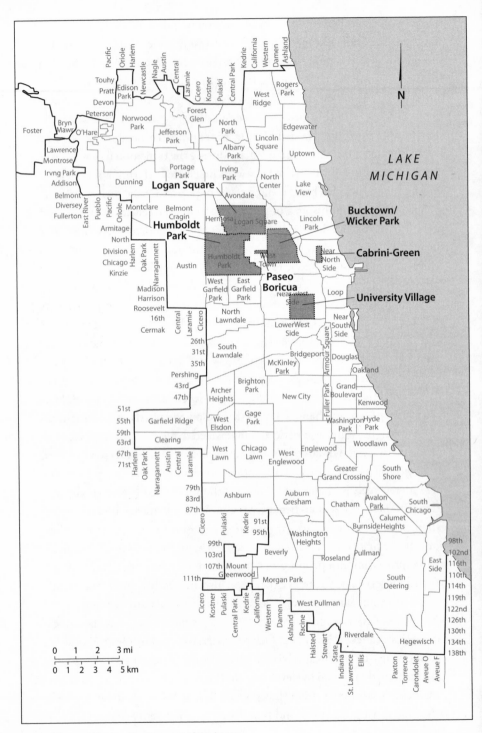

MAP 7. The gentrification frontier west of the Loop.

this Chicago differed significantly from other U.S. global cities, such as San Francisco and New York, where an emphasis on centralized planning and community participation in the rezoning process somewhat mitigated the wholesale transformation of neighborhoods in the 1980s and 1990s. New York, no less than Chicago, witnessed the rise of powerful movements for community control in the 1960s and 1970s, but, unlike in Chicago, these campaigns left a meaningful imprint on New York's zoning process, leading to the establishment of fifty-nine community boards across the five boroughs to provide aggressive public oversight of proposed zoning changes. These boards became incubators for antigentrification campaigns in the late 1980s and 1990s, when protesters in the East Village made a habit of scrawling "Die Yuppie Scum" all over the neighborhood. Moreover, without Chicago's tradition of "aldermanic prerogative," New York's council members at times found it more politically expedient to take the side of citizens protesting unwanted development—a situation that was very rare in Chicago. Chicago's city council, by contrast, did not approve a new zoning code until 2004, revising a system that had remained virtually unchanged for almost half a century. But many of the new rules added to create greater community input in the rezoning process were largely ignored. A 2008 *Tribune* investigation, for example, found that aldermen seldom enforced the requirement obligating developers to post signs on the sites of proposed zoning changes.[103]

Hence, without New York's well-established institutional framework for public participation in land use politics, Chicago saw relatively little grassroots mobilization around decisions reshaping its built environment, and this history of quiescence performed an important ideological function that quickened the city's brisk pace of real estate transactions during the Richard M. Daley era. Indeed, gentrification is made possible not only by the construction of new housing and the rehabilitation of old; it also depends on a healthy supply of buyers ready to risk their personal capital on neighborhoods on the make. Many of the white middle-class families moving into Wicker Park and other parts of West Town in the 1990s and into Logan Square in more recent years were seeking not just a lifestyle but also a good investment. And their feelings about their chances in such "frontier" neighborhoods were conditioned by what they had seen happening around them. By the mid-1990s, not only had they had seen others like themselves strike it rich in Wicker Park, but they also understood all the things that City Hall would do for them—from bringing the boot down on gangbangers to enforcing noise ordinances, to building parks and new library branches, to doing whatever was necessary to facilitate the subsequent development they depended on to raise their property values. However, the confidence they had in City Hall also came from all that they had not seen or known—in particular, concerned citizens in the streets or at zoning board hearings complaining about the condominiums and shopping centers popping up around them.

During Chicago's high years of gentrification in the 1990s residents watched neighborhoods transforming in real time before their eyes with few glitches. The typical scenario began with the construction of a multiunit condominium building—sometimes a conversion of an old factory or warehouses, at others a new structure rising up from the rubble of a teardown or a litter-strewn vacant lot. In most cases, façades were brick and balconies conspicuous; the more upscale boasted rooftop swimming pools, exercise facilities, and well-manicured gardens bounded by imposing iron fences. Then came any number of signature retail establishments catering to a middling clientele—Starbucks, for example, was the well-recognized "canary in the coal mine" for gentrification. After that, the rush was on to buy up old buildings, gut the interiors, and bedeck them with new hardwood floors, fireplaces, and spacious master bedrooms. Chicagoans living around gentrifying neighborhoods knew exactly what this process looked like, and they knew City Hall was behind it with all its might.

But in fact Richard M. Daley never had to say anything too explicit about the city's support for gentrification; the landscape was full of visual symbols conveying this very idea. A striking example was City Hall's makeover of the historically decrepit Seward Park, replete with a new state-of-the-art Chicago Public Library branch, at the very moment that the neighboring Cabrini-Green housing projects were in the midst of demolition to make way for a new "mixed-income" community.[104] For countless Chicagoans driving by the vacated projects on Halsted or riding by them on a brown-line "L" train, the neatly landscaped Seward Park, hastily erected as the city was buzzing about the demolition of one of the nation's most notorious housing projects, became a monument to City Hall's commitment to taking back the city for the middle class.

THE CHALLENGES OF DIVERSITY

The story of how the city of Chicago opened the way for a bustling middle-class neighborhood where an impoverished ghetto had been had to do with much more than building a library and renovating a park. Gazing in the early 1990s upon Cabrini-Green's ten decrepit cinder-block-like towers huddled around shabbily landscaped parks and courtyards, it was difficult to imagine that the developers eyeing the area would have their day. While white middle-class buyers had proven willing to invest in largely Latino neighborhoods around the Loop, they had largely refused to buy into black areas. Yet the city's ambitious campaign to demolish black-occupied housing projects and replace them with "mixed-income housing" under the Chicago Housing Authority's $1.6 billion Plan for Transformation purported, at least ostensibly, to achieve a level of neighborhood diversity that the private housing market had been incapable of bringing about.

Most notably, the razing of Cabrini-Green, which lay on the Near North Side, just to the west of the luxurious Gold Coast area, forced the displacement of as many as 15,000 African American residents, and, while the CHA, under the terms of its out-of-court settlement with former tenants, agreed to set aside 1,200 units of public housing in the new developments, fewer than 400 of these had been constructed as of March 2011.[105] Regardless, blacks in this area were destined to become a relatively small minority in the future neighborhood. While Cabrini-Green was certainly riddled with problems— gangs, drug trafficking, sniper attacks—the black residents living there nonetheless were the only significant concentration of African Americans on Chicago's Near North Side. Their removal cleared the way for a two-kilometer-long stretch of uninterrupted, overwhelmingly white middle-class affluence that began at the Lake Michigan shoreline and ended at the banks of the North Branch of the Chicago River, where a large cluster of upscale condominiums had been growing rapidly since the late 1990s. Touring the so-called River North area today, one would be hard-pressed to find diversity of any meaningful kind.

Launched in early 2000, the CHA's Plan for Transformation was initially conceived of as a response to decades of public housing mismanagement— more specifically, to the fact that in 1998 19,000 of the CHA's units had failed "viability inspection" and thus, according to federal law, had to be demolished within five years. This was the latest chapter in a horror story of Chicago public housing that began back in the 1940s and 1950s.[106] The situation had reached a low point in the mid-1980s, when the Department of Housing and Urban Development (HUD) cut the city's funding by 76 percent, causing the CHA to run a $1 billion maintenance backlog that included more than 30,000 unfulfilled work orders. If all this was not serious enough, the CHA had also been dragging its feet on complying with the 1969 *Gautreaux* order, which mandated that any new public housing had be located outside predominantly low-income black ghetto neighborhoods. At the time of the lawsuit, the CHA managed sixty-four projects containing some 30,000 units; sixty of the projects were 99.5 percent black, and the other four were 95 percent white.[107] By 1987, a federal court had placed the CHA in receivership, assigning the Habitat Company to control its operations. Habitat's subsequent performance drew some sharp criticism—one study, for example, found that over half of the units created under its control were located in census tracts that were at least 60 percent Latino—and the city regained control of the CHA in 1999, winning HUD's approval for its massive plan to rehabilitate or rebuild 25,000 public housing units, most within mixed-income developments.[108]

Much of the funding for this project came from the federal government's Hope IV program, whose main objective was to promote the replacement of "ghettos in the sky" with low-rise, pedestrian-friendly, mixed-income communities. This new mixed-income approach was obviously destined to pave the way for gentrification and for the kind of dramatic racial conversion of urban space that usually accompanies it. Baldwin's notion of "negro removal" comes quickly to mind when one considers that the demolitions of Chicago's three largest housing projects—the Robert Taylor Homes, ABLA, and Cabrini-Green—displaced nearly 50,000 African Americans from areas bordering some very desirable real estate.[109] While various groups of tenants pressed their claims in court for adequate numbers of replacement units and for their "right to return," the Plan for Transformation called for a net loss of some 6,000 units, and with uncertainties surrounding occupancy dates for some of the new developments, most former tenants had little choice but to take their Section 8 vouchers and move elsewhere.[110] And "elsewhere," according to scholars examining relocation patterns, usually meant either other low-income ghetto neighborhoods or economically depressed black suburbs like Harvey, Illinois, around the city's southern border.[111] Moreover, according to sociologist Sudhir Venkatesh, the CHA lost track of some 40 percent of the families displaced by the demolitions.[112]

In theory, the mixed-income communities envisioned by the plan would bring together a roughly equal mix of low-, middle-, and even high-income residents, an arrangement that would ideally serve to lift up the poor, who would acquire the kind of social and cultural capital that sociologists like William Julius Wilson had been arguing was lacking in black ghetto neighborhoods. But such objectives began to appear farfetched from the outset, when a number of incidents in some of the first mixed-income communities began to suggest that rather than creating functional communities of rich and poor, tenant and homeowner, black and white, the CHA's mixed-income solution was setting up a war of attrition between homeowners and renters in which the latter were sure to lose. The scenario resembled that which unraveled in New Orleans in the aftermath of Hurricane Katrina in 2005. According to Adolph Reed Jr., the many poor African Americans stranded on rooftops and then callously disregarded by the city's postflood reconstruction program revealed that in the "ownership society" so valorized by President George W. Bush, class and property ownership had become the most important determinants of political interest and power. "Property owners," Reed claimed, "are able to assert their interests in the polity, while non-owners are nearly as invisible in civic life now as in the early eighteenth century."[113]

Dispatches from the mixed-income gentrification frontier in Chicago offered compelling evidence for this view. For example, in the Roosevelt Square development, one of the first of several developments to be constructed to replace ABLA near Little Italy, homeowners revolted in opposition to a plan to build more rental units. According to reporters observing a meeting in late May 2010, a vocal group of largely white homeowners expressed great fears about a drop in property values, complaining about the drug-dealing, violence, and the increasing number of security cameras they felt would come with the addition of rental units. "The real question," Second Ward alderman Bob Fioretti countered, "is whether you are afraid to cross the street because there is a black guy on the other side."[114]

Such conflicts suggest that white homeowners living in these communities were continuing to oppose racial integration, as they had in Chicago since the late nineteenth century. As in the past, city authorities appeared ready to provide vital assistance towards this end. In the case of Chicago's new mixed-income communities, this aid came in the form of a draconian Admissions and Continued Occupancy Policy designed to discipline and punish low-income black residents, ultimately providing fodder for those aiming to argue for increased owner-occupied units. For example, CHA compliancy rules required public housing residents to prove that they were employed at least twenty hours per week or face eviction, and tenants faced removal if convicted of a single felony or even if a relative or guest was arrested on the premises for drug use or violent behavior.[115] In the spring of 2011 the CHA demonstrated how far it was willing to take this policy when its CEO

Lewis Jordan announced a proposal to subject subsidized housing residents to annual drug testing—a requirement that the American Civil Liberties Union (ACLU) claimed violated the U.S. Constitution's Fourth Amendment protection against police searches without probable cause. To return to a point made earlier in this chapter, that Jordan, an African American, was the face of this controversial policy helped to defuse charges of racism.

It was through such tactics that City Hall under Richard M. Daley's stewardship wielded great power over the production of space in Chicago, and the power it wielded was invariably turned towards the goal of producing the kind of space that created conditions for further development, higher tax yields, and kickbacks in the form of political contributions. While this was not exactly a new development in Chicago's history, it is important to note how the interface of power became more diffuse during the high era of neoliberalization, extending far beyond the downtown business district and into the furthest reaches of the city, where local elites of all colors served as "brokers" or "middlemen" for gentrification policies.[116] The state, moreover, added new forms of power to its arsenal in the 1990s—not merely those involving the flexible allocation of funds and modification of zoning regulations but also intrusive policing powers over the conduct of low-income residents. To be sure, public housing residents faced such regulations in the past, but in the quasi-private context of mixed-income neighborhoods, such powers took on new meaning. In the housing projects of old, residents stood on relatively equal footing; in Chicago's emerging mixed-income developments, subsidized housing tenants were forced to deal with the stigmatization created by being subjected to a different set of rules from their homeowning neighbors—specifically those regarding barbecuing, pets, and the proper use of balconies. One low-income resident described the situation:

> They watch you come in and they watch you go out. The cameras. The cameras. And if anything goes wrong and they pull you in the office, they're going to tell you every detail ... 'Cause the [property manager] told us, she said there's some other people in here paying some good, tall money for staying here, and they ain't gonna let nobody just, you know, mess up the deal. They'll throw you out and put somebody else in here.[117]

Although it would be misleading to understate the impact of policies emanating from City Hall in the making of Chicago's neighborhoods and communities, it would also be misleading to give the local state the final word in the story. Some scholars have called Chicago the "immigrant capital of the heartland," and the nearly 700,000 immigrants (1.4 million in the six-county Chicago metropolitan area) that had settled there by 2000 had a major impact in reshaping its social geography.[118] By 2010, more than one in five Chicagoans was foreign-born, and many of these immigrants had, as a result of their propensity to settle among those with whom they shared linguistic and cultural affinities, served as active agents in the process of inscribing these affinities within neighborhood spaces throughout the city. Immigrants arriving in Chicago beginning in the 1970s—after the 1965 Immigration and Nationality Act overhauled the country's exclusionary national-origins quotas and ushered in a system based on family reunification and occupational skills—reinforced existing ethnoracial communities and created new ones throughout much of the city. Generally speaking, by the late 1990s the only areas of the city not bearing the physical markings of the immigrant population—countless foreign-language signs fronting businesses, restaurants, community associations, churches, and mosques—were the solidly black neighborhoods of the West and South Sides and the overwhelmingly white ones stretching along the lakefront from the Loop up through the Lakeview area.

Mexicans had become, far and away, the largest immigrant group in the city by 2010, when Chicago's nearly 600,000 people of Mexican origin gave it the third largest Mexican population in the United States after Los Angeles and Houston. Roughly half the city's foreign-born population had arrived from Latin America, with Mexicans accounting for over 85 percent of all Latino immigrants, and this numerical strength left its mark on the city's social geography. Over the course of the 1990s and first decade of the twenty-first century, the two West Side Mexican enclaves of West Town–Humboldt Park and Pilsen–Little Village (South Lawndale) spread northward and southward respectively, creating two clusters of Mexican residential concentration where people of Mexican origin came to constitute more than 35 percent of the population in each community area. This pattern of settlement strikingly revealed that Mexicans steered clear of the heart of the West Side ghetto, settling in large numbers throughout much of the rest of Chicago's West Side, from Albany Park all the way down to the Back of the Yards area around 51st Street. The Mexican aversion to settling in and around black neighborhoods—an aversion shared by Chicago's next largest Latino group, Puerto Ricans—was so strong that by 2000 Chicago displayed the highest degree of segregation between blacks and Latinos among the hundred largest cities in the United States, with a black-Latino dissimilarity index 30 percent higher than that of New York and nearly 40 percent higher than that of Los

FIGURE 19. A mural of Benito Pablo Juárez García on 18th Street in Pilsen. RosalreneBetancourt 8/Alamy Stock Photo.

Angeles.[119] While Mexican–Puerto Rican dissimilarity was moderate by comparison, segregation between these two groups was nonetheless higher in Chicago than in any of the other cities with significant populations of Mexicans and Puerto Ricans. Moreover, according to the Lewis Mumford Center for Comparative Urban and Regional Research, Chicago ranked first among the sixty most segregated metropolitan areas for Latino-Asian segregation.[120] While Mexicans were more able and willing to settle among whites in Chicago (the Mumford Center ranked Chicago sixth for white-Latino segregation), communities like Pilsen–Little Village, with its nearly 90 percent concentration of Mexicans, seemed to speak volumes about the dynamics of ethnic clustering that were playing out in Chicago at the turn of the twenty-first century.

Indeed, many other of the city's largest foreign-born groups—the Chinese, Poles, and Indians—gravitated towards ethnoracial enclaves between the 1970s and 1990s, creating port-of-entry neighborhoods that still attract large numbers of immigrants today. In the case of the Chinese, whose population numbered just 7,000 in 1960, this period of accelerated immigration led to the emergence of a well-defined Chinatown neighborhood of Chinese restaurants, bakeries, travel agencies, and boutiques just south of the Loop

314 · A CITY OF TWO TALES

around the intersection of Wentworth and Cermak Avenue, marked by the famous red-and-gold Chinatown Gate. While most of Chinatown, strictly defined, lay primarily within the Armour Square community area, the 15,000-member Chinese community here spread westward into the Daley family's old Irish stronghold of Bridgeport, where by 2000 the Chinese and Mexican populations had reached 26 percent and 30 percent respectively (while blacks continued to remain virtually absent). During the late 1970s, moreover, another Chinese neighborhood developed quickly in the North Side Uptown neighborhood after Chinese businessman Jimmy Wong, a representative of the Hip Sing Tong, bought a strip of commercial real estate on Argyle Street between Broadway and Sheridan. By the 1980s, the area had received a large influx of immigrants from Vietnam, Cambodia, Thailand, and Laos—many of them ethnic Chinese—fleeing the postwar refugee crisis across Southeast Asia. Yet, this area—referred to by some as New Chinatown and by others simply as Argyle—largely failed to develop as a rival to the old Chinatown, which by 2010 possessed more than half the Chinese population living within the Chicago city limits.

Several other leading immigrant groups in Chicago created cohesive ethnic enclaves between the 1980s and 2010s. By 2010, Chicago was home to some 25,000 South Asian Indians, for example, and roughly one quarter of them lived around the diverse West Devon Avenue on the far North Side of the city, where Indian restaurants and stores selling everything from saris to Bollywood videos dominated a commercial strip that brought together Pakistani bakeries, Islamic bookstores, and kosher restaurants. Moreover, many of the substantial number of former Indian residents who had moved into Skokie, Lincolnwood, and other of Chicago's more affluent northern suburbs continued to frequent West Devon to buy ethnic goods and stay in touch with the community.[121] Similar arrangements also characterized the "Korea Town" neighborhood (officially designated as Seoul Drive by the city council in 1993), which stretched along Lawrence Avenue, between Kedzie and Pulaski, in the Albany Park community area, a few miles southwest of West Devon. Like West Devon, the area around Seoul Drive was a place of great ethnoracial diversity—one of the most ethnically diverse in the United States. Korean restaurants, groceries, and other businesses were prominent, but they shared the street with Mexican bakeries and taquerias, as well Middle Eastern food stores and hookah bars. In fact, Koreans constituted only about 15 percent of the population of the community area surrounding Korea Town. And yet ethnic ties exerted a relatively strong gravitational pull.

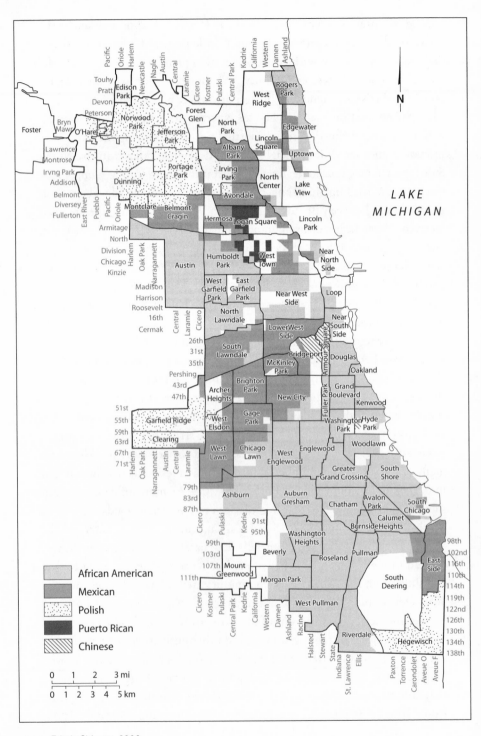

MAP 8. Ethnic Chicago, 2000.

According to one estimate, some 35,000 Koreans (out of a total of 45,000 in the city) had settled within easy reach of Seoul Drive, in the nearby community areas of Lincoln Square, Edgewater, Uptown, West Ridge, and Rogers Park.[122] Finally, during the 1980s and 1990s Arab and Assyrian immigrants, many arriving on refugee visas, had grouped together in what some referred to as "Little Arabia" communities on both the Northwest and Southwest Sides. The heart of the North Side Arab and Assyrian community, which mixed Iraqis, Assyrians, Palestinians, Jordanians, Syrians, and Lebanese, lay in the midst of Korea Town, at Lawrence and Kedzie, an area marked by a concentration of Middle Eastern restaurants, groceries, and hookah bars.[123] An older Arab neighborhood existed around the handful of mosques and Middle Eastern restaurants around Kedzie and 63rd that served Palestinians and Jordanians living in the immediate community areas of Chicago Lawn and Gage Park and in the nearby suburbs of Bridgeview and Oak Lawn.

However, perhaps no ethnic group in Chicago created a more cohesive port-of-entry neighborhood during this moment than the city's Poles. Over 100,000 Poles migrated to the Chicago area between 1972 and 2000, giving metropolitan Chicago the largest concentration of Poles in the United States. With over one hundred ethnic associations, several radio and television stations, and numerous magazines and newspapers, Chicago's Polish community (referred to as Chicago Polonia) became one of the largest and most active nodes of Polish culture in the world. Polish immigrants exhibited a strong preference for city life, even if, thanks to their whiteness, they did not have to deal with some of the racial barriers that other immigrants faced in their attempts to settle in certain suburbs. Throughout the first decade of this Polish immigration wave, the "Polish Triangle" around the intersection of Milwaukee, Division, and Ashland in Wicker Park served as the cultural center of Polonia. Anchoring the neighborhood was the powerful St. Stanislaus Kostka parish, which had been founded in 1867 and by the 1940s had grown into one of the country's largest parishes. But in the early 1990s, with Polish immigration to Chicago peaking at a rate of some 11,000 per year, the advance of gentrification in West Town began to push working-class Poles northwest up Milwaukee Avenue to a more affordable Polish enclave in the Avondale community area.

While the old Polish Triangle still retained some historical resonance, especially as it was home to the Polish Museum of America and Library, this new neighborhood, known within the Polish community as Jackowo, became the functional port of entry for Polish immigrants. Poles made up more than half of the population in the immediate area around the predominantly Polish St. Hyacinth Church, with the vast majority being foreign-born. Jackowo thus revealed a close-knit community cultivated out of shared needs for Polish-language church services, fresh pirogis, Polish ales, easy access to the latest literature out of Poland, and the kind of cutting-edge Polish rock music featured at the neighborhood's hippest nightclub, Café Lura. But once again, while the concentration of Polish businesses on the strip of Milwaukee between Central Park and Belmont gave the area a Polish feel, Jackowo nonetheless coexisted, at times uneasily, with communities of working-class Mexicans and middle-class white professionals taking advantage of Avondale's more moderately priced real estate market. With Polish immigration tapering off and Mexican immigration continuing apace, Jackowo was beginning to lose some of its Polish residents. This was due not only to rising rents associated with gentrification. Sociologist Mary Patrice Erdmans determined after interviewing numerous residents here that Poles seeking to move to the suburbs were also trying to put some distance between themselves and their Mexican neighbors.[124]

Thus, working-class immigrants and ethnic entrepreneurs continued to carve out their own ethnoracial niches in the City of Neighborhoods. Unlike the politically powerful Pilsen and Humboldt Park neighborhoods or the Disneyfied old ethnic neighborhoods such as Little Italy and Greektown, however, City Hall proved reluctant to fully embrace these more recent ethnic enclaves. Chinatown managed to become one of the city's premier tourist destinations, but it took a fund drive led by George Cheung and the Chinese-American Civic Council to raise the $70,000 to construct the Chinatown Gate in 1975. This is why the gate's founders decided to inscribe it with the phrase (in Chinese characters) "The world belongs to the commonwealth," an adage, which, according to the Chicago Chinatown Chamber of Commerce, "reflect[ed] the drive, determination and spirit of the Chinese people."[125] Likewise, Seoul Drive got its name only because Korean realtor Paul Park took the initiative to rally members of the Lawrence Avenue Korean Business Association to pressure their local alderman, Richard Mell, to propose the designation before the city council. As for West Devon, the Daley administration never embraced the district's historic or cultural significance, a situation that many local businessmen believed was largely to blame for the area's economic distress. Nor was Daley's City Hall very interested in promoting Jackowo or either of the city's rather small Arab and Assyrian districts.

Why City Hall was reluctant to place its official seal on these neighborhoods can be glimpsed in the bitter controversy that erupted over the Seoul Drive ordinance. Much to the surprise of Alderman Mell, who believed the whole affair to be a political no-brainer that would end in garnering him support from Korean merchants, non-Korean residents of Albany Park objected strongly to their neighborhood being identified as Korean. "They're singling out one group to identify a very diverse community," asserted the leader of an organization calling itself Citizens for a Democratic and Diverse Albany Park. "We're establishing chunks of territory by race. What's next: Bosnia?" The Korean merchants responded by referring to how much they had helped to raise the area's tax revenues and evoking visions of Korea Town becoming a tourist destination on par with Chinatown, which did little to appease opponents.[126]

This story explains a great deal about why City Hall never figured out an effective way to brand in any coherent way the West Devon commercial strip, where a 1.7 mile section of the avenue was segmented into four honorary streets: Sheikh Mujib Way, after the founder of Bangladesh; Mohammed Ali Jinnah Way, after the founder of Pakistan; Gandhi Marg (Way); and Golda Meier Boulevard. When Debra Silverstein finally managed to unseat long-time Fiftieth Ward Alderman Bernard Stone she spoke of "Indians, Pakistanis, Jews, Muslims all working together on the street," but this cooperation was perhaps made possible by the area's ambiguous identity. Around the Argyle Street district as well the naming issue aroused indignation, with some referring to the neighborhood as Little Vietnam and others calling it New Chinatown, a situation most civic leaders in the area resolved by employing the more neutral Argyle. And yet these same leaders complained that their neighborhood was ignored by the city, a sentiment even more commonly heard around West Devon. While Chicago's shifting, heterogeneous, "unmade" neighborhoods provided opportunities for multiethnic political cooperation, more vibrant local political cultures, and the kind of diversity idealized by realtors and urbanists alike, they remained largely excluded from the global-city agenda and were thus low priorities in the annual budget. Resources and power in Richard M. Daley's Chicago flowed to the traditional ethnic strongholds that had been able to make marketable ethnoracial order out of diversity and to inscribe that order into the landscape. To fully understand this, one need only consider the counterexample par excellence: Chicago's Filipino community. While Filipinos constituted the city's second largest Asian population, just behind South Asian Indians, their spatial dispersal throughout the city made them political and culturally invisible.

However, in considering how "the people" continued to make the city, it would be erroneous to limit the discussion to the impact of immigrants. In fact, by 2010 Chicago's foreign-born population of just over 21 percent paled in comparison to those of global cities like Los Angeles (39.4 percent), New York (36.4 percent), San Francisco (35 percent), and Boston (26.9 percent). But the city made up for this deficit by attracting high numbers of American migrants from outside the Chicago metropolitan area.[127] The 1990s was the city's first decade of population increase since the 1940s, and by the early years of the twenty-first century, Chicago had emerged as a leading destination for those seeking an urban home in the United States; in 2001, for example, only Los Angeles had more people move within its jurisdiction. The strong inflow of middle-class professionals seeking Chicago's brand of urban lifestyle helped drive the gentrification of the Near West and Near South Loop areas and to push up property values throughout the predominantly middle-class North Side, many parts of which experienced a more mild form of gentrification. The Lakeview area, for example, was a largely white middle-class community in 1990, but it was nonetheless textured by the hardly insignificant presence of Latinos (14.2 percent) and blacks (6.5 percent); ten years later, the Latino population had decreased by over 60 percent and the black population by more than 30 percent. This was a period that witnessed Lakeview's arrival as a younger, more swinging real estate rival of the more affluent Lincoln Park area to its south. But many of the young middle-class professionals moving there were not only attracted to its proximity to the lake, its tree-lined streets, and its vibrant commercial strips of eclectic restaurants, bars, cafés, boutiques, and fitness clubs along Broadway and Halsted; by the end of the 1980s, the segment of North Halsted between Clark and Addison had become the center of gay nightlife in Chicago—and of the entire Midwest for that matter. And when Boystown's real estate values rose too high and its bar scene became too raucous for some, those seeking the trappings of an urban gay community began moving north to Andersonville—a historically Swedish subsection of the Edgewater community area, where rainbow flags could be seen adorning bars along Clark Street by the mid-1990s.

A good many of those settling in neighborhoods like Boystown and Andersonville, gay and straight alike, belonged to what Richard Florida has called the "creative class": people working in design, education, arts, music, entertainment, advertising, and marketing, "whose economic function is to create new ideas, new technology and/or creative content."[128] Due to its rather large immigrant, gay, and "bohemian" populations, Florida placed

Chicago in the top twenty cities possessing the kind of creative and diverse social and cultural milieus that appeal to this new class of workers. Sociologist Terry Nichols Clark has argued that Mayor Richard Daley actively helped to make this happen by incorporating the creative class into the city's culture and politics and ultimately treating it like another ethnic group in need of space to express its identity.[129] There is no doubt some truth to this contention. One could argue that Millennium Park, with its high-concept design, was an enormous gesture in this direction. Other examples can be drawn from Daley's at times flamboyant embrace of the gay community and all his administration did to help turn Wicker Park into a national icon for hipster culture in the 1990s.[130]

But this should not blind us once again to how much the people still play a role in making Chicago's neighborhoods. Richard Sennett employs the term *disorder* to describe the kind of diverse environment cities must aspire to bring about in order to become places where people will acquire the tools to deal with social challenges.[131] Chicago, despite some very long odds, retained some of its disorder despite the rapid advance of neoliberalization during the Richard M. Daley era, and it did so, in part, because disorder was still in relatively high demand—even as those seeking this precious commodity, bohemians and yuppies alike, were unwittingly contributing to its disappearance.

Epilogue

On a spotlessly clear but unseasonably chilly Monday in May 2011, with a turquoise lake fronting its shoreline and uninterrupted blue backing its iridescent skyline, Chicago looked to those attending the inauguration of its new mayor like it rightly belonged near the top of the list of the most economically powerful cities in the world.[1] And yet things were not how they appeared on the surface. The man being sworn in that day, Rahm Emanuel, was taking the helm of a city mired in crippling financial problems. His transition team had estimated that the city faced a $700 million budget shortfall the following year, and that figure did not include unfunded pension obligations or the $700 million deficit afflicting the school system. Chicago's tax revenues had plummeted. The city had lost more than 200,000 residents in the previous decade, depleting the ranks of taxpayers. The Great Recession also hit hard, eliminating some 30,000 jobs between 2009 and 2010 alone. Chicago was also operating without the critical revenue its parking meters and downtown garages had once provided. Filling this gap was going to take some imaginative, if not supernatural, solutions. Just across the Chicago River from the Jay Pritzker Pavilion, where Mayor Emanuel delivered his first mayoral speech that day, lay a striking symbol of Chicago's financial troubles: a cavernous 110-foot-diameter, 76-foot-deep hole in the ground, where the world's second tallest building, the Chicago Spire, was supposed to have stood—before the financial crisis turned it into a local joke and urban legend. Five years later, the hole was still there and its owner, Related Midwest, was paying workers to create an artificial embankment out of dirt to hide the sight of the gaping hole from surrounding buildings. As bad as all this seemed, things could get a lot worse. In fact, a sort of doomsday scenario was lurking in the not-so-distant future, when Chicago would be forced to begin filling an even bigger hole: the nearly $20 billion gap in its public pension funds.

For all these reasons, Emanuel's transition team had planned a rather low-key inauguration—"festive but not too festive," the *Tribune* reported.[2] The chosen theme was, ironically enough for this city of stark racial segregation and economic inequality, "togetherness." The celebrations began on Saturday, May 14, with community volunteering in the neighborhoods—planting flowers and picking up trash—followed by a free concert in Grant Park. The swearing-in ceremony two days later was carefully conceived to project this same earnest spirit of civic unity and responsibility. The music for the event was provided by the Chicago Children's Choir, a "multiracial, multicultural choral music education organization" formed in 1956 by a white Hyde Park minister to symbolize the ideal of racial unity as the walls of the ghetto were hardening nearby. True to form, the group delivered its own rendition of "We Shall Overcome." When Mayor Emanuel finally took the podium, after being sworn in by—fittingly enough—Harold Washington's former floor leader Timothy Evans, now chief judge of the Cook County Circuit Court, he immediately struck the same tone. "We must face the truth," Emanuel pronounced. "It is time to take on the challenges that threaten the very future of our city: the quality of our schools, the safety of our streets, the cost and effectiveness of city government, and the urgent need to create the jobs of the future." The reasons why one of the mightiest cities in the world faced such challenges in the first place, Emanuel seemed to imply, had little to do with the city's political leadership. With former mayor Richard M. Daley by his side, he hailed the Pritzker Pavilion and Millennium Park surrounding it as symbolic of a new Chicago: "Through Mayor Daley's vision, determination and leadership, this place, like our city, was reborn."

The inauguration was neither the time nor the place to lay blame for Chicago's fiscal woes, and even if it was, Emanuel, who had been initiated into Chicago politics by Richard Daley back in 1989, was not about to go biting the hand that had fed him. This he would do in the turbulent years to come, when, for example, he would refer to Daley's parking meter privatization deal as a "lemon" that constituted "a bad deal for our city and a bad contract for our residents." For now, another kind of moral to the story was being constructed out of all this celebration of togetherness and civic duty. With little to go on in terms of an explanation about the causes of the quagmire the city now faced, Chicagoans, in some sense, were left with only themselves to blame. What else could explain all of the exhortations to residents to do their part in pulling together and improving the city? In the spirit of the neoliberal age, Emanuel called on parents to help solve the problem of failing schools through better parenting and on ordinary residents to help police deal with the problem of rising homicide rates in low-income neighborhoods by being better informants. "So today, I ask of each of you, those who live here, and those who work here, business and labor: let us share the necessary sacrifices fairly and justly," the mayor said. If this sounded a lot like a prelude to austerity, that's because that is exactly what it was.

And yet a very different message was being conveyed to Emanuel's coterie of VIPs, who, for $50,000 could buy the status of inauguration "co-chair," a deal that included a seat on stage at the Pritzker Pavilion and access to a swish reception at the Venue 1 event center in the West Loop. The message of the shadow inauguration was that there was still plenty of money to be made in the new era of austerity, and the old rules would still apply. As Richard M. Daley's senior strategist and chief fundraiser during his first successful election campaign, Emanuel had effectively ushered in the age of pinstripe patronage in Chicago. In 2010 he had used his old Rolodex to amass an $11.8 million campaign fund, a new record in Chicago politics, with sizable donations from folks like Steven Spielberg, Donald Trump, and future Illinois governor Bruce Rauner. This was four times the amount raised by his closest competitor Gerry Chico, Daley's chief of staff between 1992 and 1995 and a former president of both the Chicago School and Park District boards, and more than twenty-five times the amount raised by the leading black candidate, former Illinois senator Carol Moseley Braun. Even if Emanuel only managed 55 percent of the vote against a listless field of challengers, he had demonstrated that he clearly meant business, and business took notice.

It was thus no surprise that despite branding himself as the candidate of change during the campaign, Emanuel effectively picked up where his predecessor had left off. If something *was* new, it was the pace and intensity of austerity. Daley had wrangled with the Amalgamated Transit Union over who should pay to fill the chronic operating gap ($155 million in 2009) of the country's second largest public transit system, imposing budget constraints that led to significant service cuts, fare hikes, and the laying off of over one thousand workers in 2010. But this was mere child's play compared with the slash-and-burn austerity program Emanuel unleashed. Emanuel's 2012 budget, approved by a 50–0 vote of the city council contained "reforms and efficiencies" that would save taxpayers more than $406 million. The reforms and efficiencies, however, came with some crushing social costs. Chicago shuttered six out of its twelve mental health clinics, closed its neighborhood branch libraries on Mondays, and laid off some 32 percent of the city's library workers. Needless to say, most of the mental health clinics closed were located in low-income black and Latino neighborhoods, like Woodlawn, Logan Square, and the Back of the Yards—the same kinds of communities that had been most affected by the recent CTA service cuts. Patients transferred to the far North Side began complaining that hour-long commutes were deterring them from seeking treatment.

However, the full brunt of Emanuel's austerity program did not hit the city until after the Chicago Teachers Union (CTU) dared to challenge it in September 2012, when it rallied 26,000 teachers and support staff to conduct the first teachers' strike in the city in twenty-five years. While the Emanuel administration portrayed the strike in bread-and-butter terms, the salary and health-care cost issues were, in reality, less contentious than a range of other matters. The teachers took to the streets in large part to oppose Emanuel's grand scheme—inherited from Daley and his schools CEO Arne Duncan—to overhaul Chicago's public education system by closing public schools and replacing them with privately run charter schools. In particular, the CTU challenged the new rules and practices established by Illinois legislators at the behest of Mayor Emanuel to help pave the way towards privatization—for example, a layoff process dependent on teacher evaluations rather than seniority and an evaluation process, in the spirit of the U.S. Department of Education's Race to the Top initiative, based partly on student performance on standardized tests.

After a seven-day walkout that paralyzed the nation's third largest school system, the CTU won enough concessions from the city to claim victory— among them, a modest pay increase over the next four years, a limited right of recall for displaced teachers, the maintenance of a pay schedule based largely on seniority, no increase in health care costs, an evaluation system that followed the minimum state requirements for using student performance on standardized tests, and the right to appeal teacher evaluations. CTU president Karen Lewis referred to the deal as an "austerity contract," pointing to the fact that the 17.6 percent salary increase was much lower than the 30 percent sought.

But this was only phase one of the austerity offensive against Chicago public schools and the communities depending on them most. The following May, Emanuel's school board voted 6–0 to approve his plan to close forty-nine elementary schools, most located in black neighborhoods, a move that would entail laying off some 3,000 teachers and school personnel and forcing some 12,000 students to walk longer, and at times more dangerous, routes to school. Although school closings were sweeping the nation at the time— Philadelphia's School Reform Commission had recently voted to close twenty-three, for example—this was the biggest single round of them in U.S. history. Then, in August 2013, the school board voted 7–0 to approve a budget plan that slashed individual school budgets by 10–25 percent, a steep cut that would force the elimination of school libraries (160 schools in the city already lacked them), a sharp reduction in special education and guidance counseling services, the gutting of physical education and art and music programs, and a virtual halt on physical improvements like the badly needed installation of air conditioning.

"You never want a serious crisis to go to waste," Rahm Emanuel, during his stint as President Obama's chief of staff, told a room full of corporate chief executives in November 2008.[3] Five years later, he was practicing what he preached. In her 2007 book, *The Shock Doctrine,* Naomi Klein highlights how champions of free market reforms capitalized on the destruction wrought by Hurricane Katrina to privatize the New Orleans school system— a striking example of what she refers to as "disaster capitalism."[4] While Chicago did not have hurricane winds or floodwaters to help its privatization program along, the Emanuel administration conjured up its own crisis with school closings and deep budget cuts, rationalizing them as a painful but necessary way to deal with a now $1 billion school-operating deficit and an underfunded pension system. It was yet another doomsday scenario, following in the footsteps of the ones that had justified CTA cuts under Daley and the litany of austerity measures enacted by Emanuel during his first years in office. Yet this particular scenario was about more than just balancing the budget. Emanuel and the school board intended to induce a real crisis that would validate the transfer of schools to the private sector. With their budgets worn down to the bone, public schools were now bound to demonstrate the failings that the champions of charter schools had always attributed to them. Far more than his predecessor, Rahm Emanuel understood the brave new world of disaster capitalism. Austerity, for Emanuel, was not merely the backdrop for normal business affairs; it was a powerful wellspring of economic activities and, as such, a critical source of patronage.

But those working amidst the rubble of this policy-induced catastrophe— namely, the leadership of the Chicago Teachers Union—were not buying the crisis idea for one minute. If Emanuel had inherited a political landscape shaped over the decades by neoliberal sensibilities and forms of governance, he also faced some new conditions. Like his predecessor, Richard M. Daley, Emanuel tried to use budgetary smoke and mirrors, but many Chicagoans had peeked behind the curtain and seen that the mighty wizard was a fraud. Unimpressed by Emanuel's appeal for sacrifice in the midst of crisis, the CTU called for the mayor to use TIF funds to fill the budget gap and argued quite persuasively that a small tax on transactions made on the city's financial exchanges would quickly and easily fill the budgetary gap.

The groundswell of opposition to Emanuel's austerity education budget had been gradually building under the radar since the last few years of the Richard M. Daley era. After the CTU had failed to muster citywide opposition in 2006 to the school closings initiated by Daley's Renaissance 2010 plan, a number of disgruntled teachers within the union began to join forces and to reach out to grassroots organizations in areas affected by school closings, such as the Pilsen Alliance, the Kenwood-Oakland Community Organization (KOCO), and Blocks Together, a community organization in the Puerto Rican Humboldt Park neighborhood. By 2007, the group, led by high school history teachers Jesse Sharkey and Jackson Potter, had launched a regular forum on the school closings and convinced the CTU leadership to form a committee to address the issue. Although union leadership would swiftly abandon the cause, the teachers pressed ahead, continuing to collaborate with community organizations in neighborhoods threatened by school closings. In 2008, in the midst of the global financial crisis, members of the group, which now called itself the Caucus of Rank-and-File Educators (CORE), read Klein's *The Shock Doctrine,* engaging in a discussion of its ideas which, according to Potter, was like "a light bulb going off."[5] In May 2010, with Karen Lewis as its presidential candidate, CORE triumphed in a runoff election against the United Progressive Caucus (UPC), which had controlled the CTU for thirty-six of the previous forty years.[6] True to the organizing and ideological approach that had catapulted the movement forward from the start, CORE immediately moved the issue of publicly funded corporate subsidies and the tax increment financing (TIF) system to the center of its agenda. "Corporate America sees K–12 public education as a $380 billion trust that, up until the last ten or fifteen years, they haven't had a sizable piece of," Lewis asserted following her election. "What drives school reform is a singular focus on profit. Not teaching, not learning—profit."[7] Such views about Chicago's school system had not been voiced so loudly and clearly since the days of Margaret Haley. The CTU had become the catalyst for a broad-based multiracial movement, and Karen Lewis was quickly being bandied about as a legitimate challenger to Emanuel in the upcoming election.

Anticapitalist rallying cries were not confined to the teachers' movement. Outrage over TIFs and pinstripe patronage was increasingly being vented by neighborhood groups and political organizations dealing with affordable housing, immigrant rights, access to health care, homelessness, violence prevention, and other issues. Chicago was witnessing the emergence of a citywide movement of grassroots organizations soldered together by a sense of common struggle against the stark inequalities created by the long-standing collusion between City Hall and the downtown business crowd. When Richard M. Daley announced he would not be seeking reelection in September 2010, a new feeling spread through the ranks of activists leading the charge: hope. "The Daley legacy was so deep because people thought Chicago could never change," remarked Amisha Patel, the executive director of Grassroots Collaborative, a coalition of labor and community groups.[8] In December, Grassroots Collaborative looked to channel this new spirit by organizing a mayoral candidate forum, called New Chicago 2011, which drew 2,600 people representing more than thirty community organizations across the city.

Grassroots Collaborative was strikingly successful in bringing together unions and community organizations, including the CTU, the Service Employees International Union (SEIU), the Action Now Institute, the Logan Square Neighborhood Association, the Brighton Park Neighborhood Council, and Organizing Neighborhoods for Equality: Northside (ONE Northside). Rahm Emanuel's campaign announcement just weeks after the collaborative came together might have "crushed [the] moment"—in the words of Patel. But the movement pushed forward, picking up new momentum with the emergence of the Occupy Wall Street movement nationwide. On October 10, 2011, with Occupy Wall Street protesters camped out in the financial district along LaSalle Street, the new face of the Chicago left revealed itself. Four thousand protesters joined the Take Back Chicago marches on the Chicago Art Institute, where members of the financial futures trading industry were attending a reception for the 27th Annual Futures & Options Expo. Some four months later, in February, Grassroots Collaborative and Stand Up! Chicago, another labor-community coalition, coordinated the famous "golden toilet" demonstrations to protest the granting of $15 million in TIF funds to the CME Group in 2010 for the purpose of rehabbing bathrooms, upgrading the cafeteria, and building a fitness center at the Chicago Mercantile Exchange. As a result of the pressure, CME

Group chairman Terrence Duffy promptly announced the company would return the money. Duffy was not alone in feeling the heat. In early March, the White House suddenly announced that the Group of Eight (G8) meeting that was to take place in Chicago in mid-May would be moved to Camp David to avoid disruptive protests.

And yet, as the dust settled from this whirlwind of contentious politics that whipped through the city during this moment of regime change, Mayor Emanuel started, undaunted and relatively unimpeded, down the road paved by the neoliberalization agenda of his predecessor. In addition to keeping the school privatization program on track, with the approval of eleven charter school openings in the fall of 2014 and seven more in the fall of 2015, Emanuel's handpicked school board voted to authorize $340 million in contracts to two private firms, Aramark and SodexoMAGIC, to provide custodial and building maintenance services to the Chicago Public Schools. Shortly after the start of Aramark's contract, a survey of principals indicated shortages of supplies, dirtier schools, and teachers spending more time cleaning their classrooms. Then, after the story broke and Emanuel told Aramark to "clean out the schools or . . . clean out their desks and get out," the company announced it was laying off 476 custodians. The school board wiped its hands of the affair, claiming the privilege of public unaccountability that neoliberal governance bestows. "It's not actually CPS laying off the custodians," CPS spokesman Bill McCaffrey told the press. "It's the private contractors that work for us."[9]

But far bigger problems were coming to light as the school board sped ahead on its seemingly inexorable drive towards a privatized future. In December 2013, Juan Rangel, cochairman of Emanuel's 2011 campaign, was forced to step down from his post of executive director of the United Neighborhood Organization (UNO) amidst a federal securities probe into its use of a $98 million state grant to build charter schools—believed at the time to have been the largest government subsidy for charters in the country. The grant was merely a portion of a total of $280 million in state funds allocated to UNO between 2009 and 2014, enabling a small neighborhood organization devoted largely to housing and immigrant rights issues in the Pilsen-Little Village area to grow into the city's biggest charter school operator and the largest operator of Hispanic charter schools in the nation. Emblematic of the interplay of race and neoliberalization in Daley's Chicago, Rangel had effectively parlayed UNO's ethnoracial legitimacy—carefully cultivated by his predecessor Danny Solis—to make the organization (and himself) indispensable to Daley and then Emanuel after him. UNO would serve as middleman and fixer as the city imposed charter schools on its Latino communities, and with every charter school UNO opened, City Hall would gain legions of teachers, janitors, administrators, and parents in these communities who were, in one way or another, loyal to it. All this the CTU understood and it cried foul. But the advance of charter schools continued unabated.

Indeed, Emanuel's first term in office witnessed a litany of scandals and mishaps related to the city's privatization deals: Aramark's incompetence, Rangel's improprieties, and the rampant malfunctioning of the Chicago Transit Authority's new privatized fare collection system, Ventra, which ended up costing the city $519 million ($65 million more than expected). Yet City Hall's belief in the private sector as holding the solution to all its problems never wavered, even for a moment.

The Emanuel administration also ignored the tough talk about the injustices of the TIF system within the ranks of Chicago's new anticapitalist insurgency, not wavering in the least in its determination to keep funneling a disproportionate amount of TIF funds into the Loop while denying the areas most in need of them of their proper share. Between 2011 and 2015, almost half the $1.3 billion in TIF financing earmarked by the Emanuel administration went to the Loop district, an area that holds only 11 percent of Chicago's population and accounts for just 5 percent of its geography. The South Side, by contrast, received about 16 percent of TIF funds, the West Side only 9 percent, and the Southwest and Far South Sides just 4 percent each.[10] Moreover, TIF funds in the Loop went to projects that created few new jobs for residents of the city's poor and working-class neighborhoods during a time when the position of young African Americans in Chicago's labor market was particularly weak. In 2014, 47 percent of African Americans aged 20–24 were out of school and out of work, compared with just 31 percent in New York and Los Angeles. By contrast, only 10 percent of white Chicagoans in this same age group were unemployed and out of school.[11]

Perhaps the most controversial of Emanuel's TIF projects during his first term was his authorization of $55 million to subsidize the construction of a new 10,000-seat arena for DePaul University's basketball team. When the project was announced in May 2013, protesters took to the streets to demand "money for schools, not for stadiums." Under pressure, Emanuel rearranged the financing scheme so that the city would pay for the acquisition of land for both the arena and surrounding hotels rather than for the construction of the arena itself. The opposition fizzled. At the ground-breaking ceremony more than two years later, the whole matter had become, in the words of Third Ward alderman, Pat Dowell, "a non-issue."[12] Dowell, who represented a ward that was two-thirds African American and who was by the end of 2014 voting with the mayor's agenda nearly 90 percent of the time, supported the project, at least in part, for the 7,500 construction jobs and 2,500 permanent jobs it promised to bring to her constituents. But it was unclear how many of those jobs would be stable and well-paid enough to support working-class families in Third Ward neighborhoods like Bronzeville, Grand Boulevard, and Fuller Park.

The DePaul arena deal raised other troubling questions. Should the city subsidize an institution with an endowment approaching half a billion dollars when it was facing serious budget gaps, especially after Moody's Investors Service had downgraded Chicago's debt rating to junk grade? Not long after the city council voted almost unanimously—just three nays recorded—to approve the subsidy, it authorized a number of regressive fee and tax increases on telephones, cable television, and parking—all on top of Chicago's sales tax, one of the highest in the country.[13] In other words, the city council was approving measures to extract regressive taxes from its citizens while supporting wealthy private institutions.

Hence, if the CTU strike had appeared to usher in a new anticapitalist militancy among the ranks of community activists, the spirit of the rebellion barely touched Chicago's aldermen, who, according to political scientist and former alderman Dick Simpson, continued to wield a "rubber stamp." Between June 2011 and November 2014, the city council supported the mayor on divided roll call votes 90 percent of the time. Even the eight aldermen belonging to the so-called Progressive Reform Caucus proved reliable supporters of the mayor's program, siding with his proposals an average of 67 percent of the time.[14]

Much has been made of the tactics of intimidation, blackmail, and subterfuge that Emanuel—like Daley before him—employed to command the obedience of aldermen. And yet such factors go only so far in explaining the city council's abdication of its role as legislative body and check on executive power during Emanuel's first term. Ultimately, progressives on the city council were unable to muster enough support to challenge the mayor's policies because there was simply not enough public pressure coming from the wards that were on the losing end of them—and this despite the fact that these years saw the unions, a range of community organizations, and a pesky, talented group of investigative journalists in Chicago's mainstream and independent press unveiling the workings of pinstripe patronage and the neoliberal agenda like never before.[15] To be sure, Chicago's political culture had been reshaped by the CTU strike of 2012. But it had not been transformed in any significant way. The new insurgent style of grassroots coalition building that had crystallized around the CTU strike seemed to hold great potential, but such forms of political mobilization were difficult to normalize and sustain. The city's emerging progressive forces watched helplessly as the school board rubber stamped the school closing plan—in spite of a series of emotional public hearings—and as the city council rubber stamped just about everything that came before it. Consequently, the fatalism of old started to set in once again.

And yet some new glimmers of hope appeared in the mayoral and aldermanic elections of February 2015, when county commissioner Jesús "Chuy" García mounted a formidable challenge to Rahm Emanuel. García, the son of a Mexican farm laborer who became alderman of the heavily Mexican Twenty-Second Ward before moving on to the Illinois State Senate, managed to take enough votes (34 percent) to prevent the incumbent Emanuel from winning an outright majority. While García's ability to force a mayoral runoff race—the first in the city's history—against an incumbent who had outspent him by more than twelve times suggested that the insurgency was still alive and well, perhaps even more important was the success of the city's progressive aldermen. Chicago Forward, the super-PAC created by Emanuel supporters to defeat opposition to the mayor's policies, had funneled substantial funds to a number of pro-Emanuel candidates, but progressive incumbents had prevailed nonetheless. Progressives drew support and funds from grassroots organizations like United Working Families (UWF) and Grassroots Illinois Action (GIA). UWF, in particular, claimed to have knocked on over 153,000 doors and made over 70,000 phone calls.

With Bill de Blasio's triumphant 2013 "tale of two cities" campaign in New York's last mayoral election lingering in the air, Chicago seemed once again poised for some real change. In the weeks leading up to the runoff, García's campaign sought to script the "two cities" story for Chicago as well, referring to Emanuel by his oft-heard nickname: "Mayor 1%."[16] Emanuel countered by reminding working-class voters that he had created jobs, raised the city's minimum wage, extended the availability of preschool and full-day kindergarten, and renovated playgrounds throughout the city. The *New York Times* called the race "a test of liberalism" for the whole country.[17] When the results of the runoff election were tallied some six weeks later, few but the most naively optimistic expected any real change in the years to come. Emanuel captured just under 56 percent of the vote in an election that had— in comparison to recent mayoral elections in Chicago and other big cities— witnessed a somewhat respectable 40 percent rate of voter participation. The mayor would head into this second term with a moderately more unruly city council, but there was no doubt that the status quo had been convincingly defended.

In addition to his bloated war chest and his endorsements from President Barack Obama, legendary Chicago congressmen Luis Gutiérrez and Bobby Rush, the *Chicago Defender,* and the vast majority of black ministers and business leaders, all of whom lined up with the Democratic Party establishment, no small amount of good fortune had contributed to Emanuel's victory. Karen Lewis was, in fact, supposed to have been his challenger, and early polls had showed her running strongly. But after being diagnosed with a brain tumor, Lewis was forced to withdraw, and her heartfelt endorsement of García was no compensation. Even with endorsements from Lewis, civil rights leader Jesse Jackson, and the leading black mayoral candidate Willie Wilson, García struggled to win the support of black Chicagoans. Despite the school closings and budget cuts and despite the autocratic way the mayor had imposed them on black communities, Emanuel garnered nearly 58 percent of the black vote and carried every single black-majority ward. Turnout in black wards was especially low. The four wards that recorded turnouts under 30 percent—the Sixteenth, Twentieth, Twenty-Fourth, and Twenty-Eighth— were all between 69 and 86 percent African American.

García, who came with cred in the black community for having played an active role in Harold Washington's multiracial coalition, was simply unable to get out the vote in the black wards, as many had hoped. García's detractors pointed to a number of reasons why he had failed to inspire African Americans. The candidate had spoken vaguely about favoring "the neighborhoods versus downtown" but had never given black communities any tangible sense of what would change for them under his leadership. And in the aftermath of the August rebellion in Ferguson, Missouri, when the Black Lives Matter movement against racist police violence was spreading across the nation, García had been reluctant to address police-community issues. Unbeknownst to García was the fact that just days before he had announced his candidacy, a Chicago police officer had been filmed by a dash cam shooting a seventeen-year-old black youth name Laquan McDonald sixteen times as he was walking away. News of the incident would not leak until after the election—another "stroke of fortune" for Emanuel, who denied being aware of the matter until much later.

But Chicago provided no shortage of issues in the run-up to the election that García could have seized upon to prove his mettle to African Americans. His campaign was lethargic in its support for reparations for survivors of police torture at the Area 2 headquarters, and he remained largely silent about allegations of illegal detentions and physical abuse against black suspects at the Chicago Police Department's secret facility in the abandoned Sears and Roebuck complex in Homan Square. García was clearly out of step and out of touch with the new spirit of activism that was emerging in black Chicago around the time he launched his campaign. The grand jury decision not to indict the officer who had shot Michael Brown in Ferguson unleashed widespread anger in black Chicago about decades of rampant police misconduct. The underlying conditions of such anger were dramatically revealed in the fall of 2015, when the Invisible Institute, a group of journalists and lawyers, released a vast database of police misconduct complaint records. The findings were stark to say the least: the CPD had taken some form of disciplinary action in just 2 percent of the nearly 29,000 allegations of misconduct between 2011 and 2015. While blacks filed most of the complaints, those filed by whites were more likely to be upheld.[18]

In the weeks after the Ferguson verdict, a number of black political organizations began channeling frustrations about the situation in Chicago. Black Youth Project 100 (BYP100), an organization of young students and activists that had come together with the help of University of Chicago political science professor Cathy Cohen and a grant from George Soros's Open Society Foundation, rallied hundreds of protesters against police violence against African Americans for marches and a half-day sit-in at City Hall. Then, in February 2015, the Chicago Alliance Against Racist and Political Repression launched a series of protests at the Chicago Police Department facility in Homan Square. Meanwhile, a coalition of South Side organizations, including Fearless Leading by the Youth (FLY), Southside Together Organizing for Power (STOP), and Students for Health Equity (SHE) stepped up a campaign to force the University of Chicago to add a level-1 trauma center to the University of Chicago Medical Center (UCMC)—a struggle that had begun in 2010, after an eighteen-year old Woodlawn resident and activist, Damian Turner, had been hit by a stray bullet during a drive-by shooting and died ninety minutes later, following a long ambulance ride to the Northwestern Memorial Hospital in the North Loop.[19]

Yet regardless of García's miscues in appealing to black voters, the fact that his two-cities campaign failed revealed the limits of the multiracial coalition-building strategy that seemed so promising after the CTU strike of 2012. Chicago continued to be an ethnoracially balkanized city with an autocratic mayor, a powerless legislature, and a political culture that was, in the final analysis, stubbornly resistant to the kinds of appeals to social injustice that activists were betting the future on. Ordinary blacks and Mexicans remained as separated in the political sphere as they were in the city's social geography, and appeals to shared injustices visited upon the working class by an alliance of political leaders and business elites were failing to close the gap.

Just as importantly, middle-class and wealthy whites in the city remained as unmoved as ever about the social and economic injustices they read about in the papers. In an election that had clearly pushed such issues to the center of the debate, Emanuel crushed García in the twelve majority white wards with the highest median income, amassing a 51,492-vote margin, which accounted for nearly 80 percent of his citywide margin of 64,722 votes. In other words, most whites seemed convinced that privatization, austerity, and brutal police tactics were the best remedies for the black and brown working-class communities of the other Chicago. In view of Chuy García's rather measured challenge to the economic order—his reluctance to criticize Emanuel's austerity measures, his support of further public sector cuts, and his lukewarm support for a financial transaction tax (FTT)—the extent of his weakness among middle-class whites was remarkable, a sign that many whites still invested in cultural explanations of poverty in the other Chicago.

By the fall of 2015, when a range of local black organizations identifying with the Black Lives Matter movement rallied thousands to hit the streets in response to the revelations surrounding the Laquan McDonald shooting, the city's racial fault lines widened even further. These protests seemed to usher in a new phase of racial mobilization that moved away from the multiracial coalition-building approach that had crystallized around the CTU strike of 2012. As understandable as this shift was, in view of the unbearable state of police-community relations in black Chicago, it had the unfortunate consequence of dampening the kinds of anticapitalist mobilizations and critiques that had seemed to possess such transformative potential years earlier. Moreover, there were some strong signs that the movement against racist police violence had trouble attracting the support of both Latinos and whites. A Pew Research Center Survey conducted in early spring of 2016 found that only 15 percent of Hispanics and 14 percent of whites claimed to "strongly support" the Black Lives Matter (BLM) movement. Perhaps even more suggestive, a mere 33 percent of Hispanics expressed any support at all for BLM, a total that lagged well behind the 40 percent recorded for whites.[20]

In Chicago, moreover, the rift between blacks and Latinos was further complicated by the fact that, after forcing the firing of police superintendent Garry McCarthy, black protesters began directing their demands for justice at Cook County state's attorney Anita Alvarez, a product of the Mexican community of Pilsen, who had become the first Latina to hold her position. The following March, Alvarez lost badly in a reelection bid to Kim Foxx, an African American who had grown up in the Cabrini-Green housing project. With Foxx backed by Cook County board president Toni Preckwinkle, one of black Chicago's most influential political leaders, and Alvarez backed by most of the city's Hispanic establishment, the election emblematized the political uses of the ethnic patronage game that had been perfected by the Daley administration and handed down to Emanuel. Daley may not have fully understood back in 2008 how his slating of a Mexican American as the county's top prosecutor, and thus the head of his own local war on drugs and gangs, would play out in the years to come. But the move was now paying dividends for his successor, who was grateful for the diversion. With criticism of the War on Drugs and the mass incarceration of African Americans mounting nationwide, it would be a Mexican American who would come to symbolize the punitive excesses of such policies in Chicago.

Foxx would have her work cut out for her, as would Chicago's new police superintendent Eddie Johnson. Murders and shootings in Chicago surged by roughly 50 percent in the first six months of 2016 compared with the previous year. Such circumstances would only make matters worse for activists seeking to revive opposition to the neoliberal agenda. With working-class black communities backed against the wall in a desperate struggle for security on the streets and Mayor Emanuel embarking upon another four years of austerity and privatization, Chicago moved towards an uncertain future.

ACKNOWLEDGMENTS

Chicago on the Make is the product of more than two decades of work on a city that has never ceased to amaze me, for better or for worse. I started that time as a resident of Chicago, a young graduate student from the University of Michigan embarking on a dissertation about race and housing, and ended it in Paris as a professor of American history and civilization at the Sorbonne. I lived between two continents and passed through several institutions, accumulating numerous debts of various kinds along the way.

In the early years in Ann Arbor and Chicago, a number of people supported me both intellectually and spiritually during some times when I doubted my capacity and resolve to move forward with my research. Terry McDonald, Earl Lewis, and George Sanchez served as excellent mentors, and a number of friends in and around the graduate program in history in Ann Arbor nurtured my thinking at the outset: Chris Schmidt-Nowara, who sadly and tragically left us in 2015, John Mckiernan-Gonzalez, Riyad Koya, Steve Soper, Susan Rosenbaum, and Greg Shaya, among others. Once in Chicago, the big city for a kid from the suburbs of Boston, I was fortunate enough to have fallen in with a tight group of generous, witty, fun, and exceptionally perceptive Chicagoans that showed me another side of the city and sparked my passion for telling its stories: Edward Koziboski, Kathy Flynn, Dan Kiss, Jayson Harsin, Kevin Carollo, Lyle Rowen, Meg Zimbeck, Roshen Hendrickson, and Friese Undine. As I was conducting the research for my first book, *Mean Streets,* parts of which have been incorporated in various ways into *Chicago on the Make,* a number of scholars shared their work, read my work, or just took the time to talk with me. In particular, I am indebted to Timothy Gilfoyle, James Grossman, George Chauncey, David Roediger, Gabriela Arredondo, Chad Heap, James Barrett, Sudhir Venkatesh, Gerald Suttles, William Sites, Dominic Pacyga, and Ramon Gutiérrez.

Many of the people mentioned above continued to accompany me during the next phase, when my life moved across the Atlantic and I began to approach Chicago's history from the angle that led me to *Chicago on the Make*. In France, a number of colleagues at the Université Lille 3, the Centre de recherches internationales (CERI) at Sciences Po Paris, and more recently at the Université Paris-Sorbonne contributed in a range of ways to my work and general well-being: Thomas Dutoit, Richard Davis, Mathieu Duplay, Alexandra Poulain, Philippe Vervaecke, Angeline Escafré-Dublet, Romain Bertrand, Hélène Combes, Denis Lacorne, Christian Lequesne, Nathalie Caron, Yves Figueiredo, Thibaut Clément, Olivier Fraysse, Marc Amfreville, Juliette Utard, Claire Charlot, Joana Etchart, and Elisabeth Angel-Perez.

As I was in the process of writing *Chicago on the Make*, I was fortunate to have had numerous opportunities to bounce my ideas off some brilliant scholars during seminars and conferences, or merely over dinner or coffee. Invited talks at the Department of History at the University of Pennsylvania, the University of Chicago's Center for the Study of Race, Politics and Culture (CSRPC), DePaul University's Department of History, the Great Cities Institute at the University of Illinois at Chicago, the NYU Urban Seminar at New York University, and the University of Sydney's United States Studies Centre provided me with new and timely insights. Special thanks are owed to Teresa Córdova, Director of UIC's Great Cities Institute, for setting up the event that allowed me to exchange with Don Rose and Jesús "Chuy" García. I am also grateful to a number of scholars and others in the United States and France who shared their ideas with me as I was completing the manuscript: Mary Pattillo, Timothy Stewart-Winter, Donna Murch, N. D. B. Connolly, Kim Phillips-Fein, Thomas Jessen Adams, Sylvie Tissot, Adam Green, Michael Dawson, Pauline Lipman, Romain Huret, Emmanuel Blanchard, Sarah Leboime, Clément Petitjean, George Katito, Laurence Gervais, David Farber, Paul Schor, Jonathan Magidoff, Robert Self, Michael Foley, Sébastien Chauvin, François Weil, Nancy Green, Vincent Michelot, Julien Talpin, Hélène Le Dantec-Lowry, Marie-Hélène Bacqué, Jean-Baptiste Velut, Jeff Chang, David Huyssen, Salah Amokrane, and Frédéric Callens. My work has also benefited enormously from the fresh perspectives that my students in my master's seminars have brought to me over my past five years at the Sorbonne.

Four people, in particular, deserve my very deepest gratitude for having read most or much of the manuscript and for having offered suggestions that helped me to greatly improve it: Thomas Sugrue, Caroline Rolland-Diamond,

Bryant Simon, and Elsa Devienne. While Bryant came in towards the tail end, Tom, Caroline, and Elsa helped to keep me believing in the project from its earliest days.

No small amount of institutional support helped make this book possible. I would like to thank the École Doctorale IV, the Commission de la recherche, and the research center Histoire et Dynamique des Espaces Anglophones (HDEA) of the Université Paris-Sorbonne, as well as the Centre de recherches internationales (CERI) at Sciences Po Paris for their generous financial assistance. I would also like to extend a heartfelt thanks to the staffs at the Chicago History Museum and UIC Special Collections and University Archives, as well as to the administrative staffs of the UFR Études Anglophones and the École Doctorale IV at the Université Paris-Sorbonne. I am moreover very grateful to my editor, Niels Hooper, at the University of California Press for his unwavering support through the long years it took to bring *Chicago on the Make* to fruition.

Finally, this book would not have been possible without the encouragement and support of the people who have surrounded me closest of all over these past years—my dear friends from my neighborhood and my family. Alice, Fabrice, Julien, Charlotte, Joséphine, Marc, Johanna, Anouchka, and Guillaume, thanks for making a community out of my neighborhood. To Caroline, Clyde, and Théodore, my gratitude is endless.

NOTES

1. This kind of parody was popularized by the nationally televised comedy show *Saturday Night Live* in the 1980s.

2. On the Chicago School and its contextual approach, see Andrew Abbott, "Of Time and Space: The Contemporary Relevance of the Chicago School," *Social Forces* 75 (June 1997), 1149–82.

3. For a scathing criticism of Park's race relations paradigm for its manner of obfuscating the structures and dynamics of racial oppression, see Stephen Steinberg, *Race Relations: A Critique* (Palo Alto, CA: Stanford University Press, 2007). St. Clair Drake and Horace R. Cayton, *Black Metropolis* (1945; repr. with new foreword by Mary Pattillo, Chicago: University of Chicago Press, 2015); for an analysis of how Drake and Cayton's book redefined the concept of the ghetto within the social sciences, see Mitchell Duneier, *Ghetto: The Invention of a Place, the History of an Idea* (New York: Farrar, Straus and Giroux, 2016).

4. The so-called concentric zone model (otherwise known as the Burgess model) was developed by Chicago School founders Ernest Burgess and Robert Park in their seminal study *The City.* Robert E. Park, Ernest W. Burgess, and Roderick D. McKenzie, *The City: Suggestions for Investigation of Human Behavior in the Urban Environment* (1925; repr., Chicago: University of Chicago Press, 1984).

5. Michael J. Dear, ed., *From Chicago to LA: Making Sense of Urban Theory* (Thousand Oaks, CA: Sage, 2002). In fact, one can find the genesis of the Los Angeles School more than a decade before this when Mike Davis claimed to be "excavating the future in Los Angeles" in his classic book *City of Quartz.* Mike Davis, *City of Quartz: Excavating the Future in Los Angeles* (1991, repr., London: Verso, 2006).

6. Dick Simpson and Tom M. Kelly, "The New Chicago School of Urbanism and the New Daley Machine," *Urban Affairs Review* 44 (November 2008), 218–38. Students of New York politics have also weighed in on this discussion; see, for example, John Mollenkopf, "School Is Out: The Case of New York City," *Urban Affairs Review* 44 (November 2008), 239–65.

7. See John P. Koval, "An Overview and Point of View," in *The New Chicago: A Social and Cultural Analysis,* ed. John P. Koval, Larry Bennett, Michael I. J. Bennett, Fassil Demissie, Roberta Garner, and Kiljoong Kim (Philadelphia: Temple University Press, 2006), 3–17; and Terry Nichols Clark, "The New Chicago School," in Dennis R. Judd and Dick Simpson, *The City, Revisited: Urban Theory from Chicago, Los Angeles, and New York* (Minneapolis: University of Minnesota Press, 2011), 220–41.

8. Simpson and Kelly, "New Chicago School of Urbanism," 238.

9. Robert J. Sampson, *Great American City: Chicago and the Enduring Neighborhood Effect* (Chicago: University of Chicago Press, 2012).

10. The only other book on Chicago that moves in this direction is Larry Bennett, *The Third City: Chicago and American Urbanism* (Chicago: University of Chicago Press, 2010). While Bennett, one of the leading proponents of the New Chicago School, is not a historian, he is attentive to how Chicago's past has weighed upon the city's recent evolution. Yet *Third City* is largely concerned with the Richard M. Daley era (1989–2011) and with questions of urban form. Moreover, Bennett's minimal coverage of black Chicago leaves a large part of the Chicago story untold. To this day, the only other serious historical monograph on Chicago over the *longue durée* is Dominic Pacyga's *Chicago: A Biography* (Chicago: University of Chicago Press, 2010), but this book's treatment of the high era of globalization is rather schematic. Richard M. Daley's twenty-two years in City Hall, for example, receive merely twelve pages of a book that numbers more than four hundred.

11. Fittingly, during the twelve-year interregnum between the administrations of Richard J. Daley and Richard M. Daley, Chicago politics became quite contentious—especially during the "council wars" that broke out during the term of the city's only popularly elected black mayor, Harold Washington.

12. My conception of neoliberalization is informed by the work of Wendy Brown, who defines neoliberalism as a "rationality extending a specific formulation of economic values, practices, and metrics to every dimension of human life." Wendy Brown, *Undoing the Demos: Neoliberalism's Stealth Revolution* (New York: Zone Books, 2015), 30.

13. Eric Klinenberg, *Heat Wave: A Social Autopsy of Disaster in Chicago* (Chicago: University of Chicago Press, 2002).

14. David Harvey, *A Brief History of Neoliberalism* (New York: Oxford University Press, 2005).

15. Ibid., 42.

16. Wendy Brown, "American Nightmare: Neoliberalism, Neoconservatism, and De-democratization," *Political Theory* 34 (December 2006), 695.

17. Mahmood Mamdani, *Good Muslim, Bad Muslim: America, the Cold War, and the Roots of Terror* (New York: Pantheon, 2004).

18. See, for example, Milton Rakove, *Don't Make No Waves . . . Don't Back No Losers: An Insider's Analysis of the Daley Machine* (Bloomington: Indiana University Press, 1976); and William L. Grimshaw, *Bitter Fruit: Black Politics and the Chicago Machine, 1931–1991* (Chicago: University of Chicago Press, 1992).

19. Similar "red squads" operated in New York, Philadelphia, Los Angeles, Detroit, Baltimore, and Washington, DC, but none were as sophisticated and aggressive as that in Chicago. Surprisingly, the only study of the role played by these organizations is Frank J. Donner, *Protectors of Privilege: Red Squads and Police Repression in Urban America* (Berkeley and Los Angeles: University of California Press, 1990). Unfortunately, Donner did not have access to the Chicago Police Red Squad files, which were turned over for public scrutiny after a 1987 federal court order.

CHAPTER 1

1. Lincoln Steffens, *The Shame of Nations* (1904; repr., New York: Dover, 2004), 192, 163.

2. Daniel T. Rodgers, *Atlantic Crossings: Social Politics in a Progressive Age* (Cambridge, MA: Belknap Press, 1998), 5.

3. Daniel H. Burnham and Edward H. Bennett, *Plan of Chicago* (1908, Commercial Club of Chicago; repr., New York: Princeton Architectural Press, 1993), 1.

4. *Report of the City Council Committee on Crime of the City of Chicago,* March 22, 1915; *Chicago Tribune,* December 21, 1903.

5. *Chicago Tribune,* December 25, 1903.

6. Jeffrey S. Adler, *First in Violence, Deepest in Dirt: Homicide in Chicago, 1875–1920* (Chicago: University of Chicago Press, 2006), 15; on working-class male "sporting culture," see Timothy J. Gilfoyle, *City of Eros: New York City, Prostitution, and the Commercialization of Sex, 1790–1920* (New York: Norton, 1992), 99–106.

7. Upton Sinclair, *The Jungle* (1906; repr., New York: Dover, 2001), 15.

8. Robert Hunter, *Tenement Conditions in Chicago: Report of the Investigative Committee of the City Homes Association* (Chicago: City Homes Association, 1901), https://archive.org/details/tenementconditiooocity, 128, 132.

9. Wesley G. Skogan, *Chicago since 1840: A Time-Series Data Handbook* (Urbana, IL: Institute of Government Affairs, 1976), 24.

10. Dominic A. Pacyga, *Chicago: A Biography* (Chicago: University of Chicago Press, 2009), 61.

11. Carol Willis, *Form Follows Finance: Skyscrapers and Skylines in New York and Chicago* (Princeton, NJ: Princeton University Press, 1995), 63.

12. Daniel Bluestone, chap. 4, in *Constructing Chicago* (New Haven, CT: Yale University Press, 1991).

13. *Report on the Population of the United States at the Eleventh Census: 1890,* part I (Washington, DC: Government Printing Office, 1895), 672; *Thirteenth Census of the United States Taken in the Year 1910,* vol. 1, *Population 1910: General Report and Analysis* (Washington, DC: Government Printing Office, 1913), 829. The size of the Jewish population is estimated using the census figures for Russian-born immigrants. A tiny community before the 1890s, the foreign-born Greek population leaped forty-seven-fold between 1890 and 1920.

14. Allan H. Spear, *Black Chicago: The Making of a Black Ghetto* (Chicago: University of Chicago Press, 1967), 12–15.

15. Adler, *First in Violence, Deepest in Dirt*, 44.

16. *Chicago Socialist*, October 8, 1904, quoted in David H. Bates, "Between Two Fires: Race and the Chicago Federation of Labor, 1904–1922" (PhD dissertation, University of Illinois at Urbana-Champaign, 2012), 36.

17. *Chicago Tribune*, April 8, 1905.

18. Bates, "Between Two Fires," 55.

19. *Chicago Tribune*, May 8, 1905.

20. Frederic Thrasher, *The Gang: A Study of 1,313 Gangs in Chicago* (Chicago: University of Chicago Press, 1927), 131.

21. James R. Barrett, "Americanization from the Bottom Up: Immigration and the Remaking of the Working Class in the United States," *Journal of American History* 79 (December 1992), 996–1020; James R. Barrett and David R. Roediger, "The Irish and the 'Americanization' of the 'New Immigrants' in the Streets and in the Churches of the Urban United States, 1900–1930," *Journal of American Ethnic History*, Summer 2005, 3–33

22. *New York Times*, November 1, 1903.

23. U.S. Congress, Senate Committee on Immigration, *Report of the Immigration Commission: Immigration and Crime*, vol. 36 (Washington, DC, 1911), 144.

24. *Chicago Record-Herald*, July 31, 1906, quoted in Adler, *First in Violence, Deepest in Dirt*, 161–62.

25. Maureen Flanagan, "Gender and Urban Political Reform: The City Club and the Woman's City Club of Chicago in the Progressive Era," *American Historical Review* 95, no. 4 (October 1990), 1032–50.

26. John J. Glessner, *The Commercial Club of Chicago: Its Beginning and Something of Its Work* (Chicago: Privately printed for members of the Commercial Club, 1910), www.forgottenbooks.com/en/books/TheCommercialClubofChicago_10519965.

27. Paul DiMaggio, "The Problem of Chicago," in *The American Bourgeoisie: Distinction and Identity in the Nineteenth Century*, ed. Sven Beckert and Julia B. Rosenbaum (New York: Palgrave Macmillan, 2010), 209–32. If Chicago's brand of progressivism stood out in some ways, such activities of cultural patronage suggest its elites were more focused on changing the behavior of the laboring classes than addressing the structural roots of inequality. My thinking here thus concurs with recent work challenging the coherence and impact of the progressive era: see, for example, David Huyssen, *Progressive Inequality: Rich and Poor in New York, 1890–1920* (Cambridge, MA: Harvard University Press, 2014).

28. Joseph M. Siry, "Chicago's Auditorium Building: Opera or Anarchism," *Journal of the Society of Architectural Historians* 57 (1998), 137.

29. On the promotion of the plan, see Carl Smith, chap. 7, in *The Plan of Chicago: Daniel Burnham and the Remaking of the American City* (Chicago: University of Chicago Press, 2006).

30. Burnham and Bennett, *Plan of Chicago*, 1, 50.

31. Ibid., 8.

32. Ibid., 32.

33. Ibid., 108.

34. Ibid., 8.

35. Ibid., 50.

36. Robert Lewis, "Modern Industrial Policy and Zoning: Chicago, 1910–1930," *Urban History* 40, no. 1 (February 2013), 96–97.

37. *Chicago Tribune*, July 8, 1917.

38. William Tuttle, Jr., *Race Riot: Chicago in the Red Summer of 1919* (1970; repr., Chicago: Illini Books, 1996), 75–76.

39. Chicago Commission on Race Relations (CCRR), *The Negro in Chicago: A Study of Race Relations and a Race Riot* (Chicago: University of Chicago Press, 1922), 3.

40. James R. Grossman, *Land of Hope: Chicago, Black Southerners, and the Great Migration* (Chicago: University of Chicago Press, 1989), 178.

41. Arnold R. Hirsch, "E Pluribus Duo?: Thoughts on 'Whiteness' and Chicago's 'New' Immigration as a Transient Third Tier," *Journal of American Ethnic History* 23 (Summer 2004), 7–44; see also James R. Barrett and David Roediger, "Inbetween Peoples: Race, Nationality, and the 'New Immigrant' Working Class," *Journal of American Ethnic History* 16 (Spring 1997), 3–44.

42. Frederic Thrasher, *The Gang: A Study of 1,313 Gangs in Chicago* (Chicago: University of Chicago Press, 1927), 16.

43. Mike Royko, *Boss: Richard J. Daley of Chicago* (New York: Dutton, 1971), 37.

44. CCRR, *The Negro in Chicago*, 8.

45. *Annual Report of the Crime Commission, 1920*, quoted in CCRR, *The Negro in Chicago*, 342.

46. John Landesco, "The Gangster and the Politician," 8, Ernest Watson Burgess Papers, box 132, folder 7, University of Chicago Special Collections Research Center.

47. James R. Barrett, *Work and Community in the Jungle: Chicago's Packinghouse Workers, 1894–1922* (Urbana and Chicago: University of Illinois Press, 1987), 13–35; see also Rick Halpern, *Down on the Killing Floor: Black and White Workers in Chicago's Packinghouses, 1904–1954* (Urbana and Chicago: University of Illinois Press, 1997), 7–43.

48. Sinclair, *The Jungle*, 30.

49. Thrasher, *The Gang*, 174.

50. Ibid., 17, 194.

51. Thomas Jablonsky, *Pride in the Jungle: Community and Everyday Life in Back of the Yards Chicago* (Baltimore: Johns Hopkins University Press, 1993), 90.

52. Dominic Pacyga, "Chicago's 1919 Race Riot: Ethnicity, Class, and Urban Violence" in *The Making of Urban America*, 2nd ed., ed. Raymond A. Mohl (Scholarly Resources: Wilmington, DE, 1997), 187–207.

53. Hirsch, "E Pluribus Duo?"

54. Thomas Philpott, *The Slum and the Ghetto: Neighborhood Deterioration and Middle Class Reform, Chicago, 1880–1930* (Belmont, CA: Wadsworth, 1991), 195.

55. Pacyga, *Chicago,* 220.

56. Thomas A. Guglielmo, *White on Arrival: Italians, Race, Color, and Power in Chicago, 1890–1945* (New York: Oxford University Press, 2003), 101.

57. "Igoe Flays Negroes in Harsh Terms," *Plain Truth* 1, no. 1 (October 1930), box 102, folder 3, Charles Merriam Papers, Special Collections–University of Chicago.

58. Douglas Bukowski, *Big Bill Thompson, Chicago, and the Politics of Image* (Urbana and Chicago: University of Illinois Press, 1998), 133.

59. Ibid., 151–52.

60. *Chicago Tribune,* October 3, 1924.

61. Mary J. Herrick, *Chicago Schools: A Social and Political History* (New York: Sage, 1970), 159.

62. *Chicago Daily News,* Jan 10, 1928.

63. Arnold Hirsch, *Making the Second Ghetto: Race and Housing in Chicago, 1940–1960* (Chicago: University of Chicago Press, 1978), 4.

64. Paul M. Green, "Anton J. Cermak: The Man and His Machine," in *The Mayors: The Chicago Political Tradition,* ed. Paul M. Green and Melvin G. Holli (Carbondale: Southern Illinois University Press, 2005), 109.

65. Roger Biles, *Big City Boss in Depression and War: Mayor Edward J. Kelly of Chicago* (DeKalb: Northern Illinois University Press, 1984), 26–29.

CHAPTER 2

1. "Business in Bronzeville," *Time,* April 18, 1938. The caskets and hair-straightening products mentioned here reflect the facts that undertakers were one of most important business groups in black Chicago and beauty parlors topped the list.

2. Ibid.

3. Quoted in Wallace D. Best, *Passionately Human, No Less Divine: Religion and Culture in Black Chicago, 1915–1952* (Princeton, NJ: Princeton University Press, 2005), 87.

4. St. Clair Drake and Horace Cayton, *Black Metropolis: A Study of Negro Life in a Northern City* (1945; repr., Chicago: University of Chicago Press, 2015), 433.

5. Ibid., 438.

6. Ibid., 380.

7. Ibid., 439–43.

8. Christopher Robert Reed, chap. 3, in *The Rise of Chicago's Black Metropolis, 1920–1929* (Urbana-Champaign: University of Illinois Press, 2011).

9. Drake and Cayton, *Black Metropolis,* 217–23.

10. Ford S. Black, comp and arr. *Black's Blue Book: Business and Professional Directory* (Chicago: Ford S. Black, 1918), xv.

11. Drake and Cayton, *Black Metropolis,* 434, 438, 629. By the late 1910s churches rivaled beauty services as the most prominent "business and professional" listings in *Black's Blue Book.*

12. Ibid., 629, 650–51.

13. Best, *Passionately Human, No Less Divine,* 84.

14. Ibid., 85.

15. On the "slumming" craze in Chicago, see Chad Heap, *Slumming: Sexual and Racial Encounters in American Nightlife, 1885–1940* (Chicago: University of Chicago Press, 2009), chap. 5.

16. On the evolution of "racial uplift ideology" among black leaders and intellectuals during the interwar years, see Kevin K. Gaines, *Uplifting the Race: Black Leadership, Politics, and Culture in the Twentieth Century* (Chapel Hill: University of North Carolina Press, 1996), 234–53.

17. Davarian Baldwin, *Chicago's New Negroes: Modernity, the Great Migration, and Black Urban Life* (Chapel Hill: University of North Carolina Press, 2007), 45.

18. Ibid.

19. *Chicago Defender,* May 17, 1919. For an excellent study of how such class-biased prescriptions exemplified the Chicago Urban League's tendency to embrace behavioral models of uplift, see Touré F. Reed, *Not Alms but Opportunity: The Urban League and the Politics of Racial Uplift, 1910–1950* (Chapel Hill: University of North Carolina Press, 2008).

20. *Half-Century Magazine,* January–February 1923, 13.

21. *Chicago Defender,* April 24, 1920.

22. *Chicago Defender,* November 17, 1923.

23. Robert Park and Ernest Burgess, *Introduction to the Science of Sociology* (Chicago: University of Chicago Press, 1924), 138–39.

24. Baldwin, *Chicago's New Negroes,* 45.

25. Shane White, Stephen Garton, Stephen Robertson, and Graham White, *Playing the Numbers: Gambling in Harlem between the Wars* (Cambridge, MA: Harvard University Press, 2010), 221.

26. *Chicago Defender,* September 26, 1931; *Chicago Defender,* August 22, 1931.

27. Perhaps the most significant inquiry into "the minds of individual gamblers" during this era is White et al., *Playing the Numbers,* especially chap. 8. See also Victoria Wolcott, "The Culture of the Informal Economy: Numbers Runners in Inter-War Black Detroit," *Radical History Review* (Fall 1997), 46–75.

28. Drake and Cayton, *Black Metropolis,* 576.

29. Richard Wright, *12 Million Black Voices: A Folk History of the Negro in the United States* (1941; repr., New York: Arno Press, 1969), 106.

30. William A. Gamson, *Talking Politics* (Cambridge, UK: Cambridge University Press, 1992), 32.

31. François Ewald, "Insurance and Risk," in *The Foucault Effect: Studies in Governmentality,* ed. Graham Burchell, Colin Gordon, and Peter Miller (Chicago: University of Chicago Press, 1991), 199.

32. I borrow the term *linked fate* from Michael Dawson, who uses it to convey the feeling among African Americans that their individual interests are closely connected with the collective fate of the group. Michael C. Dawson, *Behind the Mule: Race and Class in African-American Politics* (Princeton, NJ: Princeton University Press, 1994).

33. Political Scientist Wendy Brown uses the term *economization* to describe how the advance of neoliberalism "construes subjects as relentless economic actors" or as "human capital." Wendy Brown, chap. 1, in *Beyond the Demos: Neoliberalism's Stealth Revolution* (New York: Zone Books, 2015).

34. *Chicago Defender,* June 24, 1922.

35. *Chicago Tribune,* August 4, 1931.

36. Mayor Thompson had slated DePriest to fill the vacancy opened up by Representative Martin B. Madden's death just prior to the general elections that year.

37. Harold F. Gosnell, *Negro Politicians: The Rise of Negro Politics in Chicago* (Chicago: University of Chicago Press, 1935), 236–40.

38. Douglas S. Massey, "Residential Segregation and Neighborhood Conditions in U.S. Metropolitan Areas," in *America Becoming: Racial Trends and Their Consequences,* vol. 1., ed. Neil J. Smelser, William Julius Wilson, and Faith Mitchell (Washington, DC: National Academy Press, 2001), 394. The dissimilarity index measures the relative separation or integration of groups across all neighborhoods of a city or metropolitan area. The dissimilarity index score of 85.2 means that 85.2 percent of white people would need to move to another neighborhood to make whites and blacks evenly distributed across all neighborhoods.

39. Christopher Robert Reed, *The Depression Comes to the South Side: Protest and Politics in the Black Metropolis, 1930–1933* (Bloomington and Indianapolis: Indiana University Press, 2011), 88.

40. James R. Grossman, *Land of Hope: Chicago, Black Southerners, and the Great Migration* (Chicago: University of Chicago Press, 1989), 233.

41. *Chicago Defender,* August 8, 1931.

42. Beth Tompkins Bates, *Pullman Porters and the Rise of Protest Politics in Black America, 1925–1945* (Chapel Hill: University of North Carolina Press, 2001), 72.

43. Grossman, *Land of Hope,* 230.

44. *The Messenger* 2 (August 1920), 73–74.

45. Bates, *Pullman Porters and the Rise of Protest Politics,* 80.

46. *The Messenger* 2 (October 1919), 5.

47. Cynthia Taylor, *A. Philip Randolph: The Religious Journey of an African American Labor Leader* (New York: New York University Press, 2006), 116.

48. *Pittsburgh Courier,* August 16, 1941.

49. *Chicago Defender,* November 19, 1927.

50. Bates, *Pullman Porters and the Rise of Protest Politics,* 81.

51. Jeffrey Helgeson, *Crucibles of Black Empowerment: Chicago's Neighborhood Politics from the New Deal to Harold Washington* (Chicago: University of Chicago Press, 2015).

52. Historian Earl Lewis uses the concept of the home sphere to connote a field of political activity that links up the household, the neighborhood, and the wider black community. Earl Lewis, *In Their Own Interests: Race, Class, and Power in Twentieth-Century Norfolk, Virginia* (Berkeley: University of California Press, 1991), 66–88.

53. Black, *Black's Blue Book,* 24.

54. *Chicago Defender,* September 29, 1923.

55. Quoted in Reed, *Rise of Chicago's Black Metropolis,* 96.

56. *Chicago Defender,* October 13, 1923.

57. N.D.B. Connolly, *A World More Concrete: Real Estate and the Remaking of Jim Crow Florida* (Chicago: University of Chicago Press, 2014), 11.

58. *Chicago Defender,* November 17, 1923.

59. *Chicago Defender,* May 23, 1925.

60. Helgeson, *Crucibles of Black Empowerment,* 2.

61. *Chicago Defender,* February 22, 1936.

62. Erik S. Gellman, *Death Blow to Jim Crow: The National Negro Congress and the Rise of Militant Civil Rights* (Chapel Hill: University of North Carolina Press, 2012), 25.

63. *Chicago Defender,* February 22, 1936.

64. Quoted in Michael W. Harris, *The Rise of Gospel Blues: The Music of Thomas Andrew Dorsey in the Urban Church* (New York: Oxford University Press, 1992), 89.

65. Ralph Ellison, *Shadow and Act* (1953; repr., New York: Vintage, 1995), 78–79.

66. Houston A. Baker, Jr., *Blues, Ideology, and Afro-American Literature: A Vernacular Theory* (Chicago: University of Chicago Press, 1984), 188.

67. See Angela Y. Davis, *Blues Legacies and Black Feminism: Gertrude "Ma" Rainey, Bessie Smith, and Billie Holiday* (New York: Vintage, 1998); Hazel Carby, "'It Jus Be's Dat Way Sometime': The Sexual Politics of Women's Blues," in *Unequal Sisters: A Multicultural Reader in U.S. Women's History,* ed. Ellen Carol DuBois and Vicki L. Ruiz (New York: Routledge, 1990).

68. *Chicago Defender,* April 21, 1928.

69. *Chicago Defender,* August 28, 1926; *Chicago Defender,* July 24, 1926.

70. *Chicago Defender,* June 18, 1927.

71. While Armstrong's rendition may have focused attention on white racism, it is important to note that the song was originally written for the 1929 Broadway musical *Hot Chocolates,* in which it was sung by a dark-skinned black woman who had lost her lover to a lighter-skinned woman.

CHAPTER 3

1. For an excellent critical perspective on the "good war" ideology and its dynamics of ethnic (but not racial) inclusion, see Gary Gerstle, *American Crucible: Race and Nation in the Twentieth Century* (Princeton, NJ: Princeton University Press, 2001).

2. *Life,* August 7, 1942.

3. *Chicago's Report to the People, 1933–1946* (Chicago: City of Chicago, 1947), 40.

4. For a detailed description of the war mobilization as it touched the lives of ordinary Chicagoans, see Perry R. Duis, "No Time for Privacy: World War II and Chicago's Families," in *The War in American Culture: Society and Consciousness during World War II,* ed. Lewis A. Erenberg and Susan E. Hirsch (Chicago: University of Chicago Press, 1996), 46–70.

5. Quoted in William M. Tuttle Jr., *Daddy's Gone to War: The Second World War in the Lives of American Children* (New York: Oxford University Press, 1993), 70.

6. *Chicago Tribune,* June 13, 1943.

7. On the symbolic politics of juvenile delinquency panics in the 1940s and 1950s, see James Gilbert, *A Cycle of Outrage: America's Reaction to the Juvenile Delinquent in the 1950s* (New York: Oxford University Press, 1986).

8. For further discussion of the circumstances of the Zoot Suit Riots and their meaning in wartime America, see Mauricio Mazon, *The Zoot-Suit Riots: The Psychology of Symbolic Annihilation* (Austin: University of Texas Press, 1984).

9. *Chicago Defender,* May 22, 1943.

10. *Chicago Tribune,* June 22, 1943.

11. "Meeting on Inter-Racial Situation," Friday, June 25, 1943, Welfare Council of Metropolitan Chicago Papers, box 145, folder 2, Chicago History Museum. For a study that demonstrates that such tensions escalated into violence in cities across the country during this time, see Harvard Sitkoff, "Racial Militancy and Interracial Violence in the Second World War," *Journal of American History* 58 (December 1971), 661–81.

12. "Meeting on Inter-Racial Situation," Welfare Council of Metropolitan Chicago Papers.

13. Quoted in Herbert Shapiro, *White Violence and Black Response: From Reconstruction to Montgomery* (Amherst: University of Massachusetts Press, 1988), 311.

14. *Chicago Tribune,* June 22, 1943.

15. For a detailed account of the 1943 race riot in Detroit, see Domenic J. Capeci Jr. and Martha Wilkerson, *Layered Violence: The Detroit Rioters of 1943* (Jackson and London: University Press of Mississippi, 1991).

16. *Chicago Defender,* July 31, 1943.

17. On the efforts of the CIO to create an interracial "culture of unity," see Lizabeth Cohen, *Making a New Deal: Industrial Workers in Chicago, 1919–1939* (New York: Cambridge University Press, 1990), 333–49.

18. On Mayor Kelly, see Roger Biles, *Big City Boss in Depression and War: Mayor Edward J. Kelly of Chicago* (DeKalb: Northern Illinois University Press, 1984).

19. Robin D. G. Kelley, *Race Rebels: Culture, Politics, and the Black Working Class* (New York: Free Press, 1994), 161–81.

20. Kenneth B. Clark and James Barker, "The Zoot Effect in Personality: A Race Riot Participant," *Journal of Abnormal Psychology* 40, no. 2 (1945), 143–48.

21. *Chicago Defender,* October 2, 1943.

22. *Chicago Defender,* July 7, 1945.

23. Raymond Williams, *Marxism and Literature* (Oxford, UK: Oxford University Press, 1977).

24. James Baldwin, *Notes of a Native Son* (Boston: Beacon Press, 1955), 92–94.

25. W. E. B. Du Bois, *Black Reconstruction in America, 1860–1880* (1935; repr., New York: Atheneum, 1992), 700.

26. Analysis of Chicago School Strikes, American Council on Race Relations, Welfare Council of Metropolitan Chicago Papers, box 145, folder 3, Chicago

History Museum. A number of scholars have examined the role of interracial rape rumors in triggering white mob violence against racial others between 1917 and 1943: see, for example, Marilynn S. Johnson, "Gender, Race, and Rumours: Re-examining the 1943 Race Riots," *Gender and History* 10 (August 1998), 252–77.

27. L. Stanton, "Eagles, January 20, 1942," Chicago Common Papers, box 7, folder: Clubs and Groups, 1940–42, Chicago History Museum.

28. A fascinating account of the racial politics of municipal swimming pools can be found in Jeff Wiltse, *Contested Waters: A Social History of Swimming Pools in America* (Chapel Hill: University of North Carolina Press, 2007).

29. *Chicago Defender,* May 20, 1944.

30. For a comprehensive account of the Chicago Housing Authority and its difficulties in pursuing a policy of racial integration, see Arnold R. Hirsch, *Making the Second Ghetto: Race and Housing in Chicago, 1940–1960* (Chicago: University of Chicago Press, 1998).

31. Quoted in Roger Biles, "Edward J. Kelly: New Deal Machine Builder," in *The Mayors: The Chicago Political Tradition,* ed. Paul M. Green and Melvin G. Holli (Carbondale: Southern Illinois University Press, 2005), 124.

32. For more background on the mayor of Bronzeville tradition, see Peter M. Rutkoff and William B. Scott, "Pinkster in Chicago: Bud Billiken and the Mayor of Bronzeville, 1930–1945," *Journal of African American History* 89 (Autumn 2004), 316–30.

33. For an article that examines how southern foodways offended black middle-class sensibilities, see Tracey N. Poe, "The Origins of Soul Food in Black Urban Identity: Chicago, 1915–1947," *American Studies International* (February 1999), 4–33.

34. Adam Green, *Selling the Race: Culture, Community, and Black Chicago, 1940–1955* (Chicago: University of Chicago Press, 2007).

35. Ibid., 77.

36. For a full account of these controversies, see Nadine Cohadas, *Spinning Blues into Gold: The Chess Brothers and the Legendary Chess Records* (New York: St. Martin's / Griffin, 2001).

37. The documentary *Martin Scorsese Presents the Blues: A Musical Journey* was produced by filmmaker Martin Scorsese and aired on PBS as a seven-part series between September 28 and October 4, 2003. The segment dealing with Chess, "Godfathers & Sons," was directed by Marc Levin.

38. For an account of the sense of racial militancy pervading the zoot suit milieu during the war and a provocative analysis of the link between this militancy and the rise of bebop, see Eric Lott, "Double V, Double-Time: Bebop's Politics of Style," *Callaloo* 11, no. 3 (1988), 587–605.

39. Once again, I am indebted to Adam Green for this idea, which is developed at length in Green, *Selling the Race,* chap. 2.

40. The seminal book on the "urban crisis" is Thomas J. Sugrue, *The Origins of the Urban Crisis: Race and Inequality in Postwar Detroit* (1998; repr., Princeton, NJ: Princeton University Press, 2005).

41. An instructive analysis of these arguments can be found in Eduard Bonilla-Silva, *Racism without Racists: Colorblind Racism and the Persistence of Racial Inequality in the United States* (New York: Rowman & Littlefield, 2006).

42. For two examples, see Thomas Byrne Edsall and Mary D. Edsall, *Chain Reaction: The Impact of Race, Rights, and Taxes on American Politics* (New York: Norton, 1991); and Jim Sleeper, *The Closest of Strangers: Liberalism and the Politics of Race in New York City* (New York: Norton, 1990).

43. The first major study to push the debate on the "urban crisis" back to the 1940s and 1950s was Hirsch, *Making the Second Ghetto.*

44. Chicago Commission on Human Relations, Documentary Memorandum: "Interracial Disturbances at 7407–7409 South Parkway and 5643 South Peoria Street," ACLU Papers, box 7, folder 5, Special Collections–University of Chicago.

45. "Human Relations in Chicago: Report for the Year 1946 of the Mayor's Commission on Human Relations," Chicago Urban League Papers, folder 229, Special Collections, University of Illinois–Chicago Circle.

46. Chicago Commission on Human Relations, Documentary Memorandum: "Interracial Disturbances."

47. For a recent study that argues for the key role played by youths in racist violence in Chicago during these years, see Andrew J. Diamond, *Mean Streets: Chicago Youths and the Everyday Struggle for Empowerment in the Multiracial City, 1908–1969* (Berkeley: University of California Press, 2009).

48. Mayor's Commission on Human Relations, memorandum on Fernwood Park Homes, Chicago Urban League Papers, folder 709, Special Collections, University of Illinois–Chicago Circle; *Chicago Defender,* August 30, 1947.

49. Council Against Racial and Religious Discrimination, Documented Memorandum XI: "1947 School Race Strike at Wells High School in Chicago," Chicago Commons Papers, box 31, folder 1, Chicago History Museum.

50. *Chicago Defender,* July 30, 1949; *Chicago Defender,* September 17, 1949.

51. For a full account of Mayor Martin Kennelly's years in office, see Arnold R. Hirsch, "Martin H. Kennelly: The Mugwump and the Machine," in *The Mayors,* ed. Green and Holli, 126–43.

52. Loïc Wacquant uses the term *hyperghetto* to distinguish the more recent black ghettos stricken by the disintegration of their middle-class strata, the disappearance of their economic bases, and the withdrawal of the welfare state from the "communal ghettos" of the first half of the twentieth century, which grouped together blacks of all classes around a range of vibrant institutions. Loïc Wacquant, *Urban Outcasts: A Comparative Sociology of Advanced Marginality* (Cambridge, UK: Polity Press, 2008), 2–4.

53. On the dynamics of white resistance and flight on Chicago's West Side in the postwar decades, see Amanda I. Seligman, *Block by Block: Neighborhoods and Public Policy on Chicago's West Side* (Chicago: University of Chicago Press, 2005).

CHAPTER 4

1. Arnold R. Hirsch, *Making the Second Ghetto: Race and Housing in Chicago, 1940–1960* (Chicago: University of Chicago Press, 1998).

2. *Chicago Tribune,* July 17, 1951. For a recent analysis of the events in Cicero that highlights the involvement of teenagers in the affair, see Andrew J. Diamond, *Mean Streets: Chicago Youths and the Everyday Struggle for Empowerment in the Multiracial City, 1908–1969* (Berkeley: University of California Press, 2009), 166.

3. The addresses of those arrested were published in *Chicago Tribune,* July 14, 1951.

4. Mayor's Commission on Human Relations, "Progress Report, Month of July, 1946," Chicago Area Project Papers, box 32, folder 1, Chicago History Museum.

5. Mike Royko, *Boss: Richard J. Daley of Chicago* (New York: Dutton, 1971), 56–57.

6. James Q. Wilson, *Negro Politics: The Search for Leadership* (New York: New Press, 1960).

7. Adam Cohen and Elizabeth Taylor, *American Pharaoh: Mayor Richard J. Daley: His Battle for Chicago and the Nation* (Boston: Little, Brown, 2000), 95.

8. The definitive study of the role of the black submachine in mayoral elections in Chicago is William J. Grimshaw, *Bitter Fruit: Black Politics and the Chicago Machine, 1931–1991* (Chicago: University of Chicago Press, 1992).

9. Thomas J. Sugrue, *The Origins of the Urban Crisis: Race and Inequality in Postwar Detroit* (Princeton, NJ: Princeton University Press, 2005); and Matthew D. Lassiter, *The Silent Majority: Suburban Politics in the Sunbelt South* (Princeton, NJ: Princeton University Press, 2007).

10. Confidential Report, Case # E-77, Operative L. G., April 23, 1954, ACLU Papers, box 11, folder 9, Special Collections–University of Chicago.

11. *Chicago Defender,* April 2, 1955.

12. Cohen and Taylor, *American Pharaoh,* 134–36.

13. Royko, *Boss,* 88–89.

14. Ibid., 89.

15. Cohen and Taylor, *American Pharaoh,* 141.

16. Adam Green, *Selling the Race: Culture, Community, and Black Chicago, 1940–1955* (Chicago: University of Chicago Press, 2007), 179–212.

17. Richard M. Daley, interview by Paul M. Green, *Illinois Issues* 22 (August–September 1991), 22.

18. Cohen and Taylor, *American Pharaoh,* chap. 5.

19. Milton Rakove, *Don't Make No Waves . . . Don't Back No Losers: An Insider's Analysis of the Daley Machine* (Bloomington: Indiana University Press, 1976), 5.

20. Cohen and Taylor, *American Pharaoh,* 164.

21. Jon C. Teaford, *The Rough Road to Renaissance: Urban Revitalization in America, 1940–1985* (Baltimore: Johns Hopkins University Press, 1990), 19.

22. Nelson Algren, *Chicago: City on the Make: 50th Anniversary Edition,* introduction by Studs Terkel, annotated by Bill Savage and David Schmittgens (1950; Chicago: University of Chicago Press, 2001), 23.

23. Royko, *Boss,* 93.

24. Hirsch, *Making the Second Ghetto,* 131.

25. Quoted in Hirsch, *Making the Second Ghetto,* 112.

26. Joel Rast, "Regime Building, Institution Building: Urban Renewal Policy in Chicago, 1946–1952," *Journal of Urban Affairs* 31, no. 2 (May 2009), 177–78.

27. Joel Rast, "Creating a Unified Business Elite: The Origins of the Chicago Area Committee," *Journal of Urban History* 37, no. 4, 593–96.

28. Quoted in Rast, "Creating a Unified Business Elite," 596.

29. Ibid.

30. Rast, "Regime Building, Institution Building," 180.

31. David Harvey, *A Brief History of Neoliberalism* (Oxford, UK: Oxford University Press, 2005), 47.

32. For a history of how the definition of *blight* shifted from a condition of substandard housing to a condition of "suboptimal" local economic development in the postwar decades, see Colin Gordon, "Blighting the Way: Urban Renewal, Economic Development, and the Elusive Definition of Blight," *Fordham Urban Law Journal* 31, no. 2 (January 2004), 305–37.

33. Wendy Brown, *Edgework: Critical Essay on Knowledge and Politics* (Princeton, NJ: Princeton University Press, 2005), 44.

34. Quoted in Hirsch, *Making the Second Ghetto,* 122.

35. Hirsch, *Making the Second Ghetto,* 257; and Amanda I. Seligman, *Block by Block: Neighborhoods and Public Policy on Chicago's West Side* (Chicago: University of Chicago Press, 2005), 8.

36. Cohen and Taylor, *American Pharaoh,* 189.

37. William Julius Wilson, *When Work Disappears: The World of the New Urban Poor* (New York: Vintage, 1997), 35.

38. Gwendolyn Brooks, "We Real Cool," in *The Bean Eaters* (New York: Harper & Brothers, 1960).

39. *Chicago Tribune,* March 21, 1961.

40. For similar stories in other cities, see, for example, Herbert Gans, *The Urban Villagers* (New York: Free Press, 1962); Manuel Castells, *The City and the Grassroots: A Cross-Cultural Theory of Urban Social Movements* (Berkeley: University of California Press, 1983).

41. Julian Levi, commencement address at the John Marshall Law School, Chicago, Illinois, February 18, 1961, President Beadle Administration Records, box 353, folder 5, Special Collections–University of Chicago.

42. Quoted in Robert A. Slayton, *Back of the Yards: The Making of a Local Democracy* (Chicago: University of Chicago Press, 1986), 203.

43. Quoted in Sanford D. Horwitt, *Let Them Call Me Rebel: Saul Alinsky—His Life and Legacy* (New York: Vintage, 1992), 102, 105, which provides a meticulous account of the founding of the BYNC, 102–19.

44. Jacques Maritain, "Of America and of the Future," *Commonweal* 41 (April 13, 1945), 642–45.

45. For an excellent account of the role played by parishes in the story of race relations and of the struggle of progressive Catholic leaders to promote interracialism in Chicago and throughout the country, see John T. McGreevy, *Parish Boundaries: The Catholic Encounter with Race in the Twentieth Century Urban North* (Chicago: University of Chicago Press, 1996).

46. OSC Recommendations to Superintendent Wilson, Industrial Areas Foundation Records, folder 334, Special Collections–University of Illinois–Chicago Circle.

47. Quoted in Horwitt, *Let Them Call Me Rebel*, 315.

48. Ibid., 398, 402.

49. Alain Touraine, *The Voice and the Eye: An Analysis of Social Movements* (Cambridge, UK: Cambridge University Press, 1981).

CHAPTER 5

1. Francis J. Carney, Activity Report, September 30, 1963, Chicago Youth Development Project, Hans Mattick Papers, box 3, folder 7, Chicago History Museum.

2. *Chicago Tribune*, July 3–4, 1955.

3. *Chicago Daily News,* January 25–26, 1956.

4. *Chicago Daily News,* January 27, 1956.

5. *Chicago Defender,* April 27, 1957.

6. The scholarship on the dynamics of social movements is vast. Two key works of reference are Mario Diani and Doug McAdam, eds., *Social Movements and Networks: Relational Approaches to Collective Action* (Oxford, UK: Oxford University Press, 2003); and Donatella della Porta and Mario Diani, *Social Movements: An Introduction* (Malden, MA: Wiley-Blackwell, 2006).

7. Among some of the recent fine works that have complicated the conventional civil rights story are Peniel E. Joseph, *Waiting 'Til the Midnight Hour: A Narrative History of Black Power in America* (New York: Holt, 2007); Matthew Countryman, *Up South: Civil Rights and Black Power in Philadelphia* (Philadelphia: University of Pennsylvania Press, 2007); Thomas J. Sugrue, *Sweet Land of Liberty: The Forgotten Struggle for Civil Rights in the North* (New York: Random House, 2009); and Donna Jean Murch, *Living for the City: Migration, Education, and the Rise of the Black Panther Party in Oakland, California* (Chapel Hill: University of North Carolina, 2010).

8. Frank Carney, Associate Director of Extension Work, Supervisory Report, Crane High School Riot Incident, June 15, 1962, Hans Mattick Papers, box 3, folder 5, Chicago History Museum.

9. Eric Schneider, *Vampires, Dragons and Egyptian Kings: Youth Gangs in Postwar New York* (Princeton, NJ: Princeton University Press, 1999).

10. For a discussion that challenges "race-neutral" analyses of gangs, see John M. Hagedorn, "Race Not Space: A Revisionist History of Gangs in Chicago," *Journal of African American History* 91, no. 2 (2006): 194–208.

11. For two introductions to Henri Lefebvre's thinking on the production of space, see Rob Shields, *Lefebvre, Love, and Struggle: Spatial Dialectics* (London and New York: Routledge, 1998), 141–85; and Edward W. Soja, *Postmodern Geographies: The Reassertion of Space in Critical Social Theory* (London: Verso, 1989), 76–93.

12. Manuel Castells, *The City and the Grassroots: A Cross-Cultural Theory of Urban Social Movements* (Berkeley and Los Angeles: University of California Press, 1983), 331.

13. John F. McDonald, *Employment Location and Industrial Land Use in Metropolitan Chicago* (Urbana: University of Illinois Press, 1984), 71–73.

14. Frank Carney, Report on Activities, Feb. 1, 1961 to Feb. 17, 1961, Hans Mattick Papers, box 3, folder 4, Chicago History Museum.

15. Louise Año Nuevo Kerr, "The Chicano Experience in Chicago, 1920–1970," (PhD dissertation, University of Illinois–Chicago, 1976), 166.

16. The Jones Act of 1917 granted all Puerto Ricans the right to U.S. citizenship. Many Puerto Ricans arriving in Chicago before the late 1940s had initially settled in New York City, but in the late 1940s a private Chicago-based employment agency, Castle, Barton and Associates, recruited Puerto Rican men to work as unskilled steelworkers and Puerto Rican women to serve as domestic workers in the metropolitan Chicago area. In addition to these North and West Side areas of settlement, a notable community also took shape in the South Side Woodlawn area. For a thorough account of the migration and settlement of Puerto Ricans (and Mexicans) in postwar Chicago, and of their negotiation of Chicago's racial context, see Lilia Fernández, *Brown in the Windy City: Mexicans and Puerto Ricans in Postwar Chicago* (Chicago: University of Chicago Press, 2012).

17. Felix Padilla, *Puerto Rican Chicago* (Notre Dame, IN: University of Notre Dame Press, 1987), 59.

18. For a detailed account of the racial aggression Puerto Ricans faced in Chicago in the 1950s and 1960s, see Andrew J. Diamond, *Mean Streets: Chicago Youths and the Everyday Struggle for Empowerment in the Multiracial City, 1908–1969* (Berkeley and Los Angeles: University of California Press, 2009), chap. 5.

19. Robert Orsi, "The Religious Boundaries of an Inbetween People: Street *Feste* and the Problem of the Dark-Skinned 'Other' in Italian Harlem, 1920–1990," *American Quarterly* 44 (September 1992), 314.

20. "Puerto Ricans in Chicago: A Study of a Representative Group of 103 Households of Puerto Rican Migrants on Chicago's Northwest Side—and their Adjustment to Big-City Living," June 1960, Chicago History Museum.

21. Spanish names appear prominently, for example, on the list of youths arrested at the Calumet Park race riot of 1957.

22. *Chicago Daily Defender,* May 26, 1960.

23. Stuart Hall, "New Ethnicities," in *Stuart Hall: Critical Dialogues in Cultural Studies,* ed. David Morley and Kuan-Hsing Chen (London and New York: Routledge, 1996), 441–49.

24. *Chicago Daily News,* July 29, 1963.

25. Adam Cohen and Elizabeth Taylor, *American Pharaoh: Mayor Richard J. Daley: His Battle for Chicago and the Nation* (Boston: Little, Brown, 2000), 302, 304.

26. *Chicago Defender,* October 12, 1963.

27. Alan B. Anderson and George W. Pickering, *Confronting the Color Line: The Broken Promise of the Civil Rights Movement in Chicago* (Athens: University of Georgia Press, 2008), 80.

28. John L. Rury, "Race, Space, and the Politics of Chicago's Public Schools: Benjamin Willis and the Tragedy of Urban Education," *History of Education Quarterly* 39 (Summer 1999), 130.

29. Vermont senator and 2016 presidential candidate Bernie Sanders, at the time a 21-year-old University Chicago student and CORE activist, was another of those arrested by police that day.

30. *Chicago Sun-Times,* August 29, 1963.

31. Robert O. Self, *American Babylon: Race and the Struggle for Postwar Oakland* (Princeton, NJ: Princeton University Press, 2003), 217.

32. *Chicago Daily News,* October 21, 1963.

33. A. B. Spellman, "Interview with Malcolm X," *Monthly Review* 16, no. 1 (1964), 1–11.

34. Cited in Robin D. G. Kelley, *Freedom Dreams: The Black Radical Imagination* (Boston: Beacon Press, 2002), 85.

35. *Chicago Tribune,* July 19, 1965; *Chicago Sun-Times,* July 19, 1965; *Chicago Defender,* July 23, 1965.

36. David Dawley, *A Nation of Lords: The Autobiography of the Vice Lords* (1973; Prospect Heights, IL: Waveland Press, 1992), 103, 107.

37. Noble de Salvi, "Angry Demand for Police Crackdown," *Daily Calumet,* September 28, 1966.

38. Gwendolyn Brooks, "The Blackstone Rangers," in *Blacks* (Chicago: Third World Press, 1987).

39. "A Statement Regarding the Relationship of the First Presbyterian Church and the Blackstone Rangers," Virgil Peterson Collection, box 42, folder 15, Chicago History Museum.

40. See the many photos of Lawndale street scenes in Dawley, *A Nation of Lords,* 55–96.

41. Quoted in Cohen and Taylor, *American Pharaoh,* 337–338.

42. David Garrow, *Bearing the Cross: Martin Luther King, Jr., and the Southern Christian Leadership Conference* (New York: Harper, 2004), 455.

43. One can find no better description of the relationship between the black submachine and the Daley machine in this era than William L. Grimshaw, *Bitter Fruit: Black Politics and the Chicago Machine, 1931–1991* (Chicago: University of Chicago Press, 1992).

44. Investigator's Report, Meeting at Stone Temple Baptist Church, June 6, 1966, Chicago Police Red Squad Files, box 139, file 940-B, Chicago History Museum.

45. *Chicago Sun-Times*, July 12, 1966.

46. Investigator's Report, Intelligence Division, CPD, July 11, 1966, Chicago Police Red Squad Files, box 137, file 940-B, Chicago History Museum.

47. James R. Ralph, Jr., *Northern Protest: Martin Luther King, Jr., Chicago, and the Civil Rights Movement* (Cambridge, MA: Harvard University Press, 1993), 94.

48. Investigator's Report, Intelligence Division, SCLC Leadership Conference at Holy Cross School at 65th and Maryland, May 10, 1966, Chicago Police Red Squad Files, box 137, file 940-A, Chicago History Museum.

49. Dawley, *A Nation of Lords*, 110.

50. Anderson and Pickering, *Confronting the Color Line*, 210–16; Ralph, *Northern Protest*, 109–13; Cohen and Taylor, *American Pharaoh*, 387–92.

51. Taylor Branch, *At Canaan's Edge: America in the King Years, 1965–1968* (New York: Simon & Schuster, 2006), 508.

52. Information Report, Departure and Return of Demonstrators in the Gage Park Vigil, August 5, 1966, Chicago Police Red Squad Files, box 139, file 940-D, Chicago History Museum.

53. Jon Rice, "The World of the Illinois Panthers," in *Freedom North: Black Freedom Struggles Outside the South*, ed. Jeanne Theoharis and Komozi Woodard (New York: Palgrave Macmillan, 2003), 48.

54. *New York Times*, August 6, 1966.

55. Quoted in Ralph, *Northern Protest*, 137.

56. In her analysis of the CFM's emphasis on the "open occupancy" issue, historian Beryl Satter comes to a similar conclusion: see Beryl Satter, *Family Properties: How the Struggle over Race and Real Estate Transformed Chicago and Urban America* (New York: Picador, 2009), 190–92.

57. *East Garfield Park Organization Newsletter*, July 25, 1966 (in author's possession).

58. This bit of information was revealed to me by an activist who witnessed the event but who wished to remain anonymous.

59. Investigator's Report, Washington Park Forum, August 1, 1966, Chicago Police Red Squad Files, box 156, file 973-A, Chicago History Museum.

60. John R. Fry, *Locked-Out Americans: A Memoir* (New York: Harper & Row, 1973), 19.

61. For an in-depth and balanced account of TWO's work with the Blackstone Rangers on this youth program, see John Hall Fish, *Black Power/White Control: The Struggle of the Woodlawn Organization in Chicago* (Princeton, NJ: Princeton University Press, 1973), 115–74.

62. Letter from Alfonso Alford to the Honorable Richard J. Daley, April 9, 1968, facsimile published in Dawley, *A Nation of Lords*, 122.

63. See, for example, Dawley, *A Nation of Lords*, 158–176; Fish, *Black Power/White Control*, 115–74; and Fry, *Locked-Out Americans*, chap. 4.

64. Arthur M. Brazier, *Black Self-Determination: The Story of The Woodlawn Organization* (Grand Rapids, MI: Eerdman, 1969), 125.

65. Fish, *Black Power/White Control*, 148–74.

66. James McPherson, "Almighty Black P Stone and What Does that Mean?" *Atlantic Monthly* 223 (May and June, 1969).

67. *Chicago Tribune*, June 21, 1969.

68. "Street Gangs: A Secret History," *Time Machine*, written and produced by Greg DeHart, hosted by Roger Mudd, produced by Termite Art Productions for the History Channel, 2000.

69. Self, *American Babylon*, 218.

70. A photo of Chew sitting atop his Rolls Royce appeared in the December 8, 1966, edition of *Jet* magazine.

71. For a detailed account of the negotiations between King and Daley, see Satter, *Family Properties*, 203–8. As Satter demonstrates in this pathbreaking study, gains by black Chicagoans in the racially discriminatory housing market would come not from the impetus of City Hall or the Chicago Real Estate Board but rather from a grassroots mobilization of black homeowners who had been forced into exploitive financial arrangements with panic-peddling "contract lenders" because discriminatory redlining practices by the government and the banking industry had shut them out of the conventional home mortgage market.

CHAPTER 6

1. Norman Mailer, *Miami and the Siege of Chicago* (London: Weidenfeld and Nicolson, 1968), 77, 82.

2. Studs Terkel, *Division Street America* (New York: New Press, 2006), xxx.

3. Several scholars and journalists have reconstructed the events surrounding the Democratic National Convention of 1968. The two finest accounts, to my mind, are Mailer, *Miami and the Siege of Chicago;* and David Farber, *Chicago '68* (Chicago: University of Chicago Press, 1987). For a compelling cinematic interpretation, see the film *Medium Cool* (1969).

4. Farber, *Chicago '68*, 200.

5. Mike Royko, *Boss: Richard J. Daley of Chicago* (New York: Dutton, 1971), 89.

6. The term *southern strategy* was popularized by Nixon campaign strategist Kevin Phillips, who in 1969 urged the Republican Party to abandon its liberal establishment constituency in the Northeast and pursue a race-driven strategy that would realign the South with the Republican Party and win increasing numbers of white middle-class voters in the North. A generation of political historians took this idea of a southern strategy at face value, thus viewing Barry Goldwater and George Wallace as the progenitors of a racialized conservatism that saw Republicans using racially coded appeals to mobilize working-class and middle-class white voters. More recently, historians have begun to challenge this interpretation. For an excellent study that views Republican strategy not as a racially driven southern strategy but rather as a colorblind "suburban strategy" oriented around notions of middle-class entitlement, meritocracy, and consumer rights, see Matthew D. Lassiter, *The Silent Majority: Suburban Politics in the Sunbelt South* (Princeton, NJ: Princeton

University Press, 2005). Few historians have viewed Richard J. Daley as a critical figure in the rise of reactionary populism in the 1960s.

7. For a detailed analysis of the response to Daley's handling of both the 1968 riot and the protests at the Democratic National Convention, see Farber, *Chicago '68*, 246–58; and David Farber, "The Silent Majority and Talk about Revolution," in *The Sixties: From Memory to History* (Chapel Hill: University of North Carolina Press, 1994), 291–316.

8. "The Troubled America: A Special Report on the White Majority," *Newsweek*, October 6, 1969, 31.

9. Frank J. Donner, *Protectors of Privilege: Red Squads and Police Repression in Urban America* (Berkeley and Los Angeles: University of California Press, 1992).

10. Ibid., 52.

11. Similar "red squads" operated in New York, Philadelphia, Los Angeles, Detroit, Baltimore, and Washington, DC, but none as sophisticated and aggressive as that in Chicago.

12. Quoted in Jeffrey Haas, *The Assassination of Fred Hampton: How the FBI and the Chicago Police Murdered a Black Panther* (Chicago: Lawrence Hill Books, 2009) 102.

13. See, for example, Todd Gitlin, *The Sixties: Years of Hope, Days of Rage* (New York: Bantam, 1993); Allen J. Matusow, *The Unraveling of America: A History of Liberalism in the 1960s* (New York: Perennial, 1985); and Winifred Breines, "Whose New Left?" *Journal of American History* 75 (September 1988): 528–45.

14. *Chicago Reader,* January 25, 1990.

15. Hannah Arendt, *On Violence* (New York: Mariner Books, 1970).

16. For a brilliant account of such tactics in the city of Los Angeles, see Mike Davis, *City of Quartz: Excavating the Future in Los Angeles* (New York: Verso, 2006).

17. Paul Gilroy, *"There Ain't No Black in the Union Jack": The Cultural Politics of Race and Nation* (Chicago: University of Chicago Press, 1991), 247.

18. In the original mural, the hands reached up towards the logo of the Latin American Defense Organization (LADO), a community organization that worked on housing, education, and health issues in the late 1960s and early 1970s. The sun was painted over the LADO logo during a restoration project led by original painter Weber in 2013.

19. Paul Ricoeur, *Hermeneutics and the Human Sciences: Essays on Language, Action, and Interpretation,* trans. John B. Thompson (Cambridge, UK: Cambridge University Press, 1981), 158.

20. *Chicago Tribune,* October 18, 1968.

21. John F. McDonald, *Employment Location and Industrial Land Use in Metropolitan Chicago* (Champaign, IL: Stipes, 1984), 10–11.

22. R. C. Longworth, "How Much Time Do We Have? . . . No Time," *Chicago Tribune,* May 10, 1981.

23. Gregory D. Squires, Larry Bennett, Kathleen McCourt, and Phillip Nyden, *Chicago: Race, Class, and the Response to Urban Decline* (Philadelphia: Temple University Press, 1987), 39–40.

24. McDonald, *Employment Location and Industrial Land Use,* 12.

25. The Standard Oil building was renamed the Amoco Building in 1985, when the company changed names, and then the Aon Center in 1999, when the Aon Corporation became the building's primary tenant. The Sears Tower was renamed the Willis Tower in 2009, when London-based insurance broker Willis Group Holdings, Ltd., leased a portion of the building and obtained the building's naming rights.

26. Los Angeles would never produce a signature structure of this kind, although seven out of its fifteen tallest buildings were completed in the 1970s. On these two historical moments of skyscraper construction, see Carol Willis, *Form Follows Finance: Skyscrapers and Skylines in New York and Chicago* (Princeton, NJ: Princeton Architectural Press, 1995).

27. For a detailed account of this passage from Fordism to a regime of "flexible accumulation," see David Harvey, *The Condition of Postmodernity: An Enquiry into the Origins of Cultural Change* (London: Basil Blackwell, 1990), 141–72.

28. Saskia Sassen, *The Global City: New York, London, Tokyo* (Princeton, NJ: Princeton University Press, 1991), 3.

29. Ibid., 150. These figures are for the year 1977.

30. Harvey, *Condition of Postmodernity,* 141–42.

31. Department of City Planning, City of Chicago, "Development Plan for the Central Area of Chicago: A Definitive Text for Use with Graphic Presentation" (Chicago: City of Chicago, 1958), 26.

32. Quoted in Joel Rast, *Remaking Chicago: The Political Origins of Urban Industrial Change* (DeKalb: Northern Illinois University Press, 2002), 31.

33. "Things to Do and See at Marina City," Marina City Management, 1964, archived at http://www.marinacity.org/history.htm.

34. See Adam Cohen and Elizabeth Taylor, *American Pharaoh: Mayor Richard J. Daley: His Battle for Chicago and the Nation* (Boston: Little, Brown, 2000), 294.

35. Frank Maier, "Chicago's Daley: How to Run a City," *Newsweek,* April 5, 1971.

36. Silicon Valley outside of San Francisco and the Route 128 High Technology Corridor outside of Boston are two prime examples.

37. David Bernstein, "Daley v. Daley," *Chicago Magazine,* September 2008.

38. In 1972, the old First National Bank Building next to it was razed to make space for the construction of a sunken plaza, which two years later became the site for the city's next major public art acquisition: Marc Chagall's enormous *Four Seasons* mosaic.

39. Chicago Central Area Committee, "Chicago 21: A Plan for the Central Area Communities," September 1973.

40. Cohen and Taylor, *American Pharaoh,* 531.

41. *Chicago Defender,* April 20, 1978.

42. Ibid.

43. Lawrence Bobo, James Kleugel, and Ryan A. Smith, "Laissez-Faire Racism: The Crystallization of a Kinder, Gentler Antiblack Ideology," in *Racial Attitudes in the 1990s,* ed. Steven A. Tuch and Jack K. Martin (Westport, CT: Praeger, 1997), 17.

44. For a broader discussion of the depoliticizing effects of neoliberalism, see Wendy Brown, "American Nightmare: Neoliberalism, Neoconservatism, and De-Democratization," *Political Theory* 34 (2006), 690–715.

45. The order prohibited federal contractors and federally assisted construction contractors and subcontractors who do over $10,000 in government business in one year from discriminating in employment decisions on the basis of race, color, religion, sex, or national origin. Contractors with fifty or more employees and contracts of $50,000 or more were also required to "take affirmative action" to increase the participation of minorities and women in the workplace if a workforce analysis demonstrated their underrepresentation.

46. *Chicago Defender*, July 22, 23, 1969. These gangs finally managed to bring about the long-awaited citywide gang alliance, referred to as LSD—for Lords, Stones, and Disciples. The alliance was active in CUCA's campaign against the Chicago Building Trades unions, but broke up shortly after.

47. Bernstein, "Daley v. Daley."

48. The Chicago Mercantile Exchange had evolved from the Chicago Butter and Egg Board, which some disgruntled traders at the Chicago Board of Trade formed in 1874.

49. For the full story of the Chicago Mercantile Exchange's dramatic success in the early 1970s, see Bob Tamarkin, *The Merc: The Emergence of a Global Financial Powerhouse* (New York: Harpercollins, 1993).

50. Leo Melamed, "Chicago's Future in Futures" (speech, 23rd Annual Fall Management Conference, Northwestern University, Evanston, IL, November 7, 1973), archived at http://www.leomelamed.com.

51. Douglas Franz, "A One-Issue Mayoral Race," *Chicago Tribune*, March 27, 1983.

52. *Chicago Sun-Times*, February 21, 1983; and *Chicago Tribune*, February 21, 1983.

53. For a detailed discussion of the grassroots racism that emerged during the 1983 Democratic primary, see Paul Kleppner, *Chicago Divided: The Making of a Black Mayor* (DeKalb: Northern Illinois University Press), 176–85.

54. It is important to point out that while conservatives made the most use of rationalizations that minimized racism and blamed cultural pathologies—most notably, dysfunctional family and child-rearing arrangements—for ghetto poverty, the key intellectual foundations for such ideas came from "liberals" like Daniel Patrick Moynihan and William Julius Wilson. See Nathan Glazer and Daniel Patrick Moynihan, *Beyond the Melting Pot: The Negroes, Puerto Ricans, Jews, Italians, and Irish of New York City* (Cambridge, MA: MIT Press, 1970); and William Julius Wilson, *The Declining Significance of Race: Blacks and Changing American Institutions* (Chicago: University of Chicago Press, 1980).

55. Washington was not the first black mayoral candidate to take an antima-chine candidacy on to the political stage; another black state senator, Richard Newhouse, had run against Daley in 1975, but because he was widely viewed as

having no chance against the machine, he managed to garner only 6 percent of the black vote (and 3 percent of the citywide vote).

56. Quoted in William J. Grimshaw, *Bitter Fruit: Black Politics and the Chicago Machine, 1931–1991* (Chicago: University of Chicago Press, 1992), 168.

57. Ibid, 71–78.

58. *Chicago Defender,* February 23, 1983.

59. *Chicago Tribune,* March 1, 1983.

60. *Chicago Tribune,* March 3, 4, 6, 8, 1983.

61. *Chicago Defender,* November 11, 1982.

62. Milton Rakove, *Don't Make No Waves . . . Don't Back No Losers: An Insider's Analysis of the Daley Machine* (Bloomington: Indiana University Press, 1976), 8.

63. *Chicago Tribune,* March 3, 1983.

64. Slavoj Zizek, "Eastern Europe's Republics of Gilead," in *Dimensions of Radical Democracy: Pluralism, Citizenship, Community,* ed. Chantal Mouffe (London: Verso, 1996)

65. These flyers are reproduced in Kleppner, *Chicago Divided,* 212–13. *Soul Train* was a television show that was popular among African Americans in the 1970s and 1980s and featured black soul musicians and dancers.

66. These figures are derived from a number of exit polls compiled in Kleppner, *Chicago Divided,* 217–18.

67. See footage of the incident at MediaBurnArchive, "Jane Byrne's Easter at Cabrini Green, 1981," uploaded November 4, 2009, https://youtu.be/9kCmb6tv1J4.

68. *Chicago Tribune,* August 28, 1983.

69. *Chicago Tribune,* October 5, 1983.

70. Gary Rivlin, *Fire on the Prairie: Chicago's Harold Washington and the Politics of Race* (New York: Henry Holt, 1992), 305.

71. The name first appeared in the *Wall Street Journal.*

72. Barack Obama, *Dreams from My Father: A Story of Race and Inheritance* (New York: Three Rivers Press, 2004), 197.

73. Nicholas De Genova and Ana Y. Ramos-Zayas, *Latino Crossings: Mexicans, Puerto Ricans, and the Politics of Race and Citizenship* (New York: Routledge, 2003), 47–50.

74. Ibid., 50–56.

75. *Chicago Tribune,* May 9, 1983.

76. On Washington's attempts to reach out to lakefront gays and lesbians by supporting gay rights, see Timothy Stewart-Winter, *Queer Clout: Chicago and the Rise of Gay Politics* (Philadelphia: University of Pennsylvania Press, 2016), 158–67. As Stewart-Winter argues, such efforts were even more notable in that rumors surrounding Washington's own sexuality swirled continuously around the mayor during his time in office.

77. Gutiérrez has been the U.S. congressman representing the ethnically diverse Fourth District of Illinois since 1993.

78. David Axelrod, who would become Barack Obama's campaign strategist and then senior advisor, had served as a key media consultant to Washington during the campaign.

79. Obama, *Dreams from My Father,* 287.

80. For an excellent discussion of Obama's years in Chicago, see Thomas J. Sugrue, *Not Even Past: Barack Obama and the Burden of Race* (Princeton, NJ: Princeton University Press, 2010), 58–70.

81. See Adolph Reed, Jr., *Stirrings in the Jug: Black Politics in the Post-Segregation Era* (Minneapolis: University of Minnesota Press, 1991).

82. Obama, *Dreams from My Father,* 288.

CHAPTER 7

1. Eugene Sawyer's appointment as mayor by the city council in 1987 had been only for a term of two years. In 1989, Daley had prevailed easily in a special mayoral election against Sawyer in the primary and then against independent candidate Timothy Evans and Republican candidate Eddie Vrdolyak in the general election.

2. *Chicago Sun-Times,* July 18, 1995.

3. *Chicago Tribune,* July 18, 1995.

4. This was the number that a team of epidemiologists came up with; the city's figure for heat-related deaths was 521.

5. Eric Klinenberg, *Heat Wave: A Social Autopsy of Disaster in Chicago* (Chicago: University of Chicago Press, 2002), 91.

6. Ibid., 99.

7. Ibid., 139.

8. Neil Smith, *The New Urban Frontier: Gentrification and the Revanchist City* (New York: Routledge, 1996), 45, 211. See also Mary Pattillo, *Black on the Block: The Politics of Race and Class in the City* (Chicago: University of Chicago Press, 2007), which applies this thinking to the process of gentrification in Chicago.

9. Klinenberg, *Heat Wave,* 149–53. Klinenberg conducted numerous interviews with Chicago police officers who voiced such complaints.

10. My thinking here borrows from Wendy Brown's work on tolerance. Wendy Brown, *Regulating Aversion: Tolerance in the Age of Identity and Empire* (Princeton, NJ: Princeton University Press, 2008).

11. See Neil Brenner and Nik Theodore, eds., *Spaces of Neoliberalism* (Malden, MA: Blackwell, 2002); and Jason Hackworth, *The Neoliberal City: Governance, Ideology, and Development in American Urbanism* (Ithaca, NY: Cornell University Press, 2006).

12. Evan Osnos, "The Daley Show," *New Yorker,* March 8, 2010, 41.

13. Ibid., 50.

14. Smaller cities like Detroit, Baltimore, and Washington, DC, had higher homicide rates, but Chicago's total was higher than all cities with more than one million inhabitants, including, most notably, New York and Los Angeles, both of which have larger populations than Chicago. This does not contradict the fact that violent crime rates in Chicago were down from the early 1990s; they were decreasing all over urban America, but the drop was less dramatic in Chicago.

15. *Chicago Tribune,* February 7, 1999.

16. Brookings Institution Center on Urban and Metropolitan Policy, *Chicago in Focus: A Profile from Census 2000* (November 1, 2003), https://www.brookings.edu /research/chicago-in-focus-a-profile-from-census-2000/.

17. United States Bureau of the Census, "5% Public Use Microdata Sample (PUMS)," Census 2000, https://www.census.gov/census2000/PUMS5.html.

18. *Chicago Sun-Times,* April 7, 2002; for a detailed ethnographic study of the involvement of Chicago street gangs in the underground economy of the 1990s, see Sudhir Alladi Venkatesh and Steven D. Levitt, "'Are We a Family or a Business?': History and Disjuncture in the American Urban Street Gang," *Theory and Society* 29, no. 4 (August 2000), 427–62.

19. James W. Wagner and Kate Curran Kirby, *Chicago Crime Commission Gang Book: A Detailed Overview of Street Gangs in the Metropolitan Chicago Area* (Chicago: Chicago Crime Commission, 2006).

20. Chicago Police Department, Research and Development Division, "Gang-Motivated Murders: 1991–2004," *Chicago Crime Trends* (August 2005).

21. *Chicago Tribune,* September 26, 2009.

22. Chicago, fittingly, became the first school system in the nation to appoint a "CEO" in 1995.

23. America's Promise Alliance, *Cities in Crisis 2009: Closing the Graduation Gap.* While according to this study, the national average in 2005 was 70.6 percent, the rate for the country's largest urban centers generally ranged between 40 and 60 percent. Chicago's 51 percent rate was roughly equal to that of New York but well below Philadelphia's 62.1 percent, which had gained over 23 points between 1995 and 2005.

24. Mayor's Press Office, "Chicago Public Schools Enrollment Increases Fifth Straight Year, Mayor Daley and School Officials Say," August 10, 2010, archived in Mayor's Press Releases at https://www.cityofchicago.org/

25. *Chicago Defender,* March 25–31, 2009.

26. Charter schools are publicly funded but operate independently, free from some of the rules that constrain regular schools. According to rules for charter schools in Illinois, for example, only 50 percent of the teaching staff need be certified by the state.

27. All this data is accessible on the Chicago Public Schools website, www.cps .edu.

28. Center for Labor Market Studies, "Youth Labor Market and Education Indicators for the State of Illinois," Chicago Alternative Schools Network (October 2003), archived at www.asnchicago.org.

29. Human Relations Foundation/Jane Addams Policy Initiative, *Minding the Gap: An Assessment of Racial Disparity in Metropolitan Chicago* (Chicago: Jane Addams Hull House Association, 2003), available at University of Illinois at Chicago Library. For a more detailed discussion of these reports and of Chicago school reform in the 1990s, see Pauline Lipman, "Chicago School Reform: Advancing the Global Agenda," in *The New Chicago: A Social and Cultural Analysis,* ed. John P.

Koval, Larry Bennett, Michael I.J. Bennett, Fassil Demissie, Roberta Garner, and Kiljoong Kim (Philadelphia: Temple University Press, 2006), 248–58.

30. Rick Perlstein, "Chicago School: How Chicago Elites Imported Charters, Closed Neighborhood Schools, and Snuffed Out Creativity," *Jacobin,* April 20, 2016, www.jacobinmag.com/2016/04/chicago-public-schools-charters-closings-emanuel/.

31. Jitu Brown, Eric Gutstein, and Pauline Lipman, "Arne Duncan and the Chicago Success Story: Myth or Reality," *Rethinking Schools Online* 23, no. 3 (Spring 2009).

32. By 2011, the number of military high schools had increased to six, more than any other city in the nation. Chicago also had, according to the CPS website (www.cps.edu), "the largest JROTC [Junior Reserve Officer Training Corps] in the country in number of cadets," along with more than twenty "middle school cadet corps" programs.

33. Lipman, "Chicago School Reform," 251.

34. Between 1981 and 1992, federal spending for subsidized housing fell by 82 percent, job training and employment programs were cut by 63 percent, and the budget for community development and social service block grants was trimmed by 40 percent.

35. See, for example, Shelby Steele, *The Content of Our Character: A New Vision of Race in America* (New York: HarperPerennial, 1991); Thomas Sowell, *Race and Culture: A World View* (New York: Basic Books, 1995); and William Julius Wilson, *The Truly Disadvantaged: The Inner City, the Underclass, and Public Policy* (Chicago: University of Chicago Press, 1987).

36. William Julius Wilson, *The Declining Significance of Race: Blacks and Changing American Institutions* (Chicago: University of Chicago Press, 1978); and Wilson, *The Truly Disadvantaged.*

37. Million Man March National Organizing Committee, "Million Man March Fact Sheet," in *Million Man March / Day of Absence; A Commemorative Anthology of Speeches, Commentary, Photography, Poetry, Illustrations & Documents,* ed. Haki R. Madhubuti and Maulana Karenga (Chicago: Third World Press, 1996), 152.

38. Robin D.G. Kelley, *Race Rebels: Culture, Politics, and the Black Working Class* (New York: Free Press, 1994), 224.

39. See "Nihilism in Black America" in Cornel West, *Race Matters* (Boston: Beacon Press, 1994).

40. *Chicago Tribune,* February 12, 1995.

41. Neal Pollack, "The Gang That Could Go Straight," *Chicago Reader,* January 26, 1995.

42. Ibid.

43. *Chicago Sun-Times,* May 19, 2005.

44. *Chicago Sun-Times,* January 26, 2004.

45. I borrow the term from the classic Jonathan Kozol, *Savage Inequalities: Children in America's Schools* (New York: Harper Perennial, 1992).

46. Dick Simpson, "From Daley to Daley: Chicago Politics, 1955–2006," Great Cities Institute Publication No. GCP-06-03 (May 2006), 18.

47. David Moberg, "The Fuel of a New Machine," *Chicago Reader,* March 30, 1989.

48. Cook County Clerk's Office, "City of Chicago TIF Revenue Totals by Year, 1986–2006," archived at http://www.cookcountyclerk.com/tsd/tifs/Pages/default .aspx.

49. The state of California was the first to enact TIF legislation in 1952, with six other states following suit in the 1960s. By 2000, all but three states had passed TIF legislation.

50. For a detailed discussion of how TIF laws have been transformed from "tools for eradicating substandard housing conditions to a way for municipalities to 'pad the tax base,'" see Colin Gordon, "Blighting the Way: Urban Renewal, Economic Development, and the Elusive Definition of Blight," *Fordham Urban Law Journal* 31, no. 2 (January 2004), 305–37.

51. Ben Joravsky, "Million Dollar Lies," *Chicago Reader,* August 11, 2006.

52. Ben Joravsky, "The Shadow Budget," *Chicago Reader,* October 22, 2009.

53. Ibid.

54. David Moberg, "Economic Restructuring: Chicago's Precarious Balance," in *The New Chicago,* ed. John P. Koval et al., 31.

55. City of Chicago, Department of Planning and Development, "Staff Report to the Community Development Commission Requesting Developer Designation: Brach's Redevelopment," January 8, 2008.

56. Another irony worth mentioning here was that Brach's paid wages that tripled the state minimum. By 1995 activists struggling for a citywide minimum wage had already drawn attention to the city's lack of support for Brach's in comparison with low-wage competitors like Pilsen's Farley Candy Company, which benefited from a $3 million tax abatement from the city.

57. For a detailed account of the making of Millennium Park, see Timothy J. Gilfoyle, *Millennium Park: Creating a Chicago Landmark* (Chicago: University of Chicago Press, 2006).

58. Costas Spirou, "Urban Beautification: The Construction of a New Urban Identity in Chicago," in *The New Chicago,* ed. John P. Koval et al., 297–98.

59. City of Chicago Department of Planning and Development, "The Chicago Central Area Plan: Final Report to the Chicago Plan Commission" (Chicago: City of Chicago, 2003).

60. Dennis R. Judd, "Constructing the Tourist Bubble," in *The Tourist City,* ed. Dennis R. Judd and Susan S. Fainstein (New Haven, CT: Yale University Press, 1999), 35–53.

61. Travel Industry Association of America, "Direct Impact of Travel to Chicago," www.choosechicago.com. Choose Chicago was the official destination marketing organization for the city of Chicago in 2012.

62. This estimate of manufacturing jobs lost comes from a study financed by the United States Department of Labor: Chicago Federation of Labor and Center for Labor and Community Research, "Creating a Manufacturing Career Path System in Cook County (December 2001)," archived at http://www.clcr.org/.

63. Ibid.

64. Data derived from Equal Employment Opportunity Commission Report (EEO-4) for the City of Chicago, 1980–1999, Municipal Reference Section, Harold Washington Library, Chicago.

65. Larry Bennett, *Third City: Chicago and American Urbanism* (Chicago: University of Chicago Press, 2010), 95.

66. *Chicago Tribune,* April 23, 1989.

67. Michael B. Katz, "Why Don't American Cities Burn Very Often," *Journal of Urban History* 34 (2008), 185–208.

68. This argument was made powerfully in: Adolph Reed, *Stirrings in the Jug: Black Politics in the Post-Segregation Era* (Minneapolis: University of Minnesota Press, 1999).

69. Pattillo, *Black on the Block.*

70. Katz, "Why Don't American Cities Burn Very Often," 196.

71. The best sociological study of the culture of basketball in black Chicago is the brilliant documentary *Hoop Dreams* (1994), which follows the lives of two budding basketball stars over eight years.

72. See, for example, Reuben A. Buford May, *Living through the Hoop: High School Basketball, Race, and the American Dream* (New York: New York University Press, 2007).

73. Historians are just beginning to explore how this massive wave of Mexican immigration offset the forces of deindustrialization and depopulation. See A. K. Sandoval-Strausz, "Latino Landscapes: Postwar Cities and the Transnational Origins of a New Urban America," *Journal of American History* 101 (December 2014), 804–31.

74. For a comprehensive report criticizing these privatization schemes, see Tony Dutzik, Brian Imus, and Phineas Baxandall, *Privatization and the Public Interest: The Need for Transparency and Accountability in Chicago's Public Asset Lease Deals* (Chicago: Illinois PIRG Education Fund, 2009), www.illinoispirg.org/sites/pirg /files/reports/Privatization-and-the-Public-Interest.pdf.

75. Daley claimed the action was necessary to protect the city from a possible terrorist plot.

76. Cathy J. Cohen, *Democracy Remixed: Black Youth and the Future of American Politics* (New York: Oxford University Press, 2010), 175.

77. Dominic Pacyga and Ellen Skerrett, *Chicago: City of Neighborhoods: Histories and Tours* (Chicago: Loyola University Press, 1986).

78. During these years, a list of these neighborhood festivals could be found on the City of Chicago's official tourism website www.explorechicago.org.

79. City of Chicago, Office of Tourism and Culture, *Chicago Neighborhood Tours 2009: Discover the World in Our Backyard* (Chicago: Office of Tourism and Culture, 2009), accessed from www.ChicagoNeighborhoodTours.com in 2009. In 2012, Mayor Rahm Emanuel eliminated the Office of Tourism and Culture, with its tourism functions thereafter subcontracted out to the private-sector nonprofit Choose Chicago and its culture responsibilities taken up by the Chicago Department of Cultural Affairs and Special Events.

80. Timothy Stewart-Winter, *Queer Clout: Chicago and the Rise of Gay Politics* (Philadelphia: University of Pennsylvania Press, 2016), 220. It is important to point out that Harold Washington's support of Chicago's gay community had paved the way for Daley's embrace of Boystown as a key constituency. After Washington's death, an impressive voter registration campaign called Lesbian/Gay Voter Impact had managed to add over 17,000 new voters in heavily gay areas of the Forty-Fourth, Forty-Sixth, Forty-Eighth, and Fiftieth Wards. Stewart-Winter, *Queer Clout*, 180.

81. Henri Lefebvre, *The Production of Space* (Oxford, UK: Wiley-Blackwell, 1991).

82. Stewart-Winter, *Queer Clout*, 221.

83. Neil Smith, "New Globalism, New Urbanism: Gentrification as Global Urban Strategy" in *Spaces of Neoliberalism: Urban Restructuring in North America and Western Europe,* ed. Neil Brenner and Nik Theodore (London: Wiley-Blackwell, 2002).

84. It might appear to some that the idea of an active state in the process of gentrification seems to contradict the view of Richard M. Daley's program as neoliberal. This is not the case. What distinguishes neoliberalism from classical liberalism is the key part played by the state in unleashing the forces of the free market and promoting the role of private capital.

85. Pattillo, *Black on the Block,* 259–62.

86. John J. Betancur, Isabel Domeyko, and Patricia A. Wright, *Gentrification in West Town: Contested Ground* (Chicago: Nathalie P. Voorhees Center for Neighborhood and Community Improvement, College of Urban Planning and Public Affairs, University of Illinois at Chicago, 2001), 19, www.urbancenter.utoronto.ca /pdfs/curp/Chicago_Gentrification-in-W.pdf.

87. Ibid., 20.

88. Pilsen is part of the Lower West Side community area. The Mexican community in this part of the city, however, extends westward across Western Avenue into the South Lawndale community area (also known as Little Village or La Villita), where, by the 1990s, Mexicans constituted over 80 percent of the population.

89. *Chicago Sun-Times,* May 23, 2003.

90. According to the 2010 census, African Americans constituted about 41 percent of the population of the Humboldt Park community area, but they remained largely segregated in the southwest quadrant below Grand Avenue bordering the Garfield Park neighborhood. Latinos represented over 52 percent.

91. This quote appeared in the mission statement on the Puerto Rican Cultural Center's website in 2011. The current statement mentions the importance of promoting "a holistic vision of community wellness and stability" but now omits any reference to "development" goals. See http://prcc-chgo.org/.

92. Antonio Olivo, "Edgy about 'Yuppies,'" *Chicago Tribune,* June 12, 2006; I discovered this from Bennett, *Third City,* 135.

93. John Betancur, "Gentrification before Gentrification: The Plight of Pilsen in Chicago," (White Paper, Nathalie P. Voorhees Center for Neighborhood and Community Improvement, University of Illinois–Chicago, 2005), 33.

94. On UNO's Alinskyite approach, see Wilfred Cruz, "UNO: Organizing at the Grassroots," *Illinois Issues* (April 1988). In 2011, UNO's website made no mention of the goal of affordable housing or the fight against pollution. Midwest Generation, the owner of the two coal plants, contributed $50,000 to Alderman Solis for his 2011 reelection campaign.

95. Betancur, "Gentrification before Gentrification," 26.

96. *Chicago Tribune*, November 28, 2008.

97. This was due to the fact that Logan Square's population was twice the size of Pilsen's (referred to as the Lower West Side on the Chicago community area map). According to the 2010 U.S. census, Logan Square, which was about two-thirds "Hispanic" (the term employed by the census), had a total population of over 72,000; Pilsen possessed a population of just under 36,000, nearly 89 percent of which was Hispanic.

98. In the 1980s, thirteen residents of the Humboldt Park barrio were arrested for their association with the Fuerzas Armadas para la Liberacion Nacional (FALN), a terrorist group that claimed responsibility for a series of attacks against U.S. military installations; in 1995, the FBI investigated several teachers and administrators at Humboldt Park's Roberto Clemente High School for terrorist activities—a situation that received a great deal of media scrutiny in Chicago.

99. On the gentrification of the Lower East Side, see Christopher Mele, *Selling the Lower East Side: Culture, Real Estate, and Resistance in New York, 1880–2000* (Minneapolis: University of Minnesota Press, 2000); William Sites, *Remaking New York: Primitive Globalization and the Politics of Urban Community* (Minneapolis: University of Minnesota Press, 2003).

100. Richard Lloyd, *Neo-Bohemia: Art and Commerce in the Postindustrial City* (Chicago: University of Chicago Press, 2005), 76–82.

101. Dick Hebdige, *Subculture: The Meaning of Style* (New York: Methuen, 1979), 102–6.

102. *Chicago Tribune*, January 27, 2008.

103. *Chicago Tribune*, August 21, 2008.

104. The new Near North Side branch, with an initial collection of thirty thousand titles and a number of personal computers, replaced a makeshift "reading room" occupying the second floor of the Seward Park fieldhouse.

105. *Chicago Sun-Times*, March 30, 2011.

106. For an excellent account of the policy and planning decisions that led to the failure of Chicago's public housing program between the 1940s and 1990s, see D. Bradford Hunt, *Blueprint for Disaster: The Unraveling of Chicago Public Housing* (Chicago: University of Chicago Press, 2009).

107. Brian J. Miller, "The Struggle over Redevelopment at Cabrini-Green, 1989–2004," *Journal of Urban History* 34 (May 2008), 947–48.

108. Brian Rogal, "The Habitat Company: Private Firm Keeps Tight Grips on Public Housing," *Chicago Reporter,* November, 1999.

109. ABLA is the acronym for the massive Near West Side complex composed of the Jane Addams Homes, Robert Brooks Homes, Loomis Courts, and Grace Abbott Homes.

110. Under the Section 8 voucher program, individuals or families with a voucher could rent in the private housing market and, based on their income, pay no more than 30 percent for rent.

111. See, for example, Susan J. Popkin and Mary Cunningham, *CHA Relocation Counseling and Assessment: Interim Report* (Washington, DC: Urban Institute, 2001), http://www.urban.org/sites/default/files/publication/61641/410313-CHA-Relocation-Counseling-Assesment-Interim-Report.PDF.

112. Quoted in Karen Hawkins, "Emanuel Inherits Complex Public Housing Legacy," Associated Press, May 18, 2011. Venkatesh had followed the relocation situation after spending two years at the Robert Taylor Homes to complete his pathbreaking study. Sudhir Alladi Venkatesh, *American Project: The Rise and Fall of Modern Ghetto* (Cambridge, MA: Harvard University Press, 2000).

113. Adolph L. Reed, Jr., "When Government Shrugs: Lessons of Katrina," *The Progressive,* September, 2006.

114. *Chicago Journal,* May 19, 2010; *The Gazette,* June 4, 2010.

115. The CHA Admissions and Continued Occupancy Policy guidelines can be found at www.thecha.org/.

116. These are terms employed by Mary Pattillo in *Black on the Block.*

117. Naomi J. McCormick, Mark L. Joseph, and Robert J. Chaskin, "The New Stigma of Relocated Public Housing Residents: Challenges to Social Identity in Mixed-Income Developments," *City and Community* 11, no. 3 (2012), 296–97.

118. John P. Koval and Kenneth Fidel, "Chicago: The Immigrant Capital of the Heartland," in *The New Chicago,* ed. John P. Koval et al., 97–104.

119. Brookings Institution, *Chicago in Focus,* 22. The black-Puerto Rican dissimilarity index was even higher than the black-Mexican dissimilarity index.

120. "Census 2000: Whole Population, Segregation," Lewis Mumford Center for Comparative Urban and Regional Research, the University at Albany, SUNY, http://mumford.albany.edu/census/.

121. Indians are the largest Asian subgroup in the Chicago six-county metropolitan area, with some 115,000 people.

122. Kiljoong Kim, "The Korean Presence in Chicago," in *The New Chicago,* ed. John P. Koval et al., 159.

123. The Chicago metropolitan area was a major destination for these groups. Between 1965 and 2000, 15 percent of all Palestinians and Jordanians and 13 percent of all Iraqis entering the country settled in Illinois. See Louise Cainkar, "Immigrants from the Arab World," in *The New Chicago,* ed. John P. Koval et al., 185.

124. Mary Patrice Erdmans, "New Chicago Polonia: Urban and Suburban," in *The New Chicago,* ed. John P. Koval et al., 123.

125. A description of the gate's history can be found on the Chicago Chinatown Chamber of Commerce website, www.chicagochinatown.org.

126. Ben Joravsky, "Signs of the Times: In Albany Park, a Dispute over 'Seoul Drive and Korea Town,'" *Chicago Reader,* April 29, 1993. The revolt caused the city council to rescind the initially proposed "Korea Town" designation and to shorten the part of Lawrence to be named Seoul Drive.

127. U.S. Bureau of the Census, "Table 39, Nativity and Place of Birth of Resident Population for Cities of 100,000 or More," *Statistical Abstract of the United States: 2011.*

128. Richard Florida, *The Rise of the Creative Class: And How It's Transforming Work, Leisure, Community, and Everyday Life* (New York: Perseus Book Group, 2002), 8.

129. Nichols Clark was quoted in Richard Florida, "The Rise of the Creative Class: Why Cities without Gays and Rock Bands Are Losing the Economic Development Race," *Washington Monthly,* May 2002.

130. Wicker Park's arrival on the national scene came with the release of Stephen Frears's film *High Fidelity,* in which the neighborhood is a backdrop for a love story between two young bohemians. For an excellent account of Daley's incorporation of Boystown's gay community into his coalition, see Stewart-Winter, *Queer Clout,* chap. 8.

131. Richard Sennett, *The Uses of Disorder: Personal Identity and City Life* (New York: Norton, 1992).

EPILOGUE

1. According to Richard Florida's 2011 "Global Economic Power Index" (City Lab, www.citylab.com/), a measure of economic output, global financial influence, and innovation (based on patenting activity), Chicago was the fourth most economically powerful city in the world—behind only Tokyo, New York, and London (and just ahead of Paris).

2. *Chicago Tribune,* May 10, 2011.

3. *Wall Street Journal,* November 21, 2008.

4. Naomi Klein, *The Shock Doctrine: The Rise of Disaster Capitalism* (New York: Picador, 2007), 6.

5. Micah Uetricht, *Strike for America: Chicago Teachers Against Austerity* (New York: Verso, 2014), 33.

6. For a detailed account of CORE's dramatic rise within the CTU, see Uetricht, *Strike for America;* and Jane F. McAlevey, *No Shortcuts: Organizing for Power in the New Gilded Age* (New York: Oxford University Press, 2016), chap. 4.

7. Uetricht, *Strike for America,* 37.

8. Quoted in McAlevey, *No Shortcuts,* 124.

9. *Chicago Tribune,* September 14, 2014.

10. *Chicago Reader,* March 26, 2015.

11. Teresa L. Cordova and Matthew D. Wilson, *Lost: The Crisis of Jobless and Out of School Teens and Young Adults in Chicago, Illinois and the U.S.* (Chicago: Great Cities Institute, University of Illinois at Chicago, January 2106), https://greatcities.uic.edu/2016/02/01/lost-the-crisis-of-jobless-and-out-of-school-teens-and-young-adults-in-chicago-illinois-and-the-u-s/.

12. *Chicago Sun-Times,* November 16, 2015.

13. By 2016 Chicago had the highest sales tax in the United States.

14. Beyza Buyuker, Melissa Mouritsen, and Dick Simpson, *Continuing the Rubber Stamp City Council,* Chicago City Council Report Number 7, June 8, 2011–November 15, 2014 (Chicago: Department of Political Science, University of Illinois at Chicago, December 9, 2014), 1–4, https://pols.uic.edu/political-science/chicago-politics/city-council-voting-records.

15. Among Chicago's talented group of investigative journalists are Rick Perlstein, Ben Joravsky, Dan Mihalopoulos, Mick Dumke, Whet Moser, and David Moberg.

16. The nickname "Mayor 1%" was popularized by Kari Lyderson, *Mayor 1%: Rahm Emanuel and the Rise of Chicago's 99%* (Chicago: Haymarket Books, 2014).

17. *New York Times,* March 21, 2015.

18. The data can be easily accessed on the Invisible Institute's website: http://invisible.institute/police-data/.

19. The struggle for the level 1 trauma center ended triumphantly, with the University of Chicago breaking ground on a $39 million department in September of 2016.

20. Juliana Menasce Horowitz and Gretchen Livingston, "How Americans View the Black Lives Matter Movement," *Fact Tank: News in the Numbers,* Pew Research Center, July 8, 2016, http://www.pewresearch.org/fact-tank/2016/07/08/how-americans-view-the-black-lives-matter-movement/.

INDEX

Note: Richard J. Daley is sometimes referred to as RJD. Richard M. Daley is sometimes referred to as RMD. Page numbers in *italics* indicate an illustration.

African American community *(continued)*
middle class; black power movement;
black press; black resistance to racial
oppression; black submachine politics;
civil rights movement; culturalization
of politics; migration of African Americans from the South; police (CPD)—
violence against African Americans;
violence/racial violence
African Methodist Episcopal (AME)
Church, 80, 81. *See also* Carey,
Archibald
Afro-American Student Association, 197
Airport Homes (public housing), 156
Albany Park, 315
Albert, Derrion, 268–269, 270, 282
Alford, Alfonso, 196
Algren, Nelson, *City on the Make,* 140–141,
294
Alinsky, Saul: Archdiocese of Chicago as
major donor of, 159–160, 161–162;
background of, 160; Back of the Yards
Neighborhood Council (BYNC),
158–159; Harrison-Halsted organiza-
tion and tradition of, 157; Industrial
Areas Foundation, 159; and intergroup
relations, 58; Organization for a South-
west Community (OSC), 160; and
organized labor, limitations of, 160–
161; *Reveille for Radicals,* 158–159; and
state-sponsored countersubversion, 12;
and Temporary Woodlawn Organization (TWO), 162–164, 179, 180; and
University of Chicago, 211; UNO
claim to be modeled on, 301–302
Alliance to End Repression, 212
All-Negro radio show, 71
Alpha Suffrage Club, 80
alterity, strategies of, 175
Altgeld Gardens (public housing), 257–
258, 268
Alvarez, Anita, 337
Alvarez, David, 261
Amalgamated Meat Cutters and Butcher
Workmen (AMCBW), 25
Amalgamated Transit Union, 325
American Civil Liberties Union. *See*
ACLU

American Federation of State, County and
Municipal Employees (AFSCME), 293
Americanization, 27, 40, 42, 43, 44–45
American Nazi Party, 201, 203
American Protective Association, 43
Ameritech, 283
Amoco, 233, 283
Amoco Building, 362n25
Anderson, Louis B., 77
Andersonville neighborhood, 320
Anglo-Saxonism, 29, 51, 114. *See also*
whiteness and white identity
Ann Arbor, MI, 204
anti-Catholicism, 41, 43, 52
antilynching movement, 80, 89–90
anti-Semitism, 208, 275–276
antiwar movement, 204, 205, 207
Aon Center, 362n25
Apex Club, 67, 70
Appomattox Club, 80, 85, 87
Arab and Assyrian community, 317, 318,
373n123
Aramark, 330, 331
architecture, 6; Beaux Arts,.23; Chicago
School, 6, 21–22; International Style,
232; Mies van der Rohe, 137, 228, 232;
Prairie School, 47; sense of place, and
tourism, 297–298. *See also* Burnham,
Daniel; skyscrapers
Area 2 police torture of black suspects, 7,
279, 335
Arendt, Hannah, *On Violence,* 218, 219
Argyle (aka New Chinatown, Little Viet-
nam), 315, 319
Armour, 20
Armour, J. Ogden, 28, 30
Armour, Philip, 31
Armour Square: antiblack violence, 111–112;
Chinese community in, 315
Armstrong, Frank H., 30
Armstrong, Louis, 65, 66, 89, 90, 91, *91,* 92;
"(What Did I Do to Be So) Black and
Blue," 92, 351n70; "Big Butter and Egg
Man," 92; "Heebie Jeebies," 92; "S.O.L.
Blues," 92; "Struttin' with Some Barbe-
cue," 92; "Sunset Café Stomp," 92
arson and bombings: against African
Americans, 38, 46, 78, 112, 124; against

Puerto Ricans, 175; "shoot to kill" order of RJD, 138, 203, 208, 210; by white gangs, and ethnoracial hierarchy, 45

art: community mural movement, 219–220, *220*, 302, *314*, 362n18; public art, skyscrapers and, 232, 363n38. *See also* music

Art Institute of Chicago, 31, 329

Arvey, Jacob "Jack," 55, 113–114

Asian community: cabinet of RMD including, 288; ethnoracial enclaves of, 314–315, 317, 318–319; Latino-Asian dissimilarity (segregation), 314; nationwide, 172

Associated Business Club (ABC) of Chicago, 64, 67, 69

Associated Negro Press (newswire), 67, 79, 117

Assyrian and Arab community, 317, 318, 373n123

AT&T, 233

Atlanta, GA, 249

Atlantic Era, 16

Auditorium Hotel, 30, 31

Auditorium Theater, 31

Austin (neighborhood), 47

Austin High School, 284

Austin, Junius C., 59–60, 64, 82, 84, 88

Avondale, 317–318

Axelrod, David, 265, 365n78

Ayers, Thomas G., 234

Bach, Ira, 146–147

backlash. *See* white backlash

Back of the Yards: Canaryville hostility to, 41; heterogeneity of, 24; mental health clinic closures, 326; Mexican community and, 313

Back of the Yards Neighborhood Council (BYNC), 158–159

Baker, Houston, 90

Baldwin, Davarian, 66, 70

Baldwin, James, 109; urban renewal as "Negro removal," 142, 143, 310

Baltimore, 266, 345n19, 366n14

Bangladesh, immigrants from, 319

barbecue, right to, 299

Barksdale, David, 196

Barnett, Claude A., 67, 79

Barrett, James, 27

baseball, 46, 71

basketball, 285, 289–290, 331–332

Bates, Beth Tompkins, 84

Bates, David H., 26

Bauler, Matthias "Paddy," 55

Baxter Laboratories, 97

beautification: R. M. Daley and, 266, 285, 289, 305, 308; and *Plan of Chicago* (1909), 33; and uplift of the laboring classes, 33

Begin, Menachem, 253

Bell, Lamar, 196

Ben Franklin store, 60, 61

Benito Juárez High School, 297

Benito Pablo Juárez García (mural), *314*

Bennett, Larry, 287, 344n10

Bennett, William, 269, 273

Benson, Al, 116

Berkeley, CA, 204

Bernhardt, Sarah, 1

Bernstein, David, 239

Berry, Chuck: "Johnny B. Goode," 119; "Maybellene," 119; "Rock and Roll Music," 119; "Roll Over Beethoven," 119

Best, Wallace, 64

Bethel African Methodist Episcopal Church, 82

Bevel, James, 190

Big Star (restaurant), 304–305

Bilandic, Michael, 242, 250, 261

Billboard magazine, coining "rhythm & blues," 118

Bill Haley and the Comets, 119, 166

binary racial order, development of, 45–46, 47, 58, 173

Bindman, Aaron, 123–124

Binga, Jesse, 60, 70–71, 80, 86; and black capitalism, 62, 64, 67, 69, 75–76, 82, 90

Binga State Bank, 67

Birmingham, AL, 177, 178

Black Belt: location of, 24, 38; map of, *39*; and 1919 race riot, 38, 40; and WWII housing shortage, 104, 108–109, 112. *See also* Black Metropolis

Blackboard Jungle, The (1955), 166

black capitalism: antiunionism of, 79–85; banks, 62, 67; black church alliance with, 64, 81–82; corruption and embezzlement in, 60; and culturalization of politics, 69, 78–79, 85, 87; and economization of the Black Metropolis, 75–76, 79–80, 81–82, 85, 349n32; and entrepreneurial spirit, 62–63, 78; and individualism vs. collective strategies of racial struggle, 61–62, 75; insurance business, 71, 74–75; lack of progress in white business world, 60–61; and linked fate, 75, 349n31; Negro Business Exposition (1938), 59–60, 62, 64, 88; and public assistance, lack of, 78; and race men/race heroes, black businessmen as, 60, 61, 66–67, 67, 69, 71, 74–75, 78, 80; Southern migrants and, 116–117; types of businesses in, 61, 63, 348nn1,10; as uplifting the race, 59, 61, 64–65, 67, 69, 75, 81, 86; and white-owned businesses patronized by black community, 62. *See also* Black Metropolis; Bronzeville; minority-owned businesses; real estate market

black church: alliances with black businesses, 64, 81–82; as critical of civil rights movement, 178, 189; and National Negro Congress (1936), 88; openness to Randolph and working-class solidarity, 82; opposition to Randolph and the BSCP union, 80–82; social justice movement and, 82; storefront churches, 63–64, 115, 222

black cultural expression: black middle-class disapproval of, 65–67, 69, 72, 90–91; Chicago as fountain of, 65, 117; policy wheel revenues as funding, 71; white stereotyping of, 69. *See also* music

Black Disciples. *See* Disciples (gang)

black gangs: ACT organization and, 186; antimachine activities of, 197; Black Panthers and, 197, 214–215; and black power movement, 182–183, 185–186, 187, 190, 192, *192*, 194–195, 197, 199–200; federal funding for youth services and projects, 196–197, 198–199, 210;

female branches of, 187; First Annual Gangs Convention (1966), 190; junior/midget divisions of, 187, 188; Martin Luther King and Chicago Freedom Movement attempt to enlist help of, 187–188, 189–195, 200; and labor protests, 236, 364n46; leadership talents in, 187, 195–196; LSD alliance, 236, 364n69; membership numbers and recruitment, 186–187, 188; *nation* added to names of, 187; and nonviolence vs. militancy as philosophy, 185; police brutality and, 186–187; police/government sabotage of youth/community service programs of, 197–199; police Red Squad warnings to stay away from Democratic Convention, 213; and political organizations, transformation into, 277–278; and youth services and projects, 196–200. *See also* gangs; white gangs and athletic clubs

Black Gangster Disciples. *See* Gangster Disciples (gang)

black ghettos: businesses remaining in, 153; and defiance, posture of, 108; and heat wave (1995), 261–262; hyperghettos contrasted to, 354n52; middle-class housing as barrier to encroachment of, 149–150, 154, 228, 234–235, 301; 1919 race riot and centrality of, 45; postwar geographical and demographic growth of, 101–102; white identify formation and, 47. *See also* hyperghettos; public housing

Black Lives Matter movement, 334, 336–337

Black Metropolis: economization of, 75–76, 79–80, 81–82, 85, 349n32; as inspiration during Great Depression, 64–65; insurance business, 71, 74–75; location of, 61; map of, *68*; and migrants, 66; and "old settler" vs. "new settler" ideologies, 66; policy wheels (illicit lotteries), 70–74, 75, 105, 130; population growth and, 61. *See also* black capitalism; music; Stroll, the

black middle class: as critical of the civil rights movement, 178; disapproval of black cultural expression, 65–67, 69, 72, 90–91; gentrification by, 13–14, 288–289, 298–299, 301; homeownership, 13–14, 85–86, 288–289, 361n71; incorporating via neoliberal policies, 288–289. *See also* black capitalism

black nationalism: and Black Metropolis, 61; in local positions of authority, 297; and multiethnic coalition of Howard Washington, 253. *See also* black power movement

Black Panther Party: assassination of Fred Hampton, 12, 184, 215–217; and black gangs, 197, 214–215; breakfast programs of, 217; Fred Hampton as chairman of, 214–215; perceived as threat by RJD and police, 217; "rainbow coalition" of, 12, 214–215, 217, 221, 250; reading lists of, 215; susceptibility to FBI infiltration, 215, 217; viewed as derailing civil-rights movement, 169

black power movement: and black gangs in Chicago, 182–183, 185–186, 187, 190, 192, *192*, 194–195, 197, 199–200; black nationalism, 61, 253; context of, 203; and failure of integrationist approaches, 180; Martin Luther King as opposing use of term, 190, 192; and nonviolence vs. militancy as philosophy, 180, 182–183, 185; police and FBI countersubversion of, 213–214, 215–218; and racial divide as increasing, 204; viewed as derailing civil-rights movement, 169, 180. *See also* black nationalism; Black Panther Party; countersubversion, state-sponsored

black press: development of, 117; and Emmett Till murder, 137. *See also* Associated Negro Press (newswire); *Chicago Defender*

Black P-Stones (gang), 122. *See also* Blackstone Rangers

black resistance to racial oppression: bebop jazz and, 121; and election of Barack Obama, 293–294; as structure of feeling, 109; WWII and development of, 107–108, 109, 111–112. *See also* black power movement; civil rights movement

Black's Blue Book, 63, 85, 348n10

Blackstone Rangers (gang): Martin Luther King's attempt to enlist in nonviolence movement, 190–195, 200; leadership of, 187–188, 195–196; Main 21 governing body, 195, 214–215; membership of, 186, 187, 188; *nation* added to name of, 187; and police/government investigations, 197–199, 210; and protests for minority union membership, 236; and "rainbow coalition" of Black Panthers, 214–215; and youth services/community improvement projects, 196–200. *See also* Black P-Stones (gang)

black submachine politics: and bread-and-butter political style, reproduction of, 77–78, 131; Anton Cermak as establishing patronage distribution to, 52; and Daley's actions during MLK assassination riots, 208–209; William Dawson as boss of, 188–189; death of Benjamin Lewis and, 189; Oscar DePriest as boss of, 76–77, 349n35; integration/civil rights as threat to power of, 130–131, 189; Martin Luther King opposed by, 188–189; "silent six" aldermen (Dawson), 188–189; Big Bill Thompson support, 40–41, 47–48, 71, 112–113; and Harold Washington replacement election, 256–257. *See also* Dawson, William; machine politics

Black Youth Project 100 (BYP100), 335

Blagojevich, Rod, 291

Blighted Areas Redevelopment Act (1947), 143

blight, redefined as "proper and productive economic use," 148

Blocks Together, 328

blues and jazz: blues as white tourist attraction/niche market, 118, 119, 120; Chicago blues sound, 117–119; Chicago "melting pot" of, 65–66; classical black musicians forced into jazz, 120; Delta blues, 117; dress code of respectability and, 90–91, *91*; entrepreneurial ethos and, 118–121; as floating signifier, 118; Harlem and bebop jazz, 120–121; lack of anticapitalist critique in, 92–93;

cities/global-city agenda; neoliberalization/neoliberalism

Byrne, Jane: and black community, 250–251; defeated by Washington in primaries, 242–244, 256; election of 1977, 243–244; redrawing of ward map, 255

Cabrini-Green Homes (public housing), 228, 251, 280, 308, 309, 310

Café Lura, 318

Calder, Alexander, *Flamingo,* 232

California, TIF funds, 368n49

Calloway, Cab, 66, 90; "Minnie the Moocher," 92

Calumet Community Religious Conference (CCRC), 257

Calumet Park riot (1957), 168, 176, 358n21

Cambodia, immigrants from, 315

Campbell, William, 189

Canaryville neighborhood, 41–44

Canaryville School of Gunmen, 41

capitalism: disaster capitalism, 327; spectacle of protest and, 227. *See also* black capitalism; downtown agenda; neoliberalization/neoliberalism

Capone, Al, and gang, 53, 128, 130

CAPS (Chicago Alternative Policing Strategy), 263, 289, 305

Carby, Hazel, 90

Carey, Archibald, 77, 80, 81, 82

Carey, Archibald Jr., 144–145, 149

Carl Sandburg Village (housing development), 227–228, 229

Carmichael, Stokely, 169, 180, 195, 220

Carney, Frank, 165–166, 170, 172

Carson Pirie Scott, 22, 30

Castells, Manuel, 171

Castle, Barton and Associates, 358n16

Catholic Church: anti-Catholicism, 41, 43, 52; as integrationist, 159, 161–162; and Irish control of political machine, 122; as major donor to Saul Alinsky, 159–160, 161–162; nomination of Al Smith, 52; Polish community and, 317; and production of white identity, 46; as pro-union, 121–122; as segregationist, 124, 159–160

Cayton, Horace, 3, 60–66, 70–71, 73, 102

CBOE. *See* Board of Education

CCAC (Chicago Central Area Committee), 146–147, 149–150, 234–235

CCCO. *See* Coordinating Council of Community Organizations (CCCO)

Cermak, Anton: assassination of, 53; and Great Depression, 53–54; and multiethnic political machine, 52–53, 55, 57; and Pilsen, 52; policy wheel shutdown campaign (1931), 72; progrowth, antilabor agenda of, 9–10, 53–55; victory over Thompson, 52–53

CHA. *See* Chicago Housing Authority

Chagall, Marc, *Four Seasons* mosaic, 363n38

charter schools: crisis induced to validate privatization, 327; definition of, 367n26; Latino charter schools, 330–331; Renaissance 2010 plan for, 50, 271, 305, 328; scandals and, 330; school closures and establishment of, 271, 326–328, 330, 333; teachers union and fight against, 293, 326, 327, 331

Chase corporation, 13

Chase Tower, 223, 233

Checkerboard Lounge, 118

Cheetah Gym, 304

Chess, Leonard and Phil, 119–120

Chess, Marshall, 120

Cheung, George, 318

Chew, Charles, 200, 201

Chicago: as center of national black life, 117, 137; civic pride, maintenance of, 226–227; as quintessentially American town, 1–3, 5; working-class identity of, 1–2, 13, 232. *See also* civil service, municipal; downtown agenda; gentrification; infrastructure; urban renewal; urban services provision

—NICKNAMES FOR: Beirut on the Lake, 253, 264; City of Neighborhoods, 3, 294–295, 318–319; City of the Big Shoulders, 2, 22, 204, 225, 294; City on the Make, 140–141, 294; City that Works, 2, 231, 294; Hog Butcher for the World, 2, 20, 140, 225; the known city, 117; Second City, 294; White City, 23; Windy City, 2, 294

low-income residents of mixed-income housing, 311–312; in receivership by order of federal court, 310; ruled guilty of racial discrimination, 237; transformed to redevelopment facilitator, 148–149; Elizabeth Wood as first executive director, 113, 126–127, 132, 149. *See also* public housing

Chicago Land Clearance Commission (CLCC), 144, 146

Chicago Lawn neighborhood, 47, 193, 317

Chicago Mercantile Exchange (Merc, CME), 239–241, 329–330, 336, 364n48

Chicago Merchants Club, 32

Chicago Mural Group, 220, 362n18

Chicago Neighborhood Tours program, 295

Chicago People's Church, 218

Chicago Plan (1970), 236

Chicago Plan Commission, 32, 34–35, 145, 147

Chicago Police Department. *See* police (CPD)

Chicago Public Library, 308, 326, 372n104

Chicago Public Schools. *See* schools (Chicago Public Schools, CPS)

Chicago Reader, 282

Chicago Real Estate Board, 46, 202

Chicago Record-Herald, 29

Chicago Review (UC literary magazine), 211–212

Chicago River, 23

Chicago Sanitary District, 17, 55

Chicago School architecture, 6, 21–22

Chicago School of sociology, 3, 19, 69, 113, 153, 211, 274, 294, 343n4

Chicago School of urbanism, 4–5, 6

Chicago Seed, The, 205

Chicago Skyway tolls, privatization of, 291

Chicago Spire, 323

Chicago Sun-Times, 180, 256, 279, 300

Chicago Symphony Orchestra, 31

Chicago Teachers Federation (CTF), 48, 50, 53, 54

Chicago Teachers Union (CTU): Caucus of Rank-and-File Educators (CORE), 293, 328–329; charter school teachers as barred from, 271; and R. M. Daley

school closings, 328–329; William Dever and, 50; and Rahm Emanuel's austerity program, 326, 327–329, 332, 333; fight against charter schools, 293, 326, 327, 331; and Grassroots Collaborative, 329; strike (2012), 326, 332, 333, 336; United Progressive Caucus of, 328

Chicago Title and Trust, 143–144

Chicago Transit Authority (CTA): antimachine sentiments and Byrne election, 250; R. M. Daley austerity measures and, 325; elevated municipal railway ("L"), 22, 222, 280; Rahm Emanuel austerity measures and, 325; municipal ownership of mass transit, 15; privatized fare collection system, 331; state bailout of, 291

Chicago Tribune: as antilabor, 29, 30, 56; on black strikebreakers, 26, 29; on Cermak's patronage reform, 54; crusade against Larry Hoover, 278; on education, 50; on Emanuel inauguration, 324; investigation into misappropriation of funds, 237; on juvenile delinquency, 167; on juvenile delinquency during WWII, 98–99; on murder rate, 17; Obama interview (2003), 265; on race riots, 37–38; on "rainbow cabinet" of RMD, 288; on strikes, 25–26; on Washington election (1983), 241, 245; white backlash and, 209; on zoning process, 307

Chicago 21 Corporation, 234–235

Chicago 21 Plan, 234–235

Chicago Whip, 80, 87

Chicago Women's Club, 31

Chicago Workers' Committee on Unemployment, 53

Chicago Youth Development Project, 165–166

Chico, Gerry, 269, 325

Chinatown, 314–315, 318

Chinatown Gate, 315, 318

Chinese-American Civic Council, 318

Chinese community, 314–315, 318; map (2000), *316*

Choose Chicago, 370n79

Cicero (Illinois) riot, 128–129, *129*

CIO (Congress of Industrial Organizations), 56–58, 83, 104–105
Citizens' Committee to Enforce the Landis Award, 49–50
Citizens for a Democratic and Diverse Albany Park, 319
City Beautiful movement, 33
city council: R.M. Daley and living wage ordinance, 292–293; R.M. Daley appointments to, and lack of opposition from, 281, 301; R.J. Daley reducing to rubber-stamp advisory board, 141–142; R.J. Daley severing from the planning process, 8–9, 146–147; and early urban renewal opposition, 146; and Rahm Emanuel, 332–333; gang member running for (Wallace "Gator" Bradley), 277–278; Gray Wolves, 15, 34; Progressive Reform Caucus, 332; and segregation of public housing, 126; and Harold Washington "council wars," 252–253, 254–256, 344n11; zoning changes controlled by individual aldermen, 305
City Homes Association, *Tenement Conditions in Chicago,* 19
Civic Music Association, 31
Civil Rights Act (1964), 188
civil rights movement: black veterans returning from WWII and, 106, 107, 109; and gangs, 185; guerilla tactics and, 182–183; March on Washington (1963), 180; "militants/extremists", defined, 182; and nonviolence vs. militancy as philosophy, 179–180, 182–183, 185; policy brutality protests, 183–185, 296–297; school protests, 179–180, 181–182, 184, 187, 221–222, 250, 271–272, 297, 359n29; southern movement in consciousness of Chicago, 177–178; as threat to black submachine politics, 130–131, 189; as threat to machine politics, 131–132; Emmett Till murder as "moment of simultaneity" for, 137; top-down historical perspectives on, 168–169; and TWO movement of Woodlawn, 162–163; UAW Local 600 in Detroit and, 106;

white backlash as counterforce to, 131–132; zoot suiters and, 106–108
civil service, municipal: black participation in, 77, 287; Cermak and reform of, 54; Latino participation in, 287; public pension funds, gap in, 323–324; *Shakman* case ruling preventing firing for political affiliations, 237; under RJD, 139–140; under RMD, 280, 282–283
Civil Service Commission, 77
Civil Works Administration (CWA), 57
Clark, Mark, 215
Clark, Terry Nichols, 321
class. *See* middle class; working class
CLCC (Chicago Land Clearance Commission), 144, 146
Cleveland, OH, 181
Clinton, Bill, 263, 269, 273–275
Cloud Gate sculpture, 285
Club DeLisa, 118
CME (Chicago Mercantile Exchange), 13, 239–241, 329–330, 336, 364n48
Coalition for Youth Action, 198
Coalition of United Community Action (CUCA), 236, 364n46
Cobraettes (gang), 187
Cobras. *See* Egyptian Cobras (gang)
COGLI (Mayor's Committee on Gay and Lesbian Issues), 255
Cohen, Adam, 151
Cohen, Cathy, 293–294, 335
COINTELPRO, 213–214, 215, 217
Cole, Robert, 71, 74–75
Collins, John, 29
Collins, Richard, 54
color line, 173
Commercial Club of Chicago, 30–32, 48, 54, 271; and *Plan of Chicago,* 32–36
commercial sex industry, 111
Commission on Latino Affairs, 252
Committee for Patriotic Action, 100
commodities exchanges of Chicago, 13, 239–241, 328, 329–330, 336, 364n48
Commonwealth Edison Company, 234, 261
Communist Party: anticommunism and, 79, 83, 212, 213; black presidential candidates of, 88; concerns about black capitalism, 61; membership numbers,

87; and National Negro Congress, 83, 88; social justice actions led by, 53, 76, 78, 79, 87

Communities United for Affordable Housing (CUFAH), 302

Community Action Program (CAP), 196, 209

"community areas" as term, becoming "neighborhoods," 294

community mural movement, 219–220, *220*, 302, *314*, 362n18

condominium development, 301, 304, 305, 308, 309

Condon, Eddie, 65

Congress of Racial Equality (CORE), 144, 179, 182, 183

Conlisk, James, 208, 238

Connolly, N. D. B., 86

Conservative Vice Lords. *See* Vice Lords (gang)

construction industry: affirmative action, 236, 275, 288, 363n45; Chicago Plan (1970) integrating, 236, 364n46; R. J. Daley and, 140; Rahm Emanuel and, 332; Great Depression and halt on, 104; minority-owned contractors, exclusion of, 235, 236–237, 279, 363n45; skyscrapers, 21–22, 147. *See also* Chicago Building Trades Council

consumerism: advertising industry, 204, 228; credit card debt as masking inequalities, 289; of professional sports, as diversion from inequalities, 289–290

Continental Illinois National Bank and Trust, 234

Cook, William Decatur, 82, 83–84

Cook County, 233. *See also* Democratic Party (Cook County); machine politics of Cook County Democratic Party; suburbanization

Cook County Hospital, 172

Cooperative Business League, 82

Coordinating Council of Community Organizations (CCCO), 179, 181–182, 184, 188, 189. *See also* Chicago Freedom Movement

corporate headquarters, 22, 143; suburbanization and, 232–234

corruption. *See* scandals and corruption

countersubversion, state-sponsored: overview, 12; ACLU lawsuit and destruction of files, 212; FBI (COINTELPRO), 213–214, 215, 217; frame-ups, 217–218; and gang member candidate (Bradley) for city council, 278, 280–281; Fred Hampton assassination, 12, 184, 215–217; racial tensions stirred up by, 213; Red Squad division of Police Department, 12, 212–214, 345n19; sabotage of gangs, 197, 199; as stunting development of the left, 212, 216–218

CPD. *See* police (CPD)

CPS. *See* schools (Chicago Public Schools, CPS)

crack cocaine, 267–268

Crane High School student demonstration, 169–170

Crate and Barrel, 205

creative class, 320–321

credit card debt, 289

crime and criminality: early 20th century and, 16–17, 18–19; rehabilitation model for, 19; Bill Thompson and gangsters, 53. *See also* crime rates; gangs; organized crime; scandals and corruption; underground economy

crime rates: Englewood neighborhood and, 122; gang activity and, 268; gang participation in lowering, 198; and heat wave of 1995, 262; lowering of in 2000s, generally, 366n14. *See also* homicide rates

crime syndicates. *See* organized crime

Crown Fountain, 285

CTA. *See* Chicago Transit Authority

CTF. *See* Chicago Teachers Federation

CTU. *See* Chicago Teachers Union

Cuban community, 302

culturalization of politics: overview, 246–247; antiwelfare rhetoric as, 273–274; black capitalism and, 69, 78–79, 85, 87; black intellectuals and perpetuation of, 274–275; and blaming the victims (heat wave 1995), 263–264; conservatives as tending toward, 122, 364n54; defined as attributing issues to

the politics of identity, 330–331, 337; scandals of, 330, 331; school privatization and austerity program of, 325, 326–328, 330–331, 333; and TIF funds, 328, 329–330, 331–332
emergency services, outsourcing of, 263
employers: exploiting racially motivated violence, 26, 28–29; race-baiting by, 26, 29; racism as tool of, 110; union breaking by, 26. *See also* business community; labor force; labor unions and unionization
Employers Association of Chicago, 26, 28–29
Englewood neighborhood: black population of, 127; and Catholic Church, 121–122; gangs and, 122, 277–278; and labor unions, 121–122, 123–124; of 1920s and 1930s, 121–122; and Peoria Street riot (1949), 123–124; school protests in, 179; and urban crisis, 122–124
Enright, "Moss," 42
entrepreneurialism: black capitalism and, 62–63, 78; blues music and, 118–121
entrepreneurial state, 8, 262–263. *See also* neoliberalization/neoliberalism
Epton, Bernard, 241, 245–246, 247, 248–249
Equal Rights Amendment, 242
Erdmans, Mary Patrice, 318
ethnoracial enclaves (post 1970): immigrants and growth/creation of, 313–318, *316*, 373nn121,123; reluctance of City Hall to embrace, 318–319. *See also* neighborhoods
eugenics, 45
European immigrants. *See* immigrants and immigration; southern and eastern European immigrants; whiteness and white identity; *specific communities*
Evans, Timothy, 256, 324, 366n1
eviction, antieviction riot (August 1931), 76, 78, 79
Ewald, François, 75
Executive Order No. 11246 (affirmative action), 236
Exelon Corporation, 271

Fanon, Frantz, 215
Fansteel Metallurgical Corp, 56
Farber, David, 207
Farley Candy Company, 369n56
Far North Side, 214
Farrakhan, Louis, 275–276
Far South Side, 331
Far Southwest Side, 114
Farwell, John V. Jr., 30
Farwell & Company, 30
FBI: and black power, 213–218; COINTELPRO (Counterintelligence Program) of, 213–214, 215, 217; fear of Black Panther–gang coalition, 215; Operation Silver Shovel (investigation of RMD corruption), 278–279, 284; state-sponsored repression by, 216–218. *See also* countersubversion, state-sponsored
Fearless Leading by the Youth (FLY), 335
federal courts: Byrne's redrawing of ward map declared illegal, 255; *Gautreaux* order mandating any new public housing to be located outside of ghetto, 237, 309–310; Housing Authority antiblack discrimination, 237
Federal Emergency Relief Administration, 57
Federal Employment Practices Commission, 104
federal funding: affirmative action requirements for, 236, 363n45; antipoverty programs, 209, 237; blighted land bought by government and sold to private developers, 143–144; Chicago Alternative Policing Strategy (CAPS), 263; Community Development block grants, 255; credits for urban renewal, 157; and Daley patronage expansion, 149; directed into downtown projects, 142; as drying up, 236, 238, 274, 368n34; and gang involvement in youth services (OEO), 196–197, 198–199, 210; for government building complex, 232; Great Depression and, 53, 57; homeownership housing subsidies, 127, 140, 222–223; for law enforcement initiatives, 218, 274; No

215; labor union violence, 24; map of (ca. 1919), *39*; and masculinity, 25, 43–44; nihilism of, 168; number of, 268; and "rainbow coalition" of Black Panthers, 12, 214–215, 250; Reagan administration and criminalization of youth, 218; respect and honor as factor in, 172; school closures and violence between, 271; segregation reinforced by violence of, 46; space as produced via, 170–171; supergangs, 197, 215, 364n46; turf as focus of, 170; violence against Puerto Ricans, 175; violent crime and homicide rates and, 268–269; World War II and, 108. *See also* black gangs; white gangs and athletic clubs
Gangster Disciples (gang), 122, 215, 236, 267, 277–278, 280
García, Jesús "Chuy," 256, 333–336
garment making, 22
Garvey, Marcus, and Garveyism, 61–62, 82
Gary, Indiana, 21, 86
Gary Works, 21
gay community. *See* LGBT community
Geary, Eugene, 42
Geary, J. V., 54
Gehry, Frank, 153, 285
Gellman, Erik, 88
gender, blues singers and challenges to, 90. *See also* women
Genet, Jean, 207
Gentleman brothers, 42
gentrification: overview, 10–11, 308; bohemians/hipsters and entrepreneurs and, 302–305, 320–321; bricolage and, 304–305; City Hall policies fueling, 298, 305, 307–308, 312, 371n84; and desirability of Chicago's urban lifestyle, 320; "disorder" as commodity in, 321; "edge" as commodity in, 303–304; ethnoracial identity and, 300, 302–303; at expense of working-class and low-income residents, 298–302, 311–312, 317, 371n94; global third wave of, 298, 299, 301; map of, *306*; middle-class minority homeowners and, 13–14, 288–289, 298–299, 301; middle-class white displacement of residents, 298,

300–301, 302, 303, 304–305, 311–312, 320; New York City and, 307
George Cleveland Hall Library, 61
German community: and Bungalow Belt, 47; and Englewood, 121–122; ethnoracial hierarchy and, 27, 114; Kelly-Nash machine and, 55; location of, 24; size of, 23; and whiteness/white identity, 114
Gillespie, Dizz, 121
Gilroy, Paul, 219
Gingrich, Newt, 274
Gitlin, Todd, 216
Giuliani, Rudolph, 283
global cities/global-city agenda: overview, 13, 225–226; accounting "gimmicks" used to maintain appearance of, 239; and centralization of business district, 225; Chicago as business traveler destination, 286; "City of Neighborhoods" under RMD and, 295, 318–319; and commodities markets, 13, 239–241, 329–330; definition of, 225; and donations to campaigns of RMD, 281; local context and development of, 4; "multiplier effects" of, 283; neighborhoods excluded from recognition, 318–319; subsidies via TIF funds for, 282–284, 331–332, 369n56; successes of RMD with, 264, 284–286; tax revenues and, 225; tourism and, 285–286; and "two Chicagos," 7; white-collar employment rates and, 225. *See also* service industries (global city)
globalization, 4, 225
Goins, Irene, 84
Gold Coast neighborhood, 153, 228, 229, 231, 280
Goldwater, Barry, 361n6
Gore, Bobby, 196, 199, 217–218
Grace Abbott Homes (public housing), 154. *See also* ABLA (public housing)
Graham, Donald M., 234
Granger, Lester, 88
Grant, Madison, 45
Grant Park, 35, 206, 291, 293, 324
Grassroots Collaborative, 329
Grassroots Illinois Action (GIA), 333

Holy Family Church, 165

homeowners and homeownership: cheap credit for rehabilitation of homes, 159; minority homeowners, 13–14, 85–86, 288–289, 361n71; mortgage rip-offs, 361n71; neoliberalism and transformation to financial investment, 86–87, 307–308; and political power, 311; suburbanization following federal subsidies for, 127, 140, 222–223; white homeowner associations, 46, 78; and white identity, formation of, 46; white ownership and fear of black invasion, 87. *See also* gentrification; restrictive covenants

home sphere, 85, 350n51

homicide rates: early-20th century, 16–17, 25; in early 2000s, 265, 279, 366n14; of Englewood, 122; gang-motivated, 268; immigrants blamed for, 29; in 2016, 337. *See also* crime rates

homophobia, 275–276

Honeywell, 233

Hoover, Herbert, 53

Hoover, J. Edgar, 98, 213–214, 215. *See also* countersubversion, state-sponsored; FBI

Hoover, Larry, 277–278

Hope IV program, 310

Horner, Henry, 55

Hot Doug's, 304

Hotel Grand, 61

House of Blues, 118

housing: affordable housing movement, 301, 302; Section 8 vouchers, 310, 372n110; shortage of, WWII and, 104, 108–109, 112. *See also* Chicago Housing Authority (CHA); housing developments (middle class); housing segregation; public housing; renters and rent increases

Housing Act (1949), 126, 139, 142

Housing Act (1954), 142

housing developments (middle class): overview, 227–229; as barrier to encroaching ghetto, 149–150, 154, 228, 234–235, 301; and civic pride, 227; Dearborn Park, 234–236; federal

funding and, 227; "mixed income," 234–236, 309, 310–312; urban renewal and creation of, 144–146, 227–228. *See also* gentrification; public housing

housing segregation: blockbusting tactics, 76, 87, 110, 160; block-by-block implementation of (1917), 46; catering to middle class as de facto, 154; dissimilarity index of, 78, 313–314, 350n37; gang violence reinforcing, 46; gentrification and, 311–312; "kitchenette" apartments resulting from, 76; open-housing marches to protest, 12, 47, 161, 193–195, 200–202, 208; public housing, 124–127, *125*; Puerto Ricans and, 174; restrictive covenants and homeowners associations, 46, 51, 78, 131; white identity and whiteness and, 47, 58; and WWII housing shortage, 104, 108–109, 112

Houston, service industries and, 225

Howard, Betty, 132

Howlin' Wolf, 118

HUD (Department of Housing and Development), 309, 310

Hughes, Langston, 65, 88

Hull House settlement, 16, 18, 19, 24, 31

Humboldt Park neighborhood: African American population in, 300, 371n90; Division Street riot (1966), 219, 250, 296–297; gentrification and, 300–301, 302, 303; Mexican population in, 300, 313–314, 371n90; mural movement and, 220, 362n18; physical landmarks built to identify "Paseo Boricua," 294–295, 303; police brutality in, 297; Puerto Rican community and, 174, 214, 219, 252, 254, 296, 297, 300–301, 302, 303, 372n98; rainbow coalition and, 214

Humphrey, Hubert, 207

Hungarian community, and whiteness/ white identity, 114

Hunter, Alberta, 89

Hunter, Robert, 18

Hutchinson, Charles, 31, 50

Hyde Park: racial tensions during WWII, 102–103; urban renewal resistance in, 155, 161

Hyde Park Neighborhood House, 102–103

hyperghettos: Chicago Housing Authority contributing to, 127; commercial activity of, 222; R. J. Daley and, 137; definition of, 354n52; deindustrialization and, 222; recession of 1970s and, 223; white flight and, 222–223. *See also* black ghettos

Ice Cube, 276
Ida B. Wells Homes (public housing), 112
identity. *See* politics of identity
Igoe, Michael, 48
Illinois (state): Arab and Assyrian immigration to, 373n123; bailout of Chicago Transit Authority, 291; charter school funding by, 330; charter school rules, 367n26; Chicago schools handed to RMD, 269; death penalty halt in, 279; defense contract losses (1960s-70s), 224–225; eminent domain powers granted by, 143; Great Depression and, 53; John F. Kennedy election, 158; minimum wage of, 292; no state funds to be used to subsidize public housing, 144; and *Plan of Chicago* funding, 34; and privatization of schools, 326; urban renewal subsidy funds, 143
Illinois Bankers Association, 75–76
Illinois Central Railroad, 147
Illinois Federation of Colored Women's Clubs (IFCWC), 84
Illinois Institute of Technology (IIT), 144
Illinois Steel, 21, 175
immigrants and immigration: anti-immigrant rhetoric of restrictionists and Prohibitionists, 45, 51, 52; and binary racial order, development of, 45–46, 173; and ethnoracial community growth and formation (post-1970), 313–318, *316*, 373nn121,123; ethnoracial enclaves (post-1970), and lack of political power, 318–320; foreign-born population, 23, 313, 320; percentage of population as, 313; physical markings of population of, 313, 315, 317; Thompson's anti-immigrant stance, 52; and urban crisis, RMD and avoidance of, 290; and WWII, 95. *See also* southern and eastern European immigrants; *specific communities*
Immigration and Nationality Act (1965), 172, 313
income: median (2000 census), 266; median black income, 117, 266; per capita, the 1970s and, 223; for service jobs vs. industrial jobs, 287
income inequality: census of 1980 and poorest neighborhoods, 223; census of 2000 and white/black disparities, 286–287; and spatial proximity of extremes, 222
Industrial Areas Foundation (Alinsky), 159
industrial sector: defense contracts and, 97–98, 224–225; as key driver of growth in early 20th century, 19–21; nostalgia for, 2; and "the city that works" as nickname, 2. *See also* deindustrialization
infrastructure: funding for *Plan of Chicago* (1909), 34–35; gentrification and, 305, 308; Great Fire of 1871 and destruction of, 22–23; and patronage rewards via TIF funds, 282, 287, 289; upgrade by end of 1970s, 231–232. *See also* streets/highways/expressways
Inland Steel, 283
Insull, Samuel, 49, 84
insurance: burial/funeral in black community, 71, 74–75; as sector of service industries, 225–226; white-owned companies, 74, 75
integration: of construction industry, 236, 364n46; Edward J. Kelly and, 113–114; Martin Luther King and open-housing marches, 12, 47, 161, 193–195, 200–202, 208; of leisure activities for workers in WWII, 104–105; as threat to machine politics, 130–132; of war industries in WWII, 104–105. *See also* housing segregation; school desegregation
International Amphitheater, 207
International Harvester, 21, 55, 97, 262
International Longshoremen's and Warehousemen's Union, 123
International Style, 232

Katz, Michael, 288, 289
Keane, Thomas, 189, 238
Kelley, Robin D. G., 107, 276
Kelly, Edward J.: background of, 112–113; and black policy wheel (illicit lotteries), 105; and black submachine, 105; and federal work relief funds, 57; and fisticuffs, 17; and labor relations, 56–58, 96, 106; and multiethnic political machine (Kelly-Nash machine), 55, 57–58, 112–114; and organized crime, tolerance of, 96, 105; and patronage, 57; progrowth, antilabor agenda of, 9–10, 56–58; and race relations, 102, 103–104, 105–106, 111–114; and Roosevelt 1936 election, 57, 113; scandals and, 56, 113; and WWII black veterans, 106, 112; and WWII contracts/labor, 95–96, 97, 99; and WWII mobilization, 96–97, 99, 105
Kennedy, John F.: and civil rights, 131; ties of RJD to, 138, 158
Kennedy, Robert, 209
Kennelly, Martin H.: anticorruption campaigns of, 140; and Dawson, 129–130, 133; and the Democratic machine, 133, 134; independent mayoral bid against RJD, 134; Kelly replaced by, 114; progrowth, antilabor agenda of, 9–10; reform crusade of black underground economy, 129–130, 133; and segregation of public housing, 126; and urban renewal, 145, 146
Kenwood neighborhood: gangs and, 190; mural movement and, 219–220
Kenwood-Oakland Community Organization (KOCO), 328
Kerner Commission, 122
Kerouac, Jack, 212
Keynesianism, 149, 225, 226, 240
Kimpton, Lawrence, 211–212
King, Martin Luther Jr.: assassination of, riots following, 138, 198, 208–209; black opposition to, 188–189, 201; CCCO and, 184, 188; and gangs, attempt to enlist help of, 188, 189–195, 200; and March on Washington, 180; open-housing marches in Chicago, 12,

47, 161, 193–195, 200–202, 208; residence in Chicago, 190; and state-sponsored countersubversion, 12; and summit with RJD, 200, 201–202, 208; and trust for RJD machine, 188; viewed as center of civil-rights story, 169; *Wall of Respect* as not including, 220; and white violence, 193
"kitchenette" apartments, 73, *73*, 76, 84–85, 87
Klein, Naomi, *The Shock Doctrine*, 327, 328
Klinenberg, Eric, 8, 261–263
Kluczynski Federal Building, 232
Kohl, Helmut, 264
"Korea Town" (Seoul Drive), 315, 317, 318, 319, 373n126
Kramer, Ferd, 144, 145, 146, 149

"L" (elevated municipal railway), 22, 222, 280
labor force: black population statistics, 63; heavy industries, 21; job losses between 1955 and 1963, 172; job losses due to deindustrialization, 147, 172, 222, 223, 225, 286; job losses in Great Recession, 323; manufacturing, 20–21; meatpacking sector, 20; skyscraper construction, 22; steel workers, 21. *See also* deindustrialization; economy; labor unions and unionization; service economy; service industries (global city); unemployment
labor strikes: Chicago Teachers Union (2012), 326, 332, 333, 336; hate strikes by white workers, 104, 110; Memorial Day massacre (1937), 56–57, 94, 96, 212; Pinkerton thugs hired to attack, 18; strikebreakers and antiblack violence, 25–26, 27–28, 29, 110; violence and, 18; wildcat strikes to protest racial discrimination, 105–106; World War II and, 96, 212
labor unions and unionization: Alinsky and limitations of, 160–161; Brotherhood of Sleeping Car Porters (BSCP), 79–85, 87–88; Catholic Church support for, 121–122; company unions, 80, 83; R. M. Daley austerity measures and,

325; deindustrialization and difficulty of joining, 172; Landis Award limiting, 49–50; living wage ordinance activism, 292–293; opposition to RMD, 292–293; Bill Thompson and, 48–49; work stoppages to demand more black participation in, 236, 364n46. *See also* labor strikes; *specific unions*
—ANTIUNIONISM: black capitalism and, 79–83; black church and, 80–82; William Dever and, 49–50; Employers Association of Chicago and, 26, 28–29; Edward J. Kelly and, 56–57; Landis Award contractors, 49–50; Taft-Hartley Act (1947), 161
lakefront: beautification and tourism infrastructure improvements, 266, 285–286; filling and landscaping, 35; as reserved for the public, 34, 36
Lakefront neighborhoods and Harold Washington, 249, 256
Lake Meadows (housing complex), 144–145, 146
Lake Point Tower, 223, 228–229
Lakeview neighborhood, 153, 173, 280, 295, 320, 370n80
Landesco, John, 42
Landis, Kennesaw Mountain, 49
Landry, Lawrence, 181, 182, 183, 184–185
Laos, immigrants from, 315
latchkey children, WWII and, 98–99
Latin American Defense Organization (LADO), 362n18
Latin Kings (gang), 267–268, 302, 303
Latino community: black-Latino dissimilarity index (segregation), 313–314; black-Latino social distance, 336–337; cabinet of RMD including, 288; charter schools for, 330–331; immigrants, percentage of total immigration, 313; lack of support for Black Lives Matter, 336–337; and Lakeview, 320; Latinismo, 254; Latino-Asian dissimilarity (segregation), 314; and Logan Square neighborhood, 302–304, 305, 372n97; median income (2000 census), 266; Mexican-Puerto Rican dissimilarity index (segregation), 314; migration to Chicago, 172–173; nationwide, 172; school protests and, 221–222; school reforms as leaving behind, 272–273; service economy and, 286–287; support for R. M. Daley, 7, 273, 278, 280–281, 287–289; and Harold Washington, 252–254. *See also* Mexican community; minority-owned businesses; Puerto Rican community
Latino United Community Housing Association (LUCHA), 302
Lawndale neighborhood: and gangs, 188, 198; Martin Luther King residence in, 190
Lawrence Avenue Korean Business Association, 318
Lawson, Victor, 30, 49
Lebanese immigrants, 317
Lefebvre, Henri, 170, 295–296, 297–298
Lesbian/Gay Voter Impact, 370n80
Levi, Julian, 157
Lévi-Strauss, Claude, 118
Lewis, Benjamin, 189
Lewis, Earl, 350n51
Lewis, Karen, 326, 328–329, 334
Lewis, Robert, 35
LGBT community: R. M. Daley and, 295, 321, 370n80; gentrification and, 320–321; incorporation vs. resistance to state power, 296; physical landmarks built to identify neighborhood, 295; voter registration campaign of, 370n80; Harold Washington and, 255, 370n80
Life magazine, 96
Lincoln Park neighborhood, 280, 320; Puerto Rican community and, 173, 214, 218; and rainbow coalition, 214; urban renewal in, 218
Lincoln Square, 317
Lincolnwood, IL, 315
linked fate, 75, 349n31
Lithuanian community: in Back of the Yards, 41, 44–45, 158; and Bungalow Belt, 47; ethnoracial hierarchy and, 40, 44–45; in heterogeneous neighborhoods, 24; and 1919 race riot, 40, 45; and white identity, 45
Little Hell District, 112

Little Italy, 24, 154–155, 165, 169–170
"Little Sicily," 24
Little Tokyo neighborhood, 228
Little Vietnam, 319
Little Village neighborhood, 290, 330
Little Walter, 118, 301
Little Zion Baptist Church, 111–112
living wage ordinance, 292–293
Lloyd, Richard, 303–304
Lloyd, Willie, 277
Loab, Jacob, 48
Local School Councils (LSCs), 269, 271
Locke, Alain, 31
loft conversions, 147
Logan Square neighborhood, 302–305, 307, 326, 372n97
Logan Square Neighborhood Association, 329
London, England, 16, 17, 19
Loop business district: black presence in, deemed a problem, 227; retailers, 22; size of, 225. See also downtown agenda; global cities/global-city agenda; skyscrapers; suburbanization; TIF funds (tax increment financing)
Lopez, José E., 300
Los Angeles: black-Latino dissimilarity index of, 313–314; black mayors and, 249; and black musicians forced into jazz, 120; foreign-born population of, 320; homicide rates, 366n14; migration to, 320; police "red squad," 345n19; population of, 223; service industries and, 225; skyscrapers of, 362n26; Watts rebellion (1965), 123, 184, 185, 186, 189, 190, 192, 196; Zoot Suit Riots (1943), 101, 102
Los Angeles School of urbanism, 3–4, 343n5
Louis, Joe, 59
Lozano, Rudy, 221, 252
LSD (gang alliance), 364n46
Lucas, Robert, 200
Lula Cafe, 302–303
Lyne, Sheila, 261

McAndrew, William, 48, 50, 50–51, 54
McBain, Hughston, 146

McCaffrey, Bill, 330
McCarthy, Eugene, 207
McCarthy, Garry, 337
McClellan, John, 198
McCormick Blaine, Anita, 18–19, 29
McCormick, Cyrus, 31
McCormick, Cyrus Jr., 18
McCormick Harvesting Machine Company, 18, 21
McCormick Place convention center, 143, 232, 285, 286
McCormick Place West building, 286
McCormick, Robert, 17, 56
McCormick, Ruth Hanna, 84
McDonald, Laquan, 334–335, 336
McDonald's Corporation, 232–233, 271
McDonough, Joe, 42
McDowell, Mary, 44, 84
McFetridge, William, 228
McGovern, George, 208
machine politics of Big Bill Thompson (Republican), 71
machine politics of Cook County Democratic Party: "automatic eleven" wards, 136; and biracial political order, 58; and black power, rise of, 180–181; Anton Cermak and, 52–53, 55, 57; Daley dynasty, interregnum between administrations, 344n11; Daley dynasty, length of, 6–7; integration/civil rights as threat to, 131–132; Edward J. Kelly and, 55, 57–58, 112–114; vs. national reform of, generally, 11, 53, 134; and neoliberalization, advance of, 7–8; opposition to, Red Squad neutralization of, 212–214; Harold Washington's antimachine activism, 10, 243–244, 246, 255, 259, 364n55; white gangs and, 41–42, 43; World War II mobilization eased by structure of, 96–97. See also black submachine politics; multiethnic machine
—R. J. DALEY: "accounting gimmicks" used to hide mounting deficits, 239; black power organizations as threat to, 213–214, 216–217; city services vs. social justice, provision of, 149; coded language of, 136, 150; divide and rule

logic of, 213; as dynasty, 6–7; election of 1955, 134–137, *136*; election of 1961, 157–158; election of 1963, 201; election of 1967, 197, 208; federal antipoverty programs hijacked by, 209, 237; gang services to youth as threat to, 196–199; Martin Luther King's misunderstanding of, 188; middle-class housing developments and, 227, 228; private development as shield from political fallout, 235–237; rise of, 133–134; scandals of, 136, 237–238; and white backlash, 212. *See also* patronage—of R.J. Daley machine

—R. M. DALEY: city-council appointments by, and lack of opposition to, 281; compared to machine of RJD, 281, 284; donations to campaigns, 281; as dynasty, 6–7; election of 1989, 366n1; election of 1999, 266; election of 2007, 7; and general prosperity of U.S. economy, 290; lack of opposition among African Americans and Latinos, 7, 273, 278, 280–281, 287–289; "management of marginalization" by, 288–289; Mexican immigration as benefit to, 290; opposition to, development of, 292–293, 328–329; pinstripe patronage of, 281, 282; the politics of identity and, 10–11, 287–289, 297–298, 301, 312; scandals of, 7, 278–281, 284. *See also* TIF funds (tax increment financing)

McKinley Park neighborhood, 245
MacNeal, A. C., 87
Macomba Lounge, 119
Madden, Martin B., 349n35
Madison, WI, 204
Magnificent Mile, 153, 227–228
Mailer, Norman, 203–204, 207
Majerczyk, Aloysius, 245
Malcolm X (Malcolm Little), 106–107, 169, 180, 182, 183, 220; "The Ballot or the Bullet," 180
Mamdani, Mahmood, 11
Maniac Latin Disciples, 302
manufacturing: early 20th century expansion of, 20–21; ethnoracial hierarchy in, 27; interests favoring rehabilitation

of neighborhoods vs. downtown agenda, 145–146, 147; salaries for, 287. *See also* deindustrialization
March on Washington (1963), 180
March on Washington movement (1941), 83
Marina City (housing development), 228, 229
Maritain, Jacques, 158–159
Marquette Park neighborhood, 193–194, 203
Marshall Field and Company, 22, 26, 143, 143–144, 146, 147
Marshall High School, 284
Marx, Karl, 215
Marzullo, Vito, 245, 247
masculinity, gangs and, 25, 43–44
mass incarceration of African Americans, 337
mass transit. *See* Chicago Transit Authority (CTA)
Maxwell Street flea market, 301
Mayor's Commission on Human Relations, 108, 130
Mayor's Committee on Gay and Lesbian Issues (COGLI), 255
Mayor's Committee on Race Relations (1943), 103, 108
MC5 (band), 206
meatpacking sector, 20–21, *20*, 159. *See also* packinghouses
media. *See* press/media coverage
Medill McCormick, Joseph, 29–30
Meeker, Arthur, 30
Meigs Field, 292, 370n75
Melamed, Leo, 240
Mell, Richard, 318, 319
Memorial Day massacre (1937), 56–57, 94, 96, 212
Mencken, H. L., 1
Mendell, David, 265
mental health clinics, 325–326
Merriam, Robert, 134–137, 140
The Messenger magazine, 81
Metcalfe, Ralph, 189, 238, 246
Metcalf, Gordon, 234, 262
Metropolitan Community Center, 81
Metropolitan Community Church, 82, 83–84

Montgomery Ward, 22, 25–26
Moody's bond rating of Chicago, 225, 258, 332
Morales, Jorge, 252
Morgan, J. P., 21
Morgan Park neighborhood, 102
Morgan Stanley, 291
Morris, 20
mortality rates of black vs. white Chicagoans, 75
Mortenson, Peter, 49
Morton, Jelly Roll, 66
Moseley Braun, Carol, 277, 325
Motley, Archibald, 65
Motorola, 233
Motts Pekin Theater, 67
Moynihan, Daniel Patrick, 364n54
Muhammad, Elijah, 189
multiethnic coalitions: difficulty of sustaining, 333, 336–337; Harrison High School protests and hope for, 221; the politics of identity as inhibiting, 220–221; POWER organization, 251–252; of Harold Washington, 249–250, 251–254, 255–257, 334. See also grassroots organizations, citywide coalition of
—RAINBOW COALITIONS: of Black Panthers, 12, 214–215, 217, 221, 250; as first tried in Chicago, 176–177; Jesse Jackson and, 253; Harold Washington and, 254, 255
multiethnic machine: of Anton Cermak, 52–53, 55, 57; Kelly-Nash, 55, 57–58, 112–114
Mumford, Milton C., 143–144, 145
Mundelein, Archbishop George Cardinal, 46
Municipal Voter's League (MVL), 15, 34
mural movement, community, 219–220, 220, 302, 314, 362n18
Murderers (Polish gang), 44, 45
murder rate. See homicide rates
music: blues as morphing into other forms of, 118–120; classical, exclusion of African Americans from, 120; middle-class black civic leaders disapproving of, 65–66, 90–91; race records industry, 89, 118; rap, 255, 276; rhythm & blues,

118, 119; rock íní roll, 119–120, 166; and the Stroll, 65–66, 89. See also blues and jazz
MVL (Municipal Voter's League), 15, 34

NAACP (National Association for the Advancement of Colored People): clubwomen activist support for, 87; and concerns about black capitalism, 61; Daley addressing national convention (1963), 177–178; derision of black critics of civil rights movement, 178; Hyde Park chapter and resistance to urban renewal, 155; Operation Transfer campaign, 179; pro-machine leadership of, 155; Youth Council, 169, 214
Nash, Pat, 52, 53, 113
National Guard troops, 128, 192, 207–208
National League of Cities, 264
National Mobilization Committee to End the War (MOBE), 205–206
National Negro Congress (NNC), 83, 88
Nation of Islam (NOI), 179–180, 189, 275–276
Native Americans, 175–176
Navy Pier renovation, 285
Near North Side: hippie scene and, 205; race riots and, 37; and rainbow coalition, 214; settlement house movement and, 18; Swedish community and, 24; urban renewal and, 146, 227–228, 309
Near Northwest Neighborhood Network (NNNN), 302
Near Northwest Side, gangs and, 171
Near South Side, 144, 320
Near West Side: black population of, 154; early 20th century ethnic neighborhood formation, 24; ethnoracial diversity of, 24, 165–166; gentrification of, 320; Italian community and, 176; juvenile delinquency program of, 165–166; Mexican community and, 176; Puerto Rican community and, 173–174; race riots and, 37, 102–103; settlement house movement and, 18; urban renewal of, 154–155, 172, 176; urban renewal resistance and, 155–157
Near West Side Planning Board, 146

Negro Business Exposition (1938), 59–60, 62, 64, 88
Negro Business League, 64
neighborhood effects, 4
neighborhoods: "community areas" as term for, 294; diversity lost to gentrification, 298, 300–301, 302, 303, 304–305, 311–312, 320; diversity of, and tourism, 297–298, 300; division of city into, 294; early 20th century development of, 24; effects of, Chicago Schools and, 4; heterogeneity of ethnic neighborhoods, 24, 315, 319; map of communities and gangs (ca. 1919), *39*; and nickname "City of Neighborhoods," 3, 294–295, 318–319; physical landmarks built to identify, 294–295, 303, 315, 318; "right to the city," 297; and space, production of, 170–171, 295–296, 297–298, 312, 319. *See also* ethnoracial enclaves (post-1970); housing developments (middle-class); housing segregation; *specific neighborhoods*
"Neighborhoods Alive!" program, 295
neoliberalization/neoliberalism: advancement in Chicago as rapid, aggressive, and early, 7–8; black capitalism and economization of the Black Metropolis, 75–76, 79–80, 81–82, 85, 349n32; and blight redefined as "proper and productive economic use," 148; classical liberalism distinguished from, 371n84; conventional view of turn to, 147–148; R. M. Daley and, 264, 371n84; R. J. Daley as proto-neoliberal, 147–148; definition of, 8, 344n12, 371n84; democratic governance diminished under, 13, 148; Rahm Emanuel and, 325, 327–328, 330–331, 332–333, 337; and heat wave of 1995, 263–264; and home ownership as financial investment, 86–87, 307–308; *Plan of Chicago* (1909) and, 33–34; the politics of identity incorporated into, 9–10, 288–289; populism and, 10; and primary role of city government as a mechanism to unleash private enterprise, 34, 148–149, 371n84; and public

interest realigned with downtown agenda, 148, 238–239; public unaccountability bestowed by, 235–237, 330; Reagan administration and, 8, 264; restructuring of city government to favor downtown agenda, 148, 238–239; school reform and logic of, 271–272, 289; and the state in direct service to the economy, 148–149; structural inequalities reinforced by, 236; of the underground drug economy, 267–268. *See also* downtown agenda; gentrification; global cities/global-city agenda; privatization; tourism, R. M. Daley and development of
Newark, black unemployment rate, 266
New Breed, 221
New Chicago 2011 (mayoral candidate forum), 4, 329
New Chicago School of urbanism, 4–5, 6, 344n10
New Chinatown, 315, 319
New Deal: blight defined as unsafe and unhealthy living conditions, 148; and Chicago patronage, 57; and immigrants, 95; middle-class backlash against, 57; municipal swimming pools built, 111; public housing, 112; Republican hostility to, 144. *See also* Great Depression
New Friendship Baptist Church, 193
New Haven, riots in, 209
Newhouse, Richard, 364n55
New Left: and backlash context, exposing, 218; extremist politics, move toward, 216; fractures dividing, 206; Old Left workerist vision vs., 204
New Negro ideology, 61
New Negro spirit, 81
New Orleans, 261, 266, 311, 327
Newport Jazz Festival (1960), 120
New York (state), Al Smith, governor, 52
New York City: bailout of mid-1970s, neoliberalism viewed as beginning with, 148; bankruptcy difficulties, 224; and bebop jazz, 120–121; black-Latino dissimilarity index of, 313–314; black leadership in, 188; and Brotherhood of

Sleeping Car Porters, 79; and counterculture, 204; de Blasio election, 333;
and "edge" of Lower East Side, 303;
fighting-gang subcultures in, 170;
foreign-born population of, 320; and
gentrification, 307; Giuliani subsidies
to NYSE, 283; as "great" American
city, 1; high schools, 270, 367n23;
homicide rates, 16, 366n14; insurance
industry and, 225; numbers game in,
71–72; police "red squad," 345n19;
Puerto Rican migration to, 173, 358n16;
race riots in WWII, 101, 107–108;
school boycotts, 181; tenement conditions, 19; *West Side Story,* 166
New York Life Insurance Company, 145
New York Stock Exchange, 283
nihilism, 276–277
Nixon, Richard M., 133, 361n6; white
backlash/"silent majority" and, 123, 133,
209, 210
No Child Left Behind program, 269
NOI (Nation of Islam), 179–180, 189,
275–276
Noise Abatement Commission, 99
nonviolence: Martin Luther King's
attempt to enlist gangs into, 190–195,
200; as philosophy, vs. militancy,
179–180, 182–183, 185; Bayard Rustin's
"intensified nonviolence," 180. *See also*
civil rights movement
North Halsted. *See* Boystown
North Kenwood–Oakland neighborhood,
265, 288–289, 298–299
North Lawndale neighborhood: crime rate
in, 262; deindustrialization and, 262;
and heat wave (1995), 262; population
of, 262; white flight and transformation of, 153
Northrup Defense Systems, 233
North Shore suburbs, 223
North Side: gentrification and, 320;
Puerto Rican community and, 173–
174, 358n16; South Asian Indian community and, 315; Harold Washington
election and, 245
Northwest Expressway (John F. Kennedy
Expressway), 231–232

Northwest Side, 317
NWA (Niggas With Attitude), 276

Oak Lawn (suburb), 317
Obama, Barack: on Chicago, 1; as community organizer, 253, 257–258; in congregation of Jeremiah Wright, 276; education policy of, 273; Rahm Emanuel
endorsed for Chicago mayor by, 334;
links between Daley's City Hall and
White House of, 264–265, 273,
365n76; and loss to Bobby Rush, 214,
266; meeting Michelle, 281; and
"Obama effect," 293–294; and Olympic bid of Chicago, support for, 292;
reelection as president, 249; and relocation of Group of Eight (G8) meeting,
330; state senate seat, Blagojevich
scandal of, 291; as state senator, 265;
victory speech at Grant Park, 293; on
Harold Washington's impact, 257,
258–259
Obama, Michelle, 265, 276, 281, 292
Occupy Wall Street, 329
O'Connor, Patrick, 291
Office of Civilian Defense (Chicago), 94,
96–97, 99
Office of Economic Opportunity (OEO),
grants to youth projects, 196, 197, 198,
199
Office of Tourism and Culture, 295,
370n79
O'Hare International Airport, improve-
ments to, 143, 231–232, 252–253,
285–286
oil embargo (1973), 223, 224
Okey Records, 89
Old Town neighborhood, 153, 205
Old Town School of Folk Music, 213
Oliver, Joe "King," 66, 89, 90
Olivet Baptist Church, 80, 178
Olympic Games, unsuccessful bid for,
291–292
O'Neal, William, 217
OPEC oil embargo, 223, 224
open housing. *See* integration
Open Society Foundation, 335
Operation Bootstrap, 196

Operation Breadbasket, 200–201, 236
Operation Lite, 200–201
Operation PUSH, 253
Operation Silver Shovel (FBI), 278–279, 284
Operation Transfer campaign of NAACP, 179
Opportunity Please Knock, 198
Orange, James, 191
Organization for a Southwest Community (OSC), 160
organized crime: Canaryville and ties to, 42; and corruption of RMD machine, 279; Edward J. Kelly tolerance for, 96; white gangs as manpower for, 42, 43; white takeover bid of black syndicates, 130. *See also* crime and criminality; underground economy
Organizing Neighborhoods for Equality: Northside (ONE Northside), 329
Orozco, Raymond, 261, 263
Orsi, Robert, 175
Our Lady of Nativity Parish School, 41
outsourcing of city services, 8, 13, 262–263. *See also* privatization
Overton, Anthony, 70, 74, 80, 85, 86; and black capitalism, 62, 67, 90; and Bronzeville, naming of, 115
Overton Hygienic Building, 67, *69*
Overton Hygienic Company, 62
Owen, Chandler, 81

packinghouses: ethnoracial hierarchy in, 27, 43; size of labor force, 20; street violence and, 17; strikes and strike-breakers, 25; Taylorism and, 42–43; white fear of black migrant competition, 41. *See also* stockyards
Packinghouse Workers Organizing Committee (PWOC), 57
Packingtown. *See* Back of the Yards
Pacyga, Dominic and Ellen Skerrett, *Chicago: City of Neighborhoods,* 294
Pacyga, Dominic, *Chicago: A Biography,* 233n10
Pakistani community, 315, 319
Palestinian immigrants, 317, 373n123
Palmer, Alvin, 167–168

Palmer, Lu, 251
Palmolive Building, 231
Parents Council for Integrated Schools and the Chicago Area Friends of SNCC (CAFSNCC), 179–180, 181, 182
Paris (France), 263; as influence, 16, 32, 285
Park, Paul, 318
Park, Robert, 3, 69, 343n4
Parker, Charlie, 121
parking garages, 143; privatization of income from, 291, 323
parking meters, privatization of, 291, 323, 324
Parks, Rosa, 119
Parkway Ballroom, 106, 108
Parkway Community House, 61
Patel, Amisha, 329
patronage: Anton Cermak's multiethnic machine and, 52, 55; R. M. Daley and pinstripe patronage, 281, 282; disaster capitalism as source of, 327; Rahm Emanuel and pinstripe patronage, 325, 327; national reform of, 140; and New Deal, 57; A. Philip Randolph critique of, 81, 84; Big Bill Thompson and, 53–54, 76–77, 349n35
—OF R. J. DALEY MACHINE: as chair of Cook County Democratic Party, 11–12, 141; and minority-owned businesses, exclusion of, 235–237; private development as shelter from political fallout of, 235; public housing as source of, 138–140; and quasi-Keynesian side of Daley machine, 149; and reduction of city council to rubber-stamp advisory board, 141–142; shares of pie, as substance of politics, 213; suburbanization and deindustrialization as threat to, 140–141; and urban renewal focus on property value increases, 150
Pattillo, Mary, 288–289, 298–299
Peck, Ferdinand, 31
Pekin, 70
People Organized for Welfare and Employment Rights (POWER), 251–252
People's Church, 81
People's Movement Club, 82

Peoria Street riot (1949), 123–124, 127

Pepper, Claude, 100

Perlstein, Rick, 271

Pershing ballroom, 106, 108

Personal Responsibility and Work Opportunity Reconciliation Act (1996), 263, 273–274

Pettibone, Holman, 143–144, 145, 146

Peyton, Dave, 90–91

Pfizer, 233

Philadelphia, 188, 270, 327, 345n19, 367n23

Phillips, Kevin, 361n6

Picasso, Pablo, 232

Pilgrim Baptist Church, 59–60, 82, 84, 89

Pilsen Alliance, 302, 328

Pilsen neighborhood: charter schools, 330–331; coal plant pollution and, 301, 371n94; Czech community and, 24, 52; gentrification of, 300, 301–302, 303; Mexican community and, 176, 296, 297, 300, 301–302, 313–314, *314*, 371nn88,94; Polish community and, 24; population of, 372n97; as tourist destination, 300, 301

Pistilli, Anthony, 146

Pittsburgh, PA, 82

Pittsburgh Courier, 82, 106

place, sense of, 297–298

planning, placed under mayor's control, 8–9, 146–147. *See also* Chicago—plans

Plan of Chicago (1909), 32–36

"plantation politics," 189

Playboy Club, 13, 229

Playboy Magazine and offices, 231

police (CPD): black officer recruitment, 184; Chicago Alternative Policing Strategy (CAPS), 263, 289, 305; countersubversion at Democratic National Convention (1968), 213; expansion under RJD, 167; frame-ups of black leadership, 199–200, 217–218; Gang Intelligence Unit (GIU), 184, 193, 197, 199; Gang Intelligence Unit sabotage of gang-led youth services projects, 197, 199; Fred Hampton murder/assassination by, 215–217; harassment of gang-supported city council campaign, 278; and King marches, 201; lack of protec-

tion for black victims of white violence, 38, 126, 130; Memorial Day massacre (1937), 56–57, 94, 96, 212; public housing projects and new stations for, 151; racist ideology and, 218; Red Squad and countersubversion by, 12, 212–214, 345n19; stop-and-frisk policy, 183–184; tavern shakedowns by, 238; violence against protesters at Democratic National Convention (1968), 207–208, 210–211, 218; violence against Puerto Ricans, 296–297; and World War II violence, monitoring for, 108. *See also* countersubversion, state-sponsored

—VIOLENCE AGAINST AFRICAN AMERICANS: Area 2 torture of black suspects, 7, 279, 335; black police officers and, 184; complicity with white mob violence, 38, 126, 130; and Rahm Emanuel election (2015), 334–335; federal investigation and indictment (late 1950s), 183; gangs and, 186–187; national awareness of, 334–335; pattern of physical and verbal abuse against black population, 238; police brutality protests, 183–185, 297, 335; racist ideology as justification of, 218; stop-and-frisk policy and, 183–184; and World War II, 102

policy wheels (illicit lotteries), 70–74, 75, 105, 130

Polish community (Chicago Polonia): in Back of the Yards, 41, 44–45, 158; and Bungalow Belt, 47; ethnic enclaves of (post 1970), 317–318; ethnoracial hierarchy and, 27, 40, 44–45, 114; gang violence and, 44; gentrification and, 317–318; in heterogeneous neighborhoods, 24, 318; and Logan Square neighborhood, 302, 305; map of ethnic Chicago (2000), *316*; and 1919 race riot, 40, 45; and Pilsen, 24; and Puerto Ricans, 175; settlement house movement and, 18; size of, 23; suburbanization and, 318; and Harold Washington candidacy, 245; and white flight, 153; and whiteness/white identity, 45, 114, 317

Polish Downtown, 24

Polish Museum of America and Library, 317–318
political correctness, 247
political surveillance. See countersubversion, state-sponsored
politics of identity: antimachine activism and, 10; cultural envy and, 247; R. M. Daley policies and, 10–11, 287–289, 297–298; and difficulty of uniting for social justice, 176–177; as distraction from structural inequalities, 298; ebb and flow during 1930s, 51–52; Rahm Emanuel policies and, 330–331, 337; and failure of working-class resistance in 1920s, 51; and fracturing of the left, 216, 219; institutionalization/mainstreaming of, 221–222; the machine as not affected by, 297; and neoliberal policies, incorporation into, 9–10, 288–289; power of collective identities, 219–220; as reinforcing a logic of ethnoracial difference, 220–221, 253–254; and resentment, politics of, 247; Harold Washington and, 253–254. See also ethnoracial enclaves (post-1970); whiteness and white identity
population: changes in ethnic group proportions, 23; current Chicago area, 1; decrease in (2000s), 323; gentrification and displacement of, 298, 300–301, 302, 303, 304–305, 311–312, 320; immigrants, 23, 313; Korean community, 317; living below the poverty line, 266–267; numbers of Second Great Migration, 101; urban renewal and displacement of, 146–147, 309, 310
population growth: 1990s and overall, 320; African American community, 27–28, 46, 51, 61, 117, 127, 143, 173, 178; early 20th century, 23; last quarter of the 19th century, 19; Mexican community, 173, 290; Puerto Rican community, 173
populism: antistatism, 201; neoliberalism and, 10; Bill Thompson and, 51; and urban renewal opposition, 156–157; white identity and, 10. See also white backlash (defensive localism/reactionary populism)

Potter, Jackson, 328
poverty: black/white disparity in, 266–267; blaming the victims of, 263–264; decline of (2000 census), 266; percentage of public school students in, 270; uplift of the poor, mixed-income housing developments and rhetoric of, 310–311. See also black ghettos; culturalization of politics; migration of African Americans from the South; neoliberalization/neoliberalism; public housing; renters and rent increases
Powell, Adam Clayton Jr., 88
"power to the people," 214
Prairie School Architecture, 47
Prairie Shores (housing complex), 144
Preckwinkle, Toni, 337
President's Council on Youth Opportunity, 196
Presley, Elvis, 119, 166
press/media coverage: antilabor, and antiblack violence, 28–29; and the Black Metropolis, 78–79; on civil rights movement, 177; on crime, 17; and Democratic National Convention protests (1968), 206, 207–208, 210–211; Rahm Emanuel and investigative journalism, 332–333, 375n15; and gang-member candidate for city council, 278; and gangs, 198–199; and heat wave (1995), 260–261; hippie scene press (Chicago Seed), 205; on labor strikes and demonstrations, 25–26; on patronage reform, 140; race-baiting, 26; on race riots, 37–38, 40, 103; on scandals of RJD, 237–238; Lincoln Steffens, 15–16; and "the city that works," 231; and white backlash politics, 209, 210; and WWII, 98–99, 100. See also black press; Chicago Defender; Chicago Tribune
Printing House Row, 147
printing sector, destruction of, 147
Pritzker Pavilion, 323, 324, 325
private accountability, neoliberalism and lack of, 235–237, 330
privatization: overview, 13, 290–291; Chicago Skyway tolls, 291; Chicago Transit Authority fare collection

system, 331; disaster capitalism and, 327; Rahm Emanuel budgetary problems and, 323, 324; Rahm Emanuel scandals of, 330, 331; and entrepreneurial state, 8, 13; of New Orleans' school system, 327; outsourcing of urban services, 8, 13, 262–263; parking garage fees, 291, 323; parking meters, 291, 323, 324; of public school custodial and building maintenance services, 330, 331; public unaccountability and, 325–327, 330; of tourism development, 370n79. *See also* charter schools

producer services. *See* service industries (global city)

Progressive Party, 29–30

Prohibition/Prohibitionism, 48, 51, 52, 53

Property Conservation and Human Rights Committee of Chicago, 144

property taxes: downtown agenda and increases in revenues from, 150, 235; global-city agenda and, 225; increases in, to offset suburbanization, 233; as proportion of city budget, 233; rejection of RJD bond issue, 238. *See also* TIF funds

Provident Hospital, 61, 80

Prudential Building, 140

"psychological wage" granted to whiteness, 110

Public Enemy, 276

Public Enemy (1931 film), 55

public housing: and federal requirement not to disrupt racial composition of neighborhoods, 112; integration as Housing Authority policy for, 126–127, 132, 149; Kennelly and segregation of, 126; mismanagement and maintenance problems of, 309–310; mixed-income housing developments taking the place of, 234–236, 309, 310–312; temporary housing and riot against (1946), 114; white mob rule and segregation of, 124–127, *125*

—R. J. DALEY AND: barriers created to isolate from downtown, 151; evasive rhetoric and, 135; federal funding as essential to, 138, 139, 140; high-rise

architecture of, 137, 138–139; map of, *152*; as patronage source, 138–140. *See also* urban renewal

public interest: Carter Harrison II and, 15; neoliberal realignment of, with downtown agenda, 148, 238–239; *Plan of Chicago* (1909) and expansive notions of, 34, 36; redefined to favor private interests, 144, 148; TIF program subsidies and disconnect from, 284

public participation, *Plan of Chicago* (1909) and, 34–36

public unaccountability, 325–327, 330

Pucinski, Roman, 247

Puerto Rican Agenda (activist group), 301

Puerto Rican community: African American identification and, 174; alterity, strategies of, 175; barrio along Division Street, 174, 300; black-Latino dissimilarity index (segregation), 313–314; as buffer between white and black, 174; Division Street barrio riot (1966), 219, 250, 296–297, 303; housing discrimination and, 174; independence movement for Puerto Rico and, 253–254, 372n98; lack of racial antagonism in Puerto Rico, 165; and Logan Square neighborhood, 302; map of ethnic Chicago (2000), *316*; Mexican community and, 176, 254, 314; migration to Chicago, 173–174, 358n16; mural movement and, 219, 220, 362n18; police violence against, 296–297; the politics of identity and, 253–254; racialization of and discrimination against, and consolidation into neighborhoods by, 173–175; urban renewal and displacement of, 174, 228; violence and arson against, 175; and Harold Washington, 249–250, 251–252, 253–254. *See also* Latino community; Young Lords (gang)

Puerto Rican Cultural Center, 300, 302, 371n91

Pullman, George, 28, 31–32, 80

Pullman Company, 21, 79–80, 83, 97

Pullman neighborhood, 21

Pullman porter job, 63, 79; union of (BSCP), 79–85, 87–88

Pullman Porters' Benefit Association of
America, 80
Pullman Strike (1894), 18, 28

Quinn Chapel, 80

Raby, Albert, 184, 188, 189–190, 244
race-baiting: by antiunion employers, 26,
29; by R. M. Daley, 292; and housing
segregation, 47–48; by the press, 26.
See also racism
race politics. *See* politics of identity
race riots: East Saint Louis, IL (1917), 37;
of 1919, 27, 36–38, 37, 40, 43, 45, 79;
Peoria Street riot (1949), 123–124, 127;
as spectacle, 226; temporary housing
for African Americans (1946), 114;
Trumbull Park Homes (1954), 132, 156;
during World War II, 101, 102–103,
107–108; Zoot Suit Riots (1943 Los
Angeles), 101, 102
racial order: binary racial order, development of, 45–46, 47, 58, 173; ethnoracial
hierarchy, 26–27, 40, 43, 44–45, 55,
114, 173; southern and eastern Europeans as third tier within, 45. *See also*
politics of identity; racism; segregated
racial order; structural inequalities;
whiteness and white identity
racism: culture-of-poverty rhetoric and,
274–275; and election of 1927, 47–48,
51; and fear of class position being
undermined, 109–110; general desire to
minimize appearance of, 243; laissez-
faire, 236; police terror and ideology of,
218; and rumors of robberies and rapes,
110–111; as tool of the ruling class for
exploitation of workers, 110; and
Harold Washington election, 242–243,
246–248, 364n54. *See also* culturalization of politics; police (CPD)—violence against African Americans;
race-baiting; race riots; racial order;
structural inequalities; white backlash
radio, 116, 118
Ragen, Frank, 38
Ragen's Colts (Irish athletic club), 38,
42, 44

railroad, national, and Chicago as "gate-
way," 22
Rainbow Beach, 169
rainbow coalitions. *See under* multiethnic
coalitions
Rainey, Ma, 66, 89, 90
Rakove, Milton, 138, 139, 246
Randolph, A. Philip, 79–82, 83, 88, 104
Rangel, Juan, 330–331
Rangerettes (gang), 187
rape, rumors of interracial, 110–111
rap music, 255, 276
Rauner, Bruce, 325
Razaf, Andy, 92
RCA Victor, 119, 166
reactionary populism. *See* white backlash
Reagan, Ronald, and administration:
antiwelfare crusade of, 242–243, 250,
263, 273; criminalization of youth, 218,
276; law-and-order focus of, 196, 274,
276; neoliberalism and, 8, 264; rap
critiques of, 276; shift of federal funds
from social spending to law enforcement, 274; War on Drugs, 218
real estate market: black ownership touted,
85–86; blockbusting tactics, 76, 87, 110,
160; rising values of, as increasing city
revenue, 150; World War II and decline
of values, 140. *See also* gentrification;
homeowners and homeownership;
renters and rent increases; service
industries (global city)
Rebels (Polish youth gang), 167
Rebel Without a Cause (1955), 166, 167
Reconstruction Finance Corporation, 53
red-baiting tactics, BSCP union and, 83
Redmond, James, 221–222
Reed, Adolph Jr., 258, 311
Reed, Christopher Robert, 62
Reid, Murdoch & Company, 30
Related Midwest, 323
religious community: opposition to civil
rights struggle, 189. *See also* black
church; Catholic Church
Rendell, Edward, 264
renters and rent increases: gentrification
and, 299–300; "kitchenette" apart-
ments, 73, 73, 76, 84–85, 87; mixed-

income housing developments and, 311–312; urban renewal and, 144; urban renewal and displacement of, 146–147, 309, 310

Republican Party (Illinois): Bernard Epton campaign against Washington, 241, 245–246, 247, 248–249; hostility to state funds used to subsidize public housing, 144; machine politics of, 76–78

Republican Party (national): antiwelfare crusade of, 242–243, 250, 263, 272, 273–274; law enforcement vs. social services and, 274; postwar strategy of, 101; "southern strategy" of, 210, 361n6. *See also* culturalization of politics; Reagan, Ronald, and administration

Republic Steel mill, 56, 94

resistance to racial oppression. *See* black resistance to racial oppression

respectability, as Afrian American community concern, 66, 90–91, *91*

restaurants, hipster aesthetic and, 302–303, 304–305

Restoration Act (1947), 143

restrictive covenants, 46, 51, 78, 131

retail: department stores, 22; mail-order, 22; national economy of 1970s and loss of, 223; salaries of jobs in, 287. *See also* service economy

Revolutionary Action Movement (RAM), 182–183, 197

Reyes, Victor, 280

Rhumboogie (club), 118

rhythm and blues, 118, 119

Ribicoff, Abraham, 208

Richard J. Daley Center (Chicago Civic Center), 232

Ricoeur, Paul, 221

Riis, Jacob, *How the Other Half Lives,* 19

riots: antieviction (August 1931), 76, 78, 79; police brutality protests and (1965), 185; as spectacle, 226. *See also* arson and bombings; race riots

Rittenberg, Ivan, 245

Rivera, Diego, 219

Riverview Amusement Park, 49

Robert Brooks Homes (public housing), 154. *See also* ABLA (public housing)

Roberto Clemente High School, 372n98

Robert Taylor Homes (public housing), 139, 142–143, 151, 277, 310

Robinson, Chester, 200

Rockefeller Foundation, 196

Rock Island and Pacific Railroad, 105

Rockwell, George Lincoln, 203

Rodgers, Daniel T., 16

Rodriguez, Matt, 252, 261

Roediger, David, 27

Rogers Park neighborhood, 214, 317

Roosevelt, Franklin Delano, 53, 57, 83, 104, 113, 131. *See also* Great Depression; New Deal

Roosevelt, Theodore, 29–30

Roosevelt Square (housing development), 311

Root, John Wellborn, 18, 21–22

Rose, Don, 243–244

Rose, George "Watusi," 198–199

Rosenwald, Julius, 50

Rosie the Riveter, 98, 99

Rowe, John W., 271

Royko, Mike, 41, 135, 141, 209, 216

Rubloff, Arthur, 227–228

Rubloff Company, 227–228

Rush, Bobby, 7, 214, 256, 266, 273, 277, 334; mayoral primary run (1999), 266; on "two Chicagos," 266

Rush, Otis, 119

Rush Street strip, 231

Russian-born immigrants, 345n13

Rustin, Bayard, 180, 188

Ryan, George, 279

Ryerson, Joseph, 49

St. Charles reformatory, 185

St. Cyril's Church, 162

St. Hyacinth Church, 318

St. Jarlath's Church, 165

St. Louis, MO, 266–267

St. Pascal's Catholic Church, 248

St. Patrick's Day parade, 241

Saints (gang), 267–268

St. Stanislaus Kostka parish, 317

sales tax: increases in, 141; tourism revenues, 286

same-sex relations, 90

structure of feeling: black resistance to racial oppression as, 109; definition of, 109; white backlash and, 210

student movement: antiwar organizing, 204, 205, 207; context of, 203–204; hippie scene mainstreamed in Chicago, 205; school protests and boycotts, 179–180, 181–182, 184, 187, 221–222, 250, 271–272, 297, 359n29; search for new methods, 204. *See also* Democratic National Convention protests (1968)

Student Nonviolent Coordinating Committee (SNCC), 169–170, 195, 197

Students for a Democratic Society (SDS), 204, 205, 216

Students for Health Equity (SHE), 335

subprime mortgage crisis, 290

suburbanization: corporate headquarters and, 232–234; Detroit and, 122; economically depressed black suburbs, 310; high-tech corridors and, 233; and homeownership, federal subsidies for, 127, 140, 222–223; Polish community and, 318; South Asian Indian community and, 315; as threat to patronage system, 140–141

Sullivan, Frank, 288

Sullivan, Louis, 21–22

Sun Belt, federal funding and development of, 4

Sunset Café, 67

"Super Bowl Shuffle" (Chicago Bears), 255

Supreme Court, U.S.: *Brown v. Board of Education of Topeka, Kansas,* 119, 132, 133; *Shakman* decision, 237, 281; *Shelley v. Kraemer,* 131

Swearingen, John, 233

"Swede Town," 24

Swedish community, 24

Swibel, Charles, 228

Swift, 20

swimming pools, public, 111, 113, 191–192

syndicates. *See* organized crime

Syrian immigrants, 317

Taft-Hartley Act (1947), 161

Take Back Chicago marches, 329

Target, 292

taxes: Rahm Emanuel and increases in, 332; populist backlash against paying, 238; proposed financial transaction tax, 328, 336. *See also* property taxes; sales tax

tax increment financing program. *See* TIF funds (tax increment financing)

taxis, 130

Taylor, Elizabeth, 151

Taylor, Koko, 119

Taylor, Robert, 104

Taylorism, 25, 42–43

Teamsters union, 25–26, 28, 293

telecommunication technologies, 225, 239

Temporary Woodlawn Organization (TWO)/The Woodlawn Organization, 162–164, 179, 180, 196–200

Tenants' Rights Action Group, 198

tenement conditions (early 20th century), 18–19, 21

Terkel, Studs, *Division Street America,* 205

terrorism, and Puerto Rico independence movement, 372n98

Thailand, immigrants from, 315

Thatcher, Margaret, 9, 264

The Woodlawn Organization/Temporary Woodlawn Organization (TWO), 162–164, 179, 180, 196–200

Thompson, E. P, 5

Thompson "Big Bill": "America First" campaign of, 51; anti-immigration and, 52; black voter support for, 40–41, 47–48, 71, 112–113; and Cermak, loss to, 52–53; and gangsters, 53; and Great Depression, 53; labor and, 48–49; as no friend to African Americans, 78; patronage and, 53–54, 76–77, 349n35

Thorne, Robert J., 26, 28, 30

Thrasher, Frederic, 27, 44

TIF funds (tax increment financing): overview, 13; Chicago Mercantile Exchange renovations and, 329–330; gentrification and, 305; inequalities reinforced by uneven distribution of, 282–283, 331; minority-owned businesses receiving patronage from, 287, 288; opposition to, 328–329, 331–332;

TIF funds *(continued)*
original intent of program, 282, 368n49; as pinstripe patronage, 282; proposal to dissolve, 291; public scrutiny avoided in, 282; as "shadow budget," 281–282; subsidies to downtown agenda via, 282–284, 331–332, 369n56; teachers union call to fill budget gap using, 328

Till, Emmett, 137

Tillman, Dorothy, 256, 277, 278

Touraine, Alain, 162

tourism, R. M. Daley and development of, 264; beautification, 266, 285; and "City of Neighborhoods" campaign of RMD, 294–295; and diversity of neighborhoods, 297–298, 300; Rahm Emanuel and privatization of, 370n79; infrastructure, 285–286; service jobs for, 286–287; "tourist bubble," 286

Toynbee Hall social settlement (London), 16

Trinity United Church of Christ, 276

Trumbull Park Homes, 126, 132–133, 156

Trump, Donald, 1, 325

Turner, Damian, 335

Tuthill, Richard, 16–17

21st Century Vote, 277–278

TWO. *See* Temporary Woodlawn Organization (TWO)/The Woodlawn Organization

UAW Local 600, 106

Ukrainian community, 24

Ukrainian Village neighborhood, 299, 305

underground economy: drug economy, 267–268; jitney cabs, 129–130; policy wheels (illicit lotteries), 70–74, 75, 105, 130; WWII and black market, 100. *See also* organized crime

unemployment: in 2014, 331; Great Depression and, 53, 78; rate for black males, 266, 270, 331; recessions of 1958 and 1961 and, 172; service economy ameliorating, 287; and subsidies paid to corporations, 283–284, 369n56

unions. *See* labor unions and unionization

Union Station railroad terminal, 35

Union Stockyards, 20–21, *20*

United Airlines, 147, 283

United Auto Workers (UAW), 106

United Center, 285

United Garment Workers (UGW), 25–26

United Negro Improvement Association (UNIA), 61

United Neighborhood Organization (UNO), 301–302, 330, 371n94

United States Immigration Commission (Dillingham Commission), 29

United States Post Office, 232

United Working Families (UWF), 333

Unity Hall, 82

University of Chicago (UC): and backlash, turn to, 211–212; and Citizens' Committee to Enforce the Landis Award, 49–50; economics, Chicago School of, 240; expansion of (South Campus), urban renewal and, 149, 155, 157–158, 163–164; Laboratory School (Dewey), 18, 19; sociology, Chicago School of, 3, 19, 69, 113, 153, 211, 274, 294, 343n4

University of Chicago Medical Center (UMMC), trauma center, 335, 375n19

University of Chicago Settlement, 44, 45

University of Illinois at Chicago (UIC), 155–156, 172, 176, 262, 301

University Village (middle- to upper-income housing development), 301

UNO (United Neighborhood Organization), 301–302, 330, 371n94

uplift of African Americans: black capitalism as vehicle for, 59, 61, 64–65, 67, 69, 75, 81, 86; white gaze upon, 59

uplift of laboring classes: beautification and, 33; cultural institutions and, 31–32; settlement house movement and, 18, 33

uplift of the poor, mixed-income housing developments and, 310–311

Uptown neighborhood: Asian community and, 315, 317; rainbow coalition and, 214; student movement and, 204. *See also* Young Lords (gang)

urban crisis: Detroit and, 122; Englewood as poster child for, 121–122; liberal vs. conservative views of causes, 122–123;

violence/racial violence *(continued)*
1960s escalation of intensity of, 170;
lack of protection of African Americans by law enforcement, 38, 126, 130;
map of, *125*; open-housing marches of
MLK and, 193–194; politicians and
fisticuffs, 17; postwar years and, 123–
126, *125*; prior to 1919 race riot, 38;
Puerto Ricans as victims of, 175; racist
ideology arising as justification of, 218;
against Harold Washington's campaign, 248; World War II and, 110–112.
See also arson and bombings; crime
rates; culturalization of politics; gangs;
homicide rates; police (CPD); race
riots

Violent Crime Control and Law Enforcement Act (1994), 263, 274

Visitation Parish, 124

vocational training, gang youth programs
and, 198

voter registration campaigns: black mobilization for Harold Washington, 243;
immigrant working class, rise in 1920s,
51; Lesbian/Gay Voter Impact, 370n80;
Million Man March and, 275; 21st
Century Vote, 277–278; TWO movement, 163

voter turnout, 7, 277, 280, 334

Voting Rights Act (1965), 188

Vrdolyak, Edward, 242, 245, 252, 254–256,
257, 366n1

Vrdolyak 29 bloc, 254–256, 257

Wacker, Charles, 35

Wacquant, Loïc, 354n52

wade-ins, 169

Wagner, Clarence, 134

Wagner Act (1935), 57, 83

Walker, William, 220

Wallace, George, 177, 178, 210, 361n6

Waller, Fats, 92

Wall of Respect (mural), 219–220, *220*

Wal-Mart, 292

war: antiwar demonstrations, 204, 205,
207; World War I, 38, 94–95. *See also*
veterans; World War II

War on Drugs, 218, 337

War on Poverty (Lyndon B. Johnson), 201,
209, 263

Washington, Booker T., 64, 131

Washington, DC, 345n19, 366n14

Washington, Harold: as African American politician, 241–242; antimachine
activism of, 10, 243–244, 246, 255, 259,
364n55; and "City of Neighborhoods,"
294; and community participation in
public policy making, 259; "council
wars" during term of, 252–253, 254–
256, 344n11; death of, 254, 255, 370n80;
election of 1987, 256, 365n78; Latinos
and, 252–254; LGBT community and,
255, 370n80; multiethnic coalition of,
249–250, 251–254, 255–257, 334; Barack
Obama on impact of, 257, 258–259; the
politics of identity and, 253–254;
replacement for, city council choice of,
256–257; school system and, 50, 269;
successes of, 255, 258
—ELECTION OF 1983: antimachine campaigning as factor in, 246; black community mobilization for, 243–244,
249; Latino support for, 249–250,
251–252; primary, 242–244, *244*;
racism as factor, 245, 248–249, 365n65;
and racism, cultural, 242–243, 246–
248, 364n54; racist attacks as working
to advantage of, 242–243, 249–250;
scandals and, 249; white Democrats
and machine campaigning for Republican candidate against, 241–243, 244–
246; white support, 249

water safety, Sanitary and Ship Canal and,
23

Waters, Ethel, 66, 89

Waters, Muddy, 118, 119, 120; "Hoochie
Coochie Man," 118; "I Can't Be Satisfied," 118

Water Tower Place, 223, 286

Watts rebellion (1965), 123, 184, 185, 186,
189, 190, 192, 196

Weathermen, 231

Weber, Charlie, 55

Weber, John Pitman, 220, 362n18

Webster, Milton, 84

Welfare Reform Act (1996), 263, 273–274

Wells, Junior, 301
Wells-Barnett, Ida B., 80, 83–84
Wells Club, 83–84
Wells High School, 124
"We Shall Overcome," 162, 181, 324
West, Cornel, *Race Matters,* 276
West Devon Avenue, 315, 318, 319
Western Electric, 28, 97, 233
West Garfield Park neighborhood: dein-
    dustrialization and, 283–284, 369n56;
    police brutality protests, 184–185;
    Puerto Rican community and, 174;
    schools of, 179
West Ridge neighborhood, 317
West Side: ethnoracial diversity of, 173;
    food desert problem of, 283; and loss of
    University of Illinois campus expan-
    sion, 262; Mexican community and,
    313; Puerto Rican community and,
    173–174, 175, 358n16; and rainbow
    coalition, 214; TIF funds and, 331
West Side Organization (WSO), 192
West Side riot (1966), 191–193, 208–209
West Side rioting after King's assassina-
    tion (1968), 138, 198, 208–209
West Side Story (1961), 166
West Town neighborhood: gentrification
    and, 299–300, 307, 317; Latino com-
    munity and, 173–175, 300; racial vio-
    lence in, 175
Wetten, Emil, 55–56
WGES (black radio station), 116
White, Leonard D., 54
white backlash (defensive localism/reac-
    tionary populism): antistatism of, 10,
    201; and belief in victimization by
    liberals, 132–133; blaming marchers and
    protesters for police violence, 200,
    210–211; civil rights movement as
    counterforce to, 131–132; and cultural
    racism, smear of Harold Washington
    and, 243, 249; R. J. Daley as mayor of,
    135–136, 209–211, 238; machine politics
    and balance of, with black civil rights,
    131–132; national politics of, 210; Nixon
    and "silent majority," 123, 133, 209, 210;
    Republican "southern strategy" of, 210,
    361n6; University of Chicago's turn to,

211–212; women and, 124, 156; and
    WWII war industries, 104. *See also*
    culturalization of politics; racism;
    whiteness and white identity
white Chicagoans: blaming marchers and
    protesters for police violence, 200, 210;
    lack of support for movement against
    racist police violence, 336–337; median
    income of (2000), 266; mortality rate
    of, 75; in "rainbow coalition" of Black
    Panthers, 214; "slumming" in the Black
    Metropolis, 65–66; support for Rahm
    Emanuel, 336; unemployment in 2014
    and, 331; urban renewal and clearance
    of, 154–155. *See also* gentrification;
    white backlash; white flight; white
    gangs and athletic clubs; whiteness and
    white identity
white-collar workers, making the city
    desirable for. *See* global cities/global-
    city agenda; middle-class
white flight: Alinsky efforts to stop, 160;
    deindustrialization and, 222–223; and
    ghettos, transformation to, 127, 153–
    154; and hippie scene, 205; homeown-
    ership subsidies and, 127, 222–223;
    Puerto Ricans swept by, 174. *See also*
    suburbanization
white gangs and athletic clubs, *171*; as
    adverse to packinghouse work, 42–43;
    antiblack terror by, 38, 124, 126; as
    crime syndicate manpower, 42, 43; and
    ethnoracial hierarchy, 27, 43, 45; and
    machine politics, 41–42, 43; and 1919
    race riot, 38, 40, 43, 45; and "rainbow
    coalition" of Black Panthers, 214. *See
    also* black gangs; gangs
whiteness and white identity: Catholic
    Church policies and production of, 46;
    and centrality of the black ghetto, 47;
    consolidation of (end of 1950s), 173;
    ethnic slurs within, 114; housing
    segregation and, 47, 58; interwar era
    and weakening of reform organizing,
    9–10, 58; Mexican community and,
    175, 176; "middle-class" as euphemism
    for, 150; and middle-class neighbor-
    hoods, creation of, 46–47; and

whiteness and white identity *(continued)*
nationalist fervor of WWII, 114;
progrowth, antilabor agenda enabled
by, 9–10; "psychological wage" granted
to, 110; and Second Great Migration,
114. *See also* culturalization of politics;
politics of identity; racism; white
backlash
White Sox, 285
Whoopee Era, 55
Wicker Park neighborhood: gentrification
of, 299, 300–301, 303–305, 307, 321,
374n130; Polish community and, 317
Wigwams (Polish gang), 44
Wilkins, Roy, 88
William, Lacy Kirk, 80
Williams, Eugene, 36–37
Williamson, Sonny Boy, 118
Williams, R. A., 85
Williams, Raymond, 109
Williams, Rufus, 271
Willis, Benjamin, 178, 179, 180, 181, 184
Willis, Carol, 22
Willis Tower, 283, 362n25
Wilson, James Q., *Negro Politics,* 130–131
Wilson, Orlando, 183–184, 185
Wilson, William Julius, 153, 274, 280,
310–311, 364n54; *The Declining Signifi-
cance of Race,* 274–275
Wilson, Willie, 334
Wisconsin steel, 21
women: affirmative action, 363n45; Afri-
can-American clubwomen, 80, 84–85,
87; blues singer solidarity with black
women, 90; Jane Byrne election, 242;
as Chicago Housing Authority's first
director, 113; gang branches of, 187; jobs
for black women, 63; jobs for Puerto
Rican women, 358n16; roles in WWII,
96, 97–99, 100; urban renewal opposition by, 155–157; and white resistance to
integration, 124, 156
Wonder, Stevie, 251
Wong, Jimmy, 315
Wood, Elizabeth, 113, 126–127, 132, 149
Woodlawn neighborhood: and Catholic
Church, 161–162; and gangs, 187, 188,
195; and ghetto, transformation to,
153–154, 262; mental health clinic
closures, 326; police monitoring during
WWII, 108; Puerto Rican community
and, 173, 358n16; and school conditions, 163; TWO movement/The
Woodlawn Organization, 162–164,
179, 180, 196–200; urban renewal
opposition in, 157–158, 163–164
Woodstock, 206
Woolworth's Five and Ten, 62
working class: and antiblack aggression by
Irish, 40–41; austerity cutbacks as
most affecting, 325–326; Chicago
identity as, 1–2, 13, 232; and election of
1927, 48–51; gentrification as displacing, 298–302, 311–312, 317, 371n94;
military high schools and programs,
272, 368n32; school reforms as leaving
behind, 270, 299; street violence attributed to, 17; uplift of, movement for, 18,
31–33. *See also* black cultural expression; Chicago Teachers Union (CTU);
deindustrialization; gangs; labor force;
labor unions and unionization; music;
service economy; unemployment
Works Progress Administration
(WPA), 57
World's Columbian Exposition (1893),
23, 157
World War I, 38, 94–95
World War II: class tensions and, 99–100;
consensus of support for, 94–95;
defense contracts for Chicago, 95–96,
97; Detroit and, 96, 212; Flag Day
(1942), 94; housing shortage in, 104,
108–109, 112; and juvenile delinquency
issues, 98–99; labor unions of Chicago
quiescent during, 212; mobilization by
Chicago, 96–97, 99; and morale drop
in Chicago, 99–100; race riots during,
101, 102–103, 107–108; racial discrimination in the war industries, 83; and
whiteness/white identity, 114; and
white racism, 110–112; women in the
labor force, 96, 97–99, 100; zoot suiters
and, 106–108
WPA, 57
Wright, Edward H., 76–77, 80, 84, 87